£14·95

EUROPEAN MERGERS
AND MERGER POLICY

EUROPEAN MERGERS AND MERGER POLICY

Edited by

MATTHEW BISHOP AND JOHN KAY

OXFORD UNIVERSITY PRESS

1993

Oxford University Press, Walton Street, Oxford OX2 6DP
Oxford New York Toronto
Delhi Bombay Calcutta Madras Karachi
Kuala Lumpur Singapore Hong Kong Tokyo
Nairobi Dar es Salaam Cape Town
Melbourne Auckland Madrid
and associated companies in
Berlin Ibadan

Oxford is a trade mark of Oxford University Press

Published in the United States
by Oxford University Press Inc., New York

British Library Cataloguing in Publication Data
Data available

Library of Congress Cataloging in Publication Data
European mergers and merger policy / edited by Matthew Bishop and John Kay.
p. cm.
Includes bibliographical references.
1. Consolidation and merger of corporations—European Economic
Community countries. 2. Consolidation and merger of corporations—Government
policy—European Economic Community countries.
3. Consolidation and merger of corporations—Great Britain.
4. Consolidation and merger of corporations—Government policy—
Great Britain. I. Bishop, Matthew, 1964– . II. Kay, J.A. (John Anderson)
HD2746.55.E86E94 1993 338.8'3'094—dc20 93–10516
ISBN 0–19–877345–5
ISBN 0–19–877346–3 (pbk.)

Set by Hope Services (Abingdon) Ltd.
Printed in Great Britain by
Biddles Ltd.
Guildford & King's Lynn

PREFACE

In 1989 James Fairburn and I edited a collection of readings on Mergers and Merger Policy. It was clear even then that mergers were increasingly to be a European phenomenon, and that has become truer as the European Community has adopted its own merger regulation and the dimensions of economic Europe have expanded to encompass not only a European economic area but the newly opened markets of the East. Historically, merger has been an Anglo-Saxon phenomenon, and this is reflected in the experience on which we draw, but the present volume is directed towards an understanding of the European context and draws lessons for those other European countries. I am grateful to Matthew Bishop for taking on the role of co-editor of this volume and to Barbara Lee for her assistance and support in preparing the book for publication.

J.K.

CONTENTS

FIGURES

TABLES

INTRODUCTION

Europe stands at the start of its first great merger wave. Growing international trade, accelerated by the 1992 'Single Market' programme, has seen a sharp increase in mergers across national borders between European-based firms. During the 1990s, this increase in European mergers will almost certainly continue. As it does, it is sure to raise important questions for industrial policy-makers and business strategists. Should, for instance, leading national firms merge to form 'European champions'? When does merger make good business sense, and with which firm? Are hostile take-overs a sound method for ensuring top management accountability; are alternative ownership controls preferable? What are the proper grounds for politicians to prevent a merger, and which politicians?

Many of these issues will be all too familiar to British managers, investors, and politicians, who, unlike their European counterparts, have extensive experience of the costs and benefits of mergers and take-overs. As Europe's first great merger wave begins, those guiding it should draw heavily on this British experience. Britain itself has just come to the end of its third great merger boom of the twentieth century. The first was in the 1920s when the development of mass production techniques created a steep change in the scale of production, and firms such as Unilever and ICI, which have continued to dominate the British industrial scene ever since, were brought together. The marked rise in industrial concentration in the 1920s was the product both of mergers and of internal growth.

The second boom came in the 1960s, as a response to the internationalization of the world economy. This created, it was supposed, a need to move to larger firms which were more capable of being effective in international competition. Thus, British Leyland was formed by amalgamation of the remaining indigenous UK motor manufacturers, ICL was established as flagship of the British computer industry, and GEC acquired most of Britain's strength in electrical engineering.

The lack of success of these policies should make us hesitate before we believe too easily that wider markets require larger firms. Indeed, it is now apparent that many of these developments were motivated by the most obvious of confusions. Policy-makers looked at IBM or Boeing or General Motors and concluded that they were successful because they were large—and that therefore their success could be replicated by replication of their size—rather than by recognizing that they were large because they were successful. It is a salutary reminder that in the same year that British Leyland was created to give Britain a firm of the size needed to compete in the world automobile industry, Honda produced its first motor car.

These things need to be said because the air, this time across Europe, is once again full of vague phrases about the need to create critical mass and to establish global players. We would not wish to say that what lies behind these clichés is never true, but they are clichés, and the most important point to make is that size is most certainly not the only, and it is rarely the most important, source of competitive advantage.

The third great British merger boom occurred in the 1980s. If large size had been the primary motivation of the ways of the 1920s and the 1960s, the most important element in the 1980s was the evolution of the market for corporate control. This phrase reflects a view of the world in which the management of companies is seen as a commodity for sale. As in other markets, the freedom of the market makes for efficiency of the market, and for efficiency in the allocation of resources. This analogy is more problematic than this description suggests, and we shall return later to criticize it. But it is certainly the case that in the 1980s the arguments put forward to justify mergers have rested much less on the need for scale than on the ability of the acquiring management to make effective use of the corporate assets which will come under their control.

One common feature of these three merger waves should be noted: the clearly observed, if poorly explained, correlation between the level of merger and take-over activity and the level of share prices. In broad terms, we should note that the 1920s, the 1960s, and 1980s were not only good decades for those who advised on mergers and acquisitions, they were also good decades for shareholders. One might note also that the 1930s and the 1970s were good for neither, and wonder what the 1990s hold in store. That correlation is true not only on a long-term but also on a short-term basis. Even over much shorter periods, the incidence of merger activity has tended to coincide with peaks in the stock market cycle. The most recent wave of mergers came to the crest in 1986–7, as did the great 1980s' bull market in equities. This has been true also in the United States, the only other large stock market which has an active market in corporate control.

This inter-relationship is in part puzzling because common sense might suggest that this relationship should if anything go the other way. We might expect a company to buy physical assets when the price of companies is high, and to prefer companies to new investment when the price of companies is low. This would generate the inverse of the correlation we observe. But it is what happens in certain other sectors, such as the oil sector, where there is a tendency for oil companies to choose between acquisition and exploration according to the relative prices of oil shares and oil itself. A number of theories purport to explain this relationship. The most plausible are those which base the incidence of merger activity on the prevalence of stock market misvaluations—mergers are in part a way of arbitraging stock market mistakes—and these occur more frequently in bull markets than in bear markets. In this view, possibly the fact of the merger, and certainly its timing, is influenced by these types of market failure.

The new European merger wave continues only in part the British trend. We begin our analysis with four central stylized facts about European merger (see Geroski and Vlassopoulos, this volume). The first is that merger activity is growing throughout the Community. The second is that this growth is in all types of merger. Specifically, there is little indication that cross-border mergers form an increasing proportion of the total. Although they are of rising importance, it is an importance which essentially parallels the rise in importance of all mergers. Third, cross-border mergers are typically between geographically contiguous countries. When a Spanish acquisition crosses a border, it most frequently does so to Portugal or perhaps to France. Germany and Holland form a pair. France, Belgium, and Germany form another group. When a merger crosses a border, it mostly crosses one border—it is quite rare for it to cross two.

And the fourth stylized fact is that most European mergers are still British. Through the 1980s the commonest type of merger in the European Community has been one in which one UK firm acquires another UK firm—indeed even among large mergers almost half were of that type. The next most common pair—and one which has increased very rapidly in significance—is that in which one French company acquires another. Indeed over the Community as a whole, there is only a minority of large mergers in which a British firm is not either the buyer or the seller. And more often it is the buyer, because within the European Community the UK is a net buyer of other countries' companies and other countries have typically been sellers. The United States has also been a seller of companies on a large scale and it is probably the case that Britain and Japan are the only net buyers of companies in the world. Within cross-border mergers, however, the UK is the largest buyer of non-British European companies, and the United States is the second largest buyer. Merger, in short, is—or at least has been—an Anglo-Saxon phenomenon. It remains to be seen how far this continues to be true. But it reflects a culture in which equity markets are a more significant mechanism of corporate finance and in which merger is a more important part of corporate culture, and the market for corporate control, which has never really existed outside the English-speaking world.

The analogy between the market for corporate control and other markets is one which does not, in the end, stand up to detailed scrutiny. One reason for this is information asymmetry: one party knows much more about the commodity on sale than the other. Such information asymmetry creates a problem in many markets. But the gap between the knowledge available to the incumbent management of a company and that held by its external observers is, invariably and necessarily, a very large one. Another weakness of the analogy is the essentially all-or-nothing nature of the market for corporate control. In most markets, if your product is inferior you gradually lose market share. That in turn puts pressure on you to respond to the market's verdict. In the market for corporate control, by contrast, if your performance is not up to scratch you nevertheless retain complete control over the company until, equally unambiguously, you lose control of it altogether. This discrete nature of corporate control clearly differentiates this market from the market for most other commodities.

Indeed, a better analogy with corporate governance may be found not so much in markets, as in the old style of Eastern European government. As was true there, all formal trappings of democracy exist. Shareholders have the right to elect directors, and to be consulted on major issues. In reality, these rights are essentially defunct. Shareholders re-elect incumbents certainly with the same unanimity, and perhaps with the same enthusiasm, with which the East German population re-elected Herr Hoenecker to power for many years. But as in other places where democracy is not effective, the government does change, but mostly by means of a *coup d'état*. Sometimes such a *coup* is internally generated, but more frequently it follows from external pressures. We see this in the corporate sector as we saw it in Eastern Europe. It is not a good mechanism of government, nor a good method of corporate governance.

One famous case, the 1986 acquisition of Distillers by Guinness, exemplifies all aspects—strengths and weaknesses—of the market for corporate control. On the one hand, we see a company which suffered from weak management over a protracted period. Shareholders were dissatisfied, but the company made little response to this dissatisfaction, and in the main they either shut up or reduced their holdings. At the same time, the case also reveals the inadequacies of the market for corporate control as a means of sorting out these problems. The costs of change in management by these means are very large. The corruption associated with the process implies that the victor is not necessarily the firm best suited to take control of the corporation, but rather the one most willing to stretch the rules to secure its own victory. Despite all that, it is clear that the results in this case were positive. A major British company is now significantly better run than it was before the discredited events of 1986.

A key policy objective is to achieve the desirable outcomes of contested take-overs without these undesirable mechanisms. On the one hand, this requires greater managerial accountability to shareholders, or to other external monitors on a continued basis (see Davis and Kay, this volume). At the same time, it would then be appropriate to give incumbent management greater protection against hostile take-over. There are various plausible alternative routes to achieving both these goals, including the setting up of 'supervisory boards', common in continental Europe, to oversee the firm's longer-term strategy and performance. We do not believe that the merits of any one of these alternatives are such that policy-makers should be prescriptive. However, we suggest two areas in which development is desirable. The first builds on the democratic governance structure that potentially exists in most firms.

At present, shareholders can easily 'opt out' of governance decisions, leaving top management to run the firm as they please. Shareholders would be less likely to be so 'hands-off' if they had to 'opt in'. Shareholder voting could be made mandatory, perhaps tied to dividend rights. Those seeking election, or re-election, as directors could be required to get the backing of, say, 5 per cent of shareholders in order to be nominated. Similar nomination rules could apply to chairman, chief executive, and auditors, and to changes in executive salaries and share-option schemes. Shareholders would thus have to publicly support individual managers and certain types of corporate decisions, rather than simply not object.

The second innovation could be to establish a code of practice in take-overs, akin to the Highway Code. A series of guide-lines on what constitutes responsible corporate governance could be set out, including, say, appointment of non-executive directors, salaries, and dividend policy. Provided managers stayed within these limits, shareholders could be reasonably certain that management were operating in shareholder interests, and managers could feel reasonably secure from take-over. Managers would be free to take decisions different from those suggested by the code, and might well do so profitably; however, they would in so doing be both alerting their shareholders, and increasing the riskiness of their positions.

In all this discussion, it is important to recognize that the contested bid represents only a small minority of all take-overs. The majority of acquisitions are agreed between buyers and sellers. However, the emergence of very large contested bids has the consequence that these form a much larger proportion of the total value of take-over activity than they do of its total numbers.

What then are the results of take-over activity? There are several ways in which the success of acquisitions may be appraised. One is to contrast

the combined profitability of the merged concerns with that of the independent firms which went to make it up. There is a large number of
British and American studies which attempt to assess this. The details
vary, but there is a commonality of conclusion (see Hughes, this volume).
The impact of mergers and profitability is, on average, nil to negative.
There is no major study which suggests that, overall, profits are increased
by merger. This does not, of course, imply that there are no successful
mergers—there are sufficient case studies to reveal ones that clearly are.
But these statistical analyses take us to a gloomy view of merger activity
success taken as a whole.

An alternative approach is one which concentrates, not on accounting
profits, but on influences on shareholder value (see Franks, this volume).
Here, the question is whether the value of the combined concern is more
than the value of the component parts. There are some indications here—
in contrast to the previous group of studies—that the impact may be positive. That prompts at least two questions. One is who gets these benefits,
and the answer to that seems relatively clear—that the gains overwhelmingly accrue to the shareholders of the firm which is acquired and not to
those of the acquiring firm. The second question is how these observations of a stock market impact can be reconciled with the disappointing
consequences for accounting profits. There are at least three possibilities
here. One is that mergers are indeed value enhancing, but that this
enhancement of value is not fully reflected in accounting data. Most
people's prejudices, including ours, would be that precisely the opposite
was true. There are now sufficiently many well-documented accounts of
the ways in which merger accounting can be used to enhance reported
earnings. An alternative possibility is that markets are persistently, and
unduly, optimistic about the profitability of mergers—reflecting perhaps
equivalent persistent optimism on the part of the managers who promote
them. This is an argument of some plausibility but it denies a view of
efficient markets, and suggests that the sale of companies engaged in
vigorous merger activity would be a relatively straightforward route to
stock market outperformance.

Yet another possibility is that the timing, and the fact, of mergers
involves, as we suggested earlier, the exploitation of valuation discrepancies. Mergers may occur at the end of a period during which the acquired
company has under-performed its value as perceived by the managers of
the acquirer and one in which the acquiring company has outperformed.
The stock market benefit of the merger is then the elimination of these
discrepant valuations. It is an elimination which does little for the quality
of the underlying businesses even if it does do something for market
efficiency.

We might also assess the success of mergers by asking after the event whether they are judged to be a success. This produces, on average, somewhat middling results—that 50 per cent failed, that 50 per cent succeeded. But success and failure here is of course a subjective concept. The main value of this approach is in directing us to some of the characteristics of success and failure. The probability of success is highest for horizontal merger and tends to diminish with the distance between the core business of the acquiring company and the activities of the acquisition. It is not surprising, therefore, that a prominent feature of the British market for corporate control in the 1980s has been the unpicking, or 'unbundling', of conglomerates formed by earlier mergers. Either by direct divestment of subsidiaries, or by break-up following a hostile take-over, many companies have been refocused on a few core activities (see Wright *et al.*, this volume).

The record of mergers, taken as a whole, leaves a good deal to be desired. This prompts us to consider how public policy should treat merger activity. In the UK, policy went through an erratic phase in the early 1980s (Fairburn, this volume). Lonrho was deemed unsuitable to acquire House of Fraser for reasons which were widely thought mainly to relate to the character of its chief executive. The Royal Bank of Scotland could not be acquired lest its head office move from Edinburgh, although, soon after, that was a choice that the still independent bank decided to make for itself.

In a merger between Anderson Strathclyde and Charter Consolidated, the Monopolies and Mergers Commission's (MMC) readiness to be involved as unpaid management consultants sufficiently irritated the then Secretary of State for Trade and Industry as to prompt him to overrule the MMC's recommendations and allow the merger to go ahead. The Tebbit guide-lines which followed that implied a retreat to merger policy based primarily on competition criteria and this has substantially increased the degree of predictability of merger decisions.

The European dimension of merger policy has become increasingly important. Traditionally, the basis of the Commission's jurisdiction over mergers has been dubious. From 1972 onwards, it was agreed that a merger might establish, or actions associated with it might constitute, an abusive and dominant position under Article 86 of the Treaty of Rome. An investigation of the acquisition of a minority stake in Rothmans by Philip Morris in 1987 was used to suggest that a merger might be an agreement between undertakings and hence subject to scrutiny under Article 85. The position has now been clarified through the adoption in 1990 of a Community Mergers Regulation which allows the European Commission Competition Directorate to scrutinize cross-border mergers with a combined turnover of 5 billion Ecus or more (see Bishop (a), this volume). This turnover threshold is very high; however, there are plans to reduce it substantially by the mid-1990s, reducing the effect of what remain extremely varied national merger regulations (see Bishop (b), this volume).

The key issue in framing the Regulation was the relationship between merger policy and industrial policy. This reflects a battle between those who see the 1992 programme as being primarily about the promotion of competition within the Community and those who see its important aspect as being the concentration and restructuring of European industry. This battle—reflected in a national battle between the English and Germans on the one hand and the French and Italians on the other—is largely resolved in the Regulation in favour of competition, although the degree to which this is reflected in implementation of the Regulation in practice remains to be seen. Early indications are mixed. Although a large number of mergers were quickly and uncontroversially approved, the first proposal to be blocked—the proposed acquisition of de Havilland by France's Aerospatiale and Italy's Alenia in October 1991—involved much political posturing and begged questions about the extent of the Competition Commissioner's independence from political pressures.

And yet the key issue in all this is whether the English disease is likely to afflict the European Community. Because there is a real sense in which merger activity has been an English disease. It is reflected in a preoccupation with aggressive plans for acquisition or defensive responses to potential take-over threats, a deal-driven culture founded in a financial system of impressive quality which earns its living from the promotion of transactions. Here a successful transaction means a transaction that is consummated—it does not mean a happy marriage.

This has brought us to a world in which corporate strategy is primarily about the acquisition of a portfolio of businesses. The job of the corporate manager becomes that of acquiring a collection of companies just as the job of the fund manager is to acquire a collection of shares, with equally little regard in either case for the characteristics of the underlying activity. This is not to deny that merger can play an important part in successful strategy, nor that it may well be increasingly critical to success in entering new national markets within Europe (see Davis, Shore, and Thompson, this volume). Yet we should note (see Franks and Mayer, this volume) that expansion by merger and take-over have been British and American preoccupations and have not been a primary concern of our more successful international competitors.

1

Mergers and Economic Performance in the UK: A Survey of the Empirical Evidence 1950–1990

INTRODUCTION

This chapter draws together the results of empirical research on the impact of merger on market structure and economic performance in the UK.[1] It concentrates almost exclusively on the post-war period. The chapter is organized in four sections. In Section 1, possible approaches to assessing the impact of mergers on market structure and company performance and their implications for economic welfare are briefly set out. In Section 2, the principal characteristics of post-war merger activity in the UK are described. Section 3 looks at the relationship between mergers and concentration and diversification as indicators of structural change, whilst Section 4 concentrates upon the impact of merger upon corporate performance. The final section draws the discussion of structure and performance effects together and makes some brief points relevant to competition policy matters.

1. FRAMEWORKS FOR ASSESSING THE IMPACT OF MERGER

The most common approach to assessing the impact of merger upon social welfare is the Trade-Off Model (Williamson (1968)). This is based

* Director of the Small Business Research Centre at the Department of Applied Economics, University of Cambridge.

The author is grateful to Richard Parkin for research assistance in the preparation of the original paper of which this is a substantial revision (Hughes (1989a)). Similarly valuable assistance with the current version was provided by Hong Wang. Support for this work is acknowledged from ESRC, Barclays Bank, the Rural Development Commission, the European Commission, and the Department of Employment under the ESRC Small Firms Initiative.

[1] Direct attention is not paid to the determinants of mergers. General surveys which cover this aspect of the literature may be found in Steiner (1975), Auerbach (1988), Hughes, Mueller, and Singh (1980), and Hindley (1972). Specific analyses of the determinants of the time series pattern of merger include King (1989), Nelson (1959), Geroski (1984), Melicher, Ledolter, and D'Antonio (1983), Holland and Myers (1979), and Golbe and White (1988).

upon a static, partial equilibrium trade-off, of allocative efficiency losses arising from merger-related increases in market power, against any merger-related cost efficiency gains arising from scale, from learning effects for the merging firms; and from the reallocation of output between them and other firms of differing efficiency in the post-merger industry structure (Farrell and Shapiro (1990)). This approach has its most natural application in cases of horizontal merger but is in principle extendable to vertical or diversifying merger. There are well-known problems with it. In practice, the problem of the second best, divergences between private and social benefits and costs, the exclusion from consideration of distributional issues, and the need to consider possible knock-on effects inducing further mergers must all be taken into account before reaching welfare conclusions. (See, for instance, Cowling *et al.* (1980).) Moreover, the static nature of the trade-off and the implicit assumption of a fully employed self-equilibrating economy which lies behind it has often focused attention away from explicit consideration of many of the issues of investment, technical change, export performance, and regional and national employment effects which so much exercise open-economy policy-makers in this area (Hughes, Mueller, and Singh (1980)). The result has been a preoccupation with the impact of merger on concentration as a proxy indicator for monopoly power (and hence allocative inefficiency) on the one hand, and with studies of the impact on merger on private profitability as a proxy for cost efficiency gains on the other. Neither are ideal indicators. Profitability changes are particularly ambiguous in this respect, since even within the terms of the static trade-off model itself they potentially incorporate both monopoly power and cost efficiency effects. However, if all firms face the same post-merger and pre-merger product prices, relative profitability should reflect relative efficiency, and changes in relative profitability should reflect changes in relative costs.[2] The upshot for welfare would still require an assessment of market price and output effects. The idea that mergers will have deleterious monopoly consequences is usually based on the view that they reduce the number of competitors and raise indices of market concentration. By far the most usual indicator of monopoly power used in this connection is therefore some measure of market concentration, and the impact of merger is usually assessed in terms of its relationship to concentration change. Evidence on these market structure effects is discussed in Section 2, along with a critical discussion of the links between them and monopoly power. An assessment of the corporate performance aspects of the merger trade-off is then presented in Section 3.

---

[2] In practice, of course, not all firms in an industry group may benefit equally from market power effects, and individual mergers may involve vertical and diversifying, as well as horizontal, components. The spirit of the argument remains clear enough, however.

The trade-off approach may be contrasted with another, the basic proposition of which is that 'the control of corporations may constitute a valuable asset; that this asset exists independent of any interest in economies of scale or monopoly profits; that an actual market for corporate control exists; and that a great many mergers are probably the result of the successful workings of this market' (Manne (1965)). Management teams compete for the right to control corporate assets, and operating efficiency is ensured by a natural selection mechanism in which the threat, and act, of take-over by raiders ensures the survival of the fittest teams. Poor past performance due to inefficiency or abuse of managerial discretion leads to weak share prices; potential raiders see the opportunity to alter policies and make capital gains as share prices respond to their improved management of the victims assets (Marris (1964); Alchian and Kessel (1962); Meade (1968)). For the stock market selection process to work in this way a number of conditions must be fulfilled. In particular, share prices should reflect the relative expected profitability of firms; raiders should typically be able to distinguish managerial shirking from poor performance due to unfavourable circumstances (Scharfstein (1988)), be motivated by the desire to change non-shareholder welfare-maximizing policies, and be able to obtain a sufficient pay-off to make their activity worth while. These conditions may not be realized. Whilst the market pricing mechanism may be 'efficient' in the sense of responding rapidly to changes in information for instance (Keane (1983)) there is not much to suggest that share price movements are systematically related to the current, past, or subsequent underlying performance variables of companies, or to longer-run equilibrium considerations, rather than those of short-run disequilibrium (Nerlove (1968); Little and Rayner (1966); Shiller (1981); Summers (1986); Camerer (1989)). This leaves considerable scope for take-overs based on speculative and other motives where corporate control changes hands because of differences of opinion about the accuracy of stock market valuations between sellers and purchasers of control, rather than because of proposed changes in management objectives or operating efficiency (Gort (1969); Hughes, Mueller, and Singh (1980)). It also leaves plenty of scope for promoters and arbitrageurs to attempt to manipulate, and benefit from, changes in stock prices associated with take-overs, or the threat of them, in a way unconnected with underlying performance variables (Boesky (1985); Markham (1955)).[3] As one early

---

[3] For another non-standard merger motivation model, see Cable (1977). Here it is argued that, in the case of diversifying merger especially, the search for alternative production possibilities (to allow a company to dissociate itself from an industry or product life cycle) may lead a single bidder to value more highly the investment opportunity information embodied in potential targets than those targets' shareholders themselves do (e.g. because the target's own optimal investment programme does not involve using up these opportunities or

stock market observer noted: 'Since property here exists in the form of stock, its movement and transfer become purely a result of gambling on the stock exchange, where the little fish are swallowed by the sharks and the lambs by the stock exchange wolves' (Marx (1971)).

Even where investors are rational and not fooled by share price manipulations problems can in principle still arise. For instance, where managers have some interest in preventing share price weakness (because, for example, of the threat of take-over), and where imperfectly informed investors use current earnings as a rational forecast of future earnings managerial investment decisions may become myopic. Long-term share value maximizing projects may be sacrificed to boost short-term earnings. This may be so even though the market is not fooled and discounts the current earnings in forecasting the future. The reason is that if investors assume managers do not behave myopically it will pay some managers to do so and boost earnings and share prices to try and avoid take-over. Non-co-operation leads both parties to be worse off; managers are prevented from acting in a long-term value maximizing manner by their desire to boost share prices to avoid take-over, and investors though not fooled by the share price signals that result cannot prevent the myopia that it represents (Stein (1988, 1989)). Equally, if managers are more sensitive to downward mis-pricing of their firms assets than to upward mis-pricing (e.g. because the former attracts take-over bids, and the latter perhaps a mild increase in income), then unless they are protected from these threats they may again sacrifice long-term for short-term projects. The argument here revolves around the greater uncertainty and likely persistence of mis-pricing in the relatively thin markets for long-term compared to short-term assets. Managers will avoid longer-term projects with more uncertain pay-offs so as to avoid the downward mis-pricing of their assets which could attract take-over by arbitrageurs, the gain to the latter being the ability to alter the time profile of pay-offs by cutting investments and realizing other assets of the firm. This has the effect of shortening the pay-off structure and encouraging more arbitrage activity to drive share prices back up and offer capital gains to the raider (Schleifer and Vishny (1990)).

Failures in the market for corporate control may also occur because of transactions cost considerations and because acquiring companies may not be able to capture for themselves all the benefit of the raid. Disciplinary raids are not costless; the price of identifying mismanagement and the transaction costs of correcting it through take-over can be high so that there will always be some margin of management discretion. Indeed, since contested take-overs with higher associated legal and advi-

because the acquiring company perceives possible further search gains on the basis of the information embodied in the targets).

sory costs are more likely to occur in the case of large than small bids
(Newbould (1970)), these costs may be greater for larger 'managerial'
companies giving more discretion just where it needs to be most curbed.
In more general terms, the greater the discretionary benefit of control, the
more rivalrous the market for control may be, and the more raided management may resist, and thus the higher these transaction costs may
become. To the extent that the costs of identifying mismanagement are
lower for raids within the same industry and the likelihood of contests
therefore greater (Halpern (1983)), then where monopolistic structures
exist the costs of imposing discipline will be relatively high since either
the companies involved will be within the same industry but typically
large, or the bid will involve an outsider with higher costs of information
gathering. The sums involved are not negligible. A failed diversifying contested bid for a major company in 1986 is said to have cost the raider £54
million in advisers' and other bid fees (Jay (1986)). These transaction
costs are in part a function of defensive take-over tactics which are
designed to raise either the pre- or post-acquisition costs of gaining control; such methods are well developed in the USA and have spread to the
UK. 'Shark-repellent' constitutional arrangements to protect existing
directors by staggered elections to the board, or particular voting schemes
for bid approvals; 'golden parachutes' to raise the costs of firing incumbent management and either counter-bidding against the raider, seeking a
'white knight' to contest the unwanted bid, or raiding a third party
(Greer (1986)) all throw cost-increasing sand into the works.

Whether this is a virtue or vice depends upon how genuine disciplinary
raids are, and upon the reasons for, and terms which shareholders extract
from top executives in return for offering them this sort of protection
from job loss through take-over. In principle, many of these devices could
be used as part of an overall remuneration and conditions package for
the managers which emphasized whatever incentive structure the active
shareholders desired (Jensen and Meckling (1976); Knoeber (1986);
Hirschey (1986)). This, however, may be expecting rather a lot given the
current structure of governance in the modern corporation in which managers play a leading role in determining their own remuneration and in
selecting outsider directors to serve on corporate boards (Herman 1981;
Morck *et al.* (1989)). In this respect the growth in importance in the UK
of financial institutions as shareholders assumes great significance. For it
may be argued that on the one hand they are able to exercise discipline
from within companies without the need for raiding, whilst on the other
they may impose shareholders' interests as a key factor when bids occur.
There are, however, limitations on their potential role. First, with dispersed shareholdings it may not pay a single institution to bear the costs
of monitoring and disciplining, the benefits of which accrue to all. The

bigger an institution's shareholding the less of a problem this is, but there remain difficulties of co-ordinating action across shareholders. Even amongst financial institutions, different views about possible, or appropriate remedies may exist, as well as different philosophies about taking direct action (Cosh, Hughes, and Singh (1990)). Finally, institutions themselves are subject to market and regulatory forces requiring portfolio performance which may mean that short-term financial factors may dominate their response to raids, in much the same way as other stockholders. Since the incentive to sell out in a bid is lower, the lower the transaction costs associated with subsequent portfolio readjustment, and since the effect of Big Bang will be to lower these costs for institutions, they may be even more likely to 'churn' their portfolios.

The market for corporate control may also fail where inefficiency is combined with substantial owner control at the smaller end of the spectrum of firm sizes. If the valuation placed by owner-managers upon their shares exceeds the marginal valuation ruling in the market, there will be a premium to be paid to effect control which may vary from company to company without any necessary connection with the extent of deviations from value-maximizing policies. As far as small companies are concerned it means that it may be (e.g. in the case of majority ownership) impossible to obtain control, or very costly in the face of a hostile board with large holdings (Davies and Kuehn (1977)). The upshot of these arguments is that the costs of disciplinary action might restrict its exercise to the medium size ranges of companies.

In addition to market failure problems due to transaction costs, it has also been argued that the incentive structure in bids may lead to too few bids from the point of view of disciplining management (Grossman and Hart (1980)). If each of the shareholders in the target firm in a raid believes that an individual decision to sell out will not prevent the bidder from gaining effective control then there is for each of them an incentive to hang on to their equity as minority shareholders in the post-bid situation and 'free ride' on the stock price gains following the new management's efficiency improvements. This prevents the raider from reaping all the benefits, and, in the limit, could prevent successful raids altogether if sufficient shareholders hang on for the free ride. The implication of this argument is that, *ceteris paribus*, the level of merger activity will be less than is warranted since the private return to the raider is less than the overall return which is split between the raiders and the free riders. On the other hand it may be argued that if minority rights of sellers are not protected then partial bids (e.g. for 51 per cent) will occur followed by exploitation of control at the expense of the remaining minority shareholders. This may occur whether the incumbent management are value maximizers or not since in effect the buyer gains complete control whilst paying only half the full purchase price. This could lead to too many 'undesirable' bids, in the sense that they incur transaction costs but merely redistribute wealth between the raider and the oppressed minority rather than create net social value (Yarrow (1985)).

The force of each of these arguments depends upon the institutional and legal constraints within which bidders and potential free riders must operate during and after the bid process.[4] In general, the problem in principle is how to ensure that there are costs imposed on free-riding minority interests whilst ensuring that there is no undue oppression of minority shareholders after partial bids, or unequal treatment of shareholders in the process of the bid itself. In the institutional context of the UK at least there are grounds for thinking that the free rider problem is not a serious deterrent inhibiting the level of merger activity, whilst there is some attempt to deter partial oppressive bids (Davies (1976); Yarrow (1985); Johnston (1980)). In any event the idea that free riding has seriously restricted the overall level of take-over activity does not seem very convincing in the face of the huge take-over waves of the post-war period discussed in the following section. Indeed the argument that on the contrary we have too many take-overs and alternative disciplinary mechanisms may be preferable has become widespread (Cosh, Hughes, and Singh (1990); Franks and Mayer (1990)).

So far the problems raised have all been in the context of managers, especially raiders, basically pursuing share value maximization policies. There is an alternative interpretation of take-over in which it is seen as a vehicle for empire building by growth-maximizing management. On this interpretation mature managerially controlled corporations whose preference for growth may be characterized by the use of a lower discount rate than the market as a whole, will be faced with a sea of undervalued take-over opportunities (Mueller (1969)). They may then initiate take-overs not to benefit shareholders but to satisfy their own empire-building ambitions (Rhoades (1985); Marris (1964); Roll (1986)). Moreover, it has been argued that this 'pursuit of growth may be self-reinforcing; the more managers pursue this objective, the more other managers feel they must conform . . . [thus] rather than deviant managerial behaviour being driven out by stockholder welfare-maximizing behaviour. The so-called "deviant" behaviour has more likely driven out the other' (Marris and Mueller (1980), p. 42).[5]

---

[4] Thus, corporate charter rules may allow raiders to internalize some of the free riders' gains by oppressing, or diluting, minority shareholders' interests in the post-bid situation (Grossman and Hart (1980)), or raiders may use two-tier bids with premiums for early acceptance etc. (Brudney and Chirelstein (1978)). The latter are, however, ruled out by the City Take-over Code in the UK (Johnston (1980)).

[5] This hypothesis is not without its critics either. Thus, Hindley (1972) argues that it would appear that the most likely victims of managerial raids would, because of their

There is little doubt that an active market in corporate control exists in the UK. Assessing its impact involves examining not only the change in corporate performance following merger inherent in the trade-off analysis, but also an examination of the selection process itself in terms of the pre-merger real, financial, and share price characteristics of groups of merging and non-merging firms, and of the institutional framework within which bids take place. This evidence is surveyed in Section 4, which also draws where appropriate on the insights into merger impacts which follow from the other approaches outlined in this section.

2. THE EXTENT AND CHARACTER OF MERGER ACTIVITY

There are a number of ways of measuring the extent of merger activity. The simplest count the absolute numbers of companies disappearing through merger or sum the assets sales or employment of those companies or the amounts paid in carrying out the mergers in which they are involved. For comparisons over time there are obvious shortcomings in relying on current price values of, for example, sales, so deflated series are needed. If the size of the economy is changing then it would also be preferable to express merger activity relative to appropriate population totals. Moreover, for some purposes, for instance comparing the relative importance of growth by merger and growth by investment in new plant and equipment, it would be preferable to measure expenditure on mergers as a percentage of, say, total uses of corporate funds, or of total internal and external expenditure on assets. It is possible to construct series on each of these bases for parts of the economy, especially for industrial and commercial companies, or manufacturing and distribution, and for parts of the post-war period, but there is no long run comparable series on any of them for the whole economy. Nevertheless, although the series chosen may affect the particular year in which merger activity peaked, the broad picture which emerges is clear enough.

2.1. Mergers 1945–1973

Merger activity took off in the late 1950s and early 1960s compared with the previous decade (Brooks and Smith (1963); Bull and Vice (1961);

market valuation, be managerial companies themselves, and therefore auxiliary hypotheses are needed such as that the high capital and transactions costs involved in acquiring the biggest managerially controlled corporations grant them relative immunity. However, this assumes that owner-controlled companies are necessarily more 'efficient', whatever their growth–profit combination. Moreover, the important point remains that the objective of a managerial raid would not be to pursue shareholder-orientated activity after merger. So long as there is slack in the market for corporate control as a result of the factors discussed next, then scope for this sort of behaviour exists. (See also Helm (1989) and Hughes and Singh (1987).)

Mennel (1962); Moon (1968)). It accelerated further from 1967 onwards culminating in twin peaks of activity in the late 1960s and early 1970s. In the peak years 1967–73 the spread of activity encompassed both the financial and non-financial sectors and was at least as intensive as anything previously experienced in the UK (Hannah (1976)). Of the top 200 UK manufacturing companies in 1964, 39 were acquired or merged by 1969, and of the top 200 in 1969 a further 22 were acquired or merged by 1972 (Hughes (1976)). GEC acquired two of its principal rivals, AEI and English Electric; Rowntree Mackintosh and British Leyland were formed; and the Industrial Reorganization Corporation (IRC), as a government agency charged with promoting structural change and efficiency, was directly involved in a promotional or advisory role in 22 mergers involving around £1 billion of net assets between 1967 and 1970 (Cosh, Hughes, and Singh (1980)). Extensive activity occurred in engineering, vehicles, food, drink, textiles, paper printing and publishing, and distribution (HMSO (1978); Cowling *et al.* (1980); Cosh, Hughes, and Singh (1980)). There were major banking mergers after 1968 which resulted in a reduction of the number of clearing banks from 11 to 5 and a series of mergers linking clearing and merchant banks (Aaronovitch and Sawyer (1975a)). Mergers were in the main horizontal in direction. From 1967 to 1969 inclusive, of all proposed mergers falling within the scope of the competition policy authorities, the proportion that were horizontal varied between 79 per cent and 91 per cent by value and between 80 per cent and 86 per cent by number (Gribbin (1974)). In the period 1970–3 they accounted for 74 per cent by number and 65 per cent by value (Graham (1979)). In many cases mergers had a major impact on the financial structure of merging companies, as the means of financing successful bids tended to raise gearing substantially (Cosh, Hughes, and Singh (1980); Meeks (1977)). Although there is not much evidence bearing directly on the issue it appears that foreign acquisitions played relatively little part in this wave, which was mirrored in an intensification of intra-national merger activity in nearly all the major industrial nations (Hughes and Singh (1980)).

2.2. Mergers 1969–1990

Table 1.1 takes this period of intensive activity as a base from which to update the story. It provides data on the average annual expenditure upon, numbers of, and financing of domestic and overseas acquisitions of other companies, and of subsidiaries of other companies, by UK industrial and commercial companies. As columns 1–3 of the table show, merger activity in terms of both acquisition expenditures, and numbers acquired, in the period 1974–81, was around a half its peak level of the

Table 1.1. Expenditure upon, numbers of, and financing of acquisitions and mergers by industrial and commercial companies at home and abroad, 1967–1990

Period	Within the UK									Abroad			Total		
	(1) No.	(2) Expenditure (£m.)	(3) Expenditure in 1962 stock market prices[a] (£m.)	(4) Expenditure as a percentage of gross fixed capital formation[b]	(5) Sales of subsidiaries as a percentage of all acquisitions and mergers — No.	(6) Expenditure	(7) Percentage of expenditure accounted for by — Cash	(8) Issues of ordinary	(9) Issues of fixed interest	(10) No.	(11) Expenditure (£m.)	(12) Expenditure in 1962 stock market prices (£m.)	(13) No.	(14) Expenditure (£m.)	(15) Expenditure in 1962 stock market prices (£m.)
Annual averages[c]															
1969–73	988	1,388	777	38.6	21.6	13.0	30.8	49.2	20.0	66	95.4	54.9	1,054	1,483	832
1974–81	459	947	426	7.7	26.4	16.1	61.8	33.1	5.1	50	341.4	135.2	509	1,289	561
1982–5	488	4,278	777	20.1	31.4	21.7	49.0	42.9	8.1	73	726.3	142.2	561	5,005	914
1986–9	1,301	20,500	1,930	48.8	26.7	23.3	53.3	38.0	8.8	367	6,549.3	618.8	1,668	27,049	2,594
1986	842	15,370	1,790	50.7	26.2	20.1	26.0	57.0	17.0	212	4,735	551.5	1,054	20,105	2,342
1987	1,527	16,539	1,459	44.8	22.3	28.2	35.0	60.0	5.0	282	5,972	526.9	1,809	22,511	2,207
1988	1,499	22,836	2,239	49.1	25.1	24.2	70.0	22.0	8.0	444	5,547	544.0	1,943	28,383	2,783
1989	1,336	27,253	2,231	50.6	33.0	20.8	82.0	13.0	5.0	529	9,943	813.9	1,865	37,196	3,045
1990	778	8,252	688	n.a.	43.2	35.6	75.0	20.0	5.0	n.a.	n.a.	n.a.	n.a.	n.a.	n.a.

Note: The data for activity within the UK are principally based on an analysis of press reports. From 1969 to 1985 this is also true for overseas mergers. From 1986, however, the latter are based on enquiries to companies as well as press reports and arise from exercises conducted to compile inward and outward investment flow data for the Balance of Payments tables in the national accounts. This probably increased both the scope and quality of the data analysed. Overseas acquisitions which are made indirectly via an existing overseas subsidiary are excluded. Acquisitions by UK firms of the subsidiaries of overseas companies in the UK are counted as domestic acquisitions, as are acquisitions of UK companies by UK subsidiaries of overseas firms.

[a] Actual expenditure (usually the stockmarket value of the successful offer) deflated by the FT Actuaries Industrial Ordinary Share Index, 1962 = 100.
[b] Actual expenditure as a percentage of gross domestic fixed capital formation at current prices adjusted for leasing.
[c] The first 5 rows are annual averages for the periods shown. Overseas data for 1986 to 1990 are not strictly comparable with data for 1969 to 1986. See note.

Sources: Economic Trends Annual Supplement, National Income and Expenditure, Annual Abstract, Financial Statistics, *Business Monitor MQ7*, CSO *Business Bulletin*, Acquisitions and Mergers within the UK.

years 1967–73. In the period 1982–5, however, expenditures rose significantly. By 1986 expenditure in real terms was in excess of the levels reached in the previous post-war peak years of 1968 and 1973. There was no corresponding increase in numbers acquired. The first phase of the 1980s merger wave was therefore the product of relatively few relatively massive mergers. At one stage in 1986 there were four proposed manufacturing mergers involving one or more bidders worth over £1 billion each (United Biscuits/Imperial/Hanson Trust £1.2–1.9 billion, GEC/Plessey £1.2 billion, Argyll/Distillers/Guinness £1.9 billion, and Elders IXL/Allied £1.8 billion). Of the independent companies acquired in that year 10 per cent accounted for over 85 per cent of total expenditure, whilst the top 10 per cent of subsidiaries acquired accounted for over 60 per cent of total acquisition expenditure on subsidiaries (*Business Monitor MQ7*, 1987 Q1). Of the top 200 UK quoted companies by market valuation in March 1982, 23 had been acquired by March 1986 (see further Table 1.5 below) which is on a par with the experience of the late 1960s discussed earlier. After 1986 the numbers of companies acquired rose enormously. Expenditure in real terms rose too, especially in 1988 and 1989. As a result of these trends over 1,300 companies were acquired on average in the years 1986–9 compared with around 1,000 in the 1969–73 peak, whilst expenditure in real terms was nearly three times as high. Of course between these years the economy as a whole grew too, so a comparison of real values alone may give a misleading impression of the importance of merger relative to other forms of corporate growth. In fact column 4 of Table 1.1, which expresses acquisition expenditure as a percentage of gross domestic fixed capital formation (GDFCF), does show that the 1986–9 peak was more substantial than that of 1969–73. In the late 1980s acquisition expenditure in the UK was running at around half the level of overall GDFCF, compared to around 40 per cent in the earlier peak. As the table also shows this level of expenditure was primarily funded by the use of cash and equity. The use of debt fell significantly after the peak years 1969–73. The possible implications of these financing patterns for merger motivation and outcomes are discussed further below (in the evaluation of the share price impact of merger).[6]

2.3. Sales of Subsidiaries

The growing importance of giant mergers and acquisitions as a proportion of total activity was paralleled by an increase in the number of, and

[6] The ultimate impact of merger on gearing depends not only upon the way the equity of the acquired company is replaced, but also upon the relative size and gearing of the partners to the deal. These impacts can be very substantial. For the UK wave of 1967–70, see e.g. Cosh, Hughes, and Singh (1980). The impact of the current wave has not been systematically investigated.

size of, sales of subsidiaries between companies. This increased from around 20 per cent by number and 13 per cent by value in the 1969–73 peak, to around 26 per cent by number and 23 per cent by value, by 1986–9. Moreover, whereas prior to 1979 there were few subsidiary sales of absolutely large dimensions (Lye and Silberston (1981); Chiplin and Wright (1980)), since then a number of very large transactions have occurred. Thus in 1984 when the six largest independent company acquisitions had an average value of around £100 million, the *three largest sales of subsidiaries between groups averaged £90 million (Business Monitor MQ7,* 1986 Q4). Promises to sell major divisions posing potential monopoly problems also came to play a role in a kind of pre-emptive strategy played by some would-be acquirers to forestall references to the Monopolies and Mergers Commission (MMC).

2.4. Overseas Acquisitions and Regional Patterns

The third notable feature of Table 1.1 is the growth in importance of overseas acquisitions relative to domestic ones, revealed by columns 8–11. In annual average terms in the period 1969–73 around 6 per cent by number, and value, of total independent company acquisitions were made abroad, while in the period 1982–5 these figures were over 13 per cent by number and 15 per cent by value.[7] The vast bulk of this activity was outside the EC. (*Business Monitor MQ7,* 1987 Q1). The data for the years 1986–9 are higher still. This, however, is in part a reflection of the improved system of overseas acquisition reporting noted under the table. These data none the less reveal how significant external take-over activity had become by the late 1980s. Over 25 per cent by value and 22 per cent by number of all acquisitions by UK industrial and commercial companies took place abroad in the period 1986–9. Tables 1.2–3 explore the geographical distribution of this activity, and in addition the characteristics of inward acquisition into the UK by overseas companies. As well as being somewhat more comprehensive in coverage of recorded acquisitions these data also cover the whole economy and not just the industrial and commercial sector. Table 1.2 reveals that there has been a steady increase in the numbers of overseas acquisitions by UK businesses and in total acquisition expenditure in the period 1986–90. Activity seems to have peaked in 1989. The USA and Canada were the most important destinations for this activity especially in value terms. The run-up to 1992, however, was associated with a substantial shift towards EC acquisitions, but

---

[7] This mirrors a general increase in the relative importance of investment overseas by UK industrial and commercial companies, which in the period 1979–84 was running at around 12% of total uses of funds, compared with between 5% and 7% in the previous sub-periods 1958–62, 1963–7, 1968–72, and 1973–8 (Hughes (1986)).

these acquisitions were substantially smaller than those in North America as a comparison of the percentages of numbers and values reveals. Table 1.3 shows that the UK has been a target for increasing cross-border mergers from both the EC and North America. Inward acquisition too seems to have peaked in 1989; though it has been dwarfed by the out-ward flows. In the years 1986–9 UK acquisitions overseas were over five times more numerous than inward take-overs and involved nearly three times as much expenditure, although these trends were dominated by the North America/UK pattern. The picture for the EC alone was different. Numerically UK businesses acquired nearly six times as many EC busi-nesses as the latter acquired in the UK. These UK purchases were typi-cally much smaller than the EC purchases since the total value of the latter outstripped the UK expenditure abroad. European acquirers evi-dently found much bigger targets for their activity in the UK than vice versa (for a detailed company breakdown confirming the pattern using commercial data sources see Coopers & Lybrand (1989)). Although the relative significance of the UK in terms of cross-border acquisition activ-ity involving its own businesses is fairly clear from this data, the overall significance of its position in terms of intra-national activity is much less easily identified. What scattered evidence there is suggests that the UK and USA are probably more merger-intensive than Japan and the EC economies (Hughes (1976); Hughes and Singh (1980); OECD (1984); Odagiri and Hase (1989); Franks and Mayer (1990)). From the point of view of the market for corporate control what is perhaps equally as significant is whether the take-overs which occur are hostile (i.e. against the wishes of incumbent management). Here the evidence seems more clear-cut. The UK (along with the USA) is much more characterized by hostile or contested take-overs than other advanced economies. Thus one recent study identified 26 contested bids in the EC in 1988. Of these, 23 were in the UK (Coopers & Lybrand (1989), see also Franks and Mayer (1990) and Odagiri and Hase (1989)). The fact that 5 of the 23 hostile bids in the UK were by overseas companies, and a mere 5 of the 606 overseas acquisitions by UK companies in 1988 recorded in Table 1.2 were contested (CSO (1990)) suggests that when in Rome companies do as the Romans do; in the UK that means they indulge in more contested bids than elsewhere.

Despite the difficulties of tracking international take-overs it is worth noting that the spatial incidence of merger outside the UK is much better documented than spatial incidence within the economy. This is disap-pointing in view of the emphasis on regional balance as one of the public interest issues relevant to MMC investigations. Samples of mergers for the early and mid-1970s and the 1980s do, however, suggest a distinct regional imbalance, with the South-east in particular accounting for a

Table 1.2. Cross-border acquisitions and merger by UK companies, 1986–1990

(a) *Numbers*

Period	EC		USA and Canada		Other developed economies		Developing economies		All	
	No.	%	No.	%	No.	%	No.	%	No.	%
Annual average										
1986–9	165	32.4	253	49.7	56	11.0	34	6.7	509	100
1986	62	19.6	195	61.5	26	8.2	34	10.7	317	100
1987	124	28.8	214	49.7	52	12.1	41	9.5	431	100
1988	191	31.5	311	51.3	66	10.9	38	6.3	606	100
1989	282	41.5	293	43.1	81	11.9	24	3.5	680	100
1990 (Q1–3)	148	40.4	153	41.8	36	9.8	29	7.9	366	100

(b) *Values*

Period	EC		USA and Canada		Other developed economies		Developing economies		All	
	Value (£m.)	%	Value (£m.)	%	Value (£m.)	%	Value (£m.)	%	Value (£m.)	%
Annual average										
1986–9	1,688	11.1	12,599	82.7	724	4.8	223	1.5	15,234	100
1986	643	7.2	8,151	91.2	104	1.2	41	0.5	8,940	100
1987	1,615	13.4	9,523	79.0	607	5.0	314	2.6	12,059	100
1988	1,764	10.2	14,211	82.1	1,159	6.7	183	1.1	17,317	100
1989	2,729	12.1	18,512	81.8	1,026	4.5	354	1.6	22,620	100
1990 (Q1–3)	1,972	25.7	5,145	67.0	497	6.5	70	0.9	7,683	100

Note: The data in (a) differ from that for overseas activity shown in Table 1.1 in a number of respects. They cover all businesses and not just the commercial and industrial sector analysed in Table 1.1. The data also include indirect acquisitions abroad via subsidiaries of UK companies and similar acquisitions in the UK by subsidiaries of overseas firms both of which are excluded in Table 1.1.

Source: CSO *Business Bulletin*, Cross-border Acquisitions and Mergers (Q3, 1990).

Table 1.3. Cross-border acquisitions and disposals by UK and overseas companies 1986–1990

Period	Ratio (UK/Overseas)				Average value (£m.)			
	No.		Value		UK companies		Overseas companies	
	Acquisitions	Disposals	Acquisitions	Disposals	Acquisitions	Disposals	Acquisitions	Disposals
1986–9	5.53	6.32	2.71	2.43	29.9	28.0	60.2	71.3
1986	6.10	7.80	3.07	4.40	28.2	18.6	55.3	35.7
1987	7.43	7.38	4.48	3.33	28.0	33.6	46.6	74.9
1988	6.45	5.29	3.04	5.57	28.6	35.0	60.5	31.8
1989	4.17	6.05	2.07	1.13	33.3	25.8	66.9	137.1
1990 (Q1–3)	2.88	5.31	0.80	4.09	21.0	53.2	74.0	69.5

Source: Calculated from CSO *Business Bulletin*, Cross-border Acquisitions and Mergers (Q3, 1990).

share of acquirers (and to a lesser extent acquired companies) substantially greater than would be suggested by its share in, say, total employment (Leigh and North (1978); Goddard and Smith (1978); Coppins (1991)). The net result has been an increase in the degree to which plants and companies outside the South-east are controlled by companies with headquarters in that region. The possible impact of these effects is discussed in Section 4 below.

2.5. The Industrial and Size Distribution of Merger

Table 1.1 related only to commercial and industrial companies; the companion series relating to financial companies has not been published since 1980. It showed that financial sector acquisitions fell off sharply after 1973 and had not recovered by 1980. Thus the annual average number of financial companies acquired in the period 1969–73 was 101 and the average current price value of expenditure was £342 million. In the period 1974–9 the respective averages were 47 and £180 million (*Annual Abstract of Statistics*, 1985 and 1986, tables 1750 and 421 respectively). To examine what has happened since then, and to provide an economy-wide industry breakdown of merger activity we have to make use of the Office of Fair Trading's analysis of proposed mergers falling within the scope of the Fair Trading Act. This series records merger proposals, a number of which will in the event not be proceeded with, and is restricted to those which would create or intensify a 25 per cent national or regional market share (33.3 per cent prior to 1973) or pass a minimum gross assets size test which was £5 million from 1965 to 1980, £15 million from 1980 to 1983, and was raised to £30 million in 1984. It therefore excludes a large number of the transactions recorded in Table 1.1. On the other hand its industrial coverage includes insurance, banking and finance, and building society mergers, along with other miscellaneous financial services excluded from the industrial and commercial companies data. Table 1.4 based on this source shows that target companies in finance accounted for around 25 per cent by number and 60 per cent by assets of total proposed mergers in the first half of the 1980s. After 1985 they declined significantly in relative numerical terms. The peak years of 1988 and 1989 were dominated by manufacturing bids both numerically and in terms of value.

2.6. The Industrial Direction of Merger and the Size Distribution of Merger Deaths

From the point of view of the impact of merger upon market structure it is necessary to look not only at the overall extent and industry spread of

Table 1.4. Distribution, by industry of target company, of merger proposals falling within the scope of the Mergers Panel, 1980–1989

Year	Total no.	Total asset value (£bn.)	Percentage by no.				Percentage by asset value			
			Manufacturing	All services	Distribution	Finance	Manufacturing	All services	Distribution	Finance
1980–4[a]	987(694)	218.0 (212.3)	44.0	48.2	10.8	24.9	20.5	69.9	5.6	59.5
1985–9	1,413	497.7	49.6	43.3	11.2	15.3	34.7	55.0	5.6	41.2
1985	192	57.5	44.4	50.9	13.0	24.9	35.2	64.0	5.6	53.6
1986	313	123.3	47.4	44.4	9.6	20.7	39.0	58.8	5.6	47.2
1987	321	121.9	49.4	44.6	13.1	12.8	21.5	76.0	4.3	62.4
1988	306	98.9	54.9	35.9	10.8	9.8	30.0	30.9	5.0	17.8
1989	281	96.1	52.0	40.9	9.6	8.2	47.6	45.3	7.7	24.9

[a] From April 1980 to July 1984 the asset criterion for possible referrals was £15m.: this was raised to £30m. in July 1984. The data here refer to activity measured on the £15m. cut-off. Aggregate figures that would have been produced in the period 1980–4 had the £30m. cut-off been in effect in that period are shown in brackets.

Source: Annual Reports of the Office of Fair Trading.

Table 1.5. Distribution, by type of integration, of the numbers and value of assets to be acquired in proposed mergers considered by the Mergers Panel, 1965–1989

Period	Total no.	Percentage horizontal		Percentage vertical		Percentage diversifying	
		No.	Assets	No.	Assets	No.	Assets
1965–9	466	82	89	6	5	13	7
1970–4	579	73	65	5	4	23	27
1975–9	1,003	62	67	9	7	29	26
1980–4	987	65	71	5	2	30	27
1985–9	1,413	62	57	2	2	35	41
1985	192	58	42	4	4	38	54
1986	313	69	74	2	1	29	25
1987	321	67	80	3	1	30	19
1988	306	58	45	1	1	41	54
1989	281	60	44	2	3	37	53

Sources: Annual Reports of the Office of Fair Trading; Department of Prices and Consumer Protection (1978).

activity but also at its direction and the size distribution of acquirers and acquired companies. There are great difficulties in classifying mergers by type not least because in many cases elements of horizontal, vertical, and conglomerate expansion coexist. A classification has been attempted by the Office of Fair Trading, however, using the data underlying Table 1.4, and Table 1.5 draws on this. It shows that there has been an increase in the importance of diversifying mergers since 1970. Until 1984 this showed up most noticeably in terms of numbers. In 1985, however, diversifying mergers accounted for over a half of all assets involved in proposed mergers as they also did in the peak years 1988 and 1989. Horizontal activity has remained the dominant form numerically even though its position has slipped compared to the peak years of the late 1960s and early 1970s.[8]

[8] This analysis is, of course, based upon large mergers falling within the scope of the Fair Trading Act, which is selecting partly on market share criteria and so may be biased toward identifying horizontal merger. The asset criterion ensures wide coverage, however, and any bias arising must come from different diversification rates for small rather than large acquisition. As far as sales of subsidiaries are concerned, Chiplin and Wright (1980) report that 60% of purchases in the period 1977–9 were horizontal (i.e. the acquiring company was in the same 2-digit industry as the subsidiary). Lye and Silberston (1981) on the same basis record 50% as horizontal for the year 1979. Interestingly both studies suggest that the companies selling the subsidiaries were divesting outside their primary industry. Thus 70% of the 1979 divestments are classified as conglomerate by Lye and Silberston.

We have already noted the importance of large mergers in the current wave. Table 1.6 allows us to examine the relationship between size and death by acquisition more systematically. It looks at patterns of acquisition death in three time periods spanning the years 1969–90 for successive samples of the largest UK quoted companies. The table shows quite clearly the relative invulnerability of the very largest companies. The top 50 have the lowest merger death-rate by far in every period, followed by those ranked 51–100. The middle-sized giants, ranked 101–200, experienced a substantial decline in their susceptibility to merger death in the 1970s. In the 1980s, however, this was reversed. Indeed in the period 1982–6 they experienced the highest merger deaths of all groups except those ranked 601–800, which shared a 17 per cent fatality rate. The substantial expansion of numbers acquired after mid-1986 was concentrated outside the top 200, so that the relative invulnerability of that group was re-established at levels comparable to those of the mid- and late 1960s. In the main the middle-sized giants were acquired by their larger brethren. Thus further analysis of the calculations underlying Table 1.6 show that all but one of the 23 top 200 deaths outside the top 50 in the period 1982–6 was of a smaller by a larger company. Ten of the acquirers were ranked 1–50. Goliath has continued to kill David.

2.7. Summary

In the broadest of terms we may sum up this section as showing that in the post-war period the UK has experienced two major periods of activity. Compared to the first (of the late 1960s–early 1970s) the merger wave of the 1980s was at first dominated by fewer larger acquisitions, both of independent companies and subsidiaries. After 1986 this was accompanied by a substantial increase in smaller acquisitions. The 1980s' mergers were financed predominantly by cash and equities, and were characterized by a growing proportion of overseas and diversifying mergers. Mergers in manufacturing continued to play a central role but there was a very significant level of activity in banking, insurance, and finance as well as in distribution. As in previous waves increased merger activity went hand in hand with an increased vulnerability of the middle-sized giants to raids by their bigger brethren. In the next two sections we look at the effects of mergers in the UK before, during, and after the first great merger peak.

Table 1.6. Distribution of merger death-rates by size of companies 1969–1990

Rank in terms of market value or sales[a]	Quoted companies ranked by net assets merged or acquired 1969–72	Quoted companies ranked by 1972 sales acquired 1972–82[b] (5-year average)		1,000 largest UK quoted companies by market valuation merged or acquired in the 5-year periods		
				Mar. 1982–Mar. 1986 (by Mar. 1982 rank)		Apr. 1986–June 1990 (by Apr. 1986 rank)
	%	%	No.	%	No.	%
1–50	6	3.6	1	2.0	3	6.0
51–100	10	8.0	5	10.0	5	10.0
101–200	14	10.7	17	17.0	16	16.0
1–200	11	5.6	23	11.5	24	12.0
201–400	—	13.8	22	11.0	43	21.5
401–600	—	17.8	28	14.0	57	28.5
601–800	—	19.5	34	17.0	41	20.5
801–1,000	—	20.7	30	15.0	53	26.5
1–1,000	—	15.2	137	13.7	218	21.8
Annual average	—	2.2	27.4	2.7	41.5	4.2

[a] The data relate to companies acquired or merged ranked by their opening size in successive periods. For 1969–72 the data refer to the largest 200 manufacturing quoted companies in the UK ranked by net assets. For 1972–82 the data refer to 729 quoted companies ranked by sales within the *Times* 1,000 list of largest UK companies. For 1982–6 the data relate to the largest 1,000 UK quoted companies by market valuation in Mar. 1982. For 1986–90 they refer to the largest 1,000 UK companies ranked by market valuation in Apr. 1986.

[b] The percentages acquired over the 10-year period have been divided by 2 to make them comparable to the 5-year sub-periods 1982–6 and 1986–90.

Sources: Own calculations based on *Stock Exchange Fact Book*; *Quality of Markets Quarterly*; Hughes and Kumar (1985); Hughes (1976).

3. MERGERS, CONCENTRATION, DIVERSIFICATION, AND MONOPOLY
POWER

The merger activity described in the previous section has been associated
with important variations in both aggregate and market concentration
and in corporate diversification. The nature of the relationship between
merger and concentration and the implications of this in turn for competition has attracted most attention, particularly for the period encom-
passing the upswing and peak in merger activity in the 1960s. The growth
in the importance of non-horizontal mergers has, however, also led to
similar questions being asked about the relationship between mergers
diversification and competition.[9]

3.1. Trends in Concentration and Diversification

Between 1951 and 1958 market concentration in terms of employment in
UK manufacturing industry was rising at about 0.4 per cent per annum.[10]
Between 1958 and 1968 it grew on average at double that rate (from 1958
to 1963 at 1 per cent p.a. and from 1963 to 1968 at 0.7 per cent p.a.)
(Hart and Clarke (1980)). Although less well-documented increases in
concentration in the late 1950s and 1960s also appear to have occurred in
distribution and in the financial sector (HMSO (1978); Aaronovitch and
Sawyer (1975a); Wilson (1980)). In manufacturing these increases were
followed from the late 1960s onwards by a decade of stability. The share
of the largest five employers in employment, sales, and net output hardly
changed from 1970 to 1979, and fell in the 1980s (Hughes (1990)).[11] In
terms of aggregate concentration the period 1949–58 saw the share of the
top 100 UK manufacturers in net output rise from 22 per cent to 32 per
cent (an increase of almost 50 per cent). The next decade to 1968 saw a
further rise to 41 per cent, but this represented a much slower percentage
change than in the previous period (Prais (1976)). Since 1968 aggregate
concentration, like market concentration, has shown little tendency to rise
either in the manufacturing sector or in the economy as a whole (Hughes
and Kumar (1984a,b)). In the 1980s the share of the largest 100 employers in employment sales and output all fell between 1979 and the late

---

[9] There has been much less emphasis on the link with vertical integration and its impact
on competition. See, however, the case study of Courtaulds in Cowling *et al.* (1980) for a
discussion of the issues involved.

[10] Measured in terms of changes in the average 3- or 5-firm employment concentration
ratio for samples of comparable manufacturing industries at the 3-digit level.

[11] A similar picture appears in terms of 5-firm sales concentration ratios at the 4-digit
level. Thus, Utton and Morgan (1983) report the average 5-firm sales concentration ratio
for 121 product groups in manufacturing as rising from 56.5% in 1958 to 64.8% in 1968 and
then remaining at 64.8% in 1977.

1980s (Hughes (1990)). It is interesting at this stage to note that although concentration has obviously risen substantially since the war and then stabilized, and that merger activity too has shown periods of great intensity followed by periods of stagnation, there is not a simple one-to-one match between the two. Thus although market concentration was rising fastest in the 1960s when merger activity took off, the peak period of acquisition activity between 1968 and 1973 was not reflected in especially fast increases in either market or aggregation concentration. Nor did the period of the fastest rate of change of aggregate concentration in the 1950s coincide with the peak in merger activity in the 1960s. On the other hand the slow-down in concentration after 1973 was associated at first with low merger activity. In the first half of the 1980s the upsurge in large mergers left manufacturing concentration untouched. The impact of 1988–9 mergers has yet to be evaluated.

These changes in concentration have been accompanied by important changes in the extent to which the largest companies are diversified across a spectrum of different industries, although the nature of the official UK data means that the vast majority of studies for the UK are for manufacturing companies only and relate to diversification *within* manufacturing. This excludes the impact of non-manufacturing output produced by firms primarily operating in manufacturing and vice versa. This may be a considerable omission in a world in which cigarette manufacturers buy insurance firms and hotel chains. Moreover, in practice only the crudest distinctions, if any, are made between diversification and vertical integration so that it might be more accurate to term most UK estimates as relating to non-horizontal rather than diversified activity. It does none the less appear that there has been an increase in the post-war period in the extent of diversified manufacturing production in the UK (Utton (1979); Gorecki (1975); Hassid (1975)). However, the bulk of this might be considered narrow-spectrum diversification (Wood (1971)), that is to say, outside a primary industry at a fairly fine level of disaggregation (3- or 4-digit) but inside a broader industry order (2-digit) of which it forms a part (Utton (1979)).[12] A more recent study based on a decomposition of census 3-digit employment data using the Herfindahl index measure of diversification (Clarke and Davies (1983)) confirms the tendency for overall *within*-manufacturing diversification to rise 1963–8 and suggests that within that there was a decline in the portion attributable to broad-spectrum activity, a decline which was accentuated in the period 1971–7. For the 1970s as a whole the most recent estimate available is based on an analysis of the sales of UK quoted companies (Cosh, Hughes, Kumar,

---

[12] Utton estimates narrow-spectrum diversified employment (taking mechanical and electrical engineering, vehicles, and metal goods as one approximately 2-digit group or order) as amounting to 58% of total diversified employment in 1972.

and Singh (1985)). This includes broad diversification beyond manufacturing and is based on company accounts data. For samples of the largest
100 companies and a further 110 companies drawn from the food, engineering, bricks, pottery, and glass, and the retail industries they show substantial increases in diversification on a number of bases including the
Utton and Herfindahl indices and simpler measures such as the number
of industries in which sales are made. What has been the role of merger
in these changes in concentration and diversification?

3.2. Mergers and Market Concentration

The cross-section link between mergers and industry or market concentration may be explored in terms of regression analysis, counterfactual
studies, or case studies.

3.2.1. Regression Analysis Hart and Clarke (1980) use company data on
merger expenditures as a percentage of opening net assets at the 2-digit
level of aggregation in a cross-section regression along with opening level
concentration and logarithmic changes in plant scale, industry size, and
the ratio of plants to enterprises, to explain changes in the logarithm of
the five-firm employment concentration ratio for 76 3-digit industries in
the period 1958–68. For want of better data each 3-digit industry is allocated the merger rate of the 2-digit industry to which it belongs. The
mergers proxy was statistically significant, but when added to the other
variables it increased the explained variation in concentration change by
only 4.6 per cent. Similarly Gratton and Kemp (1977) use quoted company data on the number of mergers per year at the 2-digit level to construct a dummy variable for high, medium, and low merger activity for
use in a regression along with opening concentration levels, sales growth,
and advertising intensity to explain changes in concentration at the 4-
digit level for 284 industries in the period 1963–8. The high merger
dummy is found to be statistically significant for the producer goods
industries, and for the sample as a whole, but not for the consumer goods
group. The different levels of aggregation of the merger series and the
concentration series are a problem in regression exercises of this type, and
it can be argued that using the same values for merger intensity across all
3-digit industries within a 2-digit group will lead to a systematic downward bias in the merger coefficient and in its estimated contribution to
concentration change (Hart and Clarke (1980)).[13] There is another problem, however, and that is that the merger series themselves are not well

---

[13] In effect the argument is that the 2-digit-level value of merger activity will be higher than
it would be for individual 3-digit industries and its variance will be low because the same
value is used for all industries within a given 2-digit group. (See Curry and George (1983).)

suited for the purpose in hand since they include cross-industry as well as within-industry mergers. Thus an industry with a very high level of expenditure may have a high proportion of it spent outside its primary group, and one with a low level of expenditure may have a high proportion of its members acquired by companies from other industries (see, for instance, Goudie and Meeks (1982); Cosh, Hughes, and Singh (1980)). This problem has unpredictable effects a priori on the estimated importance of merger. An alternative way of using the company merger data is to combine it with company asset size data at the same level of aggregation. Thus, Hughes (1976) correlated merger activity (measured as the percentage of an industry's assets acquired) with changes in the three-company asset concentration ratio for UK quoted manufacturing companies, both measured at the 2-digit level, and found a significantly positive relationship for the period 1954–68 as a whole and for two of three sub-periods within it (1960–4 being the odd one out). Taken as a whole these studies suggest a positive but not always inevitable link between high concentration increases and high merger activity.

3.2.2. Counterfactual Approaches The data on company asset size and acquisition activity has also been used to produce counterfactual estimates of the impact of merger (Utton (1971); Hannah and Kay (1977)). The method used is essentially as follows. Calculate an asset concentration measure on the actual company size distributions in the opening- (C_o) and end-year (C_n) of the analysis. To estimate the impact on concentration of mergers occurring between those years either demerge the end-year population using end-year size, based on assumed counterfactual growth-rates, and calculate a new concentration statistic (C_D); or merge the opening-year population as if all the mergers had occurred in the opening-year, and calculate an adjusted opening-year concentration index (C_m). In the first case the impact of merger is $C_n - C_D/C_n - C_o \times 100$ and in the second case it is $C_m - C_o/C_n - C_o \times 100$.

Depending upon the counterfactual growth-rates assumed in the first method, and the methods of concentration measurement adopted, various estimates can result. Utton, using the variance of logarithms as his concentration measure, at the 2-digit industry level, reports mergers as accounting for between one-fifth and four-fifths of concentration changes between 1954 and 1965, depending upon the industry, and upon whether the first or second counterfactual method outlined above is used. For the period 1957–69, using a variety of concentration measures[14] and the second counterfactual outlined above, Hannah and Kay report the

[14] As well as calculating concentration ratios they calculate a class of measures such that, in numbers-equivalent form,

change due to merger in many cases above 100 per cent. This implies that in many industries concentration would have fallen in the absence of merger. There is plenty of evidence pointing to increases in concentration, at times, and in industries with low merger activity (see further below). This, and the fact that Hannah and Kay themselves, after a simulation analysis of the consequences of the Gibrat effect and internal growth-rates, conclude that 'even if there were no merger and if large firms grew no faster than small, significant secular increases in concentration would still be observed' (Hannah and Kay (1977), p. 110), suggests that estimates of the effects of merger over 100 per cent are implausible. In effect the underlying counterfactual is projecting too little concentration growth in the absence of merger.[15] This interpretation is consistent with case study approaches to the problem, which suggest a less draconian role for merger.

3.2.3. Case Study Approaches Using the case study approach Evely and Little (1960) and Walshe (1974) look at high-concentration trades in 1951 and 1958 respectively and try to identify the extent to which mergers in the past led to the creation of large-firm dominance. Evely and Little concluded that 'there are few firms indeed among the leaders in the trades surveyed which were not created by amalgamation or have not resorted to acquisition and merger at some stage during their development' (Evely and Little (1960), p. 129). They analyse 36 trades with three- or four-firm employment or net output concentration ratios over 67 per cent in 1951 and conclude that in 23 of them the leading firms owed their position to a merger or amalgamation (predominantly dating from the turn-of-the-

$$HK(\alpha) = \left\{ \sum_{i=1}^{n} si^{\alpha} \right\} \frac{1}{1 - \alpha}.$$

For $\alpha = 1$ this corresponds to an entropy measure of concentration, for $\alpha = 2$ to the Herfindahl index.

[15] It is often stated (e.g. Curry and George (1983)) that the equal growth-rate assumption for acquired and acquiring firms is a reasonable counterfactual assumption to take. Since, as we shall see later, it is often found that acquiring companies are on average faster-growing pre-merger than their victims, it could at least as reasonably be argued that it is biased towards finding a high merger impact, since it may overstate the growth post-merger of the victim had it remained independent, assuming that there is some persistence in growth-rates. The same problem affects Utton (1971) to some degree, since the post-merger growth-rates attributed to merging firms based on their industry growth-rates will be the same for firms merging horizontally within the same Minimum List Heading classification. It is, of course, the variance of growth that these counterfactuals suppress and which lies behind the apparent paradox in Hannah and Kay's (1977) results discussed in the text above. There is by now a substantial literature on the fine points of this debate, focusing upon the impact that using different time periods, concentration measures, counterfactuals, and company populations has upon reported differences in the role of merger. This debate has focused upon aggregate concentration effects but the principles involved are essentially the same. (See Hannah and Kay (1977, 1981), Hart (1979, 1980, 1981), Prais (1980, 1981), and Sawyer (1979, 1980).)

century or 1920's merger waves). Walshe's reworking of this data raised
the number to 28. In contrast his own analysis of 32 products with five-
firm concentration ratios of over 90 per cent in 1958 suggested a lower
role for merger, with externally and internally expanded firms each
accounting for about half the cases. The difference, in his view, reflects
the dominance of the early merger waves in the Evely and Little sample
and the inclusion of younger new technology products in his sample
(Walshe (1974)). His reference period of course pre-dates the main post-
war periods of merger activity which are captured in the studies of Utton
(1986), Hart, Utton, and Walshe (1973), and Hart and Clarke (1980).
Utton analyses long-run trends since the inter-war period in single domi-
nant-firm market shares in 19 UK industries. Although the dominant tendency was for shares to erode, he found that in 7 cases market share had
risen or remained constant. In 4 of these, acquisitions had played a role
in sustaining dominance. In 2 of these cases, the acquisition followed
long-standing collaboration or co-operation between the firms involved
and in general the acquired companies either invited or did not resist the
take-over. He does not report the role of mergers by non-dominant firms
in eroding the market shares in the 12 industries where dominance
declined, although he notes that in 4 cases the leaders' share fell despite
their own acquisitions (wallpaper manufacturing, cigarettes, cement, and
tyres). Hart and Clarke (1980) provide an analysis of 27 randomly
selected product groups over the period 1958–68 and classify them into
an increasing concentration with mergers group, an increasing concentration without mergers group, and a decreasing concentration group. Over
half the sample (14) fell into the first category and they had an average
increase in the five-firm sales concentration ratio of 15.4 per cent compared with 7.8 per cent for the second group of 6, where internal growth
was the norm. The 7 industries in the third group experienced an average
fall of 5.1 per cent. On the assumption that in the absence of merger the
14 groups dominated by merger growth would have experienced concentration changes on a par with the non-merger-intensive second group
then concentration would have risen by 4.5 per cent for the sample as a
whole. This is around a half of the actual average concentration change
experienced (of 8.4 per cent), and therefore Hart and Clarke conclude
that mergers in this period probably accounted for around one-half of
concentration change.[16] A more sanguine counterfactual distribution of
the externally expanded industries towards the concentration decline
group would of course raise this estimate.

Mergers have certainly continued to occur in high-concentration situa-

[16] This is higher than the original estimate of Hart, Utton, and Walshe (1973) for the
period 1958–63 (using the same methodology). This reflects the higher merger activity of the
period 1963–8.

tions since the late 1960s. Between 1965 and 1978, for instance, 395 proposed mergers considered by the Office of Fair Trading are reported by
them to have either created or strengthened a statutory monopoly position in the UK economy (i.e. from 1965–73 a market share of 33.3 per
cent and from 1973 onwards a share of 25 per cent). These are narrowly
defined markets and many of them are extremely small; in 1978, for
instance, of 22 such bids one-third were in markets worth less than £25
million. Another third, however, were in markets worth over £200 million, so that even when in aggregate merger activity is low, significant
structural developments in particular industries can occur. It would be
interesting to extend the case study approach to the period 1968–73,
when as we have seen merger activity continued at extremely high levels
with a substantial horizontal component but concentration hardly
changed at all. As yet this has not been done, nor have we any work for
the 1980s.

3.3. Mergers and Aggregate Concentration

This area has been dominated by the counterfactual approach, and the
range of estimated merger impacts is as great as when this approach is
used on an industry basis. Table 1.7 illustrates the point for the 1960s as
well as covering the period 1969–73.[17]

Part of the difference between these studies for the periods in the 1960s
no doubt reflects the different years covered, but the higher estimates
should, in the light of our discussion of market concentration above, be
regarded with some reservations. As far as the period 1969–73 is concerned, Hannah and Kay argue that there were few large mergers in their
population (which is surprising in view of our earlier discussion of giant-
firm death-rates). They were none the less sufficient to prevent concentration from falling, whilst there were a large number of smaller mergers
which did not register an effect on the concentration ratio but did on
their entropy-based concentration measure covering the whole distribution. Evidence for the post-1972 period is less plentiful. Hughes and
Kumar (1985), however, echoing the findings of Utton (1972) for the
1960s, report a negative relationship between opening size and intensity
of growth by acquisition for 88 surviving companies in the *Times* 1,000 in
the period 1972–81. This, combined with their finding of a negative relationship between opening size and growth, could, *ceteris paribus*, suggest
a downward impact for merger upon the relative dominance of the
largest firms.

---

[17] For application to earlier periods see Utton (1971), Hannah and Kay (1977), Hannah
(1976), and the literature cited in n. 15 above.

Table 1.7. Effects of mergers on aggregate concentration

	Aaronovitch and Sawyer			Hannah and Kay					
	1958	1967	Percentage change due to merger	1957	1969	Percentage change due to merger	1969	1973	Percentage change due to merger
CR25	31.4	35.3	110.0	48.4	60.6	116.4	57.9	60.10	100.0
CR50	40.9	49.2	62.3	60.1	74.9	102.7	—	—	—
CR100	51.7	62.0	54.3	88.9	97.0	116.0	—	—	—

Note: Aaronovitch and Sawyer analyse the components of concentration change over the period 1958–67 for a population of 233 firms in manufacturing and distribution which were UK quoted companies with net assets of at least £5m., in terms of the effects of (*a*) the relative growth of firms that survive, (*b*) disappearances through acquisition, (*c*) births into the population of companies worth less than £5m. in 1957 but big enough to have been ranked in the top 100 quoted companies 1967, and, in order to infer trends for the population of quoted companies as a whole, (*d*) changes in the size of their population relative to the quoted sector as a whole and (*e*) the interactions between (*a*)–(*d*). The table shows the impact of (*b*) on the same counterfactual assumption as Hannah and Kay (i.e. merging the base-year population). Merger growth also affects (*a*) but the authors conclude that when an attempt is made to separate out the external element in it, neither it nor internal growth differences have a very significant impact on concentration change.

Sources: Cowling *et al.* (1980), based on Aaronovitch and Sawyer (1975b); Hannah and Kay (1977).

3.4. Conclusions on Mergers and Concentration

The broad message that these studies of aggregate and market concentration convey is that in the post-war period in many industries mergers have played a central role in the growth of leading firms and in the development and maintenance of concentrated market structures. They have also been a prime mover in changes in aggregate concentration. However, concentration can and does change in the absence of merger although spectacular changes in the UK have nearly always been associated with its presence. This does *not* mean, however, that in general concentration will always increase substantially in periods of high merger activity, as our discussions of the period 1969–73 and the first half of the 1980s make clear.[18] The direction which merger activity takes, its distribution across firms of different sizes, the overall variance and mean of growth-rates of different-sized firms, the growth of individual industries and the economy as a whole, and the pattern of births and deaths may all independently or together work to prevent that. Successive merger waves in the UK are thus best viewed in their specific historical and institutional context, which will condition each of these elements of the overall growth process and hence their structural impact relative to merger. The basic puzzle remains, however, to account for the failure of concentration to rise in the face of the high merger activity in 1968–73 and again in the 1980s. Assuming that the answer is not to be found in some measurement problem, so that big changes were being wrought in the size distribution beyond the concentration ratio cut-off, then an answer might be sought either in terms of changed relative growth-rates of large and small firms which favoured the latter; or other changes affecting the variance of growth-rates. In fact for continuous quoted companies at least, size was negatively related to growth in the period 1966–71, and especially in the years 1972–6 (though it was positive for certain sub-periods such as 1964–9 and 1966–9 (Meeks and Whittington (1976); Kumar (1984))).[19] A negative relationship holds for the periods 1975–80 and 1980–5 (Dunne and Hughes (1990)). One factor which might lie behind these patterns in the 1980s is the rationalizing activities of large firms, both through the closure of plants (Oulton (1987)) and through shrinkage via management buy-outs and divestment (Wright, Chiplin, and Thompson (this volume)). Since the 1980s saw the emergence in the UK, as in the USA, of the use of highly levered bids to purchase and then break up target companies,

---

[18] Or as the experience of the USA in the post-war period suggests. Despite experiencing a merger wave of enormous proportions in the 1960s, concentration in aggregate hardly changed (see e.g. Hughes and Singh (1980)).

[19] These results in part also reflect changes in the underlying Department of Trade and Industry population, on which the analyses are based.

this deconcentrating tendency may have been reinforced. The most detailed study available, for the United States, suggests that acquisition followed by divestiture is very common. Nearly a half of 6,000 acquisitions made between 1950 and 1976 were subsequently sold off, conglomerate purchases being especially predominant in this group (Ravenscraft and Scherer (1987)). It is apparent in general terms from Table 1.1 above that sales of subsidiaries have come to play a significant role in the acquisition scene. The net impact of all this on concentration depends, *inter alia*, on the relative size of buyers and sellers as well as upon the impact these reorganizations have on relative growth-rates. The interrelationship between these developments, the variance of growth-rates (which showed no relevant systematic shifts for quoted companies in the 1970s (Kumar (1984)), the size pattern of merger deaths, and the intensity of acquisition growth by size of firm at home and abroad would repay further work.

3.5. Mergers and Diversification

As with concentration it is easy to point to a broad connection between mergers and diversification. As diversification has risen in the post-war period in the UK so has merger activity and the proportion of activity which has been non-horizontal. There are, however, very few studies which bear precisely and directly on the link between the two compared with the concentration literature discussed above, and even fewer which deal with vertical integration. There are a number of reasons for expecting that merger might be a particularly suitable vehicle for diversifying compared with horizontal expansion. First of all, the acquisition of a going concern with an established market position and experienced management is a rapid means of expansion and may avoid important set-up costs associated with entry *de novo* via building new plant. Moreover, initially at least, competition costs may be lower as no new capacity is added to the industry total. Where expansion in market share is planned after entry, advertising costs per unit growth may be lower since there is less need to build up goodwill and market presence. Some support for these ideas comes from Hill (1985). He provides case study material for 12 of the largest most diversified UK firms relating to the 1970s.[20] In all cases he identifies merger as the main vehicle for their diversified expansion often via the purchase of market leaders in the industries entered. This study does not, however, quantify changes in diversification or the relative importance of different growth strategies towards it. The implication that merger is the principal vehicle for growth in diversification

---

[20] The firms are Booker McConnell, BTR, Cope Allman, Grand Metropolitan, Arthur Guinness, Imperial Group, Norcros, S. Pearson and Son, Reckitt and Colman, Reed International, Thomas Tilling, and Tube Investments.

strategies does not appear to generalize to wider samples of firms. Thus Cosh, Hughes, Kumar, and Singh (1985), using individual company diversification measures, find no evidence of a systematic relationship between acquisition intensity at the individual company level in the years 1971-7 (measured as acquisition expenditure over the period relative to opening net assets) and either diversification levels in 1971 or 1980, or the change in diversification 1971-80. Thus the simple correlation coefficients relating acquisition activity to the Utton index of diversification for the full sample of 210 firms in 1971 was 0.17 and in 1981 0.07. The growth by acquisition variable had the right (positive) sign in regression equations seeking to explain changes in diversification (as measured by the Utton or Herfindahl indices or changes in the number of industries operated in) but was never statistically significant (Cosh, Hughes, Kumar, and Singh (1985)). There are a number of ways these results could be refined, for instance by distinguishing different directions of merger expenditure or extending the analysis to include more industries or later periods. As it stands, however, they suggest that in general the most rapidly diversifying companies have not been especially merger-intensive. This is not to deny that for some companies this has been the case or that some companies with currently very high levels of diversification have adopted merger-intensive strategies in the past, but that diversification and merger need not inevitably go together.

An interesting conjecture which arises out of this literature and our earlier discussion of the direction of divestment,[21] is that firms may acquire more extensively diversified interests as a result of merger than they wish, because, for example, their target company is bundled up with others and is not available separately. They may then use the market in subsidiaries to unscramble unwanted parts. This might satisfy a reported desire to keep diversification within relatively related areas (Hill (1985)). Equally the break-up and sale of the target may be the object of the raid. In either event it means that in assessing the links between merger and diversification the direction of both acquisition and divestment activity must be relevant.

3.6. The Outcome in Terms of Monopoly Power

The impact of mergers on monopoly power cannot be deduced simply from an analysis of their role in the structural changes we have discussed

---

[21] Which suggested a high proportion of subsidiary sales were conglomerate whilst purchases were horizontal. The most recently publicized offers of divestment have, however, been horizontally connected subsidiaries of large companies where the divestment has been aimed at avoiding a merger reference.

in the previous section. We need to trace possible connections between them and behaviour and the competitive process.

3.6.1. Concentration As far as concentration is concerned, a proper assessment requires an analysis of the conceptual and empirical links between structure and performance and an analysis of other changes occurring in the competitive environment of UK firms. In my view the evidence for a strong and consistent link between monopoly power and market structure as measured by concentration ratios or other measures of the size distribution of firms in the UK is relatively weak, is primarily based on cross-section static comparisons, and does not readily capture the essence of competitive rivalry as a dynamic process. I have set the conceptual arguments out elsewhere for emphasizing this last point (Hughes (1978)) and will simply make a few observations here on the competitive environment generally. First, the merger waves and changes in concentration which characterized UK industry in the 1960s followed a period of widespread abandonment of restrictive practices, so that part at least of what was observed was a replacement of one sort of market control by another. That is not to say that a decline in such control might not have been preferable but that the structural changes observed did not necessarily imply an *increase* in market power.[22] Second, increased merger activity was associated with a growth in the openness of national economies to international competition and direct investment (Hughes and Singh (1980)). It is difficult to argue for a *general* increase in market power of UK firms (manufacturers in particular) in a period when they consistently lost out in terms of their share of world and UK markets, and of their representation amongst the ranks of the world's largest companies. The downward impact of adjusting for trade on concentration ratios for the UK is now well known.[23] Finally, to the extent that countervailing buyer power constrains producers, the tendency for concentration to increase amongst distributors and their customers may have been mutually offsetting. It is difficult to disagree with Utton's conclusion after

[22] Thus Elliott and Gribbin (1977) report that UK industries with terminated price agreements show faster concentration increases in the 1960s than do other industries. They also show that the largest mergers in the 1960s frequently involved companies that were formerly common members of abandoned agreements. In the same vein, Hope (1976) shows how the 1965 Crittal/Hope merger was explicitly designed to replace a faltering agreement. Both Heath (1961) and Swann, O'Brien, Maunder, and Howe (1974) suggest on the basis of questionnaires, interviews, and case studies that merger was a common medium-term response to the abandonment of agreements, although O'Brien, Howe, and Wright (1979) cannot find a significant link between acquisition intensity and abandonment in a cross-section statistical analysis.

[23] See e.g. Utton and Morgan (1983) and the references therein. As is clear from their work, however, identifying the competitive consequences of these adjustments is not straightforward in view of the possible connections between domestic producers and apparently independent importers.

his analysis of long-term trends in 19 dominant firm positions over 30–40 years ending in the 1970s that, although in all cases they retained their opening lead positions, 'the forces of erosion have been stronger than those of reinforcement' (Utton (1986)).

All of this is not to deny that in individual cases merger may have inhibited the competitive process or prevented the erosion of the dominant firms' market share, but instead to argue that the identification of those cases requires a pragmatic, case-by-case approach. It cannot be presumed that merger-induced concentration change inevitably changes monopoly power in the same direction, and that all assessments of post-merger performance effects in the UK must be predicated upon an assumption that because domestic concentration levels have risen so must monopoly power. Even in its own terms that argument would of course imply no changes in the competitive environment on average between the late 1960s and the 1980s, when, as we have argued, concentration was stable or fell. It is also striking to note that long-run studies of the evolution of market share in United States manufacturing in the period 1950–72 suggests that merging firms have suffered *declines* compared to other companies (Mueller (1985)), a result consistent with the Ravenscraft and Scherer sell-off findings reported earlier, especially when it is noted that market share falls were more significant where the merger was non-horizontal. These paradoxical results of the deconcentrating impact of merger in the long run should alert us to the distinction between the *short-run impact* when post-merger changes in growth performance may be slight but the immediate market share impact of joining two firms together may be high, and *long-run impacts* when possibly adverse influences of merger upon growth performance may lead to decline or divestiture.

3.6.2. Diversification By definition conventional single-market monopoly power effects are likely to be minimal in genuinely conglomerate expansion. Nevertheless, potentially adverse impacts on the competitive process may be identified for multi-product growth. For example, conglomerate firms may impose reciprocal buying pressures upon suppliers to encourage them to use as inputs the products of subsidiaries of the parent conglomerate. Diversified firms may also employ predatory pricing in newly entered markets, and practise mutual forbearance with other conglomerates. More difficult to document are effects arising from reductions in potential competition, where it is argued, for instance, that entry by a large conglomerate firm may deter other likely entrants, or lead to subsequent anti-competitive behaviour which could not, or otherwise would not, have occurred. Where entry of this kind is by merger it may also be argued that this is at the expense of new investment in the market, either by incumbents or by the new entrant itself. (See, for instance, Scherer and Ross (1990); Steiner (1975); Markham (1973).) All of these effects may have implications for market structure. Estimating the nature of it in terms of levels and trends in industry concentration is, however, fraught with empirical difficulties. These arise principally from lack of precise data on the market shares of individual firms in different industries and the evolution over time of those shares. Similar problems limit attempts to measure the impact of diversifying new entry either by merger or by new investment. What evidence we have suggests that conglomerate mergers have had little impact on levels of or trends in market concentration in the US (Goldberg (1973, 1974); Adams and Heimforth (1986)), whilst in the UK and the USA neither the presence of diversified firms, nor new entry by diversification, seem to lead to increased levels of concentration. If anything the reverse seems to be the case (Berry (1975); Utton (1979)). Moreover, we have already noted the extent to which divestment in conglomerate merger is a frequent follow-on from purchase, although the evidence is more systematic for the USA than the UK on this point. In structural terms, therefore, the case against conglomerate merger remains unproven. Effects on competitive behaviour, however, especially pricing, are a little better documented. Examples can be found in the USA, and to a lesser extent in the UK, of most of the anti-competitive practices referred to earlier. There is little to suggest, however, that these are typical or pervasive features of diversified firms' market behaviour. Where such effects have been most prominent they appear to be due as much to individual market power as to overall diversified strength. Thus in the seven cases investigated by the MMC where the possibility of discriminatory or predatory pricing was examined, the companies involved held extremely dominant positions the smallest market share being 51 per cent (Utton (1979)).[24] In these terms the conglomerate merger problem collapses back to the single-market monopoly power problem.

There is, however, a broader issue. The growth of conglomerate organization is a replacement of the market by organizational hierarchy. Two questions then arise: Is the internal economy of the diversified firm an 'as if' competitive environment?; and What impact on competitive stock market efficiency arises from the loss of information inherent in replacing separate accounting units by a consolidated group account? The second

---

[24] The cases considered involved British Match Company (95% domestic production controlled plus 85% of imports), British Oxygen Company (90% of total UK supplies of oxygen and dissolved acetylene plus trade protection via high transport costs and 30% import duty), Metal Box Company (78% of the market analysed), Courtaulds (over 90% of the UK supply of cellulosic fibres plus tariff protection), Roche Products (over 90% of the market for librium and valium), and Joseph Lucas (51% of the motor vehicle electric wiring harness market and a more dominant position in certain other sectors of the motor vehicle electric equipment market).

question depends on how effective company disclosure rules are. There is not much cause for complacency here. It also depends, however, on how effective the market itself is in evaluating and using such information. In the context of this survey it is perhaps best to address this question in terms of the market for corporate control; the empirical evidence bearing on this is discussed in the next section. As far as the competitive impact of the internal economy of firms is concerned, we have evidence of considerable variation in its nature (Hill and Pickering (1986a)) and some evidence suggesting private profitability gains from superior management organization (Steer and Cable (1978)), but nothing to suggest particular anti-competitive impacts which are not covered by our discussion of product market behaviour discussed above.

3.7. Conclusion: Mergers, Structural Change, Market and Extra-market Power

Merger movements have played a major role in transforming the nature of business organization and market structure in the UK in the post-war period, but in my view the problems that this raises are not primarily ones of a *generalized increase* in market power as manifested in changes in market concentration. Such effects in individual markets have occurred, and will occur, as a result of horizontal and non-horizontal merger. A case-by-case approach is needed to identify them. We should not, however, make a universal background assumption of increased market power in making a net assessment of the average welfare effects of merger.[25]

There is more at stake, however, than market power. The enormously increased scope of the largest business organizations in the post-war period and the role that merger has played in creating and restructuring them raise questions of their extra-market power which goes beyond the summation of lost consumers' surplus. As Jacquemin and de Jong ((1977), p. 198) put it 'big firms represent a concentration of power in private hands rather than in democratically chosen governments. Such private power can cross economic boundaries and poses the threat of an extra-market power which can change the rules of the game in favour of the dominant corporations.' Assessing the force of this argument and

[25] It is often argued that a merger could not decrease market power. This view is based on an essentially static conception of market power. Viewed in a dynamic sense, it is intuitively easy to see how an increase in rivalry could be produced by newly merged firms who would otherwise have declined, or left the market altogether. There is plenty of case study evidence to this effect. See e.g. the discussion below of the international rivalry impact of mergers in bearings, and computers in the UK based on Cowling *et al.* (1980) and Utton's discussion of the possible outcomes of mergers in the glass and plasterboard industries (Utton (1986), p. 65). For the general point, see Hughes (1978).

appropriate ways of dealing with the problems it raises go beyond the scope of this paper. It should not, however, be lost sight of in the discussion that follows.

4. MERGERS EFFICIENCY AND ECONOMIC PERFORMANCE

In this section we examine in turn the stock market selection process and post-merger performance (including real resource impacts, profitability, investment, trade technical change, and regional and stock price impacts).

4.1. The Stock Market Selection Process

Analysing the stock market selection process involves looking at the pre-merger financial characteristics of various groups of firms defined by their involvement in merger activity, and in addition examining their post-merger performance. In this section we look at size, profitability, growth, and stock market prices. This is partly for reasons of space and partly because it is these variables which figure most prominently in discussions of the market for corporate control. Before turning to the empirical evidence, however, a couple of methodological points are worth making. These relate to the choice of control groups, to sample design, and to techniques available for discriminating between groups of firms. Figure 1.1 summarizes the classification possibilities within a population in any year where companies are identified as either acquiring (AG), or acquired (AD), or neither acquiring nor acquired (R). The possibility that a company may both make an acquisition and itself be acquired is captured by the shaded intersection of sets AG and AD. Since some companies may

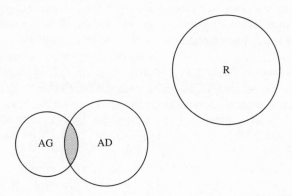

Fig 1.1. Classification of sample.

make more than one acquisition the AG and AD groups need not be the same size.

In terms of the natural selection model the most natural comparisons to make are between AG and AD and between each of these and a control group (C) representing the characteristics of the non-acquiring and non-acquired members of the population respectively. For a comparison with AG, C may be drawn from R or from R plus the unshaded portion of AD; similarly for a comparison with AD, C may be drawn from R or from R plus the unshaded portion of AG. This choice may affect the results significantly if the group characteristics of AG and AD differ from one another and from R. This will become relevant when we discuss studies using different control groups, and which report differing results. As we have seen, the overall incidence and nature of take-overs, and the institutional framework in which they occur, vary significantly over time and between industries and different sizes of firm. There are also important differences between industries in the average characteristics of firms. There are therefore strong reasons for believing that comparisons of pre-merger (or other) performance characteristics will be subject to aggregation bias unless specific allowance is made for these factors in the sample design. One way of doing this is to choose firms matched by industry, year, and size with the acquiring (MAG) and acquired (MAD) companies. Other ways are to carry out comparisons on an individual year, or industry, or size class basis, or using individual company data normalized by industry averages. Evidence on each of these bases is available for the UK. Finally, in seeking to discriminate between groups it is important to bear in mind that statistically significant differences in group averages may conceal very large overlaps between the groups. Moreover, variables which show up well on a univariate basis may prove more or less successful on a multivariate basis when the pattern of intercorrelations between variables is taken into account. Bearing these issues in mind we can examine in turn evidence relating to the comparative characteristics of acquired and acquiring companies on the UK stock market.

Acquired Companies Table 1.8 drawn from Singh (1975) summarizes the pre-merger characteristics of acquired companies relative to their industry median in terms of size, profitability, the short-term change in profitability, and growth in a sample of industries for two periods of take-over activity in the UK 1955–60 and 1967–70. In 1955–60 on an aggregate basis, taking all industries together, the proportions of acquired firms with below median size, profitability, and growth were significantly greater than 50 per cent. In 1967–70 the differences were weaker. Although the proportion of companies with below median value remained above 50 per cent, it was only significantly so for profitability

Table 1.8. Percentage of taken-over companies below or equal to their industry median, 1967–1970 and 1955–1960

Variable[a]	1967–70				All 4 industries 1967–70	All 5 industries 1955–60[b]
	Non-electrical engineering	Drink	Food	Clothing and footwear		
Size	52.4	61.1	43.8	73.3	55.4	60.5***
Profitability	60.3	55.6	50.0	66.7	58.9**	64.4***
Growth	58.7	52.9	62.5	46.7	56.8	63.3***
Changes in profitability	55.6	61.1	50.0	73.3	58.0*	n.a.
No. of companies taken-over	63	18	16	15	112	181

Significant levels: *10%; **5%; ***1%.
[a] Size is measured as net assets. With the exception of the change in profitability, which is measured in the year before merger, the remaining variables are averages over the 3 years prior to merger. Profitability is the pre-tax rate of return on net assets; growth is the growth of net assets.
[b] The data for 1955–60 relate to the 4 industries analysed for 1967–70 plus electrical engineering.
Source: Singh (1975).

and the change in profitability in the year before merger. Nor were any of the proportions significant on an individual industry basis.

These results may be compared with those of a number of other studies covering later periods. The tendency for acquired companies to be smaller than average gets some support from Meeks (1977) in an analysis of 233 acquisitions in the period 1964–72, Kumar (1984) for a sample of 354 mergers in the period 1967–74, and Levine and Aaronovitch (1981) for a sample of 69 mergers worth over £3 million in 1972. Kuehn (1975), however, reports little difference between 1,554 acquired companies in the period 1957–69 and non-acquired companies as a whole. This result, though, probably reflects some degree of aggregation bias because when size is expressed relative to industry it becomes a significant variable in explaining the incidence of take-over in a number of industries in his sample (Kuehn (1975), p. 77); Cosh, Hughes, and Singh (1980) compare around 290 acquired companies in the period 1967–70 with all non-acquiring non-acquired companies and find no significant size difference in terms of assets, though in terms of sales the acquired are smaller. In this case the insignificant differences in size arise largely from the deliberate exclusion of relatively large acquiring companies from the control group. Their inclusion would produce results similar to those cited above for other studies using the broader control group concept, that acquired companies are relatively small.[26] Evidence for periods since the mid-1970s is much sparser. For 1981–3 and 1986, however, Cosh, Hughes, Lee, and Singh (1989) analyse 136 mergers and report acquired companies as significantly smaller than industry averages. The relative smallness of the targets in acquisition activity is therefore a robust result in this literature.

In terms of growth the evidence is also fairly clear-cut. The acquired companies are always less dynamic pre-merger than their respective control groups even though the difference is not always statistically significant (Kuehn (1975); Cosh, Hughes and Singh (1980); Levine and Aaronovitch (1981); Cosh, Hughes, Lee, and Singh (1989)).

The evidence on profitability is more mixed. Meeks (1977) reports acquired companies as having somewhat below average profitability in the year before merger and somewhat higher profitability in the second and third years before, although none of these differences are statistically significant. He also reports acquired firms in non-horizontal mergers as *more* profitable than the average in their industry for the three years prior to merger (though like other victims they had experienced a short-term deterioration in the year before merger). These results are consistent with Singh's (1975) finding of significant short-term deterioration in profitabil-

---

[26] It is worth remembering, however, that, as we saw earlier, the relative vulnerability of different size classes of firm may vary considerably during merger waves, so that different time periods could easily produce different results too.

ity immediately before acquisition in the period 1967–70. Kuehn's analysis for the period 1957–69 shows the acquired companies as less profitable than the rest, whilst Cosh, Hughes, and Singh (1980) find them less profitable than the non-acquiring non-acquired firms in the years 1967–9. Their result holds for both horizontal and non-horizontal mergers and in 12 of the 14 industries they analyse. For the 1980s Cosh, Hughes, Lee, and Singh (1989) report acquired firms in the period 1981–3 as indistinguishable from industry averages in returns to an equity share, but significantly inferior in terms of the return on net assets. They were indistinguishable on either basis in the high merger activity year of 1986, which echoes the findings of Levine and Aaronovitch (1981) for the peak year of 1972. The latter study also concurs with Meeks's (1977) findings that the targets in conglomerate bids were *more* profitable than industry averages. All of this suggests that whatever overall tendency there is for the least profitable companies to be acquired, it is weakest in periods of merger boom and strongest in the case of horizontal acquisitions. Empirical studies which pool across years of varying merger activity or type of merger may therefore conceal important features of the selection process.

We have so far only discussed financial accounting and share return data, whereas the corporate control theory in effect collapses these underlying indicators as far as stockholders' welfare is concerned into a single variable, the market value of the company. Singh (1971), Kuehn (1975), Levine and Aaronovitch (1981), Buckley (1972), and Newbould (1970) have all attempted to discriminate between groups of firms involved in the take-over process in terms of the valuation ratio, that is, the ratio of the stock market value of assets to their reported book value. *Ceteris paribus*, the lower the valuation ratio, the higher the probability of acquisition should be. Singh (1971) found a statistically significant but weak inverse relationship for the period 1955–60; thus 63 per cent of the taken-over companies had a valuation ratio less than their industry average and 37 per cent a higher one. Kuehn also found a weak inverse relationship between a company's valuation ratio relative to its industry valuation ratio, and the probability of take-over for the period 1957–69, whilst Buckley (1972), for a sample of 65 non-financial mergers in 1971, again reports the acquired as having lower valuation ratios than the non-acquired. Newbould, on the other hand, in an analysis of 64 mergers in the period 1967–8, reports that only 41 per cent of the acquired firms had a lower than industry average valuation ratio and 59 per cent a higher one. Levine and Aaronovitch (1981) report acquired companies as having lower valuation ratios (VR) than acquiring companies, but they are not compared with industry averages. They, and a number of other authors, have also compared the acquired and acquiring companies in terms of the related concept of the price earnings ratio (PE) (VR = PE × post tax rate of return on equity assets). Cosh, Hughes, and Singh (1980), for instance, find no systematic differences for three or two years before a bid between a sample of 28 acquired and 28 size- and industry-matched non-acquiring non-acquired companies in the period 1967–9 but a significant tendency for the acquired to have a *higher* PE ratio in the year before. Even in that year, however, half the acquired companies had lower PE values. Levine and Aaronovitch report similarly for 1972. Their analysis of a size- and industry-matched sample of acquiring and acquired firms suggests that whilst the former had higher PE ratios than the latter they both had higher ratios than the average for companies in manufacturing and distribution industries as a whole. This evidence is inconsistent with a bargain theory of purchase based on low market valuation.

In the very broadest terms these results suggest that, whilst there are some important variations across time periods and type of merger, the acquired companies have worse short-term profitability growth records and are smaller, less dynamic, and somewhat less highly valued than companies on average. They are not always less profitable on a medium-term basis. What about the acquirers?

Acquiring Companies In terms of growth, acquiring or merger-intensive, companies appear to be more dynamic both pre-merger and on a cross-sectional basis over a given time period than those less heavily engaged in merger. Acquirers are also generally larger than non-acquirers. The contribution of merger to overall growth, however, appears if anything to be negatively related to size (Cosh, Hughes, and Singh (1980); Meeks (1977); Kuehn (1975); Kumar (1985); Utton (1972); Levine and Aaronovitch (1981)). The picture in terms of profitability is less clear. When the acquiring companies are compared with companies in general, they appear to be as profitable or more profitable (Meeks (1977); Cosh, Hughes, and Singh (1980); Levine and Aaronovitch (1981)). The result is consistent for the 1980s and the 1970s (Cosh, Hughes, Lee, and Singh (1989)). Interestingly, however, in Cosh, Hughes, and Singh's study, and in Meeks's study, disaggregation of the sample into horizontal and non-horizontal acquirers (i.e. making acquisitions across 2-digit industry boundaries) suggests that only the latter have a superior pre-merger profits performance. In fact in the former study the horizontal acquirers were if anything less profitable than comparable non-acquirers. The overlap between acquirers and the rest in terms of profitability again emerges when attention is focused on the performance of acquisition-intensive companies compared over a given period to internal growers (instead of just looking at pre-merger data). Kuehn, in an analysis of a sample of 117 raiders making three or more acquisitions in the period 1957–69, finds them as likely to be below their industry median as above it. Similarly, Meeks reports that companies with above-median growth by acquisition in the periods 1948–64 and 1964–71 are neither more nor less profitable than those relying less on external growth. However, within the former group the 100 most merger-intensive were more profitable in the period 1964–71 than other acquiring or non-acquiring companies.[27] The acquirers are therefore larger and faster-growing but (with the exception of those merging most intensively or involved in diversifying merger) not especially profitable compared to companies in general. From the point of view of the market for corporate control this latter finding is not particularly encouraging since the non-horizontal acquirers, who appear relatively the most profitable, also appear according to our discussion above to have sought out partners who were relatively profitable compared to their industries. The question remains, however, whether the acquirers can be distinguished from their victims.

Acquired versus Acquiring Companies Table 1.9 considers differences between the characteristics of acquired and acquiring companies in the same industries and time periods as Table 1.8. In 1955–60 the acquired companies were significantly smaller, less dynamic, and less profitable than the acquiring companies. By 1967–70, when, as we have seen, the acquired had become less distinguishable from companies on average, so had the gap between them and acquiring companies as a group. They were still smaller and also had a worse performance in terms of profitability growth. They were not, however, significantly less fast-growing or less profitable. The neutrality of the last finding is reflected in other studies for the late 1960s and early 1970s, which suggest that sometimes the acquiring and sometimes the acquired have a superior profit performance relative to each other and that sometimes they are indistinguishable, at least on a univariate basis. Thus, Rose and Newbould report for a sample of 46 mergers in 1967 that the acquiring are *less* profitable than the acquired. Newbould (1970) for 1967–8 and Levine and Aaronovitch (1981) for 1972 parallel Singh's (1975) finding that there is no significant difference between the groups, whilst Cosh, Hughes, and Singh (1980) for the period 1967–9, Meeks (1977) for the period 1964–71, and Holl and Pickering (1988) for a sample of 50 mergers in the decade 1965–75 suggest that the acquiring are either as profitable or more

[27] Utton (1974) reports 39 acquisition-intensive companies in the period 1961–5 as having lower profits than 39 non-acquirers both in that period and in the subsequent years 1966–70. There may, however, be an aggregation bias here. The samples are not matched by industry. If, as Aaronovitch and Sawyer (1975a) suggest, industry acquisition intensity varies inversely with industry profitability, then acquisition-intensive firms may have lower profit rates. In fact, when Utton does compare profitability between the acquiring firms and their industry, he is unable to distinguish between them (Utton (1974), pp. 22–3).

Table 1.9. Differences between acquired and acquiring companies, 1955–1960 and 1967–1970

Variable[a]	1955–60		1967–70	
	$\frac{d^b}{s}$	*t*-statistics	$\frac{d^b}{s}$	*t*-statistics
Size (logarithms)	–1.35	–6.21*	–1.50	–10.60*
Profitability	–0.29	–1.33	–0.41	–2.93*
Growth	–0.35	–1.60	–0.69	–4.91*
Change in profitability	–0.70	–3.20*	n.a.	n.a.

*Significance level: 1%.

[a] The variables are defined as in Table 1.10 except that profitability and the change in profitability are measured over 2 years rather than 3 years and 1 year respectively.

[b] d is the difference in the means of the acquired and acquiring group, and s is their common standard deviation. A minus sign for d/s indicates acquired firms had a mean value below acquiring firms. When d/s is zero the groups are indistinguishable: the larger d/s is in general the greater the differences between them.

Source: Singh (1975).

profitable than the acquired. In terms of growth, the acquiring companies appear relatively dynamic pre-merger compared to acquired companies, though not always significantly so (Cosh, Hughes, and Singh (1980); Levine and Aaronovitch (1981); Holl and Pickering (1988)).

A more consistent picture emerges in terms of size differentials. All studies for the 1960s and 1970s show the acquirers to be larger, especially for non-horizontal merger (Singh (1971, 1975); Rose and Newbould (1967); Kuehn (1975); Meeks (1977); Levine and Aaronovitch (1981); Cosh, Hughes, and Singh (1980); Kumar (1984)).

The evidence for the 1980s in terms of performance and size is more clear-cut than for earlier periods. Acquired companies as a whole underperform the companies that acquire them in terms of growth, profitability, and share return. The statistical significance of these differences is, however, typically lower in 1986 than the lower merger activity years 1981–3 (Cosh, Hughes, Lee, and Singh (1989)).

The Market for Corporate Control: An Assessment of Pre-merger Characteristics In the very broadest of terms the evidence we have examined suggests that the big and fast-growing companies acquire their smaller and less dynamic brethren. The acquirers are not, however, always especially profitable relative either to companies in general or to their victims. The non-horizontal acquirers in the 1970s are a possible exception to this rule but, whilst they appeared to be relatively profitable compared to other acquirers, there is also evidence to suggest they were selecting companies as victims which were *more* rather than less profitable than the average. In so far as profitability does enter the picture, it appeared in the 1960s and 1970s to be in the guise of short-term adverse *changes* in the year or so before merger for the acquired companies and not in terms of medium- to long-run profit levels. Finally in the broadest of terms the differences between the various categories of company are smaller in periods of merger boom and greatest in periods of relatively low merger activity. It has been argued that, if the market for corporate control was working well, then the threat of discipline for poor profitability would in fact produce the results reported for profitability levels. Thus, with a perfectly effective disciplinary threat, all firms would be making maximum potential profits and the remaining take-overs would be occurring for other non-disciplinary reasons. Therefore the data cannot, it is argued, distinguish between the view, on the one hand, that the deterrent is ineffective because the threat is unreal and, on the other, that the deterrent is very effective and so is the threat (Hannah and Kay (1977), pp. 123–5). This is not particularly convincing. In so far as a deterrent is perceived it must be based on learning from the nature of take-over activity, so that punishment and crime can be connected. If the thousands of mergers which have occurred in the UK have been essentially random as far as efficiency criteria are concerned, upon what evidence is the notion of the threat of take-over based, and what sort of behaviour will it induce? Of course, as we have seen, the incidence of merger is not random when variables other than profitability are considered; this is especially so in relation to size.

Before considering the behavioural consequences of this it is appropriate to consider the relationship between the incidence of take-over and the various characteristics of companies taken together. There are essentially two reasons for adopting a multivariate approach to supplement univariate comparisons. First, it may be possible that when variables are considered *together* we can to distinguish more clearly between acquiring, acquired, and other firms. Second, many of the characteristics are or may be intercorrelated so that a good discriminator on a univariate basis may fail to be so on a multivariate basis when the pattern of intercorrelations is taken into account. Equally in a multivariate context the relative importance of discriminators may be assessed. In fact, Singh (1975), Levine and Aaronovitch (1981), Cosh, Hughes, Lee, and Singh (1989), and Holl and Pickering (1988) find that when an attempt is made to distinguish between the acquiring and acquired firms on a multivariate basis the most powerful single discriminator is once again size and *not* a performance variable such as profitability or a stockholder variable like the valuation ratio. Thus, on the basis of size alone, one could expect to classify firms correctly as either acquired or acquiring companies 75 per cent of the time in Singh's 1967–70 sample, and 73 per cent of the time in

Levine and Aaronovitch's 1972 sample. This is compared with 50 per cent on the basis of random allocation.[28] Adding other variables to size increases the percentage correctly classified, but not by much. Thus, in Singh's sample, adding the short-term change in profitability raises the figure from 75 per cent to 80 per cent, whilst then adding growth, profitability, liquidity, gearing, and retention raises it only to 83 per cent. Similarly, in the Levine and Aaronovitch sample, adding growth, profitability, liquidity, and gearing raises the correctly classified proportion only from 73 per cent to 80 per cent. If, on the other hand, size is left out, the maximum correctly classified on the basis of *all* other variables taken together is 61 per cent in the Levine and Aaronovitch study compared to 50 per cent achievable on a random allocation. Size rather than profitability or market valuation emerges clearly as the most consistently successful discriminator between acquiring and acquired companies. What kind of behaviour on the part of managers might the *threat* of a take-over based on this sort of selection mechanism induce?

One way of bringing this out is (following Singh (1975)) to compare the actual probability of acquisition by size class of firm and by profitability class. Table 1.10*a* shows variations in the probability of being taken over by relative size within a firm's own industry in the period 1967–70 and Table 1.10*b* shows the variations in the same probability by average profitability class. Two things emerge from this; the very largest and smallest quoted firms are the most safe from take-over. In the case of the latter this may well be because of their relatively highly concentrated and/or family-dominated shareholding patterns (Davies and Kuehn (1977)). Increasing size from the third quintile onwards significantly reduces the probability of take-over.[29] This suggests that if large size is associated with market power, then discipline on the stock market may be most restricted in just those cases where the size of the companies involved suggests that product market constraints will be weakest. Table 1.10*a*, on the other hand, shows that once a company

[28] In Singh's 1955–60 sample, size was also the most important single discriminator, followed by growth. In 1967–70, after size, changes in profitability were the most important. In fact, a function taking only profitability, growth, and the change in profits together in 1967–70 would have classified correctly 70% of the time, compared with 75% on the basis of size alone. Tzoannos and Samuels (1972) also report high probabilities of misclassifying companies on the basis of multivariate combinations of financial variables.

[29] This is consistent with our conceptual arguments at the beginning of this section that the sanction might only be effective in the middle ranges. The discussion in the text, of course, relates to quoted companies. The limited evidence for other companies suggests that, for the 1960s at least, similar annual death-rates from merger (i.e. 2–3% p.a.) characterized the small non-quoted company sector and the lower end of the quoted size range. Attitudes to small firm take-overs are, not surprisingly, less based on questions of management discipline but more on the need to ensure managerial succession and access to financial and other resources (Bolton (1971), Merrett Cyriax Associates (1971), Boswell (1972), Hughes (1989b)).

Table 1.10. Average probability of being taken over within a year, by size class and by profitability class, 1967–1970

(a) Size class

	Lowest 20%	Next 20%	Next 20%	Next 20%	Top 20%	Top 10%	Top 5%	All
Probability of take-over	3.0	10.1	9.7	6.5	4.5	2.6	1.4	6.7

(b) Profitability[a] class

	Lowest 10%	Next 10%	Next 10%	Next 10%	Next 10%	Next 10%	Next 10%	Next 10%	Next 10%	Top 10%	All
Probability of take-over	8.6	11.0	9.8	4.3	5.5	7.4	4.9	6.1	4.9	6.1	6.9

[a] 2-year pre-merger profitability.
Source: Singh (1975).

moves out of the bottom 30 per cent of companies in terms of profitability there is no systematic gain in terms of increased immunity. This is consistent with evidence that managers of large companies do not link poor *long-run* profit performance with the threat of take-over. Minimizing the threat of take-over was chosen as the least significant of 10 possible *long-run* corporate objectives by senior executives of 18 large UK quoted companies in an interview and questionnaire study carried out in the period 1974–6. Moreover, minimizing the risk of take-over was also thought to be the least important of 9 possible reasons for pursuing profits as a *long-term* objective (Francis (1980)).[30] To the extent that profitability is a selection criterion which managers observe, our earlier analysis suggests that *short-term* profit levels and changes should cause them more concern. Recent survey evidence for the 1980s suggests that managers do indeed feel that investors place too much emphasis on short- compared to long-term performance (Cosh, Hughes, and Singh (1990)), and we have discussed earlier theoretical models (Stein (1988, 1989); Schleifer and Vishny (1990)) which can provide a rationale for this out- come. Even if high profitability and increases in size were both perceived by managers as reducing the probability of take-over, then it is possible to argue that, where they have some degree of internal discretion, they will prefer increases in size. This is because their remuneration status and

[30] This study relates to a period of low merger activity and managers may respond differ- ently in a take-over boom. Equally, however, the companies sampled had just lived through the 1968–72 merger wave, so that at best the threat complex seems to be highly transient.

power are more closely related to size than to profitability. Since size and
the variability of profitability over time are also inversely related, increasing size would also help reduce the threat of take-over due to *short-term*
swings in profits. Making an acquisition to increase size might then itself
become a tactic to avoid acquisition (Greer (1986)). Interestingly,
Pickering (1983) reports that the pursuit of growth (by merger or new
investment) rather than enhanced profitability was typical of the post-bid
reaction of a sample of UK firms surviving failed take-over attempts in
the late 1960s and early 1970s, whilst surviving a bid is better for post-bid
performance than being acquired (Holl and Pickering (1988)). For all
these reasons, therefore, we should expect that the market for corporate
control will be at best a highly imperfect disciplinarian. We need, however, to look at post-merger performance before making a final assessment.

4.2. Post-merger Performance

We examine in turn: real resource effects; the impact on profitability and
investment; trade, technical change, and regional impacts; and the effect
on returns to stockholders. But before doing so it is worth emphasizing
that any study of the impact of merger on company performance requires
some view to be taken about what would have happened in the absence
of merger; just as assessment of the impact of merger on concentration
the outcomes reported may be sensitive to the counterfactuals used. In
practice, as we shall see, the counterfactual against which merging companies are assessed is usually a control group of non-merging firms, or
the performance of all firms on average. Thus if, say, the joint profitability of two merging firms *relative to their industry profitability* is higher
before merger than after it, a decline in performance is deduced. Here the
counterfactual is that without merger unchanged relative performance
would have ensued. Whilst this approach seems intuitively sensible, and
has been widely used, it is as well to be aware of a potential difficulty
with it. If in any time period there exists a distribution of profit rates
across firms, and if in subsequent periods profit differences persist but
with some tendency for extremes to be pulled back towards mean values,
then acquiring companies, if they are relatively profitable on average,
could be expected to have some regression of their performance to the
mean. Projecting their counterfactual performance on the basis of companies in general will be biased against finding a positive merger impact.
The counterfactual will be too severe, since without merger some deterioration in their relative performance might be expected in any event. A
similar argument will hold for acquired companies but in reverse if they
are typically less profitable. In practice very few studies have attempted to

control for this effect. (Ravenscraft and Scherer (1987) and Cosh, Hughes, Lee, and Singh (1990) make attempts to do so for the USA and the UK respectively, but the other studies reported below do not.) This must be borne in mind in interpreting the results which follow.

Real Resource Effects The most detailed study attempting to estimate the real resource effect of merger is that of Cowling *et al.* (1980). They estimate changes in 'unit factor requirements' (K), where

$$K = P_0/P_I (1 - TP/R),$$

with P_0 an index of revenue per unit output, P_I a fixed weight price index of inputs (reflecting an assumption of fixed factor proportions in production), TP is total production profits, and R total production revenue. In effect K is average unit costs deflated by input prices, and changes in it over time are inversely proportional to 'efficiency' in the sense of the ratio of inputs to outputs.[31] Estimates of K are used in the context of individual case study material to evaluate a sample of large primarily horizontal mergers. With one exception these took place in the period 1966–9 and had been considered by the Mergers panel for possible referral to the MMC. In general the combined market shares of the merging firms was over 30 per cent and there were significant changes in market share arising from the merger. The size of the mergers meant that in several cases they had been referred to the MMC for investigation, or the industry in which they operated was the subject of an investigation. In addition a number had been aided and abetted by the Industrial Reorganization Corporation (IRC).[32]

The principal comparison made is between the pre- and post-merger efficiency of the merging firms. Lack of data and suitable comparators meant that in general the authors could not systematically compare the pre-merger performance of the merging companies *relative* to other companies with their *relative* post-merger performance. Instead the impact of merger on the merging firms is compared with an assumed counterfactual

---

[31] This index is sensitive to changes in capacity utilization and to changes in vertical integration and factor proportions. Therefore the authors stress that their assessment of the impact of merger in terms of K is based on its use in the context of particular case studies where the impact of the possible biases in the measure can be evaluated.

[32] In all, 12 individual mergers are analysed (* means merger referred to the Monopolies and Mergers Commission or industry investigated subsequently; † means IRC involvement): London Brick/Marston Valley†; Ransome/Hoffman Pollard† (RHP); BICC/Pyrotenax*; Tube Investment/Coventry Gauge (TI); Berger Jensen Nicholson (BJN)/British Paint; Rowntree/Mackintosh†; Johnson/Richards Campbell; Thorn/Radio Rentals*; Courtaulds/British Celanese (this merger took place in 1957); Leyland Motor Company/BMH Ltd† (BL); GEC/English Electric/AEI†; and the formation of ICL† (K is not calculated for ICL). An industry case study is also provided for the series of mergers affecting the brewing industry, as well as an analysis of Courtaulds' vertically integrating mergers in textiles.

growth-rate of efficiency of 1.5 per cent p.a., and/or the post-merger performance of the merged company is compared with industry or compara-
tor firms in the same post-merger period. In 5 of the 11 individual case
studies where K is calculated, the merging companies showed gains in
efficiency considered by the authors to have been in excess of the 1.5 per
cent p.a. counterfactual.[33] In 4 of these cases, where a comparison with
other firms is possible, they do as least as well as their comparators.[34]
This broadly neutral outcome is mirrored in a study of building society
mergers. Barnes (1985) compares changes in the operating cost ratios of
merging societies in the period 1970–8 relative to average operating cost
changes for other societies allowing for the possible gains to be had by
changing size. He finds no tendency for relative unit operating costs to be
lower (or for that matter higher) after merger than before, or for any
improvement in growth of assets to accrue from possible improvements in
service quality (see also Gough (1979); Barnes and Dodds (1981); Gough
(1981)). These real effect studies suggest that *on average* there is not a
systematic efficiency gain with at least as many cases of no change or
deterioration as there are of enhanced performance. There are, however,
some success stories and the merit of the case study approach is that
some pointers to the reasons why might be found from a close reading of
them. I return to this below in considering accounting measures of performance.

The Effects of Merger on Corporate Profitability There are well-known
objections to the use of accounting rates of return on assets in assessing

[33] This is on the basis of a relatively weak test comparing the best post-merger year with
the year of merger itself. In fact, in only one case (BJN) is this test failed on a simple evaluation of the raw data for K, and in this case the picture is confused by the fact that the
merged company itself was acquired within the comparison period by another company. In
4 cases (BICC, Courtaulds, Radio Rentals, TI) the gains are more than 1.5% but the
authors reject the data as either unreliable or misleading, or because the gain is completely
reversed after the best post-merger year. BL passes the test set out in the text, but a detailed
comparison of averages of K pre- and post-merger shows no significant differences. The
statement in the text therefore refers to the GEC, London Brick, RHP, Johnson/Richards,
and Rowntree/Mackintosh mergers. The indicator K was not calculated for the ICL merger
but it is clearly regarded on other grounds as successful by the authors.

[34] Thus in the RHP case the authors' opinion is that it is unlikely the merging companies
could have kept up with their rivals in the absence of merger (Cowling *et al.* (1980), p. 104).
In the cases of GEC and Johnson/Richards, the firms clearly outperformed their rivals in
the post-merger period Cowling *et al.* (1980), pp. 140–1, 200–1). In the case of
Rowntree/Mackintosh the merged firm does at least as well as its rivals Cowling *et al.*
(1980), pp. 135–6). In the fifth case (London Brick), where a 20% improvement in unit factor requirements occurred in the 5 years following merger, no sensible comparison could be
made since, as a result of this and other mergers, the company became the sole supplier of
Fletton bricks. The separate case study of the brewing industry suggests that, for the industry as a whole, there was declining efficiency (as measured by K) until improvements
occurred in the 1970s which took place to the same degree in merger-intensive as well as
internally growing firms (Cowling *et al.* (1980), p. 223). See also Cubbin and Hall (1979).

company performance generally. These arise from their lack of correspondence to economists' concepts such as the internal rate of return.[35] They remain, however, an essential starting-point for internal and external analysts of company performance, and evidence based upon them is therefore of some interest. But the usual problems are compounded in the case of take-over by variations in accounting practices and other difficulties arising with respect to consolidating acquired companies in the parent's accounts. There are two principal effects at work here. First, in the merger year, if the acquired company's earnings are incorporated into the acquirer's accounts for whatever proportion of the year remains after acquisition, but only its end-year assets are included in striking the profit rate (on the average of opening- and end-year assets of the newly merged combination), then reported profit may be biased either up or down relative to a measure for the merger year which incorporated all the earnings and both opening and closing assets. The direction will depend on the distribution and scale of earnings over the year and the value of the assets. Secondly, there is a downward bias arising whenever the acquired companies are bought for more than their book value and corresponding 'goodwill on acquisition' is added to the assets of the merging firm. These and other arguments related to the way in which mergers are financed and in which accounting practices may be harmonized post-merger lead Appleyard (1980) to conclude on conceptual grounds that there will be on average a downward bias to reported profit following acquisition in the 1960s and 1970s. Meeks's (1977) earlier study of the problem concurs in this view and he demonstrates the impact empirically for the goodwill point in his careful study. Although on average in the case of a firm making a single acquisition the effect on profitability is small (profitability adjusted for goodwill being, for instance, between 1.3 per cent and 5 per cent higher on average than raw profitability in the second year after merger), in individual cases it could be very large (for example, in the case of the GEC/AEI merger the adjustment amounted to over 20 per cent). Moreover, in the case of multiple acquirers the effect would be cumulative (Meeks (1977)). For accounting developments relevant to acquisitions in the 1980s and the biases to which they give rise, see Carty

---

[35] See e.g. Harcourt (1965), Fisher and McGowan (1983), and, for a more optimistic view under certain strict assumptions, Kay (1976). Meeks and Meeks (1981) set out a number of objections to other rates of return derivable from accounts (e.g. profit margin on sales, and the post-tax return on equity). Their main concern is with the usefulness of these rates as guides to 'efficiency', taking as given that mergers enhance monopoly bargaining power and thus profits, and they consider various biases which might arise in measuring them. Whatever the merits of profitability measures as a guide to 'efficiency', it is clear that the margin on sales and return to equity may have uses in relation to other specific objectives (e.g. estimates of monopoly power or of gains to shareholders from reorganizing capital structure) which make them preferable to the return on net assets, notwithstanding any biases in measurement which arise.

(1990), Higson (1990). It is important to bear these in mind in interpreting the results that follow when unadjusted data are used.

There are six studies to which we can refer. Utton (1974) compares the
unadjusted pre-tax profit performance of 39 quoted UK companies growing intensively by a series of mergers in the period 1961–5 and then by
internal means in the period 1966–70, with 39 randomly selected companies growing primarily without merger over the period 1961–70 as a
whole. He found that the merger-intensive firms had lower profitability
than the non-merging firms in their merger-intensive period and that the
gap widened subsequently. Thus, the average profitability of the merger-
intensive group fell from 13.6 per cent to 11.5 per cent and of the control
group from 15.4 per cent to 14.2 per cent. However, the industrial composition of the two groups of companies is not the same, so that, in addition to any downward accounting biases, there is some aggregation bias
(arising perhaps from the fact that mergers occur more frequently in low-
profit or falling-profit industries).[36] Interesting though Utton's counterfactual comparison is as an attempt to measure the effects of merger
intensity over a period of time, it does not pick up the profitability effects
on the assets of the acquiring and acquired firms under common management after merger, compared with their estimated combined profitability
when they were independent. The other five studies for the UK (Singh
(1971); Meeks (1977); Cosh, Hughes, and Singh (1980); Kumar (1985);
Cosh, Hughes, Lee, and Singh (1989)) all make attempts to do so, and to
deal with the problem of aggregation bias by comparing the profitability
of merging companies after merger with their weighted average pre-
merger profitability, either relative to their industry average or to size-
and industry-matched non-merging companies. The first two studies
(Meeks (1977) and (Singh (1971)) also attempt to adjust for the accounting bias. Of these five studies all but Cosh, Hughes, Lee, and Singh
(1989) refer to the 1970s or earlier. It is convenient to discuss these as a
group first before turning to the latter study, which covers the 1980s.

Allowing for accounting biases, Singh found, for a sample of 77 companies making a single horizontal acquisition in the period 1955–60, that
a little over 50 per cent of them suffered a decline in their relative pre-
and post-tax return on net assets after merger. He did not report the
magnitude of the changes but concluded that the impact overall was
likely to be neutral. Some illustrative results of two studies using methodology similar to Singh's for the later periods 1964–74 are shown in Table
1.11. These studies show negative effects. They are, however, not always

---

[36] The accounting biases would need to be very substantial to account for the differences
observed. Interestingly, the Sturgess and Wheale (1984) share price study reported below,
which is based on a subset of the Utton sample, shows that these reported profit differences
were not reflected in similar differences in terms of shareholder returns.

Table 1.11. Changes in normalized profitability[a] after merger in the UK, 1964–1974

Post-merger year	(1) Meeks 1964–71			(2) Kumar 1967–74		
	No. of companies (n)	Change in normalized profit	Percentage negative	No. of companies (n)	Change in normalized profit	Percentage negative
$t + 3$	164	−0.06**	52.7	241	−0.08*	61†
$t + 5$	67	−0.11**	64.2†	186	−0.06	60†

† Significantly different from 50% at the 5% level.
* Significantly different from zero at the 5% level.
** Significantly different from zero at the 1% level.

[a] Net income/net assets.

statistically significant and a high proportion of mergers show positive effects. Thus, in the period 1964–71, whilst the mean fall in normalized profitability was significantly negative three years after merger, 47 per cent of merging companies by then, nevertheless, showed improvements. Equally, in the period 1967–74, the fall in relative profitability by the fifth post-merger year was insignificant and 40 per cent of mergers showed improvement. The effects are also small and in the case of the second study are biased against finding positive effects because they do not adjust for the downward post-merger accounting bias discussed earlier. Thus in the case of the period 1967–74, for instance, if pre-merger industry profitability was around 16 per cent (as it was in the period 1966–71), then the pre-merger profitability of the merging firms would have been around 19.5 per cent and would on average have fallen by the third year after merger to around 18.2 per cent on an unadjusted, and only 19.2 per cent on an adjusted, basis.[37]

There is not much support here for the view that merger raises relative profitability. The clear impression is of a small, variable, but negative impact. The remaining study of profitability effects for the late 1960s, summarized in Table 1.12, presents merger overall in a slightly more favourable light, especially when it is noted that no adjustment is made for the downward accounting bias. It covers a sample of 211 firms in manufacturing and distribution in the period 1967–70, which overlaps with the two studies of Table 1.11. The years it covers represent the peak of the first major post-war merger wave and exclude the relatively low merger years of the mid-1960s and mid-1970s. In this study each pair of merging companies is compared with a control group which consists of those companies which were neither acquiring nor acquired in the five years prior to and following the merger. The profitability of the merging companies (AGAD) is calculated for five years pre-merger and compared with profitability for the average of three and five years after merger. Normalization is then effected by comparing the average change for merging firms with that of the unweighted average change for the control group as a whole (C) or with that of industry- and size-matched pairs of companies (MAGMAD) drawn from the control group.[38] This differs

[37] The figures in the table represent the differences between the ratios of merging company profitability to industry profitability pre- and post-merger. In year $t + 3$ the pre-merger ratio in the Kumar study was 1.22 and the post-merger ratio 1.14, giving a fall of 0.08. Hence with industry profitability assumed as 16%, pre-merger profit for the merging companies is $1.22 \times 16 = 19.52\%$ and post-merger profit $1.14 \times 16 = 18.24\%$. Meeks (1977) estimates that profitability adjusted for goodwill for a single merger in the second post-merger year varies between 1.5 and 5%. Taking the upper figure, in view of the inclusion of multiple acquirers in the Kumar study, raises post-merger profitability to $1.05 \times 18.24 = 19.15\%$.

[38] Thus, whilst the data in Table 1.11 refer to differences in the normalized profit ratios, in Table 1.12 the data represent mean changes in actual profit rates.

Table 1.12. Change in profitability[a] due to merger, 1967–1970

Merger comparison	3-year mean change in profitability (P)				Difference in mean changes	Percentage of industries where difference positive	5-year mean change in profitability (P)				Difference in mean changes	Percentage of industries where difference positive
	Merging		Non-merging				Merging		Non-merging			
	n	Change in P	n	Change in P			n	Change in P	n	Change in P		
All v. C	225	−0.26	1,186	−1.13	0.87*	57	211	0.63	1,185	−0.74	1.38*	71
All v. MAGMAD	225	−0.26	225	−1.78	1.52**	64	211	0.63	211	−0.24	0.87	50
Horizontal v. MAGMAD	109	−0.71	109	−1.89	1.18	64	98	0.47	98	+0.15	0.32	50
Non-horizontal v. MAGMAD	116	+0.16	116	−1.67	1.83**	57	113	0.78	113	0.58	1.35*	61

*Significantly different from zero at 10% on a 2–tailed test.
**Significantly different from zero at 5% on a 2–tailed test.

[a] Net income/net assets. For definition of the control groups, see the text.

Source: Cosh, Hughes, and Singh (1980).

from the control group used in the studies of Table 1.11, which was the weighted average profitability of the relevant industry population including the acquiring and acquired companies themselves. This difference probably accounts for the bulk of the discrepancy between the studies,[39] which is in any case most marked only for the non-horizontal merging group, which dominates the results for the sample as a whole and forms a bigger proportion of the Cosh, Hughes, and Singh sample than that, for instance, of Meeks. The horizontal mergers show no significant changes in profitability either up or down, compared to non-merging firms.[40] This distinction between the performance of horizontal and non-horizontal mergers is also mirrored in the Meeks study. He reports smaller and less statistically significant falls in profitability for mergers crossing 2-digit industry boundaries (corresponding to the definition of Table 1.12).

If these results for non-horizontal mergers prove robust to further empirical work they are an interesting finding. It must be remembered, however, that the differences are quite small, and high proportions of non-horizontal acquirers have negative post-merger performance changes. Nevertheless, their relative superiority may be rationalized. It may, for instance, reflect the relative characteristics of the acquiring and acquired firms in this type of take-over compared to others. In both the Meeks (M) and Cosh, Hughes, and Singh (CHS) samples the acquirers in these mergers were relatively more profitable pre-merger than horizontal

[39] The profitability change discrepancies hold for both the matched pairs and the overall control group comparisons, which is inconsistent with an explanation based on difficulties of matching for size. Of more relevance is the possible relative downward effect on control group profits in the other studies arising from taking weighted averages (if profits are negatively related to size) and the possible regression towards mean performance of the control group companies in the Cosh, Hughes, and Singh study which were relatively profitable in the pre-merger period compared with *both* the acquiring and acquired companies.

[40] It should be remembered that these profit effects are probably biased downward because they are not adjusted for the accounting problems discussed earlier and they include multiple acquisitions which compound these effects. To the extent that multiple acquisition is associated with learning by doing and persistent success, their exclusion from the Meeks study would bias his results downward and, as we have seen above, there is some evidence that the most intensive acquirers are relatively profitable. However, the other study in Table 1.11 included them without dramatically changing the results. Cosh, Hughes, and Singh also report the effects of merger on the sales margin (insignificantly positive for both non-horizontal and horizontal merger) and the ratio of post-tax income to equity assets (significantly positive for non-horizontal and insignificantly so for horizontal). The latter was investigated as part of an analysis of the impact of changes in leverage as a determinant and effect of merger, and gains in this measure reflect the use of debt as part of the purchase consideration to effect capital restructuring. Meeks and Meeks (1981) criticize the sales margin as being biased upwards in the event of vertical merger since some sales are internalized, whilst profits on them are still recorded. The force of this may depend upon the extent to which the control group is vertically integrating. As it happens, the non-horizontal mergers do no better in terms of sales margin changes than horizontal mergers, whilst in terms of the rate of return on assets they do outperform them.

acquirers or companies in general. In CHS they acquired significantly below-average profit victims. In M their victims were distinctly above average in profitability. The post-merger evidence suggests that these acquirers were able in the former case on average to turn poor performance around and in the latter more or less to maintain good performance. As far as horizontal mergers are concerned the situation was a bit different. In the CHS sample *both* the acquiring and acquired companies were below-par performers, whilst in M the acquiring were above par and the acquired below. In neither case on average did performance improve after merger and in the M study it fell. If the CHS horizontal mergers were failing-firm, rationalizing, or defensive ones, they served only to maintain, not improve, relative performance.

These estimated differences in outcome between horizontal and non-horizontal mergers may understate the actual differences in the presence of any regression to the mean. The counterfactuals against which performance is being measured is more biased against finding positive effects for conglomerate than non-conglomerate acquisitions. This is because in these samples the conglomerate acquirers are superior performers. If regression were present, their performance, *ceteris paribus,* should have declined towards mean levels. In the M study this would have been reinforced by a similar effect for the acquired companies who were also superior profit performers pre-merger. How might the superior performance of the non-horizontal group be rationalized? One possible explanation is simply that the non-horizontal acquisitions were made by a superior subset of firms (whose relatively superior pre-merger performance reflects superior management skills). This is consistent with a market for corporate control role for diversifying firms. However, as we noted earlier, on average they exercised 'discipline' over the weak only in the CHS case. In M's sample the way to avoid their attention would have been to pursue lower, not higher, profits. More plausibly the differences between the studies reflect the multi-causal nature of merger motives, in some cases acquirers seeking to turn around poor performers, in other acquirers seeking to maintain overall performance by buying into successful ones. The dominant motives varying from time period to time period and company to company. A further question remains, however, and that is why whatever superior performance horizontal acquirers may have relative to their victims does not lead to gains, or produces losses, whilst the impact for non-horizontal acquirers is more favourable.

It may be argued that this reflects the superior ability of diversifying firms to absorb new companies. This in turn depends upon the extent to which they have internally divisionalized management structures more readily adapted to the integration of new concerns. There is little doubt that inadequate post-merger management planning and decision-taking can be a key factor in determining the success or failure of merger and that divisionalized firms may have an advantage in this respect (Kitching (1967, 1974); Newbould (1970); Cowling *et al.* (1980); Grinyer and Spender (1979); Hunt *et al.* (1987); Samuels (1971); Hope (1976); Pratten (1970); Hill (1984)). The divisionalized form was, of course, growing in importance in the 1960s and its adoption is linked to diversification (Steer and Cable (1978); Thompson (1982); Channon (1973)). In the case of the sample of mergers discussed above, any advantage in absorbing acquired companies arising from product-based divisionalization would be strengthened in comparing non-horizontal to horizontal acquirers. This is because the former were typically acquiring companies relatively much smaller than themselves than were the latter (Cosh, Hughes, and Singh (1980); Meeks (1977)). The horizontal acquirers therefore may have experienced greater integration costs, because of both inadequate management structures and a greater relative size of victim.

A further factor may also have been at work. In horizontal mergers there may have been upward wage drift arising from parity bargaining between the plants of newly merged firms in the same industry. Thus Millward and McQueeney (1981) in a case study of five mergers in the period 1971–4, where the acquirers employed over 15,000 workers, and where some degree of diversification was involved, found some slight evidence of an increase in parity claims post-merger. They speculate that these would be more widespread in horizontal mergers, where the scope for such claims is greater. Moreover, if, as Geroski and Knight (1984) argue, the divisionalized form itself is a management response to gain enhanced control over pay and conditions of work, then not only would the parity claims be lower, but the response to them in general might be more effective. In these terms non-horizontal mergers may show superior performance because the internal distribution of income is shifted towards the managers and/or the stockholders. This would reflect a distributional rather than an efficiency impact.

Merger Profitability and Investment A further clue to the relative success of the non-horizontal group in the 1960s and 1970s may be traced to their investment performance. In their case study work Cowling *et al.* (1980) noted that on a number of occasions where post-merger productivity improvements occurred this was in association with the introduction of expansionary or restructuring programmes of capital expenditure.[41] They concluded that the link between merger, investment, and improved relative productivity was more than coincidental. Their evidence related

[41] The cases in question were London Brick/Marston Valley, RHP, and Johnson/Richards Campbell.

to horizontal mergers and would imply, if generalizable, that post-merger success in that group will be related to post-merger investment performance.[42] Equally, if non-horizontal mergers have a better post-investment record than horizontal mergers, then as a second hypothesis we might argue that this might help account for their superior profit performance too. Some evidence bearing on these issues is provided in Table 1.13. Column 3 shows (for the same sample of companies whose profit changes were analysed in Table 1.11 above) evidence relating to changes in the share of industry investment for merging firms pre- and post-merger both in total and for a breakdown between horizontal and non-horizontal merger. It also shows for mergers as a whole the profitability changes following merger and the correlation between them and investment share changes.

A number of points emerge. First, for the sample as a whole there is a small positive change in investment share for merging firms. By the fifth year after merger 58 per cent show increased investment performance (significantly different from random expectations on the binomial probability test). This is consistent with a number of other studies which have shown on a cross-section basis that there is a positive and significant relationship between growth by acquisition and growth by new fixed investment, and that overall asset growth post-merger is maintained at least at pre-merger rates (Meeks (1977); Cosh, Hughes, and Singh (1980)).[43] Table 1.13 also shows, however, in keeping with the first hypothesis outlined above, a small but statistically significant correlation between improvements in investment share and changes in normalized profit (column 4). Finally, it is noticeable that when the merging sample is split into horizontal and non-horizontal groups the former have a negligible investment share change, whilst the latter show a larger and statistically significant improvement. This gives some support to our second conjecture; that these firms may be more successful post-merger because they invest more. At least two possible explanations may be relevant here. The first would emphasize again the superior management form argument. If fewer managerial resources are required to integrate and plan the development of acquisitions in non-horizontal merger, then more are available for planning net expansion. Thus, any trade-off between the two forms of

[42] In what follows it is implicitly assumed that it is investment which permits the efficiency and profit improvements, rather than better profit performance permitting higher investment.

[43] Meeks reports, for instance, that in the period 1964–71 the 100 most acquisition-intensive companies also had the highest rate of growth by net investment, and that for 17 industries out of 18 a regression of growth by new investment on growth by acquisition showed a positive coefficient on the acquisition variable. In 9 cases the coefficient was statistically significant. It might be argued that this could reflect the acquisition of dynamic companies rather than an effect of merger. However, the result reported in the text compares pre- and post-merger investment *shares* for both partners, which avoids this problem.

Table 1.13. Mergers, profitability, and investment

Post-merger year	No. of mergers	All mergers					Horizontal mergers		Non-horizontal mergers	
		Change in normalized profit	Percentage positive	Change in investment share	Percentage positive	Correlation coefficient between (2) and (3)	Change in investment share	Percentage positive	Change in investment share	Percentage positive
	(1)	(2)		(3)		(4)	(5)		(6)	
$t + 3$	241	−0.008***	39*	0.26	54	+0.133***	0.02	53	0.55***	57
$t + 5$	186	−0.06	40*	0.21	58*	+0.102**	0.07	55	0.47***	56

* Significantly different from 50% at the 5% level.
** Significantly different from zero at the 10% level.
*** Significantly different from zero at the 5% level.

Source: Calculated from Kumar (1985), tables 5.3–5, 5.8.

growth may be reduced. Second, non-horizontal merger itself may be the way in which entry into sectors offering new profitable investment opportunities is effected. However, all of this requires further work to establish both the strength of the underlying relationships themselves as well as the possible reasons for them.

All the results so far surveyed pre-date the merger wave of the last decade. The only study using accounting data for the 1980s (Cosh, Hughes, Lee, and Singh (1989)) produces results for post-merger performance changes which are similar to those for the 1970s. Thus Table 1.14 shows that for mergers in the period 1981–3 profitability was if anything lower after merger than before. However, this study was designed to probe behind these average changes and to assess the impact on the merger process of a substantial change in UK stock markets between the 1960s and the 1980s: the growth in the importance of institutional investors. As Table 1.14 shows, acquiring companies which numbered one or more 5 per cent holdings by financial institutions amongst their equity holders were associated with a superior post-merger performance compared with those which did not. Further analysis also showed that the presence of financial institutions was associated with relatively high pre-merger profitability compared to other acquirers, and the acquisition of the least profitable target companies. In that sense their presence was more consistent with disciplinary raiding in the shareholders' interest than was the activity of acquiring companies without significant holdings by financial institutions. Moreover, for merging companies as a whole a subsequent study of the same sample showed that post-merger success was most likely where *both* parties were relative under-performers and that this result held even when allowance was made for the effects of regression back to mean values of profitability which these companies might in any event have been expected to make (Cosh, Hughes, Lee, and Singh (1990)).

Technical Change, Trade Performance, Small Firms, and the Regional Dimension With the exception of the discussion of investment effects, the emphasis so far has been essentially static. It has, moreover, focused primarily upon benefits and costs at the level of the individual large quoted company. In terms of the wider public interest issues with which economic policy is concerned in an open-economy, dynamic and spatial effects are clearly of central interest, as is also the impact of mergers involving small as well as large businesses.

Technical Change Small Firm Acquisitions, and Trade To the extent that merger has had a positive association with investment performance then it may have improved productivity via embodied technical change,

Table 1.14. Change in normalized profitability in the UK, by type of acquirer, 1981–1983

Variable	Whole sample			Sample of killers with financial holding			Sample of killers without financial holding		
	Sample size	Comparison of after with before	Significance level (two-tail) (%)	Sample size	Comparison of after with before	Significance level (two-tail) (%)	Sample size	Comparison of after with before	Significance level (two-tail) (%)
(1)	(3)	(4)	(5)	(6)	(7)	(8)	(9)	(10)	(11)
1-year profitability	59	Lower	—	25	Same	—	34	Lower	10
3-year profitability	59	Lower	—	25	Same	—	34	Lower	—
Change in profitability	59	Worsens	10	25	Same	—	34	Worsens	5
Share returns	47	Lower	—	19	Higher	—	28	Lower	10

Source: Cosh, Hughes, Lee, and Singh (1989).

benefits accruing both through the scrapping and replacement of old plant and via net investment. There is some scattered case study evidence to this effect. Thus the London Brick/Marston Valley merger of 1968 led to a gain in efficiency from a post-merger investment and rationalization programme involving a modernization of plant and equipment. (Cowling *et al.* (1980)). Evidence that merger may enhance the effectiveness of inputs into the process of technical improvement is also available. The impact of the government-sponsored formation by merger of ICL in 1968 appears to have improved the effectiveness of the UK industries' R & D effort, and that of the government's funding, by reducing competitive replication of expenditure. The resulting effect on product quality served to enhance the ability of ICL to match its international rivals in domestic and foreign markets (Stoneman (1978); Cowling *et al.* (1980)). These are, however, particular cases which focus on large-firm effects.

More recently attention has focused on the impact upon the innovative capacity of smaller businesses following their absorption into larger units. The vast majority of take-overs in the UK and the USA do not involve disciplinary raids on giant companies or even companies listed on the stock exchange (Hughes (1989b)). In these take-overs the decision to sell is made by the owners, who are usually also the key managers. Here the evidence, in so far as it relates to innovative small firms, suggests that selling out may meet the needs of the owners of smaller businesses to secure adequate financial resources for innovative or restructuring invest-ment strategies. It is, of course, in these areas that capital market failures to supply the necessary funds are most prevalent (ACOST (1990); Ashcroft, Love, and Scouller (1987); Granstrand and Sjölander (1990)). It has been argued, however, that in filling this market gap bureaucratic large businesses stifle the companies they acquire (Williamson (1985)). The evidence on this issue is scattered and unsystematic. In a recent series of case studies of barriers to growth in 25 small and medium-sized com-panies in the UK, over a third had been acquired. Nearly all cited the pursuit of financial resources as a key factor. Two had suffered significantly in the process but the majority reported improved ability to develop their plans for expansion and innovation (ACOST (1990)). Post-acquisition failure is most common where care is not taken to integrate the new acquisition and to manage effectively the clash between the infor-mal innovative small-firm culture of the business selling out and the inter-nal control mechanisms of the parent (Hunt *et al.* (1989)). Interesting case study material relating to the acquisition of UK hi-tech companies suggests that this may have been more easily achieved when the acquiring companies are themselves free of the short-term pressures of a stock mar-ket quotation. (See, for instance, the series of detailed studies by Garnsey, Roberts, and their associates covering hi-tech acquisitions in the UK by listed and private German companies and publicly listed US and UK firms (Garnsey and Roberts (1990, 1991); Garnsey, Alford, and Roberts (1991)). Recent evidence from Sweden is favourable to the notion that there may be a symbiotic relationship between large and small firms in the innovative process in which acquisition plays a positive part. Studies of samples of hi-tech firms reveal faster growth-rates after acquisition by large firms than before, and compared to non-acquired hi-tech firms (Granstrand and Sjölander (1990)).

The evidence on trade effects is also scanty. The case studies of Cowling *et al.* (1980) again suggest some cases where merger enhanced or sustained the ability of the firms concerned to meet international competition. (In addition to ICL these included mergers in machine tools and bearings where management reorganizations and restructuring played an important role). Equally, there were others where such claims were made pre-merger, but the evidence did not suggest that much improvement materialized subsequently. There is also some statistical cross-section material for individual companies bearing on this issue. Kumar (1984) reports a positive and significant correlation between acquisition intensity and export growth for large samples of continuing quoted UK companies in the period 1968–72 and 1972–6. The relationship between acquisition intensity and the growth of the export to sales ratio was, however, weaker and not statistically significant. This, of course, does not get directly at the issue of the impact of merger upon subsequent performance. However, for a sample of 311 firms divided into high- and low-acquisition-intensity groups in the period 1965–70 Kumar reports a higher subsequent growth in exports and in export intensity in the period 1971–6 for the merger-intensive group. The differences are not, however, statistically significant.

Regional Impacts The impact of merger upon the regional balance of activity and employment is one of the criteria which the MMC is asked to take into account in its evaluation of the public interest impact of a merger. It has been a significant issue, for instance, in a number of reports where the possibly adverse implications of a proposed merger for the Scottish regional economy were at stake (Charter Consolidated/ Anderson Strathclyde, and Royal Bank of Scotland/Hongkong and Shanghai Bank). It also figured prominently in the abandoned BTR bid for Pilkingtons. The subject has been relatively neglected by industrial economists. Cowling *et al.* (1980) consider employment rationalization in a general sense in a number of their case studies and provide a specific account of the labour reorganization within GEC following the major mergers involving that company in the late 1960s. Their concern is not, however, with estimating regional impacts as such, but more with considering the extent to which the social costs of community unemployment and job opportunity effects are taken into account in the merger decision. Their answer to which is not a lot.

Massey and Meegan (1979), on the other hand, provide an explicitly spatial analysis of the short-term employment effects over the period 1967–72 of 14 mergers in the electrical engineering and aerospace industries which the IRC sponsored in the period 1967–70.[44] They stress the historical and industrial specificity of their study and the difficulty of generalizing across space and time in the face of changes in macro-economic conditions and regional policy. The overwhelmingly dominant short-term impact of the mergers they studied was reduced employment, with 38,000 jobs lost and only 4,500 transferred between UK standard regions. The concentration of closed plants in relatively prosperous areas, however, plus the existing strong regional policy incentives to relocate towards the development areas, meant that the latter gained most from the limited job-switching which occurred. The short-term result was thus a slight decrease in regional unemployment inequality. Similarly, Leigh and North (1978) argue on the basis of an analysis of 263 food, clothing, textiles, and chemical acquisitions in the period 1973–4 that in the development areas superior short-term output and productivity performance following merger may have emerged.

Other studies covering later or longer time periods and different industries are less favourable. They suggest higher closure rates in the development areas for externally acquired or controlled plants compared to indigenous ones (Healey (1982); Smith and Taylor (1983); Smith (1979)), and lower rates of employment growth (Fothergill and Gudgin (1982)). Moreover, it has been argued on the basis of an analysis of plants employing over 100 people in the northern region in the period 1963–73 that where externally acquired plants do show a superior employment growth performance to those which remain independently and locally owned, this may reflect the superior pre-merger growth performance of the acquired plants (Smith (1979)). This would imply a transfer of control outside the region for the most dynamic ones within it.[45] There is evidence both for England and Scotland that such effects may have occurred.

For England an interview-based case study of five non-horizontal mergers in the period 1971–4 by Millward and McQueeney (1981) shows a general upward shift of decision-making to the new parent company. This affected, in particular, capital spending, financing, insurance, legal services, data processing, and clerical and management-training functions.

---

[44] They included the formation of ICL (under the Industrial Expansion Act (1968)) because of its links with other companies involved in IRC-sponsored rationalization.

[45] For some further informal illustrations of the point see Smith (1986).

In a similar vein Massey and Meegan (1978) suggest that these and other post-merger restructuring changes in their sample of IRC mergers could give rise to short- and long-run effects weakening growth prospects in the regions outside the South-east. Thus in the post-merger period the regional branch plant was left as a production unit with relatively few high-skilled employment opportunities, whilst the higher-level management control and technical and scientific support functions were switched elsewhere, especially to the South-east. Supporting conclusions emerge from the analysis by Leigh and North (1978) of 141 acquisitions by 61 companies in the food, chemicals, textiles, and clothing industries in the early 1970s. They show by means of an interview and case study approach that although there was some variation between region, industry, and type of take-over (e.g. horizontal or non-horizontal), in general low-level managerial decision-making relating to material inputs and production was retained locally. As a result, in the short term, local economy sourcing for these inputs was maintained in over 80 per cent of cases. On the other hand, over 80 per cent of service linkages affecting marketing, banking, insurance, advertising, legal advice, transport, and security were broken and either internalized by the central parent company or transferred to suppliers in the headquarters region. Relocation of headquarters and related staff changes can also have intraregional implications, with a shift of activity away from inner city to outer ring and suburban locations (Massey and Meegan (1978, 1979); Leigh and North (1978); Gripaios (1977)).

The evidence for Scotland supports the broad thrust of these results for the English regions, but is based more firmly on an attempt to distinguish and evaluate three separate sets of effects (see, for instance, Love (1990a)). The first are those familiar in the merger literature which arise from the impact of merger upon the competitive performance of the acquired firms. These are what may be termed the internal or private effects. The second group of effects arises from the impact upon suppliers of inputs and labour to the acquired firm as a result of post-merger reorganization. The third are the local multiplier implications consequent upon the first two groups of changes for which only the Scottish studies provide guidance. The evidence for the Scottish mergers suggests that the profitability effects of intraregional merger are much the same as for mergers as a whole (neutral or negative), although there is some evidence for improved sales-growth performance. Post-merger reorganization, however, leads, as in England, to major changes in input supplier relationships; once again in services, especially in the form of banking and auditing arrangements. These effects are strongest in failing-firm horizontal mergers (Ashcroft (1988); Ashcroft, Love, and Scouller (1987); Love (1990a)). This has led to an increased centralization of these functions in the financial centre of the South-east of England and away from the peripheral regions of England and of Scotland. Whilst the linkage effects have negative multiplier impacts, the Scottish work suggests they are smaller than the multiplier effects consequent upon post-merger sales changes in the acquired firms. Where the latter are positive they outweigh the direct linkage effects (Love (1990b)). This is clearly an area meriting further work, especially in the light of the increasingly cross-border nature of European activity.

Stock Price Effects and Market Returns The difficulties of estimating changes in accounting profitability, and of real effects in terms of resource use, have led some investigators to emphasize the virtues of using stock price movements as a better guide to the performance impact of merger. There is a growing body of work adopting this approach, though as I shall argue, it is not without its own important limitations.

Cosh, Hughes, and Singh (1980) and Cosh, Hughes, Lee, and Singh (1989) complement their accounting data tests with a comparison of shareholder returns (capital gains plus reinvested dividends). The first study compares five years before and after merger for 63 acquiring companies and 63 size- and industry-matched non-acquiring companies in the period 1967–9. For the pre- and post-merger periods the acquiring companies had higher shareholder returns. For the pre-merger period and one year after merger these positive differences were statistically significant. Thereafter the performance of the acquirers deteriorated relative to the control group. The second study, for 47 mergers in the period 1981–3, reports an insignificant worsening of share returns for the three years post-merger compared with three years before. Sturgess and Wheale (1984) compare for each year in the period 1961–70 shareholder returns for two groups of 26 companies which differ in that one experienced intensive merger activity in the period 1961–5 and the other did not. They find no significant differences between the groups in either period. Their results, however, show that in three of the years 1961–5 the merger-intensive group significantly over-performed, and in two of them significantly under-performed, relative to the non-merging group. In the 1966–70 period this is so in only one year. This pattern of performance between periods is consistent with the Cosh, Hughes, and Singh results, which suggest post-merger declines for the acquirers.[46] With these and one or two other exceptions, studies of the impact of merger based on stock price movements have not used return comparisons between merging and non-merging groups but have preferred 'event' study

---

[46] Adjusting their returns for risk using the Sharpe measure reverses the periods, in the sense that the internal growers now outperform the acquirers in the merger-intensive period and vice versa (Sturgess and Wheale (1984)).

methodology applied to samples of acquiring and acquired companies.[47] A model of stock price returns is estimated excluding data for a period before and after merger, and then actual returns for the firms involved are compared with the counterfactual returns based on the estimated equation. The deviation between the actual and counterfactual returns are termed abnormal (AR) and their cumulative sum (CAR) relative to some reference point is taken as the market's reaction to the 'new information' contained in the 'event' of the merger. Thus positive CARs associated with merger are taken to show that the merger is expected to create value for the shareholders reflecting economic efficiency gains. As Marsh (1986) puts it, 'Quite simply, if acquirers' shareholders gain, and if (at worst) acquirers' shareholders do not lose, there must therefore be net gains to shareholders from acquisition. Put another way, acquisitions have historically allowed companies to reap economic and efficiency gains.'

The most frequently used counterfactual models on which judgements such as this are based are the capital asset pricing model (CAPM), the market model, and the mean-adjusted return model. Actual returns may also be simply compared directly with a market index. These various models may be set out as follows, where P is the security price, D represents dividends, r_{jt} is the return on security j in month t, r_j is its average value over some period of months, rm_t is the return on a market index, rf_t is the risk-free rate of return, and a and b are coefficients of a regression equation used to estimate $R_{jt}{}^*$ (the counterfactual 'normal' return) so that

$$AR_{jt} = r_{jt} - R_{jt}{}^*$$

and

$$r_{jt} = \frac{(P_t - P_{t-1}) + D_t}{P_t.}$$

$R_{jt}{}^*$ and hence AR_{jt} may then be calculated using:

1. Mean-adjusted return model $\quad (R_{jt}{}^* = r_j)$

$$AR_{jt} = r_{jt} - r_j.$$

2. Market model[48] $\quad (R_{jt}{}^* = a_j + b_j rm_t)$

$$AR_{jt} = r_{jt} - (a_j + b_j rm_t).$$

3. Capital asset pricing model $\quad (R_{jt}{}^* = rf_t + b_j(rm_t - rf_t))$

$$AR_{jt} = r_{jt} - (rf_t + b_j(rm_t - rf_t)).$$

---

[47] Firth (1978), however, combines both. See the discussion of his results below.
[48] In some cases an industry-specific index may be added to the estimating equation:

$$R_{jt}{}^* = \alpha_j + b_j rm_t + c_j r^{zt}.$$

4. Simple market index model $(R_{jt}{}^* = rm_t)$

$$AR_{jt} = r_{jt} - rm_t.$$

With few exceptions in the UK the Market Model is estimated using OLS to obtain the counterfactual values.[49] We can look at the results of these studies for the acquired and acquiring firms separately and then at the net outcome taking both together.

Effects on Acquiring Companies Barnes estimates the effects of making a bid on 39 acquiring companies in the period June 1974 to February 1976 using a simple index model (Barnes (1978)) and the market model plus an industry index (Barnes (1984)). He reports small positive abnormal returns in the year before merger and offsetting or more than offsetting cumulative negative returns lasting up to five years afterwards, although none of these effects are statistically significant. This is in keeping with the declining post-merger results of Cosh, Hughes, and Singh reported earlier using shareholder returns relative to a non-merging control group. Franks, Broyles, and Hecht (1977) also use the market model plus a market index in a study of 70 mergers in the period 1955–72 in the UK brewing industry. Like Barnes, they find positive abnormal returns in the immediate run-up to the bid announcement, which persist for a few months after. There then follow negative effects, chiefly in the period between five and ten months after the bid so that by the fourth year after merger the CARs are negative. Similar post-bid results are reported by Dodds and Quek (1985). They analyse 70 acquisitions using the market model in the same period of low merger activity in the mid-1970s as the Barnes sample. They report that after initially positive post-merger effects the CARs are negative by the fifth year, with 58 per cent of the acquirers showing negative returns. Again, however, as in Barnes, none of this is statistically significant. Franks and Harris (1986), again using the market model, also report positive abnormal returns over the immediate bid announcement period in a sample of 1,048 mergers in the period 1955–85, a similar result to Meadowcraft and Thompson (1986) for 67 mergers in the period 1982–4. In the Franks and Harris study this is followed by cumulatively negative effects so that by two years after the mergers the CARs are significantly negative and outweigh the pre-merger gains.[50]

---

[49] Recent simulation studies suggest that the simpler estimation techniques and models (such as the mean-adjusted return) are as powerful as the more complex ones in identifying abnormal security performance (Brown and Warner (1980), Malatesta (1986)).

[50] They do not find this result using CAPM, or a simple index model, and speculate that this is due to the fact that if bidders time their bids to coincide with relative highs in their own prices, then the estimated α in the market model will be 'too high' so that there is an inevitable drift downwards after merger compared with counterfactual returns based on the estimated market model. The force of this must depend to some extent on how the estimation period is chosen, and the date from which the abnormal returns are then

Finally, Firth (1979, 1980) for samples of 224 successful bids in the period 1972–4, and 434 in the period 1969–75 respectively, reports positive abnormal residuals prior to merger for bidders using equity as the means of payment, substantial losses at the time of bid announcement, and cumulatively negative residuals after the bid, so that for his 1969–75 sample, for instance, by the end of the third year 64 per cent of the acquiring companies have negative CARs. (See also Firth (1976).) Taken as a whole these studies suggest that acquirers launch their bids when their prices are relatively high (either by accident or by design), but that whatever positive short-term effects are associated with the bid, in the longer run they are followed by cumulatively negative effects. Franks, Harris, and Mayer (1988) present results consistent with this interpretation. They analyse 954 UK acquisitions in the period 1955–85 split into two groups, those making all-equity bids and those making all-cash bids. In the all-equity bids high pre-merger constant terms in the market model are associated with significantly negative effects on acquirers' returns two years after the bid. Using the Capital Asset Pricing Model the effects are mildly positive. Similarly for cash offers the market model shows no change in acquirer returns and the Capital Asset Pricing Model significantly positive effects.

Acquired Companies Firth (1979, 1980) reports mildly negative deviations from expected returns in the first ten months of the year prior to the bid with around 55 per cent of the acquired companies showing negative CARs. In the two months prior to the bid announcement, however, positive abnormal returns occur, becoming very large and statistically significant in the merger month itself, so that by the announcement date 99 per cent of acquired companies show positive CARs, suggesting gains of around 22–8 per cent due to the merger event. Similarly, Franks, Broyles, and Hecht (1977) report abnormal gains of 26 per cent on average over the five months up to and including the offer date; Franks and Harris (1986) report bid premia in the 25–30 per cent range over the interval from four months prior to one month past the first approach or first bid date, and Meadowcroft and Thompson (1986) report similar gains over a slightly shorter period straddling the bid date. In the case of Franks, Broyles, and Hecht (1977) and Meadowcroft and Thompson (1986) these gains follow periods of negative residuals which are, however, rarely statistically significant. The picture here is fairly clear-cut, the acquired companies have a mildly below-par performance in the year before merger, but as the bid date approaches they gain in performance, perhaps as a result of leaks, insider trading, or the build-up of pre-bid

cumulated. For a critique of the capital asset pricing itself and possible biases in estimating the counterfactual equations, see Conn (1985).

strategic shareholdings. The bid period itself then generates substantial positive premia. These premia appear to be substantially higher in all-cash bids than in all-equity bids (Franks, Harris, and Mayer (1988)). This result, combined with the superior post-merger performance of cash bids noted above, suggests that bidders use cash in bids they expect to be relatively successful. They hope to capture thereby all the gains for themselves. In equity bids greater uncertainty about success leads to a willingness to share gains (and losses) with equity holders (Fishman (1986) cited in Franks, Harris, and Mayer (1988)).

The Net Effects Firth (1979, 1980) judges the immediate *short-term* effects on the acquiring and acquired companies together in the late 1960s and early 1970s to have been neutral or negative. That is to say, allowing for the relative sizes of the companies involved, the losses to the acquirers in the one month prior to and after the bid matched, or more than offset, the gains to the acquired company over the same period. This neutral or negative impact was maintained up to two years post-merger, so that 'The stock market viewed takeovers as having little overall impact on corporate profitability' (Firth (1980)). This view is consistent with the actual profit outcomes discussed above. Meadowcroft and Thompson (1986), and Franks and Harris (1986) analysing the early 1980s and the period 1955–85 respectively, conclude, on the other hand, that there are net benefits in the short-term (i.e. one month before to two or three months after the bid). In their samples, the acquirers either gain slightly or at least do not lose, whilst the acquired have substantial positive residuals. Thus, Meadowcroft and Thompson suggest net gains of around 7–8 per cent on the pre-merger total market capitalization of the companies involved. These are very short-term effects, however. By the end of the second year the Franks and Harris (1986), and Franks, Harris, and Mayer (1988) acquirers are showing significantly negative residuals at least using the Market Model (Meadowcroft and Thompson provide no data beyond month 12). It is difficult to argue that these studies taken together and in their own terms suggest that the market expected fundamental long-term gains to occur, and if they did they revised their opinions as far as the acquirers are concerned. Such gains as did occur accrued to the shareholders in the acquired company.[51]

[51] Interestingly, gains of a similar or greater extent seem to be made by shareholders in target companies where the bids fail, as well as those in which they succeed (Firth (1980)). This may reflect pepped-up performance following the bid, and suggests that the threat may be as effective as the fact of take-over. Thus Pickering (1983) reports some target companies as effecting managerial and other changes after surviving bids, and in the majority of his 20 case studies he reports some improvement in performance. (See also Holl and Pickering (1988).) It is notable, however, that many of the targets sought purchase by third parties, went for short-term growth, or acquired other companies as ways of reducing future vulnerability, rather than pursuing improved profitability.

The idea that merger has insignificant effects on the processes generating expected returns receives further support from another study by Firth. He estimated the parameters of the market model for 24 months prior to merger, and 24 months after, for 150 merging companies and a similar number of size- and industry-matched non-acquiring companies in the period 1972–4. He could find no systematic significant differences between the merging group and the control group in the mean or variance of stock market returns either pre- or post-merger, or in the estimated parameters of the market model (Firth (1978)).

Even if it were accepted that in the short run the joint effects of merger on abnormal returns may be positive, a fundamental problem of interpretation remains. The underlying methodology of the event studies assumes that demand curves for stocks are horizontal so that normally trading investors may buy or sell any amount of stock without systematically affecting the price. The marginal price reflects average opinion; when sharp movements in price occur in association with an event (e.g. a take-over) they are then interpreted as a response to the 'new information' imparted by it. Positive abnormal returns associated with bids may therefore be interpreted to suggest that the market expects improved performance to follow from merger and shareholders benefit accordingly. The distribution of these gains between the acquired and acquiring is then determined by the competitiveness of the bid market, the presence or absence of rival bids, or contests, and so on.

If, however, there are, for instance, divergences of expectations and opinion over security values so that the marginal trading valuation reflects marginal opinion, then the market demand curve slopes downwards to the right and some investors will require a price above that at the margin before selling (Hughes, Mueller, and Singh (1980); Cragg and Malkiel (1982); Miller (1977); Black (1986); Schleifer (1986); Mayshar (1983)). Premia will therefore be necessary simply to effect the ownership transfer in a take-over, and they may vary with the dispersion of stockholdings and the dispersion of divergent opinion across the various blocks of shares. These premia will therefore be highly ambiguous guides to expected efficiency gains when taken either on average or in relation to particular mergers. They tell us merely what the short-term windfall wealth effects of merger are relative to a particular counterfactual for the small number of individuals directly involved as shareholders (or the larger number indirectly involved via changes in pensions and insurance policy premia following financial institutions' portfolio responses to bids). There is no necessary connection between the direction and magnitude of these premia and underlying real changes in the management and performance of the assets over which the property rights embodied in the stock give control.[52] All we can deduce is that for *some* reasons the bidders felt it worth while to offer the premia and the sellers felt it worth while to accept. These reasons, as we saw in Section 2, may be as much related to the pursuit of monopoly power, and empire building, as to enhanced management techniques, scale and scope economies, or other efficiency-enhancing targets. The existing UK stock price evidence does not help us distinguish between them.[53] It is an act of faith to argue on the basis of it alone that acquisitions have in general allowed companies to reap economic or efficiency gains.

5. CONCLUSIONS ON THE IMPACT OF MERGER: STRUCTURE, PERFORMANCE, AND POLICY

Mergers have played a major role in the post-war structural transformation of the UK economy. They have had an impact upon the concentration of market sales, the diversification of corporate output, and the regional and international distribution of corporate activity. Concentration at the market and aggregate level rose substantially to the late 1960s. This was in large part due to the scale and incidence of merger activity in the decade following the first increases in merger in the late 1950s. The peak years of merger activity from 1968 to 1973 were not, however, associated with contemporaneous or subsequent increases on the same scale. Nor was the merger wave of the 1980s associated with an increase in concentration. But we do not have any systematic studies of the role that merger has played in these later years. Reconciling high rates of merger and stability in domestic concentration is possible if, for instance, *inter alia*, a considerable portion of the activity is directed overseas, or contributes either to a faster rate of growth for smaller firms or a reduced variance of growth-rates. In the 1960s and early 1970s we have seen that merger growth and internal growth were if anything complementary. If in the depressed years of the late 1970s and early 1980s net investment has been severely constrained and merger growth has substituted for it at the individual firm level, then extremely high growth-rates combining both internal and external expansion might be less frequent, and the drift towards domestic concentration reduced. Similar effects may occur if merger and other forms of expansion by large firms are

[52] It is interesting in this connection to note that Kuehn (1975) could not find any systematic relationship between the financial and performance variables of acquiring, and acquired, firms and the size of the bid premium.

[53] It is possible, however, by choosing appropriate control group samples, to try to isolate monopoly effects, etc.; for a relevant survey of US evidence, see Jensen and Ruback (1983).

increasingly diverted abroad, or if merger is followed by the break-up and
divestment of constituent companies. In several instances changes in concentration may have led to increased market power. It is difficult to sustain the argument, however, that the degree of monopoly in the UK
domestic market has increased in the last two decades. At best it might
be argued that merger has served to maintain whatever power existed
previously, but even that seems overly generous. Diversifying activity has
increased in importance and some firms have grown spectacularly fast by
non-horizontal merger. The implications for market power of these
changes are ambiguous and probably less important than their broader
impact on the nature of resource allocation, in particular for investment
goods and productive resources. Much here depends upon how optimistic
a view one takes of the virtues of the stock market allocation process
versus the internal administrative market of conglomerate firms, and the
damage that information loss in consolidated accounts causes to the
former. Take-over or the threat of it, as a disciplinary stock market
device leaves a lot to be desired. Except at the height of booms its discipline appears constrained to the middle size ranges of companies.
Moreover, the most favourable route to avoid nemesis is to grow bigger
and seek stabler profits in the short run rather than to go for higher
medium-term profitability. The disciplinarians are bigger and faster-
growing but not on average more profitable, and their shareholders gain
little or even lose as result of their companies' acquisitions. The shareholders of acquired companies, on the other hand, make windfall gains
that on average have no counterpart in improved resource use or corporate profitability. If these gains are supposed to represent expected performance improvements then direct evidence on the latter suggests that the
market gets it wrong and is on average too optimistic. Neutral net effects
on stockholder welfare would be more consistent with average post-
merger performance effects. All this evidence seems at least as consistent
with an inducement to empire building by growth-minded managers as
much as discipline in the stockholders' interests. Within this story the
non-horizontal acquirers appear in a less unfavourable light. They are
more successful pre-merger than other acquirers and they improve or sustain performance post-merger better than other acquirers, in terms of
both profitability and post-merger investment, though the differences in
either direction are not terribly large. Against this, some information loss
might seem a small cost, especially since it is in principle remediable by
improved reporting and disclosure requirements. Despite the much publicized success of some conglomerates, not all conglomerates are efficiently
run internally, and their victims are not always those mismanaging their
affairs, so that the growth and success of these acquirers may come to
depend on the capture of ever bigger and more successful companies to

maintain a given proportionate expansion in size and performance. Nor does the existing evidence tell us much about the sources of the gains to profits for these companies. Some may be consistent with a convergence of private and public gain, others may not, or may represent internal redistributions of income. Moreover, anyone with a memory stretching back to the heady days of the merger boom of the late 1960s will recall how the shining captains of today's industry can become tomorrow's over-ambitious failures. And there are always problems of succession. As with profits, so with growth-rates, there is some evidence of regression towards the mean. Compared to conglomerate mergers, those which have been horizontal have produced neutral or negative performance effects at the micro-economic level. To the extent that horizontal merger activity is more widespread and frequent, it could be argued that neutral results are to be expected, since, on average, over long periods of time one sort of expansion (internal) should show the same sort of return as another (external). If, in addition, there are management diseconomies and industrial relations problems then over-indulgence in periods of high activity may produce some losses overall. There might be something in this, but it should apply to other forms of merger growth too, so that non-horizontal expansion should be no more successful than other kinds. It is possible to argue here that in fact it too will converge towards the norm, once it becomes the predominant form and there are more rivalrous predators pursuing the same prey. This may be one reason why performance gaps narrow in merger booms. All this assumes a distribution of entrepreneurial talent and empire building drive that may in the UK context be overly optimistic. In any event, the fact that horizontal mergers are as likely to fail as to succeed, whilst they have obvious potential for market power effects, suggests that on these grounds there should be an appropriate case-by-case application to them of existing merger policy powers. In the case of non-horizontal mergers where market power effects are suspected, close consideration should be paid to the nature of the company's past success as well as the internal features of its management structure, since these seem likely to be closely connected with the likelihood of any prospective efficiency gains. In both cases the power to require undertakings and to monitor post-merger activity should be actively pursued.

All this, however, is very much in terms of private gains and losses, and set in a static context in which efficiency gains are to be traded off domestically against presumed allocative welfare losses (forgone consumers' surplus). There are broader issues. Merger waves bring with them huge windfall gains acquired both legally and illegally by market participants. At the same time, the decision upon which these redistributions of wealth occur may affect the location of industry and the associated regional distribution of job opportunities and growth prospects within the

UK, as well as the ability of industry to compete effectively both domestically and abroad. All of these issues quite properly feature in the list of matters which the MMC must bear in mind in evaluating the public interest effects of merger once a reference is made. They have, however, been largely neglected in empirical research, which has focused excessively, as we have seen, on the monopoly power–efficiency trade-off and upon an analysis by proxy using stock market returns as a guide to welfare. They have also been ignored most recently in the application of merger policy where references have been based almost exclusively on competitive effects. Such evidence as we have on these broader issues suggests that there are potentially damaging effects upon regional vitality which may arise after take-over, and, on the other hand, that in certain circumstances merger can have a central role to play in the reorganization and revitalization of particular sectors. As I have argued at length elsewhere (Hughes (1978)), to be most effective competition policy must be operated on principles complementary to those adopted in industrial policy generally and be integrated with it. At the very least, the criteria for reference should be consistent with the public interest criteria to be used in evaluating a merger once a reference is made. There is little sense in investigating trade or regional impacts in horizontal merger because a separate market power impact is suspected, but ignoring them in conglomerate mergers because no competition issue is raised.

Finally. it must be recognized that the many issues to which mergers in general, and the current merger wave in particular, give rise cannot be resolved by an appeal to competition policy alone. Much broader questions about the relationship between management and major investors, the internal governance of the modern corporation, and the regulation and organization of capital markets are at issue. As portfolio 'churning' increases in the period of adjustment to Big Bang it is worth while recalling the views of one well-known market operator.

As the organization of investment markets improves, the risk of the predominance of speculation does, however, increase. Speculators may do no harm as bubbles on a steady stream of enterprise. But the position is serious when enterprise becomes the bubble on a whirlpool of speculation. When the capital development of a country becomes a by-product of the activities of a casino, the job is likely to be ill done. (Keynes (1936), pp. 158–9)

REFERENCES

Aaronovitch, S., and Sawyer, M. C. (1975a), *Big Business*, London: Macmillan.
—— —— (1975b), 'Mergers, growth and concentration', *Oxford Economic Papers*, **27**, 136–55.

ACOST (1990), *The Enterprise Challenge: Overcoming Barriers to Growth in Small Firms*, Advisory Council on Science and Technology, London: HMS0.

Adams, J. W., and Heimforth, K. (1986), 'The effect of conglomerate mergers on changes in industry concentration', *Antitrust Bulletin*, Spring.

Alchian, A. A., and Kessel, R. A. (1962), 'Competition, monopoly, and the pursuit of pecuniary gain', in *Aspects of Labour Economics*, Princeton: National Bureau of Economic Research.

Appleyard, A. R. (1980), 'Takeovers: accounting policy, financial policy and the case against accounting measures of performance: a synopsis', *Journal of Business Finance and Accounting*, 7, 541–54.

Ashcroft, B. K. (1988), 'External takeovers in Scottish manufacturing, the effect on local linkages and corporate functions', *Scottish Journal of Political Economy*, May, 35, No. 2, 129–48.

—— Love, J. H., and Scouller, J. (1987), *The Economic Effects of the Inward Acquisition of Scottish Manufacturing Companies 1965–80*, ESU Research Paper No. 11, Industry Department for Scotland.

Auerbach, A. J. (ed.) (1988), *Corporate Takeover: Causes and Consequences*, Chicago: Chicago University Press.

Barnes, P. A. (1978), 'The effect of a merger on the share price of the attacker', *Accounting and Business Research*, 8, 162–8.

—— (1984), 'The effect of a merger on the share price of the attacker, revisited', *Accounting and Business Research*, 15, 45–9.

—— (1985), 'UK building societies: a study of the gains from merger', *Journal of Business Finance and Accounting*, 12, 75–91.

—— and Dodds, J. C. (1981), 'Building society mergers and the size-efficiency relationship: a comment', *Applied Economics*, 13, 531–4.

Berry, C. H. (1975), *Corporate Growth and Diversification*, Princeton, NJ: Princeton University Press.

Black, F. (1986), 'Noise', *Journal of Finance*, 41, 529–43.

Boesky, I. F. (1985), *Merger Mania*, London: Bodley Head.

Bolton (1971), *Small Firms: Report of the Committee of Inquiry on Small Firms*, Cmnd. 4811, London: HMSO.

Boswell, J. (1972), *The Rise and Decline of Small Firms*, London: Allen and Unwin.

Brooks, D., and Smith, R. (1963), *Mergers, Past and Present*, London: Acton Society Trust.

Brown, S. J., and Warner, J. B. (1980), 'Measuring security price performance', *Journal of Financial Economics*, 8, 205–58.

Brudney, V., and Chirelstein, M. A. (1978), 'A restatement of corporate freeze-outs', *Yale Law Journal*, 87, 1354–76.

Buckley, A. (1972), 'A profile of industrial acquisition in 1971', *Accounting and Business Research*, 2, 243–52.

Bull, A., and Vice, A. (1961), *Bid for Power*, London: Elek Books.

Cable, J. R. (1977), 'A search theory of diversifying merger', *Recherches Économiques de Louvain*, September.

Camerer, C. (1989), 'Bubbles and fads in asset prices', *Journal of Economic Surveys*, 3, No. 1, 32–40.

Carty, J. (1990), 'Accounting for takeovers', in *Takeovers and Short Termism in the UK*, Industrial Policy Paper No. 3, Institute for Public Policy Research, London.

Channon, D. F. (1973), *The Strategy and Structure of British Enterprise*, London: Macmillan.

Chiplin, B., and Wright, M. (1980), 'Divestment and structural change in UK industry', *National Westminster Bank Review*, February, 42–51.

Clarke, R., and Davies, S. W. (1983), 'Aggregate concentration, market concentration and diversification', *Economic Journal*, **93**, 182–92.

Conn, R. L. (1985), 'A re-examination of studies that use the capital asset pricing model methodology', *Cambridge Journal of Economics*, **9**, 43–56.

Coopers & Lybrand (1989), *Barriers to Takeovers in the European Community*, Department of Trade and Industry, London: HMSO.

Coppins, B. (1991), 'An Investigation into the Spatial Distribution of Acquisition Activity in the UK Economy: 1969, 1977 and 1985', M.Phil. dissertation, Napier Polytechnic, Edinburgh.

Cosh, A. D., Hughes, A., Kumar, M. S., and Singh, A. (1985), 'Conglomerate organisation and economic efficiency: a report to the Office of Fair Trading', mimeo, Cambridge.

—— —— Lee K., and Singh A. (1989) 'Institutional investment, mergers and the market for corporate control', *International Journal of Industrial Organization*, March, pp. 73–100.

—— —— —— —— (1990) *Predicting Success: Pre-merger Characteristics and Post-merger Performances*, Small Business Research Centre Working Paper No. 6, Department of Applied Economics, Cambridge.

—— —— and Singh, A. (1980), 'The causes and effects of takeovers in the UK: an empirical investigation for the late 1960's at the micro-economic level', in D. C. Mueller (ed.), *The Determinants and Effects of Mergers*, Cambridge, Mass.: Oelschlager, Gunn and Hain.

—— —— —— (1990), 'Takeovers and short termism: analytical and policy issues in the UK economy', in *Takeovers and Short Termism in the UK*, Industrial Policy Paper No. 3, Institute for Public Policy Research, London.

Cowling, K., Stoneman, P., Cubbin, J., Cable, J., Hall, G., Domberger, S., and Dutton, P. (1980), *Mergers and Economic Performance*, Cambridge: Cambridge University Press.

Cragg, J., and Malkiel, B. (1982), *Expectations and the Structure of Share Prices*, Chicago: University of Chicago Press.

CSO (1990), *Business Bulletin: 'Cross Border Acquisitions and Mergers'*, Q3, 1990, London: HMSO.

Cubbin, J. S., and Hall, G. (1979), 'The use of real cost as an efficiency measure: an application to merging firms', *Journal of Industrial Economics*, **28**, 73–88.

Curry, B., and George, K. D. (1983), 'Industrial concentration: a survey', *Journal of Industrial Economics*, **31**, 203–55.

Davies, J. R., and Kuehn, D. A. (1977), 'An investigation into the effectiveness of a capital market sanction on poor performance', in A. P. Jacquemin and H. W. de Jong (eds.), *Welfare Aspects of Industrial Markets*, Leiden: Martinus Nijhoff.

Davies, P. L. (1976), *The Regulation of Take-overs and Mergers*, London: Sweet and Maxwell.

Department of Prices and Consumer Protection (1978), *A Review of Monopolies and Mergers Policy*: A Consultative Document, Cmnd. 7198, London: HMSO.

Dodds, J. C., and Quek, J. P. (1985), 'Effect of mergers on the share price movement of the acquiring firms: a UK study', *Journal of Business Finance and Accounting*, **12**, 285–96.

Dunne, P., and Hughes, A. (1990), *Age, Size, Growth and Survival: UK Companies in the 1980s*, Small Business Research Centre Working Paper No. 4, Department of Applied Economics, Cambridge.

Elliott, D. C., and Gribbin, J. D. (1977), 'The abolition of cartels and structural change in the United Kingdom', in A. P. Jacquemin and H. W. de Jong (eds.), *Welfare Aspects of Industrial Markets*, Leiden: Martinus Nijhoff.

Evely, R. A., and Little, I. M. D. (1960), *Concentration in British Industry*, Cambridge: Cambridge University Press.

Farrell, J., and Shapiro, C. (1990), 'Horizontal mergers: an equilibrium analysis', *American Economic Review*, March 1990, pp. 107–26.

Firth, M. (1976), *Share Prices and Mergers*, Farnborough: Saxon House/ Lexington Books.

—— (1978), 'Synergism in mergers: some British results', *Journal of Finance*, **33**, 670–2.

—— (1979), 'The profitability of takeovers and mergers', *Economic Journal*, **89**, 316–28.

—— (1980), 'Takeovers, shareholder returns and the theory of the firm', *Quarterly Journal of Economics*, **94**, 235–60.

Fisher, F. M., and McGowan, J. J. (1983), 'On the misuse of accounting rates of return to infer monopoly profits', *American Economic Review*, **73**, 82–97.

Fishman, M. J. (1986), 'Pre-emptive bidding and the role of medium of exchange in acquisitions', mimeo, North Western University, Evanston, Illinois, July.

Fothergill, S., and Gudgin, G. (1982), *Unequal Growth*, London: Heinemann Educational Books.

Francis, A. (1980), 'Company objectives, managerial motivations and the behaviour of large firms: an empirical test of the theory of managerial capitalism', *Cambridge Journal of Economics*, **4**, 349–61.

Franks, J., and Mayer, C. (1990), 'Capital markets and corporate control: a study of France, Germany and the UK', *Economic Policy*, April, 191–231.

Franks, J. R., Broyles, J. E., and Hecht, M. J. (1977), 'An industry study of the profitability of mergers in the United Kingdom', *Journal of Finance*, **32**, 1513–25.

—— and Harris, R. S. (1986), 'Shareholder wealth effects of corporate takeovers: the UK experience 1955–85', London Business School and University of North Carolina at Chapel Hill Working Paper.

—— Harris, R. S., and Mayer, C. (1988), 'Means of payment in takeover: results for the United Kingdom and the United States', in A. J. Auerbach (ed.) *Corporate Takeovers: Causes and Consequences*, National Bureau of Economic Research, Chicago: University of Chicago Press.

Garnsey, E., and Roberts, J. (1990), 'Growth through acquisition for small high technology firms: a case comparison', in S. Birley (ed.), *Building European Ventures*, Amsterdam: Elsevier..

—— —— (1991) *Aftermath of Acquisition of High Technology Ventures: A Further Case Comparison*, Small Business Research Centre Working Paper No. 10, Department of Applied Economics, University of Cambridge.

—— Alford, H., and Roberts J. (1991) *Acquisition as Longterm Venture: Cases from High Technology Industry*, Small Business Research Centre Working Paper No. 9, Department of Applied Economics, University of Cambridge.

Geroski, P. A. (1984), 'On the relationship between aggregate merger activity and the stock market', *European Economic Review*, **25**, 223–33.

—— and Knight, K. G. (1984), 'Corporate merger and collective bargaining in the UK', *Industrial Relations Journal*, **15**, 51–60.

Goddard, J. B., and Smith, I. J. (1978), 'Changes in corporate control in the British urban system, 1972–77', *Environment and Planning*, **A10**, 1073–84.

Golbe, D. L., and White, L. J. (1988), 'A time series analysis of mergers and acquisitions in the UK economy', in A. J. Auerbach (ed.), *Corporate Takeovers: Causes and Consequences*, National Bureau of Economic Research, Chicago: University of Chicago Press.

Goldberg, L. G. (1973), 'The effect of conglomerate mergers on competition', *Journal of Law and Economics*, **16**, 137–58.

—— (1974), 'Conglomerate mergers and concentration ratios', *Review of Economics and Statistics*, **56**, 303–9.

Gorecki, P. K. (1975), 'An inter-industry analysis of diversification in the UK manufacturing sector', *Journal of Industrial Economics*, **24**, 131–46.

Gort, M. (1969), 'An economic disturbance theory of mergers', *Quarterly Journal of Economics*, **83**, 624–42.

Goudie, A., and Meeks, G. (1982), 'Diversification by merger', *Economica*, **49**, 447–59.

Gough, T. J. (1979), 'Building society mergers and the size-efficiency relationship', *Applied Economics*, **11**, 185–94.

—— (1981), 'Building society mergers and the size-efficiency relationship: a reply', *Applied Economics*, **13**, 535–8.

Graham, J. (1979), 'Trends in UK merger control', *Trade and Industry*, 14 September.

Granstrand, O., and Sjölander, S. (1990), 'The acquisition of technology and small firms by large firms', *Journal of Economic Behaviour and Organization*, **13**, 367–86.

Gratton, C., and Kemp, J. R. (1977), 'Some new evidence on changes in UK industrial market concentration 1963–68', *Scottish Journal of Political Economy*, **24**, 177–81.

Greer, D. F. (1986), 'Acquiring in order to avoid acquisition', *Antitrust Bulletin*, Spring.

Gribbin, J. D. (1974), 'The operation of the Mergers Panel since 1965', *Trade and Industry*, 17 January.

Grinyer, P. H., and Spender, J. C. (1979), *Turnaround: The Fall and Rise of the Newton Chambers Group*, London: Associated Business Press.

Gripaios, P. (1977), 'The closure of firms in the inner city: the south-east London case 1970–75', *Regional Studies*, **11**, 1–6.

Grossman, S. J., and Hart, O. D. (1980), 'Takeover bids, the free-rider problem and the theory of the corporation', *Bell Journal of Economics*, **11**, 42–64.

Halpern, P. (1983), 'Corporate acquisitions: a theory of special cases? A review of event studies applied to acquisitions', *Journal of Finance*, **38**, 297–317.

Hannah, L. (1976), *The Rise of the Corporate Economy*, London: Methuen. 2nd edn. 1983.

—— and Kay, J. A. (1977), *Concentration in Modern Industry*, London: Macmillan.

—— —— (1981), 'The contribution of mergers to concentration growth: a reply to Professor Hart', *Journal of Industrial Economics*, **29**, 305–13.

Harcourt, G. C. (1965), 'The accountant in a golden age', *Oxford Economic Papers*, **17**, 66–80.

Hart, P. E. (1979), 'On bias and concentration', *Journal of Industrial Economics*, **27**, 211–26.

—— (1980), 'Lognormality and the principle of transfers', *Oxford Bulletin of Economics and Statistics*, **42**, 263–7.

—— (1981), 'The effects of mergers on industrial concentration', *Journal of Industrial Economics*, **29**, 315–20.

—— and Clarke, R. (1980), *Concentration in British Industry, 1935–75*, Cambridge: Cambridge University Press.

—— Utton, M., and Walshe, G. (1973), *Mergers and Concentration in British Industry*, Cambridge: Cambridge University Press.

Hassid, J. (1975), 'Recent evidence on conglomerate diversification in the UK manufacturing sector', *Manchester School of Economic and Social Studies*, **43**, 372–95.

Healey, M. J. (1982), 'Plant closures in multi-plant enterprises: the case of a declining industrial sector', *Regional Studies*, **16**, 37–51.

Heath, J. B. (1961), 'Restrictive practices and after', *Manchester School of Economic and Social Studies*, **29**, 173–202.

Helm, D. (1989), 'Mergers, takeovers and the enforcement of profit maximization', in J. A. Fairburn and J. A. Kay (eds.), *Mergers and Merger Policy*, Oxford University Press, Oxford.

Herman, E. S. (1981), *Corporate Control Corporate Power*, Cambridge: Cambridge University Press.

Higson, C. (1990), *The Choice of Accounting Method, in UK Mergers and Acquisitions*, London: Research Board of the Institute of Chartered Accountants in England and Wales.

Hill, C. W. L. (1984), 'Profile of a conglomerate takeover: BTR and Thomas Tilling', *Journal of General Management*, **10**, 34–50.

—— (1985), 'Diversified growth and competition: the experience of 12 large UK firms', *Applied Economics*, **17**, 827–47.

—— and Pickering, J. F. (1986a), 'Conglomerate mergers, internal organisation and competition policy', *International Review of Law and Economics*, June 6.

—— —— (1986b), 'Divisionalization, decentralization and performance of large UK companies', *Journal of Management Studies*, **23**, 26–50.

Hindley, B. (1972), 'Recent theory and evidence on corporate merger', in K. Cowling (ed.), *Market Structure and Corporate Behaviour: Theory and Empirical Analysis of the Firm*, London: Gray-Mills.

Hirschey, M. (1986), 'Mergers, buyouts and fakeouts', *American Economic Review*, Papers and Proceedings, **76**, 317–22.

Holl, P., and Pickering, J. F. (1988), 'The determinants and effects of actual, abandoned and contested mergers', *Managerial and Decision Economics*, **9**, pp. 1–19.

Holland, D. M., and Myers, S. C. (1979), 'Trends in corporate profitability and costs', in R. Lindsay (ed.), *The Nation's Capital Needs: Three Studies*, New York: Committee for Economic Development.

Hope, M. (1976), 'On being taken over by Slater Walker', *Journal of Industrial Economics*, **24**, 163–79.

Hughes, A. (1976), 'Company concentration, size of plant, and merger activity', in M. Panic (ed.), *The UK and West German Manufacturing Industry, 1954–72*, NEDO/HMSO: London.

—— (1978), 'Competition policy and economic performance in the UK', in NEDO, *Competition Policy*, London: HMSO.

—— (1986), 'Investment finance, industrial strategy and economic recovery', in P. H. Nolan and S. H. Paine (eds.), *Rethinking Socialist Economics*, Cambridge: Polity Press.

—— (1989a), 'The impact of merger: a survey of empirical evidence for the UK' in J. A. Fairburn and J. A. Kay (eds.), *Mergers and Merger Policy*, Oxford: Oxford University Press.

—— (1989b), 'Small firms merger activity and competition policy', in J. Barber, J. S. Metcalfe, and M. Porteous (eds.), *Barriers to Growth in Small Firms*, London: Routledge.

—— (1991), 'UK small businesses in the 1980s: continuity and change', *Regional Studies*, October, 471–8.

—— and Kumar, M. S. (1984a), 'Recent trends in aggregate concentration in the UK economy', *Cambridge Journal of Economics*, **8**, 235–50.

—— —— (1984b), 'Recent trends in aggregate concentration in the UK economy: revised estimates', *Cambridge Journal of Economics*, **8**, 401–2.

—— —— (1985), 'Mergers, concentration and mobility amongst the largest UK non-financial corporations 1972–82: a report to the Office of Fair Trading', mimeo, Department of Applied Economics, University of Cambridge.

—— and Singh, A. (1980), 'Mergers, concentration and competition, in advanced capitalist economies: an international perspective', in D. C. Mueller (ed.), *The Determinants and Effects of Mergers*, Cambridge: Oelschlager, Gunn and Hain.

—— Mueller, D.C., and Singh, A. (1980), 'Hypotheses about mergers', in D. C. Mueller (ed.), *The Determinants and Effects of Mergers*, Cambridge: Oelschlager, Gunn and Hain.

Hunt, J. W., Lees, S., Grumbar, J. J., and Vivian, P. D. (1987), *Acquisitions: The Human Factor*, London: Egon Zehnder International.

Jacquemin, A. P., and de Jong, H. W. (1977), *European Industrial Organisation*, London: Macmillan.

Jay, J. (1986), 'Argyll recounts the cost', *Sunday Times*, 21 December, 27.

Jensen, M. C., and Meckling, W. H. (1976), 'Theory of the firm: managerial behaviour, agency costs and ownership structure', *Journal of Financial Economics*, **3**, 305–60.

—— and Ruback, R. S. (1983), 'The market for corporate control: the scientific evidence', *Journal of Financial Economics*, **11**, 5–50.

Johnston, Sir A. J. (1980), *The City Take-over Code*, Oxford: Oxford University Press.

Kay, J. A. (1976), 'Accountants, too, could be happy in a golden age: the accountant's rate of return and the internal rate of return', *Oxford Economic Papers*, **28**, 447–60.

Keane, S. M. (1983), *Stock Market Efficiency: Theory, Evidence and Implications*, Bath: Philip Allan.

Keynes, J. M. (1936), *The General Theory of Employment, Interest and Money*, London: Macmillan.

King, M. A. (1989) 'Takeover Activity in the United Kingdom', in J. A. Fairburn and J. A. Kay (eds.), *Mergers and Merger Policy*, Oxford: Oxford University Press.

Kitching, J. (1967), 'Why do mergers miscarry?', *Harvard Business Review*, November–December, 84–101.

—— (1974), 'Why acquisitions are abortive', *Management Today*, November, 52–7, 148.

Knoeber, C. R. (1986), 'Golden parachutes, shark repellents and hostile tender offers', *American Economic Review*, **76**, 155–67.

Kuehn, D. A. (1975), *Takeovers and the Theory of the Firm*, London: Macmillan.

Kumar, M. S. (1984), *Growth, Acquisition and Investment*, Cambridge: Cambridge University Press.

—— (1985), 'Growth, acquisition activity and firm size: evidence from the United Kingdom', *Journal of Industrial Economics*, **33**, 327–38.

Leigh, R., and North, D. J. (1978), 'Regional aspects of acquisition activity in British manufacturing industry', *Regional Studies*, **12**, 227–45.

Levine, P., and Aaronovitch, S. (1981), 'The financial characteristics of firms and theories of merger activity', *Journal of Industrial Economics*, **30**, 149–72.

Little, I. M. D., and Rayner, A. G. (1966), *Higgledy Piggledy Growth Again*, Oxford: Basil Blackwell.

Love, J. H. (1990a), 'External takeover and regional economic development: a survey and critique', *Regional Studies*, **23**, No. 5, 417–29.

—— (1990b), 'External takeover and regional linkage adjustment: the case of Scotch whisky', *Environment and Planning A*, **22**, 101–18.

Lye, S., and Silberston, A. (1981), 'Merger activity and sales of subsidiaries between company groups', *Oxford Bulletin of Economics and Statistics*, **43**, 257–72.

Malatesta, P. H. (1986), 'Measuring abnormal performance: the event parameters approach using joint generalized least squares', *Journal of Financial and Quantitative Economics*, **21**, 27–38.

Manne, H. G. (1965), 'Mergers and the market for corporate control', *Journal of Political Economy*, **73**, 693–706.

Markham, J. W. (1955), 'Survey of the evidence and findings on mergers', in G. J.

Stigler (ed.), *Business Concentration and Price Policy*, New York: National Bureau of Economic Research.

Markham, H. G. (1973), *Conglomerate Enterprise and Public Policy*, Boston, Mass.

Marris, R. L. (1964), *The Economic Theory of 'Managerial' Capitalism*, London: Macmillan.

—— and Mueller, D. C. (1980), 'The corporation, competition and the invisible hand', *Journal of Economic Literature*, **18**, 32–63.

Marsh, P. (1986), 'Are profits the prize of the prey or the predator?', *Financial Times: Mergers and Acquisitions*, May.

Marx, K. (1971), *Capital: A Critique of Political Economy*, iii, London: Lawrence and Wishart.

Massey, D. B., and Meegan, R. A. (1978), 'Industrial restructuring versus the cities', *Urban Studies*, **15**, 273–88.

—— —— (1979), 'The geography of industrial reorganisation: the spatial effects of restructuring the electrical engineering industry under the IRC', *Progress in Planning*, **10**, 155–237.

Mayshar, J. (1983), 'On divergence of opinion and imperfections in the capital market', *American Economic Review*, **73**, 114–28.

Meade, J. S. (1968), 'Is the "New Industrial State" inevitable?', *Economic Journal*, **78**, 372–92.

Meadowcroft, S. A., and Thompson, D. J. (1986), 'Empirical analysis of returns to pre-merger shareholdings', mimeo, Institute for Fiscal Studies.

Meeks, G. (1977), *Disappointing Marriage: A Study of the Gains from Merger*, Cambridge: Cambridge University Press.

Meeks, J. G., and Meeks, G. (1981), 'Profitability measures as indicators of post merger efficiency', *Journal of Industrial Economics*, **29**, 335–44.

—— and Whittington, G. (1976), *The Financing of Quoted Companies in the United Kingdom*, Background Paper No. 1, Royal Commission on the Distribution of Income and Wealth, London: HMSO.

Melicher, R. W., Ledolter, J., and D'Antonio, L. J. (1983), 'A time series analysis of aggregate merger activity', *Review of Economics and Statistics*, **65**, 423–30.

Mennel, W. (1962), *Takeover*, London: Lawrence and Wishart.

Merrett Cyriax Associates (1971), *Dynamics of Small Firms*, Research Report No. 12, Committee of Inquiry on Small Firms, London: HMSO.

Miller, E. (1977), 'Risk, uncertainty and divergence of opinion', *Journal of Finance*, **32**, 1151–68.

Millward, N., and McQueeney, J. (1981), *Company Takeovers, Management Organization and Industrial Relations*, Department of Employment, Manpower Paper No. 16, London: HMSO.

Moon, R. W. (1968), *Business Mergers and Take-over Bids*, London: Gee & Co.

Morck, R., Schleifer, A., and Vishny, R.W. (1989), 'Alternative mechanisms for corporate control', *American Economic Review*, September, **79**, No. 4, 842–52.

Mueller, D. C. (1969), 'A theory of conglomerate mergers', *Quarterly Journal of Economics*, **83**, 643–59.

—— (1985), 'Mergers and market share', *Review of Economics and Statistics*, **67**, May, 259–67.

Nelson, R. L. (1959), *Merger Movements in American Industry 1895–1956*, Princeton, NJ: Princeton University Press.

Nerlove, M. (1968), 'Factors affecting differences among rates of return on investment in individual common stocks', *Review of Economics and Statistics*, **50**, 312–31.

Newbould, G. D. (1970), *Management and Merger Activity*, Liverpool: Guthstead.

O'Brien, D. P., Howe, W. S., and Wright, O. M., with O'Brien, R. J. (1979), *Competition Policy, Profitability and Growth*, London: Macmillan.

Odagiri, H., and Hase, T. (1989), 'Are mergers and acquisitions going to be popular in Japan too? An empirical study', *International Journal of Industrial Organization*, **7**, No. 1, 49–72.

OECD (1984), *Merger Policies and Recent Trends in Mergers*, Paris: OECD.

Oulton, N. (1987), 'Plant closures and the productivity miracle in manufacturing', *National Institute Economic Review*, August, No. 121, 53–9.

Pickering, J. F. (1983), 'Causes and consequences of abandoned mergers', *Journal of Industrial Economics*, **31**, 267–81.

Prais, S. J. (1976), *The Evolution of Giant Firms in the United Kingdom*, Cambridge: Cambridge University Press.

—— (1980), 'Industrial concentration: the role of statistical theories (a comment on Mr Sawyer's note)', *Oxford Bulletin of Economics and Statistics*, **42**, 269–72.

—— (1981), 'The contribution of mergers to industrial concentration: what do we know?', *Journal of Industrial Economics*, **29**, 321–9.

Pratten, C. F. (1970), 'A case study of a conglomerate merger', *Moorgate and Wall Street*, Spring, 27–54.

Ravenscraft, D. J., and Scherer, F. M. (1987), *Mergers, Sell-offs and Economic Efficiency*, Washington: Brookings Institution.

Rhoades, S. R. (1985), *Power, Empire Building and Mergers*, Lexington, Mass.: Lexington Books.

Roll, R. (1986), 'The hubris theory of corporate takeovers', *Journal of Business*, **59**, 197–216.

Rose, H. B., and Newbould, G. D. (1967), 'The 1967 takeover boom', *Moorgate and Wall Street*, Autumn, 5–24.

Samuels, J. M. (1971), 'The success or failure of mergers and takeovers', *Journal of Business Policy*, Spring.

Sawyer, M. C. (1979), 'The variance of logarithms and industrial concentration', *Oxford Bulletin of Economics and Statistics*, **41**, 165–81.

—— (1980), 'The variance of logarithms and industrial concentration: a reply', *Oxford Bulletin of Economics and Statistics*, **42**, 273–8.

Scharfstein, D. (1988) 'The disciplinary role of takeovers', *Review of Economic Studies*, **55**, 185–99.

Scherer, F. M., and Ross, D. (1990), *Industrial Market Structure and Economic Performance*, 3rd edn., Boston: Houghton Miffin.

Schleifer, A. (1986), 'Do demand curves for stocks slope down?', *Journal of Finance*, **41**, 579–90.

—— and Vishny, R. W. (1990), 'Equilibrium short horizons of investors and firms', *American Economic Review*, May, **80**, No. 2, pp. 148–53.

Shiller, R. J. (1981), 'Do stock prices move too much to be justified by subsequent changes in dividends?', *American Economic Review*, **71**, 421–36.

Singh, A. (1971), *Takeovers: Their Relevance to the Stock Market and the Theory of the Firm*, Cambridge: Cambridge University Press.

—— (1975), 'Takeovers, economic "natural selection", and the theory of the firm: evidence from the post-war UK experience', *Economic Journal*, **85**, 497–515.

Smith, I. J. (1979), 'The effect of external takeovers on manufacturing employment change in the northern region between 1963–73', *Regional Studies*, **13**, 421–37.

—— (1986), 'Takeovers, rationalization and the northern region economy', *Northern Economic Review*, Winter 1985/6.

—— and Taylor, M. J. (1983), 'Takeover, closure and the restructuring of the UK iron foundry industry', *Environment and Planning*, **A15**, 639–61.

Steer, P. S., and Cable, J. (1978), 'Internal organization and profit: an empirical analysis of large UK companies', *Journal of Industrial Economics*, **27**, 13–30.

Stein, J. C. (1988), 'Takeover threats and managerial myopia', *Journal of Political Economy*, February, **96**, 61–80.

—— (1989), 'Efficient stock markets, inefficient firms: a model of myopic corporate behaviour', *Quarterly Journal of Economics*, November 1989, **104**, 655–70.

Steiner, P. O. (1975), *Mergers: Motives, Effects, Control*, Ann Arbor: University of Michigan Press.

Stoneman, P. (1978), 'Merger and technical progressiveness: the case of the British computer industry', *Applied Economics*, **10**, 125–39.

Sturgess, B., and Wheale, P. (1984), 'Merger performance evaluation: an empirical analysis of a sample of UK firms', *Journal of Economic Studies*, **11**, 4.

Summers, L. H. (1986), 'Does the stock market rationally reflect fundamental values?', *Journal of Finance*, **41**, 591–601.

Swann, D., O'Brien, D. P., Maunder, W. P. J., and Howe, W. S. (1974), *Competition in British Industry*, London: Allen and Unwin.

Thompson, R. S. (1982), 'The diffusion and performance impact of the multidivisional form in the UK', Ph.D. thesis, University of Newcastle upon Tyne.

Tzoannos, J., and Samuels, J. M. (1972), 'Takeovers and mergers: the financial characteristics of companies involved', *Journal of Business Finance*, **4**, 3, 5–16.

Utton, M. A. (1971), 'The effects of merger on concentration in UK manufacturing industry 1954–65', *Journal of Industrial Economics*, **20**, 42–58.

—— (1972), 'Mergers and the growth of large firms', *Oxford Bulletin of Economics and Statistics*, **34**, 189–97.

—— (1974), 'On measuring the effects of industrial mergers', *Scottish Journal of Political Economy*, **21**, 13–28.

—— (1979), *Diversification and Competition*, Cambridge: Cambridge University Press.

—— (1986), *Profits and the Stability of Monopoly*, Cambridge: Cambridge University Press.

—— and Morgan, A. D. (1983), *Concentration and Foreign Trade*, Cambridge: Cambridge University Press.

Walshe, G. (1974), *Recent Trends in Monopoly in Great Britain*, Cambridge: Cambridge University Press.

Williamson, O. E. (1968), 'Economies as an anti-trust defense: the welfare trade-offs', *American Economic Review*, **58**, 18–36, repr. with corrections in C. K. Rowley (ed.) (1972), *Readings in Industrial Economics*, London: Macmillan.

—— (1985), *The Economic Institutions of Capitalism*, New York: Free Press.

Wilson, H. (1980), *Report of the Committee to Review the Functioning of the Financial System*, London: HMSO.

Wood, A. J. B. (1971), 'Diversification, merger and research expenditure: a review of empirical studies', in R. L. Marris and A. J. B. Wood (eds.), *The Corporate Economy*, London: Macmillan.

Wright, M., Chiplin, B., and Thompson, S. (1993), 'The market for corporate control: divestments and buy-outs', in J. Kay and M. Bishop (eds.), *European Mergers and Mergers Policy*, Oxford: Oxford University Press.

Yarrow, G. K. (1985), 'Shareholder protection, compulsory acquisition and the efficiency of the takeover process', *Journal of Industrial Economics*, **34**, 3–16.

2

The Market for Corporate Control: Divestments and Buy-outs

MIKE WRIGHT,* BRIAN CHIPLIN,†
and STEVE THOMPSON‡

1. INTRODUCTION

The merger wave of the second half of the 1980s was marked by several features not seen in previous upsurges in acquisition activity. Besides the unprecedented size of some take-overs, new sources of transactions and new organizational forms, accompanied by new initiators and enabled by innovations in financing techniques, appeared. Divestment of subsidiaries, whilst an important component of previous merger waves (Chiplin and Wright (1980)), took on a much higher profile as the size of subsidiaries being sold off rose significantly. A major development in the market for corporate control, particularly for divestment, was the acquisition of such subsidiaries by their own managers—the management buy-out. For example, three of the largest management buy-outs in the UK arose on the shift of core activities by their respective parents. MFI-Hygena was divested to management by Asda in 1987 for £717 million. Reedpack was the subject of a £690 million management buy-out as the parent Reed International shifted the focus of its attention. Similarly, Bricom was sold to its management by B & C.

In simple terms, the market for corporate control may be categorized as follows:

1. Acquisition of independent companies:
    (i) by another existing company;
    (ii) by a newly formed company where it includes existing managers

* Professor of Financial Studies, and Director of the Centre for Management Buy-out Research, School of Management and Finance, University of Nottingham.
† Pro-Vice Chancellor and Director of the School of Management and Finance, University of Nottingham.
‡ Senior Lecturer in Business Economics, UMIST, Manchester..

Financial support from Barclays Development Capital Limited and Touche Ross Corporate Finance for the Centre for Management Buy-out Research, from whose database the buy-out material in this chapter is derived, is gratefully acknowledged. Thanks are also extended to Chris Ennew, Paul Dobson, and Pauline Wong for comments on an earlier draft.

of the target as equity-holders, often largely debt-financed (leveraged buy-out); *and/or* a new management team has a substantial equity holding in the new company (management buy-in).
2. Acquisition of part of an existing company—divestment:
   (i) by another existing company;
   (ii) by a newly formed company where it includes existing managers of the target as equity-holders, often largely debt-financed (management buy-out); *and/or* a new management team has a substantial equity holding in the new company (management buy-in); *or* the parent of the target takes an equity stake in the new company which may or may not number managers, either incumbent or new, amongst its equity-holders (spin-off).

Thus, management buy-outs and the related management buy-ins or leveraged buy-outs were not only associated with divested subsidiaries but were also as an alternative form of acquisition of companies quoted on a stock market. In some cases, such as Haden, these buy-outs were a response to a hostile take-over bid, whilst in others, for example the Magnet Group, management took the initiative.

Towards the end of the 1980s, the highly leveraged bid for an underperforming company emerged. The Isosceles bid for the Gateway supermarket chain successfully received institutional support against competition from a management buy-out. The leveraged take-over bid by Hoylake for BAT was the largest ever seen in the UK and although it failed, prompted significant restructuring action which arguably may not otherwise have occurred. Both these bids involved companies specifically created to effect the acquisition, funded by various forms of debt and quasi-debt finance, in common with many buy-outs. They also marked an important development of the concept of 'unbundling', whereby significant assets were to be resold following the successful acquisition in order to reduce high levels of debt. In the case of Isosceles/Gateway, an agreement was made prior to the bid whereby Asda would purchase a certain number of stores.

The above developments reflect increasing flexibility in the boundaries of firms and a more dynamic approach to the concept of firm and industry structure. These 'voluntary' changes have also been accompanied by increasing attention by anti-trust (Director-General of Fair Trading; Monopolies and Mergers Commission (MMC)) and other authorities (Bank of England; the Takeover Panel) on structural issues, including financial structures, and their impact on the market for corporate control and on product market competition. Hence, for example, recent developments in merger policy have emphasized enforced divestment and there extensive attention has been addressed to the implications for shareholders when managers attempt to buy a company quoted on a stock market in the absence of competing bidders. In its latest annual review, the MMC notes that companies selling non-core businesses to buyers in the same industry helped to make 1990 the busiest year yet for the Commission and that companies tend to find that the best price offered for an unwanted subsidiary comes from competitors in the subsidiary's own industry.

This chapter analyses a number of issues relating to divestment. Section 2 reviews, in turn, trends in UK divestment and buy-outs, the direction and nature of divestment, continental European buy-out trends, and financial developments in buy-outs. Section 3 analyses buy-outs and buy-ins of quoted companies, Section 4 reviews the extensive literature on the effects of divestment and buy-outs, and Section 5 draws some conclusions.

2. DIVESTMENT AND BUY-OUT TRENDS

To place divestment and buy-out activity in the context of the general market for corporate control, Table 2.1 presents data on the four main forms of ownership transfers: independent acquisitions, sales of subsidiaries between industrial parent groups (sell-offs), management buy-outs, and management buy-ins.

The merger wave of the late 1980s reached its peak in 1989 with a total

Table 2.1. The UK market for corporate control

(*a*) Value of transactions (£m)

Year	Independent acquisitions	Sell-off of subsidiaries	Buy-outs	Buy-ins	Total	Real value[a]
1982	1,373	804	348	316	2,841	761
1983	1,783	436	365	8	2,592	550
1984	4,252	1,121	404	3	5,780	1,032
1985	6,281	793	1,141	39	8,254	1,192
1986	12,279	3,089	1,188	316	16,872	1,965
1987	11,861	4,668	3,214	308	20,051	1,769
1988	17,300	5,534	3,715	1,232	27,781	2,724
1989	21,026	5,340	3,877	3,588	33,831	2,769
1990 Q2	3,068	1,641	1,419	290	6,418	518

[a] Deflated by FT Actuaries Industrial Share Index, 10 April 1962 = 100.

Sources: CMBOR, an independent research centre founded by Touche Ross and Barclays Development Capital Ltd at the University of Nottingham; *Business Monitor QM7*.

Table 2.1. (*cont.*)

(*b*) Number of transactions

Year	Independent acquisitions	Sell-off of subsidiaries	Buy-outs	Buy-ins	Total
1982	299	164	238	8	709
1983	305	142	235	8	690
1984	398	170	238	5	811
1985	340	134	262	29	765
1986	621	221	313	51	1,206
1987	1,187	340	344	90	1,961
1988	1,123	376	371	112	1,982
1989	725	352	359	144	1,580
1990 Q2	322	183	214	57	776

Sources: CMBOR; *Business Monitor QM7*.

(*c*) Average size of transactions (£m)

Year	Independent acquisitions	Sell-off of subsidiaries	Buy-outs	Buy-ins	Total
1982	4.6	4.9	1.5	39.5	4.0
1983	5.8	3.1	1.6	1.1	3.8
1984	10.7	6.6	1.7	0.7	7.1
1985	18.5	5.9	4.4	1.3	10.8
1986	19.8	14.0	3.8	6.2	14.0
1987	10.0	13.7	9.3	3.4	10.2
1988	13.1	14.7	10.0	11.0	14.0
1989	29.0	15.2	10.8	24.9	21.4
1990 Q2	9.5	9.0	6.6	5.1	8.3

Source: CMBOR.

value of all mergers and acquisitions in the UK of £33.8 billion, which in real terms[1] represents a 235 per cent increase over the peak of an earlier merger wave in 1972. All types of acquisitions, except sales of subsidiaries to other groups, reached their highest ever values. However, there was a 20 per cent fall in the volume of take-overs with all forms except management buy-ins declining from their 1988 levels. All types of take-over reached peak average values in 1989. Against this background, the share of all take-overs accounted for by buy-outs and buy-ins rose sharply to account for almost a third of volume (31.8 per cent in 1989 from 24.4 per cent the previous year) and 22.1 per cent of value.

[1] Where the values are reflated by the FT-Actuaries Industrial share index.

In the first half of 1990 the market for corporate control changed dramatically, with independent companies and buy-ins in particular experiencing sharp falls in both value and volume. The value of sales of subsidiaries fell significantly on a simple annualized basis, although numbers remained reasonably constant on this basis. In this context, buy-outs held up reasonably well, narrowing the gap with the value of sales of subsidiaries to other groups and exceeding them by a substantial margin in volume terms. As a result of these developments, buy-outs and buy-ins together accounted for their highest ever share of the value of all takeovers at 26.6 per cent and their highest share in volume terms since 1985 at 34.9 per cent. Whilst the number of acquisitions of independent companies in the second quarter of 1990 fell sharply to its lowest level for four years and sales of subsidiaries dipped, the number of buy-outs was at its highest ever level at 119 deals.

Wide dispersions around these averages and shifts over time are worth noting. As can be seen in Table 2.2, 16.6 per cent of the acquisitions of independent firms were at values of £10 million or more in 1986, whereas the figures for sell-offs, buy-outs, and buy-ins were 16.8 per cent, 7.9 per cent, and 9.8 per cent respectively. With the development of the merger wave between 1986 and 1989, some shifts in these distributions could be observed. Whilst there was some drift upwards in the proportion of inde-

Table 2.2. Size distributions of various types of acquisitions, 1986 and 1989 compared (actual prices)

Size band	Independent acquisitions		Sell-offs		Buy-outs		Buy-ins	
(£m)	No.	%	No.	%	No.	%	No.	%
1986								
Over 100	18	2.9	3	1.4	—	—	1	2.0
10–100	85	13.7	34	15.4	25	7.9	4	7.8
1–10	256	41.2	92	41.6	167	53.4	23	45.1
1 or less	262	42.2	92	41.6	121	38.7	23	45.1
TOTAL	621	100.0	221	100.0	313	100.0	51	100.0
1989								
Over 100	29	4.0	10	2.8	7	1.9	2	1.4
10–100	106	14.6	63	17.9	50	14.0	15	10.3
1–10	328	45.2	153	43.5	204	56.8	79	54.1
1 or less	262	36.2	126	35.8	98	27.3	50	34.2
TOTAL	725	100.0	352	100.0	359	100.0	146	100.0

Sources: Business Monitor QM7 and CMBOR.

pendent acquisitions at transaction prices of at least £10 million, which is only partially explained by inflation, other forms of acquisition displayed marked increases in these upper bands. Over a fifth of sell-offs in 1989 were at prices above £10 million, whilst the proportion of buy-outs in these bands doubled between 1986 and 1989.

Buy-outs themselves come from several different sources with the majority being divestments (Table 2.3). In 1989, buy-outs from family firms increased their share of the market to the highest ever level at 30.6 per cent of all transactions. Buy-outs of companies quoted on the stock market also achieved their most important position at 2.5 per cent, with those arising from foreign parents falling to their lowest ever share of the market at 6.5 per cent. Privatization buy-outs fell further from their 1987 peak to 4.2 per cent in 1989. A marked shift occurred in the first half of 1990 with a resurgence of buy-outs of companies in receivership to account for 9.1 per cent of the market, a level last seen in the early 1980s. Buy-outs from family businesses fell to 26.4 per cent and from UK parents to 46.2 per cent. Buy-outs of public sector activities recovered to 5.8 per cent of transactions as more local authority and public sector buy-outs were completed and the sale of the Scottish Bus Group got under way. Buy-outs of companies quoted on a stock market ('going privates'), despite the new Takeover Panel rules, retained their share of the market. Transactions of the Magnet type were absent but there was an increase in deals where managers or founding directors already held significant stakes (we return to these transactions below).

The trebling of the overall buy-in market in value terms and the sharp uplift in deal volume in 1989 was followed by a sharp decline in 1990. In 1989 and 1990 the sources of buy-ins became much more varied, going beyond the dichotomy of buy-ins of quoted companies and buy-ins of family-owned businesses which characterized early growth in the market. In particular, subsidiaries of larger groups became more evident as sources for such transactions. Partial or full buy-ins of companies quoted on the stock market declined sharply from 1987, when 43 were recorded, to 28 in 1988 and 29 in 1989. Their value increased dramatically in 1989 as a result of a small number of exceptionally large transactions, causing the average size of public buy-ins to rise fivefold between 1988 and 1989 to over £100 million. However, in the first half of 1990, only six public buy-ins were completed. The rapid growth of private buy-ins continued up to 1989 when 115 deals were completed, an increase of 36.9 per cent on the previous year. The volume of private buy-in activity in the period to June 1990 was at 51 completions almost the same as for the first half of 1989. Whilst the majority of private buy-ins involve family businesses, their relative importance has been falling as parent groups have increasingly divested subsidiaries to buy-in teams. In 1989, 30 per cent of private

Table 2.3. Sources of management buy-outs

Source	Number (%)										
	Pre-1982	1982	1983	1984	1985	1986	1987	1988	1989	1990 Q2	Total
Receivership	12.6	14.3	7.0	10.0	2.2	1.7	0.7	2.0	0.4	9.1	5.0
UK parent	59.2	62.8	66.0	63.0	61.4	59.5	51.1	52.0	55.8	46.2	57.0
Foreign parent	14.1	10.2	11.5	12.5	12.0	13.8	10.7	9.7	6.5	9.6	10.8
Family ownership	11.0	8.7	11.0	12.5	21.0	19.4	25.8	28.6	30.6	26.4	21.0
Privatization	3.1	4.1	4.5	2.0	3.0	4.8	10.4	5.7	4.2	5.8	5.1
Going private	0.0	0.0	0.0	0.0	0.4	0.7	1.3	1.7	2.5	2.9	1.1
Total	100.0	100.0	100.0	100.0	100.0	100.0	100.0	100.0	100.0	100.0	100.0
Number	191.0	196.0	200.0	200.0	233.0	289.0	309.0	350.0	354.0	208.0	2539.0

Source: CMBOR.

buy-ins arose on divestments from UK firms but in the first half of 1990 36.7 per cent of buy-ins came from this source. The period from the beginning of 1989 has seen a marked increase in large buy-ins of divested subsidiaries. Ten of the largest 25 buy-ins of all time have involved divestments of subsidiaries. In July 1990, the £186 million buy-in of Jarvis Hotels from Allied-Lyons was completed.

The Direction and Nature of Divestment

From the viewpoint of merger policy, the direction of divestment in relation to the main activity of the vendor and acquirer may be important. In the USA, studies by Duhaime and Grant (1984) and Ravenscraft and Scherer (1987), which addressed the strategic rationale behind divestments in the form of sell-offs, concluded that they were likely to involve more peripheral businesses and that it was unusual for divested units to have had a vertically integrated relationship with their parent group. Evidence from UK divestments by sell-off (Chiplin and Wright (1980)) indicates that about one-third had a horizontal relationship with the former parent, i.e. were in the same market sector, a fifth were unrelated, a tenth were related in a vertical manner, and the remainder were divestments by financial companies, breweries, hotels, etc. These figures are broadly supported by a subsequent study covering a later period and using the same methodology (Lye and Silbertson (1981)).

Conventional wisdom held that buy-outs which arose on divestment involved peripheral activities, often unwanted parts of larger organizations. The evidence from two surveys covering the first half of the 1980s (Wright (1986b), Wright, Chiplin, Thompson, and Robbie, (1990b)), shows that almost two-fifths of buy-outs of divisions or subsidiaries sold their products and services to the former parent. Around one-quarter of buy-outs were found to purchase goods from their former parent. For the most part, these links accounted for a relatively small share of the buy-outs' sales and purchases. In at least 10 per cent of cases in the earlier study and in 15 per cent of buy-outs in the later one, the parent accounted for at least ten per cent of sales, with some buy-outs being very heavily dependent upon their former parent. Buy-outs from non-UK parents were found on average to have a higher proportion of sales and supplies with their former owners than was the case for those acquired from UK parents (Wright, Chiplin, Thompson, and Robbie (1990b)). For those buy-outs from UK parents, the former parent was more likely to be a customer, whilst for buy-outs from non-UK parents a supplier relationship was more probable.

Of course, the sale of a subsidiary does not necessarily imply that the divestor is exiting completely from a market, especially if it has several subsidiaries operating in a particular sector. But whether partial or complete exit reduces market concentration depends upon the nature of the purchaser. The evidence from sell-offs (Chiplin and Wright (1980)) suggests that horizontal or vertical divestments by one firm are likely to augment horizontal integration in the new parent. The issue of search for an optimal set of assets raises the question as to the extent of subsequent divestment of subsidiaries which had previously been acquired and the extent of simultaneous acquisition and divestment activity. A detailed study of 33 companies by Porter (1987) showed that on average corporations divested more than half of their acquisitions in new fields, more than three-fifths of their acquisitions in entirely new fields, and almost three-quarters of their acquisitions in unrelated areas. Ravenscraft and Scherer (1987) also show that many divested units were previously acquired rather than having been generated internally. In respect of buy-outs, Wright (1988) showed that the majority had been owned for a small proportion of their lives by the divesting parent. However, about 30 per cent of buy-outs had always been owned by their former parent. There is thus some support for the view that buy-outs are unwanted parts of acquisitions, but also indications that they have occurred in response to strategic shifts and control difficulties. This view is supported by a survey carried out by the Centre for Management Buy-out Research (CMBOR), which asked managers who bought out subsidiaries of groups why the vendors wished to sell. Redefinition of core activities of the group was clearly the most important reason for sale, followed by other factors relating to performance.

Divestment activity may be a single or multiple event, possibly associated with acquisitions. In respect of sell-offs, Chiplin and Wright (1980) show that in the late 1970s, over a quarter of firms which divested in the two-year sample period engaged in more than one divestment, with 4 per cent undertaking at least four sales of subsidiaries. This picture seems likely to have increased in the 1980s, especially with the growth of buy-outs. Buy-outs, like sell-offs, may be part of major and continuing restructuring programmes involving multiple divestments of unwanted subsidiaries, and may be alternatives. Twenty-one companies have been identified as having sold seven or more subsidiaries as buy-outs up to June 1990, one more than in 1991. Thorn EMI continues to be the most intensive divestor by means of a buy-out in the UK, selling a further three subsidiaries in this manner in the eighteen months to June 1990. It is noteworthy that the eight buy-outs to have come from Cope Allman were effected prior to the buy-in. The most notable private sector groups to have divested by means of a buy-out up to mid-1990 are Thorn EMI (19 buy-outs), BET (16), Hanson (15), Guinness (12), TI (12), BICC (11), Sears (11), Plessey (10), and Elbar (10). Many of these groups have also sold subsidiaries to other groups (Wright, Coyne, and Robbie (1987)). BET's strategy of focusing on the provision of a total service package for industrial customers has produced several buy-outs as it seeks to exit from activities which, though once key areas, are no longer seen as core businesses. Hanson Trust has produced buy-outs as a result of both initial and subsequent restructuring of major acquisitions.

Besides the association with shifts in corporate strategy, divestments may be associated with acquisition activity. Where acquisitions are simultaneously being conducted, divestment may be a convenient way of disposing of those parts of a recently purchased group that are peripheral to the main areas of interest. As regards firms engaged in acquisition and divestment activity in the same period, evidence suggests that this is quite widespread. In the period from January 1984 to June 1986, some 16 per cent of acquiring firms in the UK divested subsidiaries either to another group or to incumbent management.

The growth of leveraged acquisitions and of large buy-outs and buy-ins in particular has given impetus to the notion of unbundling whereby, following the transfer of ownership, significant parts of a group are divested. The rationale for the exercise depends upon the divestment market holding up to allow the new owners to exit and repay their debt. Indeed, such buy-outs in the USA are often predicated on the ability to make sell-offs, at prices which will allow the investing parties to achieve their target returns on investment within a relatively short period of time. Such an approach was slow to develop in the UK, primarily because financiers were not confident of achieving the required prices for assets on bust-up. At the end of the first decade of buy-outs in the UK, there were indications of divestment programmes being introduced after completion in a number of the larger transactions. For example, major buy-outs completed in 1988, such as Hollis, Dwek, Virgin, Invergordon, Bricom, and Argus all made significant divestments (Chiplin, Wright, and Robbie (1989b)). The case of the predicated sale of Asda superstores following the hostile buy-in by Isosceles has already been noted.

Continental European Buy-out Trends

The continental European buy-out market scarcely existed until the 1980s (see Table 2.4). Before any national market in buy-out and restructuring transactions can develop at all, certain conditions must be met (Wright, Thompson, and Robbie (1992)). Conceptually, a buy-out market may be considered as requiring three main factors to be present if it is to develop:

1. the generation of buy-out opportunities;
2. the infrastructure to complete a transaction; and

3. opportunities for the investors in a buy-out to realize their gains.

These factors further imply:

4. a supply of vendors willing to sell and manager-investors willing to buy;
5. the existence of a development capital and financial infrastructure to fund the transactions;
6. a legal and taxation environment which facilitates debt-financed changes in control; and
7. the existence of suitable exit routes for investors of all types.

At present, in continental Europe only France, Sweden, and the Netherlands can be considered as having a developed market for buy-out transactions. Lower levels of activity can be observed in Denmark, Italy, Switzerland, Germany, Belgium, and Finland, but elsewhere in Europe any corporate restructuring activity is rudimentary.

The European market is dominated by the UK, which has experienced more restructuring activity by value and volume than all other European countries combined (Table 2.4). In 1989, there were 504 UK buy-outs and buy-ins with a total value of £7.5 billion ($15 billion). In the same year, the total comparable activity elsewhere in Europe has been estimated at 369 deals with a value equivalent to £3.23 billion.

Table 2.4. Estimated number of buy-outs and buy-ins in Europe to the end of 1989

Country	1987	1988	1989	Total 1980–89	Estimated value 1989 ($m)
Austria	3	5	5	15	69
Belgium[a]	4	10	12	52	107
Denmark[a]	5	20	31	63	226
Finland	5	14	16	40	113
France[a]	50	100	130	430	1,358
Germany[a]	8	36	25	111	654
Ireland[a]	21	14	12	131	34
Italy[a]	3	10	21	53	523
Netherlands[a]	30	30	41	245	310
Norway	7	8	8	29	11
Spain[a]	4	8	12	35	85
Sweden	18	22	32	127	1,332
Switzerland	2	5	21	46	107
UK[a]	434	482	504	2,992	12,334

[a] Member of the European Community.

Source: CMBOR.

Just as the European markets vary in size, so they also differ in the principal sources of restructuring transactions—see Table 2.5. In the UK a large proportion of deals arise from the voluntary divestiture of divisions or subsidiaries by domestic- or foreign-owned multi-product firms, but the UK has long had an active take-over market.

Although comprehensive information remains difficult to obtain in continental Europe, the Netherlands, and Sweden—both economies with a sector of large quoted companies—also exhibit high levels of divestment transactions. In France, Germany, and Italy, in contrast, the market for corporate control has until quite recently been almost completely non-existent (see Franks and Mayer, this volume for details). In France, for example, the ability to vary voting rights, the frequent practice of hard-core (*noyau dur*) friendly shareholders and interlocking shareholdings have tended to form an effective barrier to such transactions. Successful hostile bids have now begun to appear but remain difficult. In Germany, the power of managers and employees to frustrate unwelcome raiders, because of the potentially adverse effects on their employment contracts, is not inconsiderable. Germany has only recently experienced its first hostile take-over attempts let alone successful ones. As a result, there are few true conglomerates in the private sectors of these economies—and hence few voluntary divestitures. In Germany, the commercial banks play a pivotal role as stock owners and proxy stockholders (Cable (1985)). Since they obtain the benefits of portfolio diversification directly, *ceteris paribus*, it is against their interests to permit indirect diversification via merger.

In much of continental Europe, buy-outs have developed as a means of dealing with succession problems in the large private and family-run company sector. In France, for example, by the mid-1980s, thousands of family-run companies established in the post-war boom years found themselves with ageing or infirm owner-executives. A traditional reluctance to cede control to an outsider, reinforced by the absence of an orthodox take-over market, led to specific legislation in 1984 (Heuze, Wright, and Dupouy (1990)) to facilitate debt-financed transfers of control via buy-outs.

Buy-outs of public sector activities have been heavily influenced by individual countries' political commitments to privatization as a means of restructuring industries, enhancing incentives, and improving control. Again it has been in the UK where this activity has been at its most intense. Elsewhere in Western Europe, including France, Italy, Spain, and Sweden, privatization restructurings have tended to involve the divestment of subsidiaries from unwieldy groups and State-run holding companies.

Two recent developments are likely to stimulate European restructurings in the near future. First, the momentous events in Eastern Europe

Table 2.5. European buy-out sources, 1989
%

Country	Sample	Local divisions	Foreign divisions	Family/ private	Privatization	Going private	Other	Total
Austria	n.a.	n.a.	n.a.	n.a.	n.a.	n.a.	n.a.	100
Belgium	8	37.5	50.0	12.5	—	—	—	100
Denmark	29	58.6	27.5	10.3	—	3.4	—	100
Finland	14	78.6	14.3	7.1	—	—	—	100
France	58	20.7	10.3	44.8	3.5	15.5	5.2	100
Germany	18	16.7	44.4	38.9	—	—	—	100
Ireland	11	18.2	72.7	9.1	—	—	—	100
Italy	18	5.6	33.3	50.0	11.1	—	—	100
Netherlands	39	69.2	18.0	12.8	—	—	—	100
Norway	3	66.7	33.3	—	—	—	—	100
Spain	4	—	—	75.0	25.0	—	—	100
Sweden	29	69.0	6.8	6.9	6.9	10.4	—	100
Switzerland	21	52.4	19.1	28.5	—	—	—	100
UK	350	56.0	6.8	29.7	4.3	2.6	0.6	100

Source: CMBOR.

and the increased pressure for industrial change there have led to interest in the idea of the buy-out as a means of dealing with control and incentive problems (see Ellerman (1990), Buck and Wright (1990)). Buy-outs would introduce active owners to replace passive State owners and avoid the problems of diffuse and potentially ineffective ownership that various proposed models for the free distribution of shares might bring (Lipton and Sachs (1990)). As yet there are severe practical difficulties relating to the establishment of who actually owns assets; passing enabling legislation for privatization; establishing a financial infrastructure, which amongst other things would include a basis for valuing assets; and there is a need to deal with the problem that buy-outs may be perceived as asset-stripping by members of the old regimes (Wright and Thompson (1991)). As in Western Europe, buy-outs may become more important in some countries (for example Slovenia, where the relevant privatization legislation places emphasis on this kind of transaction given the former self-management system in that country, and Hungary) than others.

The other major development likely to stimulate restructuring through divestments and buy-outs is the Single Market. In anticipation of a united Western Europe, there has been a higher level of cross-border merger and joint venture activity (see Geroski and Vlassopoulos (1990)). Since these international link-ups tend to have high failure rates, it may be expected that many will be sold on to local management teams in subsequent years.

Financing Developments and Buy-outs

In the UK, development capital firms played a significant role in the establishment of the buy-out market. Only in the late 1980s did debt become important. Subordinated debt was added to the traditional mezzanine layer of convertible and redeemable preference shares, but a high yield (junk) bond market such as existed in the US was not established in Europe (Altman (1990), Molyneux (1990)). In this period, debt levels in larger UK deals began to approach those seen in their counterparts in the US (Table 2.6), enabling very large transactions to be completed, accompanied in some cases by subsequent divestment of unwanted subsidiaries (Chiplin *et al.* (1989a)). The shifts in fortunes of the large end of the buy-out market from mid-1989 produced major changes in financing structures (Table 2.6). After a resurgence in the senior debt element in larger buy-outs in 1988, 1989 witnessed a major growth in the use of mezzanine finance in the UK. In the first half of 1990, mezzanine experienced a major reversal to account for a little over one-tenth (10.8 per cent) of the finance in larger buy-outs, with equity and quasi-equity recovering to over one-fifth of the total (22.2 per cent).

Table 2.6. UK management buy-out deal structures

Type of finance (average %)	Size of buy-out					
	Less than £10m financing			Over £10m financing		
	1988	1989	1990 Q2	1988	1989	1990 Q2
Equity	39.3	32.1	32.8	25.4	17.4	24.0
Mezzanine	5.2	8.1	8.4	6.8	18.0	11.7
Debt	49.3	46.4	42.4	62.6	58.6	58.3
Loan Note	0.7	2.8	10.3	0.9	3.4	3.3
Other Finance	5.5	10.4	6.1	4.3	2.6	2.7
TOTAL	100.0	100.0	100.0	100.0	100.0	100.0
Within which: Funding:						
Average vendor contribution	5.2	6.5	8.4	4.9	5.3	5.4
Average management contributions	6.3	7.1	8.4	0.9	1.3	1.1
Average proportion of equity held by management	52.3	60.1	58.4	25.8	32.7	27.5

Source: CMBOR.

Various factors contributed to these changes: substantial amounts of equity funds have become available and been taken up as the emphasis of buy-out investment has shifted from the short to the longer term. As the price earnings ratios at which deals can be completed have fallen, the goodwill element has been reduced. At the same time there has been a marked reluctance on the part of senior debt lenders to enter into highly leveraged deals to the same extent as seen in recent years. Whilst this has tended to mean continuing demand for mezzanine finance, mezzanine lenders have been reluctant to extend their position, partly because of the adverse effects on their prospective internal rates of return when performance targets are not met, as seen in certain recent deals. By the same token, deal arrangers have been reluctant to borrow mezzanine at the returns looked for by mezzanine lenders to compensate themselves for what they perceive as increased risk. Links with difficulties in the US junk bond market have also not helped the mezzanine market. The proportion of finance accounted for by senior debt has hovered around the 60 per cent level in the last two and a half years.

Although mezzanine debt may contribute to the financing of smaller buy-outs, its main use is in buy-outs completed for prices of at least £10 million. The number of buy-outs in this larger category, which comprised an element of mezzanine finance, increased by a half in 1989 to 30 as against 20 in 1988. Between these two years the value of mezzanine debt in £10 million plus buy-outs rose more than fivefold from £172 million to £892 million. However, in the first half of 1990 this trend was sharply reversed, with both numbers and values on a simple annualized basis returning to 1988 levels. The size of the market meant that multi-layer mezzanine debt, reflecting the different levels of risk in a deal, only made a notable contribution in a small number of buy-outs (for example, Magnet) and buy-ins (for example, the bid by Isosceles for Gateway stores) in 1989. As in the US, larger deals in the UK market became affected by various adverse factors from late 1989.

Mezzanine debt was slower to develop in continental Europe principally because of the relatively underdeveloped state of big transactions in these markets, as noted earlier. Access to adequate accounting information to establish clearly the stability and viability of potential deals is also a key issue, as the investors in at least one major deal subsequently discovered (Graeper (1990)). Nevertheless, pioneering deals have been completed in France, Germany, and Belgium, for example. In addition, more recently there has been the establishment of a number of domestic and cross-border European specialist mezzanine funds, to add to the already significant number of specialist equity funds (Wright *et al.* (1991)). These cross-border developments, to which may be added the establishment of joint ventures between institutions in different countries as well as a number of other transnational initiatives, reflect the perception of considerable further restructuring opportunities by several types of institution. The development of expertise in newly emerging markets such as France has enabled domestic players to engage in cross-border initiatives. The form and extent of these strategic moves is part of many of these firms' parent institutions' approaches to the European Community's Single Market, with some seeking to be Europe-wide leaders, and others niche players either in several countries, one country, or in a particular type of deal (Wright and Ennew (1990)). The full scope of these changes is yet to manifest itself and will depend significantly on the future development of individual markets, and particularly on the scope for completing large deals within them.

3. BUY-OUTS AND BUY-INS OF QUOTED COMPANIES

Buy-outs and buy-ins of quoted companies were a major feature of the US market for corporate control throughout the 1980s, culminating in

the $23 billion RJR-Nabisco leveraged buy-out in 1989. In the UK, rela-
tively few such cases have occurred, as noted in Section 4. However, their
significantly larger size in comparison with buy-outs and buy-ins generally, the innovative techniques used, and the new implications they introduce mean that they have attracted attention from the authorities.
Elsewhere in Europe only five other countries have experienced this type
of deal, and then only rarely (Table 2.7). The UK apart, stock markets
are generally less well developed in Europe than in the US. Such buy-outs
and buy-ins may occur in a number of circumstances, as shown in Table
2.8. The first three types have attracted the most attention and in particular Type 2—opportunistic ventures by incumbent management.

Table 2.7. Buy-outs of quoted companies in Europe[a]

Country	1985	1986	1987	1988	1989	1990 Q3
UK[b]	1	2	4	8	12	9
France	1	2	2	8	5	2
Sweden	—	1	—	2	2	9
Netherlands	—	—	—	1	0	—
Denmark	—	—	—	1	1	—
Switzerland	—	1	—	—	—	—

[a] As recorded on CMBOR database.
[b] Excluding partial buy-ins.

Source: CMBOR.

In continental Europe particularly, various forms of poison pills and
shark repellents have hitherto made successful hostile take-overs
extremely difficult to achieve (see Franks and Mayer, this volume).
Despite the move towards a single European market, these barriers are
only slowly being removed. Hence Type 1 deals (hostile take-over
defences) are unusual. More common practice in Europe is for buy-outs
of companies quoted on a stock market to involve friendly changes in
ownership. In continental Europe, many quoted companies remain under
family control. Buy-outs may be used to allow succession without control
passing to an outsider. Several buy-outs in France have been of this kind.
    Buy-outs of listed companies, especially Type 2, frequently raise con-
tentious issues relating, amongst other things, to the conflict between the
interests of the management and shareholders. In the absence of an outside bidder, there is serious concern that shareholders will not receive a
fair price. These arguments arise notwithstanding the substantial premia
which usually ensue when a buy-out is proposed and completed, and

Table 2.8. Types of buy-outs of companies quoted on a stock market

Type	Features	Main UK examples
1. Hostile take-over bid defence (actual or anticipated)	Management likely to need to satisfy institutional shareholders that they have not underperformed and that needed restructuring could not have been achieved beforehand. An LBO may be a 'white knight' rescue	*Successful*: Haden against bid by Trafalgar House (1985) *Failed*: McCorquodale against Norton Opax (1987); Newgateway against Isosceles; Lowndes Queensway (1989)
2. Opportunistic venture by incumbent management	Institutional shareholders may be unwilling to sell in absence of competing bidders or appropriate safeguards as to price being paid. May prompt hostile bid	*Successful*: Magnet; Ryan Int; Tyzack; British Syphon (1989) *Failed*: Molins (1985)
3. Hostile buy-in or LBO	Institutional support critical and enhanced when incumbent management perceived to have underperformed. Likelihood of subsequent unbundling	*Successful*: Lowndes Queensway; Isosceles/Gateway (1989) *Failed*: Valuedale/Simon Engineering (1986); Hoylake/BAT (1989)
4. Response to severe performance difficulties	Likely to take form of a buy-in with new managers replacing old to enable needed restructuring to occur	*Successful*: Executex clothes (1990)
5. To permit transfer of significant/controlling shareholdings	May be appropriate where only a small proportion of equity is in outside hands and attempts to sell large blocks in absence of a bidder would be impractical. May also be means of retaining independence in what are effectively family controlled quoted firms	*Successful*: Wickes (1987); Invergordon (1988)
6. Key shareholder dissatisfaction with aspects of stock market quotation	Founder or directors are likely to have significant equity stakes prior to buy-out	*Successful*: Virgin Group; Dwek Group (1989); Really Useful Group (1990)

which are in line with those paid in hostile take-over bids. Key potential problems are that management may not make proper disclosure of information before an offer is made and/or may artificially depress the firm's performance and share price in order to acquire the firm at a lower price than may otherwise be the case. Whilst such potential for misleading shareholders exists, it is not clear whether it actually occurs. Managers' inside knowledge may not necessarily be such that it could be made public or form the basis for an insider-dealing strategy. The existence of the buy-out makes it possible for the increased value to be released to the advantage of existing shareholders. If a buy-out attempt signals there is unreleased value, it may trigger a competing bid, so enhancing further the premia to shareholders.

Kaplan (1989) shows that in the US buy-outs improve performance after the transaction is completed, but contrary to the manipulation hypothesis fail to meet their forecasts. Managers would, therefore, appear to be overestimating rather than underestimating expected performance and hence value. An examination of the potential manipulation of accounting data by De Angelo (1986) found no evidence of biased information. The evidence on whether share prices display under-performance before a buy-out attempt is made is mixed. Support for the argument is provided by Kieschnick (1989) and Maupin *et al.* (1984), whilst Amihud (1989) finds that a sample of firms which went private outperformed the market prior to the announcement of the bid. For the UK, Thompson, Wright, and Robbie (1989) found that the majority of a sample of all buy-outs improved trading profit above their business plan, although almost a third were performing under plan. Even where performance is above plan, this does not necessarily indicate manipulation. It may equally be consistent with management underestimating profit recovery in the period of buoyant economic conditions which characterized the mid-1980s onwards.

Methods of dealing with the potential public interest issues arising in 'going private' buy-outs range from a complete ban through requirements for disclosure of the nature of conflicts of interest, requirements for submission of a proposed deal to independent assessment and expression of a fair value opinion, or to an auction, to requirements that management should pay a price equal to the value that would be placed on the company if shareholders themselves were to refinance the company with debt and the use of instruments to give existing shareholders a stake in future gains.

Arguments for a complete ban on buy-outs may be countered by citing the gains which may accrue both to shareholders and the economy generally. Nevertheless, there may be grounds for reform to remove abuses and prevent marginal cases without the loss of the major gains from the buy-outs which would continue to be completed (Auerbach (1989), Summers (1989)). Where fair value opinions are expressed, the key question arises as to how such opinions are derived. An examination of procedures in US 'going privates' (De Angelo (1990)), showed that investment bankers overwhelmingly made use of accounting information in conjunction with share price information, prices paid in other acquisitions, management forecasts, etc. De Angelo concludes that the ultimate buy-out price is constrained to fall within the approximate range of values implied by a broad variety of valuation techniques.

In the US, concern about losses to shareholders led to the proposal for a mandated auction. However, Amihud (1989) points out that whilst premia are higher in competitive bidding contests, mandated auctioning may actually reduce the probability that an initial offer is made. Potential bidders who perceive that the likelihood of success is reduced in a competitive bidding situation, and that their expected returns are also likely to be reduced as they have to outbid competitors, are less likely to initiate the bid in the first place. The result of a mandated auction may be fewer buy-outs and consequent economic losses from the non-occurrence of benefits they can create.

In the UK, the controversy surrounding the Magnet buy-out in particular led to the development of new rules published by the Takeover Panel in late 1989 which govern proposed buy-outs of firms quoted on a stock market. These rules include: a requirement to appoint an independent adviser to the offeree board; secrecy relating to the organization of a buy-out; prohibitions on share dealings by those with privileged information; a requirement that information supplied to prospective financiers should be given to all shareholders and other bidders; and a description of the proposed financing structure. These new rules raise important issues as to the desirability of passing commercially sensitive information to a bidder who is also a competitor, and whether the property right on management's projections rests with the company or its management. It is worth reiterating that buy-outs still involve an element of risk to management. There is a need to make a bid at a price which will be recommended by non-executive directors and which will not encourage a significantly higher competing offer. If a competing offer materializes and succeeds, management risk losing their jobs.

A further element in protecting shareholders is the use of some form of retained participation in the future prospects of the buy-out or other form of payment in kind. 'Stub equity' was an important element in the completion of the Magnet and Isosceles transactions. Instruments of the payment in kind type have the benefit for the buy-out attempt of helping to bridge a gap between the maximum price that management can pay, based on the ability to raise and service external finance, and what is considered a fair price by shareholders. As for buy-out bids generally, valuation problems arise with stub equity.

Buy-outs of companies quoted on a stock market raise the wider issues of the control of such companies. The question arises as to what alternative approaches can be used to monitor management adequately and to obtain the gains which buy-outs offer without the need to change the organizational structure.

Some have considered whether the benefits of improved performance from increased managerial equity ownership can be achieved whilst retaining a public listing. Amihud (1989) suggests that management and the buy-out specialist could buy the controlling interest in the firm without going private and so achieve the appropriate incentive structure and control mechanisms. However, there may be institutional reasons why such an approach is not pursued. For example, there may be difficulties in obtaining the necessary asset security on loans. An alternative route may be to engage in a partial share repurchase, funded by increased borrowing.

More generally, buy-outs link into the vexed issue of corporate governance and the role of the market for corporate control in controlling managers and maximizing shareholder wealth. Major question marks have been raised in the UK and the US about the effects of the behaviour of institutional shareholders and of an active market in hostile take-overs in stressing short-term performance at the expense of the long term. Institutional churning of portfolios and views that take-overs are a blunt instrument for dealing with poor managerial performance have led to concern in some quarters about the current system. Suggestions and proposals for dealing with these issues have including banning hostile take-overs, introducing quinquennial shareholders' meetings to replace annual meetings, the separation of the role of chairman and chief executive, and greater and more active institutional investor involvement through non-executive directors. However, the ability and availability of non-executive directors to undertake a closer and more active role is open to debate, and an appropriate solution to the problem remains to be identified. A strength of buy-outs, according to the Jensen hypothesis, is the introduction of more active investor monitoring over a long period, but the applicability of such arrangements may be limited.

4. EMPIRICAL STUDIES OF THE EFFECTS OF DIVESTMENTS AND BUY-OUTS

The evidence on the effects of more traditional mergers has been the subject of considerable debate (Jensen and Ruback (1983), Chiplin and

Wright (1987), Hughes (1989)), with the general view appearing to be that gains to selling shareholders significantly exceed those to acquirers. Over the longer term, the performance improvements by acquirers are more questionable (Mueller (1988), Franks and Harris (1989)). A substantial body of evidence is now available regarding divestments, but the empirical evidence on the performance impact of such a new phenomenon as the management buy-out has until recently been somewhat fragmentary. However, a number of studies have recently been completed.

Voluntary Sell-offs

Empirical studies of the performance effects of sell-offs relate predominantly to American experience. The main focus of attention has been the impact of announcements of sell-offs on shareholder wealth. The 'announcements effects' approach adopts an efficient markets framework and examines abnormal share price behaviour around the time of the announcement of the sell-off. Different reasons for divestment may be expected to produce varying impacts on shareholder wealth. Voluntary sell-offs or indeed spin-offs might be expected to result in an upward movement in the share price of the divestor, as the action should have an expected positive net present value in comparison with retaining the activity.

These results may be expected given the evidence that divested entities are often poor performers and peripheral to core interests (Harrigan (1980), Duhaime and Grant (1984)). Studies of voluntary sell-offs generally show a positive effect on announcement (Table 2.9). Alexander, Benson, and Kampmeyer (1984) found weak evidence of positive announcement effects whilst Rosenfeld (1984) found stronger evidence. The study of sell-offs by Montgomery *et al.* (1984) found that the reason for sale was more important than the act of sale itself. The significant effects were related to the underlying corporate strategic reason for the divestment. Sell-offs linked to clearly defined strategic decisions were valued positively by the market, whilst those that apparently involved the sale of unwanted assets without clear strategic goals were valued negatively. Divestments arising as a response to liquidity problems did not give rise to significant announcement effects. Sell-offs are thus seen as firm-specific events, their effects depending on various underlying strategic motivations, a view also supported by the work of Hearth and Zaima (1986). Denning (1988) also shows that the effect of divestment is significantly related to the motivation behind it. Where loss-making operations are divested, management may achieve significantly positive effects on shareholder wealth. Where units are sold to managers, as a means of dealing with agency cost problems, positive but insignificant improvements in shareholder wealth occur.

Table 2.9. Results of voluntary divestiture studies on divesting firm

Study	Methodology[a]	CAR (%)	Event dates[b]	Stat.	Sample size	Sample dates
Sell-offs						
Heart and Zaima	SIM	3.55	[−5, 5]	t = 3.1416[c]	58	1979–81
Rosenfeld	MAR	2.33	[−1, 0]	t = 4.60[c]	62	1969–81
Alexander,	MAR	0.17	[−1, 0]	t = 0.6795	53	1964–73
Benson, and	MKTADJ	0.40	[−1, 0]	t = 1.48		(single
Kampmeyer		−0.31	[−1, 0]	t = 1.04	39	divestments only)
Montgomery et al.	SIM	7.25	[−12 mths, + 12 mths]	Insignificant at 5%	78	1976–9
Jain	SIM	−0.40	[−10, −6]	t = −2.40[c]	1,064	1976–8
		0.70	[−5, −1]	t = 4.04[c]		
		−0.20	[+1, +5]	t = −1.03		
Klein	SIM	0.19	[−10, −3]	Insignificant at 5%	202	1970–9
		0.45	[+1, +10]	Insignificant at 5%		
		1.12	[−2, 0]	t = 2.83[c]		

	Model[a]	CARS[b]	Event window[b]	z-statistic	N	Period
Hite, Owers, and Rogers	SIM	1.66 0.82	[-1, 0] [T -1, T]	z = 4.08[c] z = 1.88[c]	55 42	successful sellers only 1963–83
Denning and Shastri	MKTADJ	-0.014 0.016	[-6, +6] [T-6, T+6]	Insignificant Insignificant	50	1970–81 Single divestment announced and completed in a two-year period
Hite and Vetsuypens	PredErr[d]	1.12[e]	[-1, 0]	z = 9.13[c]	468	1973–85
Divestment buy-outs						
Hite and Vetsuypens	PredErr[d]	0.55[e]	[-1, 0]	z = 2.48[c]	151	1973–85
Madden, Marples, and Chugh	SIM	8.4 20.7	[-12 months, 0] [-12 months, +12 months]	z = 0.94 z = 1.80	30	1973–78

[a] MAR = mean adjusted returns model; SIM = single index model; MKTADJ = market adjusted returns model.
[b] Event days in brackets [ ] are defined relative to the announcement day, t = 0, or the completion day, T. CARS (cumulative average residuals) are those reported in the original research. Not all authors report CARS for [t = -1, 0] separately.
[c] Statistically significant at $\alpha = 0.05$ or better
[d] Authors note that other models were tested and results remained robust.
[e] Average cumulative prediction error.

Zaima and Hearth (1985) found positive but not significant returns for a sample of 75 firms which purchased divested units. Rosenfeld (1984), in a sample of 30 firms, found statistically positive gains in shareholder wealth to acquirers. Jain (1985), whilst confirming the positive effects, found that gains to buyers were smaller than those accruing to sellers. Although the buyer must expect to be able to manage the acquired entity better than the vendor, there is an element of asymmetric information which affects the buyer's perception of how much better he can do and which the market is taking into account. Analysis by Sicherman and Pettway (1987) found significant positive announcement effects for acquirers of 147 divested assets which had product-line relatedness and negative effects for the acquisition of unrelated divested assets. In addition, this latter group of firms had smaller proportions of inside equity ownership than firms acquiring related divested assets, suggesting that an economically significant agency conflict exists in decisions to purchase unrelated divested assets. Purchases of related assets from strong sellers resulted in significant positive changes in shareholder wealth.

An analysis by Hite *et al.* (1987) shows positive benefits for both sellers and buyers when transactions are completed. However, when announced intentions to divest were abandoned, all the announcement gains disappeared, suggesting that the market had not previously valued the subsidiary incorrectly and had recognized the loss of benefits resulting from the divestment not taking place.

It has been suggested that the weak results obtained by Alexander *et al.* (1984) may be due to the size of the unit divested relative to the parent (Rosenfeld (1984)). In both the Jain and the Hite *et al.* samples, divestments were large relative to parent asset value. Klein (1986) also points to the important implications of the relative size of the divestiture and whether the transaction price is initially announced. Klein shows that if the transaction price is initially announced or the divestment is relatively large, abnormal returns are significant and positive. Where price or relative size are not specifically isolated, smaller or insignificant announcement effects are evident.

A further difficulty has been suggested by Denning and Shastri (1990), who point out that statistically significant announcement period returns may be due to an examination of multiple divesting firms and/or firms with simultaneous news announcements, such as poor firm or unit performance. In their examination of firms making single, large divestments with no other announcements in the relevant period, Denning and Shastri (1990) find no significant announcement effects.

Voluntary Spin-offs

Spin-offs may produce gains to shareholders in several ways. Besides improvements in the efficiency of productive organization, they may also bring benefits from the increased opportunity set they present to shareholders who are able to adjust their holdings in the separated entities. There may also be wealth transfers from bondholders and relaxations in regulation following spin-off. The evidence from announcement effect studies appears to support the efficiency improvement argument, positive gains to shareholders being identified in the US by Boudreaux (1975), Miles and Rosenfeld (1983), Schipper and Smith (1983), and Hite and Owers (1983). Rosenfeld (1984) found that gains from spin-offs were greater than those seen in sell-off announcements. Case study evidence in the UK, where demergers of quoted companies are still unusual, indicates that in respect of Bowater, at least, similar benefits to those found in the US are obtained (Wright (1986a)).

Management Buy-outs

The available evidence tends to support the view that buy-outs improve performance. In this section we cover the broad spectrum of buy-outs, paying particular attention to those arising on divestment and to those involving firms quoted on a stock market ('going privates'). The largest batch of studies relate to 'going private' deals in the USA ((De Angelo *et al.* (1984), Smith (1989), and others reviewed in Amihud (1989) and Yago (1989)). These typically examine the announcement effects of LBO offers on the stock price of the target. In itself, this exercise is somewhat trivial—because since a bid premium is necessary to secure the stock and the bidder is unquoted, a positive market response is inevitable. However, the size of the average bid premium is as much as 40 per cent, which appears to exceed by a considerable margin any gains made by downgrading senior debt (Marais *et al.* (1989), Jensen (1989)) or from tax benefits of the buy-out (see KKR (1989)). Amihud (1989), in a survey of several studies, reports substantial excess stock market returns on the announcement of the buy-outs (Table 2.10). An announcement effect study of divestment buy-outs in the US by Hite and Vetsuypens (1989) found small but significant wealth gains to vendor shareholders in the two days surrounding the announcement of the sale. At an average 0.55 per cent the premium for divestment buy-outs compares with an average premium of 1.12 per cent for inter-firm divestments in the same period. UK bid premia for 'going private' buy-outs are in line with those for hostile take-over bids.

In addition to the market-based literature, there are now some LBO

Mike Wright, Brian Chiplin, Steve Thompson

Table 2.10. Excess (net-of-market) stock returns at the announcement of a stock market ('going private') leveraged (management) buy-out

Study[a]	Period of study	Event period[b]	Number of cases	Cumulative excess return (%)
De Angelo, De Angelo and Rice (1984)	1973–80	–1, 0 days	72	22.27
		–10, +10 days	72	
Grammatikos and Swary (1986)	1975–84	–1, 0 days	131	14.04
		–10, 0 days	131	19.52
Lehn and Poulsen (1987)	1980–4	–1, 0 days	93	13.93
		–10, +10 days	93	20.76
Marais, Schipper, and Smith (1987)	1974–85	–1, 0 days	79	13.00
Torabzadeh and Bertin (1987)	1982–5	0 month	48	18.64
Travios and Milion (1987)	1975–83	–1, 0 days	56	16.20
			56	19.24
Amihund (1989)[c]	1983–6	–20, 0 days	15	19.60

[a] The results of these studies are not independent due to partial overlapping of samples.

[b] Date 0 is when the announcement about the offer appeared in the *Wall Street Journal*. The sign on the days is relative to day 0.

[c] Sample of 15 largest LBOs.

Source: Adapted from Amihud (1989).

studies available which use operating performance. These appear to confirm the beneficial effect of the LBO on profitability (De Angelo *et al.* (1984)), return on equity (Lowenstein (1985)), and productivity (Yago (1989)). A recent study by Singh (1990) of performance in the first three years before entry to a stock market found that buy-outs tended to out-perform their corresponding industry averages in terms of revenue growth, inventory management, operating income, and debtors. Buy-outs of former divisions of larger groups tended in particular to grow faster than industry averages whilst maintaining the same levels of operating income. Scherer (1986) undertook a series of case studies of buy-outs on divestiture. He found evidence of important improvements, including a reduction of delays and distortions in decision-making and resource utilization. However, he expressed concern that over-strict financial control could jeopardize advertising and R & D budgets. Direct evidence on this point is hard to come by. Lichtenbert and Siegel (1989) find no evidence that manufacturing firms which have undergone an ownership change reduce their R & D spending. However, a small sample study by the National Science Foundation, reviewed by Yago (1989), reported lower growth rates in R & D for LBO firms. More generally, it is unlikely that any reduction in research spending will be substantial since American LBO activity is overwhelmingly concentrated in low R and D intensity industries.

Across all buy-outs in the UK, a questionnaire study of the initial consequences of buy-out for 111 private sector cases up to late 1983, a period largely characterized by recession, showed improvements in profitability, trading relationships, cash and credit control systems, and evidence of new product development. The sample showed considerable changes in employment and management structure (Wright and Coyne (1985)). These findings are supported by a second survey of 57 buy-outs over the same period undertaken by Hanney (1986). A subsequent survey by CMBOR of 182 UK buy-outs completed between mid-1983 and early 1986, a period of industrial recovery, lent support to these earlier studies, but also found certain differences. For the majority of respondents, trading profits and turnover were found to be 'better' or 'substantially better' than before the buy-out and in excess of expectations contained in the business plan (Thompson, Wright, and Robbie (1989)).

In respect of those buy-outs with trading relationships with the vendor, evidence indicates that both product development and customer bases are enhanced by separation from the restrictions imposed by a parent (Wright (1986b)). Moreover, the general state of trading relationships between customers and suppliers, is found to improve significantly after buy-out, whether or not these relationships are with the former parent. However, about one-third of buy-outs which arose on divestment experienced cash-flow problems after the buy-out, with pre-buy-out difficulties caused by central control of cash flow, often being replaced by problems relating to the servicing of highly leveraged financial structures (Thompson and Wright (1987)). A little under a half of buy-out on divestment made managerial adjustments after the transfer of ownership, roughly in line with buy-outs generally. A more detailed study of the short-term changes in accounting control systems following a buy-out provides evidence that the remarriage of ownership and control involved enables more appropriate systems to be introduced, especially at the more strategic level (Jones (1988)). There is also evidence of a perpetuation of standard performance reports, influenced to a great extent by the requirements of financial backers who wished to ensure that buy-outs were effectively controlled in order to meet their finance servicing costs. There was clear evidence that whilst management were freed from group constraints, and had the ownership incentive to make improvements, the bonding to meet financial targets was also a key influence on the action they took. Case study evidence from the US (Scherer (1986)), shows benefits from the removal of delays and distortions in decision-making and the draining away of resources to other parts of a larger organization.

A study of the longer-term performance of buy-outs (Warwick Business School (1989)) in the UK using operating performance data confirmed the short-term results but found that after three years profitability declined. However, this study has to be treated with care as the longer-term results are based on samples below double figures.

A subsequent study by 3i, the leading buy-out financier in the UK, of 366 of its management buy-out investments found that average rates of return on assets were above those for all 3i companies and for all large UK companies. Average rates of return on assets were found to fall initially and then fluctuate around a rising trend to year four after the buy-out (Bannock (1990)). The study was unable to confirm the results of the Warwick study.

Studies of UK buy-outs which have exited by flotation on a stock market show that performance as measured by increases in company value exceeds market indices both prior to flotation (Thompson, Wright, and Robbie (1989)) and afterwards (Lloyd et al. (1987), Parker (1988), Wright et al. (1987)), although post-flotation performance tended to slow down. Evidence concerning performance after the ownership change in UK management buy-ins indicates a less positive out-turn than has generally been found in respect of buy-outs. A recent survey by CMBOR of 58 buy-ins of private companies (i.e. excluding those involving quoted companies) found that although restructuring activity was greater than for buy-outs (for example, 95 per cent had reorganized control systems; 73 per cent had reduced debtor payment periods; 84 per cent had added new products, etc.), operating profit was worse than forecast at the time of the buy-in in 53 per cent of cases, and more than 10 per cent worse in a third of cases (CMBOR (1991)). Whilst the cost of finance was easily the most serious post-buy-in problem, discovery of unexpected problems was clearly second in importance.

The crucial question as to whether greater managerial equity stakes lead to higher levels of performance has attracted a great deal of general attention beyond management buy-outs. The authors of a major study of chief executive incentives and company performance conclude that 'what really matters is the percentage of the company's outstanding shares the Chief Executive Officer owns' (Jensen and Murphy (1990)). In structuring a typical management buy-out, various devices are used to try and ensure that performance targets are met, and we return to them below in the context of controlling for exit. Besides the incentive to management from owning equity, debt and quasi-debt instruments introduce a commitment to meet demanding servicing costs. In addition, other control devices such as institutional representation on the board of the buy-out, detailed informational requirements by institutions, and equity ratchets are frequently used to monitor the buy-out. By allowing management's equity stake to increase if certain pre-defined targets are met, ratchets may give management an enhanced incentive to improve performance. It has recently been shown that the size of the management equity stake is the most important factor in explaining improvements in performance after buy-out (Thompson, Wright, and Robbie (1990)) and that control devices such as equity ratchets and high levels of debt were generally insignificantly related to increases in company value.

A more controversial performance issue concerns the impact of buy-outs on labour. In the USA, where the highly leveraged deals might be expected to create redundancy, the evidence is unclear. Jensen (1989) reports that employment *increased* 4.9 per cent among a sample of LBOs, but fell 6.2 per cent after adjustment for industry factors (although making such an adjustment is itself problematical when many LBOs are conglomerates and job losses are frequently concentrated at their corporate headquarters). Yago (1989) examined profiles for the cohorts of LBOs occurring in each of the years 1984, 1985, and 1986. In the first two cases there was an overall increase in employment after an initial shake-out, and in the latter year a worsening. Yago suggests that there is an initial shake-out, associated with reorganization, followed by subsequent repositioning of the firm and new recruitment. Kaplan (1989) found almost no change in employment, whilst Muscarella and Vetsuypens (1989) found a slight decline. After adjusting for industry factors, Kaplan found that relative employment declined sharply. A clearer picture is provided by Smith (1989) who, after allowing for the decline which may result from asset sales, found that although sample firms did not tend to reduce the number of employees after buy-out, they tended to hire fewer new employees than other firms in the same industry.

A common assertion is that LBOs are followed by ruthless plant closures. Again the evidence does not support this. Yago (1989) reports that LBO firms have a slightly lower incidence of closure than other manufacturing plants. In the UK there appears to have been a marked reduction in the proportion of buy-outs shedding labour, which is related to a shift away from distress sales to management and to the general recovery in profitability in the mid- to late 1980s. In the earlier survey by Wright and Coyne (1985), 44 per cent of firms reduced employment whereas in the later CMBOR study this had fallen to 25 per cent (Wright, Chiplin, Thompson, and Robbie (1990a)). With respect to the amount of job losses, the CMBOR survey also shows an improved position. In the earlier survey, 18 per cent of pre-buy-out jobs were found to have been lost on the transfer of ownership, whereas in the later study only 6 per cent of jobs disappeared. The Wright and Coyne survey also found, however, that after buy-out there had been some recovery in employment levels, but that this had not reached the levels prevailing prior to the transfer of ownership. At the time of the CMBOR survey, total employment was some 4.5 per cent below pre-buy-outs levels, and 2 per cent above the level immediately after buy-out. The UK firms, being generally smaller than their American counterparts, are less affected by sell-offs of assets. However, when considering comparative employment effects, it is important to bear in mind what might have happened in the absence of buy-out. There is some indication in the literature reviewed above that buy-outs occur in relatively weaker sectors. To the extent that this is true, the effects of buying-out may be to prevent further adverse changes in employment.

A further aspect of the divestment issue concerns its use as a means of controlling labour and reducing trade-union power. Buy-outs may to some extent be considered as an attempt by senior managers to deal with aspects of control by externalizing, either completely or partially, certain activities. Where a trading relationship exists, control may be reasserted through a market relationship. The break from the parent created by a buy-out may enable conditions of employment to be renegotiated, the Transfer of Undertakings Regulations permitting, to reflect the specific market conditions of that entity, which may not have been possible under the central bargaining arrangements of the parent (Frank (1984)). The extent of direct market control may be limited because of the generally low level of trading between buy-out and former parent (Wright, Chiplin, Thompson, and Robbie (1990a)). But the managers who buy out the company now have the incentive and the ability to make changes. Managers may take a more indirect route to changing employment conditions by deciding to close certain activities and obtain supplies from contractors or from former employees who establish themselves in a self-employed capacity. Although there are incidences of this kind of action, there is as yet no systematic evidence of its extent (Drummond (1988)). In any case, evidence suggests that industrial relations improve substantially after a buy-out from what were generally satisfactory conditions beforehand (Wright *et al.* (1984), Wright, Chiplin, Thompson, and Robbie (1990a)). There may be some selection bias in the sense that firms without satisfactory industrial relations may have difficulty in obtaining funding; however, the extent of industrial relations disputes in buy-outs is not out of line with levels found for non-buy-outs of similar sizes and industries.

④ Divestitures Enforced by Regulators

For enforced divestitures, it can be argued that if a dominant firm has been enjoying its market power, the firm's shareholders will lose from the removal of that power. However, a possible counter-effect emanating from a subsequent relaxed regulatory framework also needs to be taken into account. Studies of the effects of enforced divestitures in the US have produced conflicting results. Burns (1977, 1983) found positive share-holder wealth effects, whilst Kudla and McInish (1981) and Boudreaux (1975) have observed a negative impact. Negative effects on shareholder wealth may, of course, be insufficient to outweigh large positive abnormal returns accumulated over the years prior to the divestiture (Ellert (1976)). Montgomery, Thomas, and Kamath (1984) found the consequences of enforced divestiture on shareholders to be insignificant. The most notable enforced divestiture involved the break-up of AT and T into eight sepa-rate companies. The authorities had been grappling with the regulation of the company over a long period and as O'Brien (1986) shows, under this regime AT and T had shown notable signs of organizational slack and the use of cross-subsidization of equipment as a barrier to entry. At the same time the company had been prevented from competing in other areas. The rationale for the structure adopted on break-up was to increase competition, reduce entry barriers, and encourage competition in other heavily concentrated markets by allowing AT and T to compete with IBM in the computer market. The individual companies created on divestiture were still very large and it was unclear as to whether the impact on market efficiency and competition would derive from technical change or from the change in structure. Moreover, the benefits of divesti-ture have to be offset against the costs, particularly the burden on AT and T of the expense of the transition to the new regime.

Chen and Merville (1986) use an announcements effect approach to examine the impact of deregulation, the dropping of anti-trust charges, and the reversal of the co-insurance benefits which stem from having an integrated set of activities. Hence, a variety of events occur during the break-up process. The authors find positive transfers of wealth from con-sumers and the US government to AT and T shareholders and bond-holders, but no evidence of wealth transfers from bondholders to shareholders. The buffering effect which arises from the reduction in riski-ness as a result of deregulation was reduced as AT and T passed through the total deregulation process. The shareholders of the post-break-up operating companies also experienced positive gains from consumers. Notable asset swaps prompted by anti-trust action in the US have been the exchange of breweries between Stroh and Pabst (Davis (1986)). Pabst became more competitive after the trade but was not able to maintain its independent existence. Stroh shook off anti-trust action and was placed in a stronger competitive position.

5. CONCLUSIONS

In this chapter we have reviewed recent developments in the market for corporate control which have introduced new organizational forms. These developments merit attention for a number of important reasons. First, they reflect increasing flexibility in the boundaries of the firm and a more dynamic approach to the concept of the firm and industry structure. Second, the developments highlight important asymmetries between the acquisition of an independent company and divestment.

The third issue concerns the particular case of buy-outs and the question as to whether they represent a new longer term organizational form or whether they are merely a short-term device. There is a view that debt and quasi-debt intensified incentives in buy-outs gives managers a short-term perspective which is appropriate merely during a transitory phase. However, this considerably underestimates the scope of the buy-out in corporate restructuring. Buy-outs which remain with their original structures may not necessarily be the best performers. Such buy-outs may be the classic case of a mature, long-term stable sector with low investment needs or requirements which can be met from cash flow. For many companies, the buy-out structure may be only one, albeit legitimate, stage in the life cycle of the firm. In the UK, a substantial proportion of buy-outs, especially those with development capital firm involvement, may have significant growth prospects which require substantial capital investment that can only be met from stock market flotation or sale to another group. In addition, what is a credible independent market position may change over time, as has become particularly evident as firms develop their strategies in relation to the European Community's Single Market. Whilst larger buy-outs exit considerably sooner than smaller ones, the majority of buy-outs in the UK and especially in continental Europe retain their original structures.

REFERENCES

Alexander, G. J., Benson, P. G., and Kampmeyer, J. M. (1984), 'Investigating valuation effects of announcements of voluntary corporate sell-off', *Journal of Finance*, **39**, 503–17.

Altman, E. (1990), 'Setting the record straight on junk bonds', *Journal of Applied Corporate Finance*, **3**, No. 2, 82–95.

Amihud, Y. (1989), *Leveraged Management Buy-outs: Causes and Consequences*, New York: Dow Jones Irwin.

Auerbach, A. (1989), 'Testimony to the Senate Finance Committee on LBOs and corporate debt', *Journal of Applied Corporate Finance*, **2**, No. 1, 52–7.

Bannock, G. (1990), 'The long-term performance of management buy-outs', 3i Occasional Paper, London.

Boudreaux, K. J. (1975), 'Divestiture and share price', *Journal of Financial and Quantitative Analysis*, **10**, 619–29.

Buck, T., and Wright, M. (1990), 'Vertical hierarchies, soft budgets and management buy-outs', Economic Analysis and Workers' Management.

Burns, M. R. (1977), 'The competitive effects of trust-busting: portfolio analysis', *Journal of Political Economy*, **8**, 717–39.

—— (1983), 'An empirical analysis of stockholder injury under S.2 of the Sherman Act', *Journal of Industrial Economics*, **31**, 333–62.

Cable, J. (1985), 'Capital market information and industrial performance: the role of West German banks', *Economic Journal*, **95**, 118–32.

Chen, A. H., and Merville, L. J. (1986), 'An analysis of divestiture effects resulting from deregulation', *Journal of Finance*, **41**, 997–1010.

Chiplin, B., and Wright, M. (1980), 'Divestment and structural change in UK industry', *National Westminster Bank Review*, February.

—— —— (1987), *The Logic of Mergers: The Competitive Market for Corporate Control in Theory and Practice*, IEA Hobart Paper 107, IEA.

—— —— and Robbie, K. (1989a), 'Management Buy-outs in 1989: the Annual Review from CMBOR', CMBOR, Nottingham.

—— —— (1989b), *Realisations from Management Buy-outs: Issues and Prospects*, CMBOR, Nottingham.

CMBOR (1991), 'Management buy-ins: characteristics, performance and problems', Research Report, CMBOR, Nottingham.

Davis, G. (1986), 'Strategic trading: rationalisation in US brewing', in J. Coyne and M. Wright (eds.), *Divestment and Strategic Change*, Oxford: Philip Allan.

De Angelo, H., De Angelo, L., and Rice, E. (1984), 'Shareholder wealth and going private', *Journal of Law and Economics*, **27**, 367–402.

De Angelo, L. (1986), 'Accounting numbers as market valuation substitutes: a study of management buy-outs of public stockholders', *Accounting Review*, **61**, 400–420.

—— (1990), 'Equity valuation and corporate control', *Accounting Review*, **65**, No. 1, 93–112.

Denning, K. (1988), 'Spin-offs and sales of assets: an examination of security returns and divestment motivations', *Accounting and Business Research*, No. 73, Winter, 32–42.

—— and Shastri, K. (1990), 'Single sale divestments: the impact on stockholders and bondholders', *Journal of Business Finance and Accounting*, **17**, Winter, 731–43.

Drummond, R. (1988), 'Buy-in case study: Southnews', in *MBOs, LBOs and Buy-ins*, Euromoney Seminar Transcripts, Euromoney, London.

Duhaime, I., and Grant, J. (1984), 'Factors influencing divestment decision making: evidence from a field study', *Strategic Management Journal*, **5**, 301–18.

Ellerman, D. (1990), 'Perestroika with worker ownership', *Annals of Public and Cooperative Economy*, **61**, No. 4, 519–36.

Ellert, J. C. (1976), 'Mergers, antitrust law enforcement and shareholders returns', *Journal of Finance*, **31**, 715–32.

Frank, R. H. (1984), 'Are workers paid their marginal products', *American Economic Review*, **74**, 549–71.

Franks, J., and Harris, R. (1989), 'Shareholder wealth effects of corporate takeovers: the UK experience 1955–1985', London Business School and University of North Carolina at Chapel Hill Working Paper.

Geroski, P., and Vlassopoulos, A. (1990), 'European merger activity: a response to 1992', in London Business School, *Continental Mergers are Different: Strategy and Policy for 1992*.

Governor of the Bank of England (1990), 'Management buy-outs', *Bank of England Quarterly Bulletin*.

Graeper, M. (1990), 'Management and employee buy-outs in Germany', paper presented to Council for European Studies Conference, Washington, DC, March.

Hanney, J. (1986), 'Management buy-outs: an offer you can't refuse', *Omega*, **14**, No. 2, 119–34.

Harrigan, K. (1980), *Strategies for Declining Businesses*, Lexington, Mass.: Lexington Books.

Hearth, D. P., and Zaima, J. K. (1986), 'Divestiture uncertainty and shareholder wealth: evidence from the USA', *Journal of Business Finance and Accounting*, **13**, 71–86.

Heuze, C., Wright, M., and Dupouy, P. (1990), 'Management buy-outs in France', *Acquisitions Monthly-Buy-out Supplement*, November.

Hite, G., and Vetsuypens, M. (1989), 'Management buy-outs of divisions and shareholder wealth', *Journal of Finance*, September, **44**, No. 4, 953–970.

—— and Owers, J. (1983), 'Security price reactions around corporate spin-off announcements', *Journal of Financial Economics*, **12**, 409–36.

—— —— and Rogers, R. (1987), 'The market for inter-firm asset sales: partial sell-offs and total liquidations', *Journal of Financial Economics*, **18**, 229–52.

Hughes, A. (1989), 'The impact of merger: a survey of empirical evidence for the UK', in J. A. Fairburn and J. A. Kay (eds.), *Mergers and Merger Policy*, Oxford: Oxford University Press.

Jain, P. C. (1985), 'The effects of voluntary sell-off announcements on shareholder wealth', *Journal of Finance*, **40**, 209–24.

Jensen, M. C. (1989), 'Eclipse of the public corporation', *Harvard Business Review*, September/October, 61–74.

—— and Murphy, K. (1990), 'CEO incentives—it's not how much you pay, but how', *Harvard Business Review*, May/June, 138–49.

—— and Ruback, R. S. (1983), 'The market for corporate control', *Journal of Financial Economics*, **11**, 5–50.

Jones, C. S. (1988), 'Accounting and organisational change: an empirical study of management buy-outs', *European Accounting Association*, Nice, April.

KKR (1989), 'Leveraged buy-outs', *Journal of Applied Corporate Finance*, **2**, No. 1, 64–70.

Kaplan, S. (1989), 'The effects of management buy-outs on operating performance and value', *Journal of Financial Economics*, **24**, No. 2, 217–54.

Kieschnick, R. L. (1989), 'Management buy-outs of public corporations: an analysis of prior characteristics', in Y. Amihud (ed.), *Leveraged Management Buy-outs: Causes and Consequences*, New York: Dow Jones Irwin.

Klein, A. (1986), 'The timing and substance of divestiture announcements: individual, simultaneous and cumulative effects', *Journal of Finance*, **61**, 685–95.

Kudla, R., and McInish, R. (1981), 'The microeconomic consequences of an involuntary corporate spin-off', *Sloan Management Review*, **22**, 41–6.

Lichtenberg, F., and Siegel, D. (1989), 'The effect of takeovers on the employment and wages of central office and other personnel', Columbia University Graduate School of Business and NBER, January, 1–36.

Lipton, D., and Sachs, J. (1990), 'Creating a market economy in Eastern Europe: the case of Poland', *Brookings Papers on Economic Activity*, No. 1.

Lloyd, S., Coyne, J., and Wright, M. (1987), *Trends in Management Buy-outs*, London, CMBOR/Venture Economics.

Lowenstein, L. (1985), 'Management buy-outs', *Columbia Law Review*, May, **85**, 730–84.

Lye, S., and Silbertson, A. (1981), 'Merger activity and sales of subsidiaries between company groups', *Oxford Bulletin of Economics and Statistics*, **43**, 257–72.

Marais, L., Schipper, K., and Smith, A. (1989), 'Wealth effects of going private for senior securities', *Journal of Financial Economics*, **23**, No. 1, 155–91.

Maupin, R. J., *et al.* (1984), 'An empirical investigation of the characteristics of publicly quoted companies which change to closely held ownership through management buy-outs', *Journal of Business Finance and Accounting*, **11**, 435–50.

Miles, J., and Rosenfeld, J. (1983), 'The effect of voluntary spin-off announcements on shareholder wealth', *Journal of Finance*, **38**, 1597–606.

Molyneux, P. (1990), 'US high yield debt and the case for a European market', *National Westminster Bank Review*, February, 2–15.

Montgomery, C., Thomas, A., and Kamath, R. (1984), 'Divestiture, market valuation and strategy', *Academy of Management Journal*, **27**, 830–40.

Mueller, D. C. (1988), 'The Corporate Life-Cycle', in S. Thompson and M. Wright (eds.), *Internal Organisation, Efficiency and Profit*, Deddington: Philip Allan.

Muscarella, C., and Vetsuypens, M. (1989), 'Efficiency and organisational structure: a study of reverse LBOs', Working Paper, Southern Methodist University.

O'Brien, D. (1986), 'Divestiture: the case of AT and T, in J. Coyne and M. Wright (eds.), *Divestment and Strategic Chance*, Oxford: Philip Allan.

Parker, P. (1988), 'Floating to market: a study of 12 management buy-outs', *Financial Times*—Mergers and Acquisitions, August.

Porter, M. (1987), 'From competitive advantage to competitive strategy', *Harvard Business Review*, May/June.

Ravenscraft, D. J., and Scherer, F. M. (1987), *Mergers, Sell-offs and Economic Efficiency*, Washington: Brookings Institution.

Rosenfeld, J. (1984), 'Additional evidence on the relation between divestiture announcements and shareholder wealth', *Journal of Finance*, **39**, 1437–48.

Scherer, F. M. (1986), 'Mergers, sell-offs and managerial behavior', in L. G. Thomas (ed.), *The Economics of Strategic Planning*, Lexington, Mass.

Schipper, K., and Smith, A. (1983), 'Effects of recontracting on shareholder wealth: the case of voluntary spin-offs', *Journal of Financial Economics*, **12**, 437–67.

Sicherman, N., and Pettway, R. (1987), 'Acquisitions of divested assets and shareholders wealth', *Journal of Finance*, **42**, 1261–74.

Singh, H. (1990), 'Management buy-outs and shareholder value', *Strategic Management Journal*, July/August, 111–30.

Smith, A. (1989), 'Corporate ownership structure and performance: the case of management buy-outs', University of Chicago Working Paper.

Summers, L. H. (1989), 'Taxation and corporate debt', *Journal of Applied Corporate Finance*, **2**, No. 1, 45–51.

Thompson, S., and Wright, M. (1987), 'Markets to hierarchies and back again: the implications of management buy-outs for factor supply', *Journal of Economic Studies*, **14**, 5–22.

Thompson, S., Wright, M., and Robbie, K. (1989), 'Buy-outs, debt and efficiency', *Journal of Applied Corporate Finance*, **2**, No. 1, 76–85.

—— —— —— (1990), 'Management equity ownership, debt and performance: some evidence from UK management buy-outs', CMBOR Occasional Paper.

Warwick Business School (1989), *The Long-Term Performance of Management Buy-outs*, Touche Ross.

Wright, M. (1986a), 'Demerger: the case of Bowater', in J. Coyne and M. Wright (eds.), *Divestment and Strategic Change*, Oxford: Philip Allan.

—— (1986b), 'The make-buy decision and managing markets: the case of management buy-outs', *Journal of Management Studies*, **23**, No. 4, 434–53.

—— (1988), 'Redrawing the boundaries of the firm', in S. Thompson and M. Wright (eds.), *Internal Organisation, Efficiency and Profit*, Deddington: Philip Allan.

—— Chiplin, B., Thompson, S., and Robbie, K., (1990a), 'Management buy-outs, trade unions and employee ownership', *Industrial Relations Journal*, Summer.

—— —— —— —— (1990b), 'Management buy-outs and large-small firm relationships', *Management International Review*.

—— and Coyne, J. (1985), *Management Buy-outs*, London: Croom-Helm.

—— —— and Robbie, K. (1987), 'Management buy-outs in Britain', Long Range Planning, August.

—— and Ennew, C. (1990), '1992 and strategic bank marketing', *International Journal of Bank Marketing Special Issue*, **8**, No. 3.

—— *et al.* (1991), *Buy-ins and Buy-outs: New Strategies in Corporate Management*, London: Graham & Trotman.

—— and Thompson, S. (1991), 'Privatisation through asset sales', in C. Price and P. Jackson (eds.), *Privatisation Policy*, forthcoming.

—— —— and Robbie, K. (1992), 'Management led leveraged buy-outs: a European perspective', *Journal of Business Venturing*, **7**, No. 1, 47–72.

Yago, G. (1989), 'Leveraged buy-outs in focus: empirical findings and policy issues', Senate Revenue and Taxation Committee State of California, 7 April.

Zaima, J. K., and Hearth, D. P. (1985), 'The wealth effects of voluntary sell-offs: implications for divesting and acquiring firms', *Journal of Financial Research*, **8**, 227–36.

3

Shareholder Wealth Effects of UK Take-overs: Implications for Merger Policy

JULIAN FRANKS*
and ROBERT HARRIS†

1. INTRODUCTION

This chapter has three objectives. First, it discusses concerns about the aggregate level of merger activity, and how institutional changes might provide more effective alternatives to take-overs as a way of remedying managerial failure. Second, it estimates the costs to shareholders arising from referrals of proposed mergers to the Monopolies and Mergers Commission, hereafter referred to as the Commission. Third, it offers an overview of UK merger activity and the role of the Commission in take-overs.

In the empirical section, a sample of mergers from the period 1965–85 is examined in order to answer three questions. First, what costs do shareholders bear when a bid is referred to the Commission and is subsequently permitted to proceed? Second, does the rejection of a merger by the Commission involve the loss of a bid premium which shareholders would have realized in a successful merger? Third, do bids which fail because of management and shareholder discretion perform better or worse than bids which fail as a result of rejection by the Commission?

In Section 2 of the chapter, historical statistics on merger activity in the UK and a brief description of the role of the Commission and the level of its intervention are provided. In Section 3, data, methodology, and results for the analysis of referred mergers are described. In Section 4, some of the policy issues which are raised by the recent high level of merger activity are explored. In particular, some institutional changes that might reduce the level of merger activity by providing a less costly means of capturing perceived merger benefits are discussed.

* National Westminster Bank Professor of Finance at the London Business School.
† C. Stewart Sheppard Professor of Business Administration and Associate Dean of Academic Affairs at Darden School of Management, University of Virginia.

2. MERGER ACTIVITY AND THE ROLE OF THE COMMISSION

Past Merger Activity

Table 3.1 reports statistics from the Department of Trade and Industry (DTI) on the level and value of UK merger activity from 1963 to 1990. From these time series, it is apparent that the value of acquired firms' assets is more volatile over time than is the number of acquisitions. In 1968, one of the peaks of merger activity, the pound sterling value of mergers (at 1985 prices) is more than 13 times the value of acquisitions transacted in the trough of 1975. In comparison, the number of acquisitions in 1968 is only 3 times that recorded in 1975.

The level of merger activity can be put in a different perspective if one considers that in 1985, the value of merging firms' assets was about 4 per cent of total non-financial corporate assets calculated on a replacement cost basis. The result is that merger activity has been a formidable force in changing the ownership of British industry.

In Table 3.2, we report the annual statistics provided by the Takeover Panel. These provide some guide as to the number of UK bids involving a target which were traded on the London Stock Exchange. The Panel came into operation in 1968 to administer the City Code on Takeovers and Mergers. Column 2 of the table reports the number of bids notified to the Panel which involved formal documents being issued to the target's shareholders; other bids were withdrawn without the issuance of formal documents. As column 3 suggests, about 80 per cent of all offers were for targets of UK quoted companies. The final column reports the number of successful bids. An estimate of the number of quoted targets can be made by multiplying the numbers in column 4 by those in column 3. Since there are only about 2,000 UK quoted companies traded at any one time (excluding the unlisted securities market), the death-rate from merging has been substantial. An interesting question is whether this high rate of activity has beneficially influenced the restructuring of British industry.

In Table 3.3 statistics on cross-border acquisitions both into and out of the UK are given. The size and value of UK acquisitions abroad is large compared with the aggregate figures given in Table 3.1. For example, in 1989, UK companies acquired £22.8 billion of overseas companies compared with UK transactions valued at about £26 billion.

This level of merger activity is not confined to the UK. In the US, similar levels of merger activity have been seen. Table 3.4 documents the last decade of merger activity in four Western countries, together with the rising trend of that activity.

Table 3.1. Take-overs of UK companies, 1969–1988

Year	No. of completed mergers and acquisitions[a]	Value as [b] a proportion of replacement cost of capital[c] (£bn)	Value as [d] a proportion of market capitalization of securities (%)
1969	744	0.97	2.8	2.0
1970	614	1.00	2.9	2.3
1971	620	0.74	1.7	1.8
1972	938	2.35	4.5	3.7
1973	951	1.06	1.6	1.8
1974	367	0.46	0.6	0.8
1975	200	0.22	0.2	0.6
1976	242	0.35	0.3	0.7
1977	372	0.73	0.6	1.3
1978	441	0.98	0.7	1.5
1979	417	1.47	0.8	1.7
1980	368	1.26	0.6	1.7
1981	327	0.88	0.4	0.9
1982	299	1.40	0.6	1.3
1983	305	1.91	0.8	1.4
1984	398	4.35	1.7	2.4
1985	340	6.30	2.2	2.8
1986	537	12.13	3.9	4.0
1987	905	11.28	3.4	2.7
1988	937	16.87		4.2

[a] An alternative source of information on acquisitions in the UK is *Acquisitions Monthly* (AM Data):

Year	No.	Value (£bn)
1984	187	3.98
1985	495	7.62
1986	794	15.73
1987	1,260	18.10
1988	1,465	15.84

[b] This is the replacement cost capital stock of the total UK corporate sector. Source: CSO, National Accounts.

[c] Figures represent the market value of the consideration paid by the bidder which represents the value of the equity and the publicly traded debt instruments.

[d] The securities include equities, preference, and marketable debt. Bank borrowings are not included, thereby overstating the measure as a proportion of firms' assets.

Source: Department of Trade and Industry, *Business Monitor MQ7*, 1989. But see note d.

Table 3.2. Number of bids processed by Panel on Takeovers and Merge

Year ending March	Number of bids notified to Panel	Proportion of merger proposals for publicly quoted targets (%)	Succe bids
1970	363	85	239
1971	296	83	186
1972	393	85	240
1973	356	74	214
1974	266	79	163
1975	142	83	107
1976	139	90	117
1977	189	90	138
1978	214	87	159
1979	158	75	117
1980	141	78	99
1981	134	76	97
1982	135	78	81
1983	113	88	88
1984	158	85	116
1985	192	92	160
1986	197	86	138
1987	275	87	211
1988	222	n.a.	171
1989	246	n.a.	184

Source: Based on reports of the Takeover Panel.

The Role of the Commission in Merger Activity

Takeovers are regulated through a number of institutions and mechanisms. The Commission regulates mergers primarily as part of its competition policy, although it may intervene on the basis of other considerations, such as national security. The Takeover Panel provides rules on bid procedures, for example the circumstances under which a company must make an offer to another company's shareholders when its own stake reaches a particular level (currently 30 per cent). The Stock Exchange may influence take-overs by listing both requirements for new companies and rules for existing companies which wish to raise new funds such as equity. It is a widespread perception that the Stock Exchange has used these listing requirements to discourage the issuance of non-voting shares. The Department of Trade is responsible for

Table 3.3. Cross-border acquisitions by UK companies overseas and overseas companies into UK

Year	Acquisitions overseas by UK companies		Acquisitions in UK by overseas companies	
	No.	Value (£bn)	No.	Value (£bn)
1986	317	8.9	52	2.9
1987	431	12.1	58	2.7
1988	606	17.3	94	5.7
1989	682	22.8	163	10.9
1990 (Q1–Q2)	259	5.4	66	6.3

Source: Central Statistical Office 'Business Bulletin'. Cross-Border Acquisitions and Mergers (Quarter 3, 1990).

Table 3.4. Number of acquisitions in selected countries

Year	Canada	Germany	Netherlands	United States
1975	264	445	n.a.	2,297
1976	313	453	n.a.	2,276
1977	395	554	n.a.	2,224
1978	449	558	n.a.	2,106
1979	511	602	n.a.	2,128
1980	414	635	n.a.	1,889
1981	491	618	296	2,395
1982	576	603	328	2,346
1983	628	506	296	2,533
1984	641	575	370	2,543
1985	712	709	318	3,001

developing government policy on insider-trading laws and other laws that protect minority shareholders. For example, legislation requires companies to disclose their share stake in other companies when it reaches 3 per cent of the target's share capital, thereby making it more difficult for prospective bidders to accumulate shares without the target company's knowledge. Finally, the European Commission has responsibility for competition policy (as well as national governments) within the common market and has recently issued a draft directive which would harmonize take-over regulation within the Community.

The Monopolies Commission was established in 1948 by Act of Parliament, its name subsequently being changed to the Monopolies and Mergers Commission. Merger control, as we know it today, was introduced in 1965, although some new provisions were introduced in the Fair Trading Act (1973).[1] A primary responsibility of the Commission has been the investigation of mergers. However, it only investigates mergers that are referred to it by the Secretary of State for Trade and Industry (the Minister), who usually (but not necessarily) acts on the recommendation of the Director-General of the Office of Fair Trading (OFT). The OFT completes a preliminary study of announced bids after consultation with representatives of public and private institutions, and as a result the Director may recommend a referral. If the Minister agrees to a referral, the bid is investigated by the Commission.

Although companies are not obliged to inform the OFT of a bid for another company, it is in their interests to do so since a completed merger can be referred; if it is found against the public interest, the Minister can require the merger to be unwound. The OFT can provide confidential guidance to individual companies prior to any referral. Such guidance may include information on whether a referral is likely before a bid is publicly announced. Such 'guidance' is given in an increasing number of cases.

Criteria for referral are broad. Any bid is eligible if the combined market share of the merged firms exceeds 25 per cent, or if the assets of the acquired company are greater than £30 million (raised in 1984 from £15 million). As a result, only a small proportion of the mergers reported in Table 3.1 qualify; up to 1985, the number was about 200 each year, although subsequently it has risen to 300.

On the basis of the report, the Minister makes the decision to accept or reject the merger. The Minister does not have to accept the report of the Commission, and in a number of cases has not done so. The Minister can, however, only disallow a merger if the Commission report makes an adverse judgement with at least a two-thirds majority.

Once a referral is made, three possible results may ensue. The bid may be rejected, accepted, or laid aside. In the last case, no report is made because the bid lapses, usually because the acquiring company has indicated that it does not wish to proceed with the acquisition. In considering a bid, the Commission must take into account the general public interest. An important criterion is the effect of the bid on competition. Such a consideration embraces not only mergers which would lead to horizontal and vertical integration, but also conglomerate mergers. However, current policy is that vertical and conglomerate mergers are unlikely to be

[1]   For a discussion of the UK merger legislation and the role of the Commission, see Office of Fair Trading (1985).

referred unless they raise 'special' concerns of wider public interest. Other considerations may also play a role, such as those of employment (and regional considerations), international competition, foreign ownership and its implications for the national security, and the survival of failing firms.

Up to November 1985, only 93 mergers have been referred to the Commission (excluding newspaper mergers which are considered under separate provisions). Although the rate of referral has increased in recent years, referrals represent only about 2 or 3 per cent of those mergers eligible for consideration by the Commission. Table 3.5 documents the timing, number, and outcome of Commission referrals. Though only about one-third of referrals lead to rejection, the rejection rate understates the Commission's deterrence capacity since it is possible that bids laid aside would have borne a high probability of rejection. Furthermore, an unknown number of bids have not materialized because the OFT has given informal advice that a referral would be likely to be recommended. While a minority of mergers were rejected, the average value of a rejected bid was more than 5 times the size of an accepted bid (using equity market value of the target firm as the bench-mark).

Table 3.5. Timing and number of referrals and outcomes, 1965–1990[a]

	1965–9	1970–4	1975–9	1980–4	1985–90[a]	Total
Total referrals	13	19	21	35	71	159
Acceptances	7	5	7	14	27	60
Rejections	5	5	7	15	19	51
Laid aside	1	9	7	7	16	40
Report awaited					9	9

[a] Up to 12 October 1990.

3. MERGERS, SHAREHOLDER VALUE, AND COMMISSION DECISIONS

Neo-classical economic theory holds that a voluntary decision by market participants to merge is based on some perception of shareholder benefits. Activity by the OFT and Commission designed to monitor, and at times prohibit, mergers may deprive shareholders of these benefits—the social calculus being that undesirable anti-competitive effects will occur if the merger is undertaken.

Grossman and Hart (1981) draw a distinction between 'acquisitional' take-overs, motivated solely by inside information held by the bidder, and 'allocational' take-overs where the prospective merger benefits require a reallocation of real resources. If a take-over is 'acquisitional', the bidder's incentive to acquire and process information is based on gains to be reaped when the information is released and the currently 'undervalued' target company is revalued upwards. Why is a merger required to realize these benefits? Grossman and Hart point out that any small shareholder's incentive to gather and process information about a company is limited by the ability of other shareholders to free-ride. Shareholders free-ride if they gain from the revelation of new information but do not bear the costs of gathering it. To avoid this free-rider problem, at least in part, a single bidder may be motivated to acquire an entire company. Thus, purely acquisitional take-overs may play a role in improving information reflected in financial market prices.[2]

On the other hand, 'allocational' take-overs involve changes in real asset markets (such as cost savings or increased monopoly power). In allocational take-overs, increases in financial market value reflect planned changes in real asset markets, and not merely changes in the market's information about those markets.

If an acquisitional merger is referred to the Commission and rejected by it, would the value added by the bidder's information be eroded as a result of the rejection? We would not expect any erosion if the information gathered and processed by the bidder is revealed by the bid process. Alternatively, if the information is retained by the bidder and is never made public, then the value added would be eroded by the rejection. We believe the former is the more realistic case, since information (such as an undervaluation of the assets) would be revealed by the announcement that a bidder had gathered and processed information, and had been intending to bid. Moreover, the time delays and investigation surrounding Commission deliberations would be likely to reveal the information.

If mergers referred to the Commission are allocational, then two outcomes of Commission rejection are possible. If the value-creating resource reallocation is not unique to the proposed merger, Commission rejections may not significantly erode shareholder wealth if another merger (where rejection by the Commission is not anticipated) can accomplish the same reallocation. On the other hand, if the real resource reallocation is unique to the proposed pairing (or to any merger that would be rejected by the Commission), shareholder wealth would be eroded upon Commission rejection.

---

[2] There is a further question of how much value gain a bidder can reap, given that a bid may reveal some of the inside information. This may explain why bidders often obtain sizeable 'toehold' interests prior to making a formal bid. Rules about disclosure of such toehold interests thus can be interpreted as ways to limit a bidder's profit from inside information. Such rules may discourage acquisitional take-overs which improve the efficiency of the information market.

In Commission referrals, we would expect the proposed merger to be allocational rather than acquisitional. Furthermore, in Commission rejections, we would expect a likely benefit of merger to be enhanced market power. Such market power enhancement is likely to be unique to the merger (or to that set which would be referred to the Commission). As a result, we would expect value gains to be eroded as a result of Commission rejection.

The Evidence on Take-overs to Date

Accounting studies (Meeks (1977), Singh (1971, 1975)) of UK mergers have generally concluded that, on average, mergers produce zero or negative shareholder benefits; only a study by Cosh, Hughes, and Singh (1980) suggests an increase in post-merger profitability. In addition, UK studies of share price performance have produced conflicting results. Franks, Broyles, and Hecht (1977) found mergers to be value creating, but their work was restricted to a single industry. Firth (1979, 1980), on the other hand, found that any gains to target shareholders were offset by losses to bidders, and concluded that mergers are most likely 'motivated by maximization of management utility reasons' (1980, p. 235). Using a sample of 39 mergers from the period 1974 through to 1976, Barnes (1984) found small gains to the bidder around the merger announcement date but greater losses during the subsequent six months. Dodds and Quek (1985) used a larger sample for the same period and found residuals around the announcement date similar to those of Franks *et al.* (1977) and contrary to those of Barnes.

However, the latest study by Franks and Harris (1989) includes a much larger data set and a much longer time series than previous studies. Using methodology similar to that described earlier, they examined nearly 1,900 UK mergers with the results shown in Table 3.6. Target shareholders have significant positive gains as a result of mergers. There are 22 per cent value gains to targets in the bid month and 30 per cent gains over the six-month period around the bid month (the bid month is month zero). The higher bid premium over the longer time period may reflect the market's anticipation of a bid. The bidder's shareholders obtain a small value increase in the bid month and a 7 per cent gain over the six-month period, with two-thirds of the individual bidders showing gains for the period. To some extent, the bidder's gains prior to the bid may reflect positive earnings trends or other favourable developments which coincided with the bid or which influenced the bidder's timing of a bid. As a result, it is not clear how much of the 7 per cent gain is attributable to the anticipation of merger benefits. What is clear is that there is no evidence of shareholder losses by the bidder. Franks and Harris also show

Table 3.6. Average value changes

	Average value changes		Percentage of firms with value increases	
	Bid month (%)	6 months (−4 to +1)	Bid month	6 months
Acquiree	22[a]	30[a]	86	85
Acquirer	1[a]	7[a]	50	65

[a] Significantly different from zero at 95% confidence level.

that gains to target shareholders are larger in contested and/or revised bids than in the single bid case, but that there is no reduction in returns to the bidding firm's shareholders. This evidence suggests that contested and/or revised bids are more a manifestation of larger merger benefits than of an increase in competition for corporate control. In summary, Franks and Harris's work shows positive gains to shareholders in merging firms, with most if not all of the gain going to target shareholders.[3]

What is the post-merger performance of these acquiring firms? In an efficient stock market, we would expect the market to price the anticipated gains from merging in an unbiased way; thus we would expect no abnormal performance post-merger (positive or negative). Franks, Harris, and Mayer (1988) examine shareholder returns for bidders two years subsequent to merger, beginning after the bid becomes unconditional. Their results show that bidders, on average, outperform the market prior to the merger but that this abnormal performance does not continue post-merger; thus, a bench-mark for bidders based on pre-merger performance produces losses of 10 to 13 per cent over a two-year period.[4] However, if the bench-mark is altered to represent the performance of all firms (i.e. a market index), then bidding firms outperform the market by only about 4 per cent over the two years subsequent to merger. It should be apparent

[3] Franks and Harris (1989) report that on average the bidder is 7 to 8 times as large as the target, based on market value of equity; thus, a direct comparison of percentage value gains does not give a full picture of the split of value gains. They show, however, that value gains still go largely to the target after controlling for the relative size of merging firms.

[4] Franks and Harris (1989) show that bidders' shares appear to outperform the market in the five- to six-year period prior to making a merger bid. This corresponds to high pre-merger α values in the model market (see Appendix 3.1). They suggest that this may, in part, indicate managers' timing of take-over bids following favourable developments in their stock price, perhaps to capitalize on what they perceive as advantageous financing conditions. It may be that the management of acquiring firms have superior information to other market participants about the economic value of their assets and therefore about the value of their financial securities.

that the post-merger performance of acquiring firms is very sensitive to the bench-mark used.

Sample and Methodology

To provide evidence on shareholder wealth effects in mergers and on the impact of Commission decisions, we obtained a comprehensive list of mergers (excluding newspaper mergers) referred to the Commission through early 1986. For each merger we obtained the following key dates: the *bid date*, when the bidder announces its bid; the *referral date*, when the merger is referred to the Commission; and the *report date*, when the Commission publishes the report, accepting or rejecting the merger. When the merger is laid aside, no report is published although the 'laid aside' date was collected.

Mergers are typically referred to the Commission within a month or two of the bid. Over 90 per cent of all referrals come within two months of the bid. The lag between referral and the final reporting date could be up to a year, but a six- or seven-month lag is more typical. In cases where all three dates exist in our sample, the median lag between bid date and report is eight months. These lags show that, subsequent to initial bids, shareholders are subject to uncertainty and possible delays to both referral and to the ultimate fate of the merger.

For our analysis of effects of Commission decisions on shareholder wealth, we require share prices which we obtained from the London Share Price Database (LSPD). LSPD includes all UK companies quoted since 1975, in addition to a large sample of companies from 1955. Although there were over 90 mergers referred in the period examined, the sample used in this study was smaller. Some companies were not quoted (because they were private or foreign), while in other cases share price data were not available in the LSPD. Finally, in other cases we were unable to obtain necessary information on key dates. As a result, for companies with return data, we had bid dates for 86 mergers, referral dates for 82, and report (including laid aside) dates for 75 companies.

To measure the impact on shareholders, we use a model to predict how share prices would have performed if a merger had not taken place and then subtract this predicted return (control return) from the realized return. The difference between the prediction and the realization is a measure of the percentage shareholder value gain attributable to the merger.

$$\text{Value gain} = \text{Realized return} - \text{Control return}$$

Returns include both dividends and capital gains (or capital losses). We calculate these value gains on a monthly basis with time defined relative to a particular event. The particular event is referred to as 'month zero' (since monthly share price data is being used) for all companies in the sample. Thus month 'minus one' for a company is one month before the event for that company, irrespective of the actual calendar date. To measure value gains arising from the bid announcement, we define month zero as the bid month. Alternatively, when we study the effects of Commission decisions, month zero could be defined as the report date. In the latter case, the value gain in month zero is interpreted as the effect of the Commission report on shareholders' wealth. Due to possible anticipation by the market of forthcoming events, we also report value gains accumulated over periods of months surrounding the event date.

The approach described above requires a control or predicted return. We use the so-called 'market model' which controls for general equity market movements, adjusting for both company risk and the company's expected performance, given movements in a market index. If a company were of similar risk to the market index, and, prior to the event, had average stock returns equal to returns on the market, then the control (or forecast) return would be defined as the return on an equally weighted index of all stocks covered in LSPD. If the control return is less than the return actually realized in a month, we can say the security has outperformed the market. If in the event month, on average, a sample of companies (for example, bidders) outperforms the market, we attribute the 'value gain' to the event. Our procedures are described in more detail in Appendix 3.1.

Why use share price data rather than accounting data? The accounting methodology measures rates of return on assets before and after the merger. The advantage of this method is that *realized* rates of return are being measured, which should reflect actual changes in the profitability of assets employed. The major disadvantage is that accounting rates of return are rarely equal to economic rates of return (see Kay (1976), Solomon and Laya (1967)). Not only are accounting profits different from free cash flows, but more important, the initial and final book values of assets may be poor proxies for their economic values.

Given the measurement problems in accounting studies, share price studies offer an alternative to measuring the effects of merger. Provided that share prices reflect the underlying economic values of assets, changes in equity values will properly capture expected changes in the economic profitability of the firm. Notwithstanding the substantial empirical evidence supporting the efficiency of the stock market, efficiency is still a controversial proposition (see Summers (1986)). Furthermore, stock market prices reflect both current levels of profitability and anticipated changes. As a result, it is difficult to disentangle expectations from realizations.

Even if share prices do not properly anticipate changes in the profitability of assets, it may still be possible to make statements about whether mergers add value to shareholder wealth. However, it would not be possible to claim that these changes in shareholder wealth reflect changes in the underlying profitability of the firm's assets associated with the merger. In this study, we rely on share price data.

Results

Table 3.7 reports value changes around the bid month for Commission referrals (bid month is month zero). For all Commission referrals, average value changes in target firms are 15 per cent in the bid month and 26 per cent over the six-month period. These are somewhat lower than Franks and Harris's (1989) estimates of target value changes in mergers generally, but are still significantly positive, suggesting that the market does place value on the prospective merger. At 20 per cent, initial value gains to targets are lower for bids ultimately rejected than those accepted (32 per cent). This pattern of gains around the bid month may result because the market is, at least in part, successful in discriminating between bids that are likely to be referred to and rejected by the Commission and those that are not. For example, suppose a merger would produce a £1 million value gain if the market knew it would be consummated. The value gain at the bid would, however, be less than £1 million and could be approximated as the product of the £1 million and the perceived probability of the merger taking place. Thus the lower bid month gains realized in our sample may reflect perceptions of possible Commission rejection and hence lower probabilities of an actual takeover.

Table 3.7. Bid value changes to shareholders in mergers referred to the Commission in the announcement month

	Bid month value changes		6-month (−4 to +1) value changes		Percentage of firms with bid month value increases	
	Target (%)	Bidder (%)	Target (%)	Bidder (%)	Target (%)	Bidder (%)
All referrals	15[a]	0	26[a]	1	70	43
Accepted	26[a]	2	32[a]	6	88	50
Rejected	5[a]	−2	20[a]	−1	48	33
Laid aside	14[a]	−1	26[a]	2	68	53

[a] Significantly different from zero at 95% confidence level.

Turning to bidders in Commission referrals, value gains to bids that are ultimately accepted or laid aside appear comparable to those in mergers generally—about zero in the bid month and small positive gains over a six-month period. Given our sample size, these figures are not, however, significantly different from zero. For rejected bids, there are no bidder gains; this again suggests market anticipation of Commission referral and rejection. In general, Table 3.7 shows that proposed mergers eventually referred to the Commission are viewed at the bid date as value-creating for shareholders. However, the market's capitalization of those gains is likely to be attenuated by the perception of a relatively high probability of the mergers not taking place (compared with those mergers that are not referred).

To see how OFT and Commission decisions affect shareholder value, we examined value changes in the referral and report months, with the results shown in Table 3.8. In all categories, value gains are eroded on the referral date by approximately 8 per cent to targets and 1 per cent to bidders. There is significant further erosion to targets when the bid is rejected (–9 per cent in the report month) and a small positive (though statistically insignificant) gain to the target upon acceptance. Value changes to bidders are small in both the referral and report months and are generally not significantly different from zero.

Table 3.8. Value changes on referral and report

	Value changes in referral month		Value changes in report month	
	Target (%)	Bidder (%)	Target (%)	Bidder (%)
All referrals	–8[a]	–1	–3[a]	1
Accepted	–9[a]	–1	2	2
Rejected	–8[a]	0	–9[a]	1
Laid aside	–9[a]	–2	(No report)	

[a] Significantly different from zero at 95% confidence level.

There are two possible interpretations of our results for rejected mergers. The first is that a value-enhancing merger has been rejected, and the costs of the rejection by the Commission are borne by the shareholders of the target company. The second is that the merger was not value-enhancing and the loss to the target is simply the disappearance of (an undeserved) bid premium. The latter explanation is not easy to sustain, however, because if it held, we would expect to see value losses to bidders in the bid month. In a merger that is not value-enhancing, a target's gain should be equal to a bidder's loss. However, in Table 3.7 we do not find any appreciable losses to bidders around the bid month. The evidence thus indicates a cost to shareholders of Commission deliberations and rejections—a cost that falls upon target shareholders.

A difficulty in measuring value changes in Commission referrals and rejections is that information about a merger is revealed by a series of events rather than by one single event. In Table 3.9, we report an esti-mate of the entire effect of the three events (bid, referral, and report) for the period from twelve months prior to the report date, through to one month thereafter (a total of fourteen months). Given lags between bid and report dates, this corresponds to a beginning date for our analysis, on average, four months prior to the bid date.

Table 3.9. Value changes over whole inquiry

	Average value changes through report date (−12 to +1)	
	Target (%)	Bidder (%)
Commission accepted	38[a]	6
Commission rejected	9[a]	−6

[a] Significantly different from zero at 95% confidence level.

The results show markedly different patterns based upon the Commission's decision. For Commission acceptances, as expected, value increases arise as the result of the consummated bid. Furthermore, these value changes are quite comparable to value gains in successful mergers generally. In contrast, Commission rejections ultimately erode a large part of value gains initially manifested at the bid stage. The 9 per cent figure for target shareholders in rejections is well below the bid premiums measured in Table 3.7; furthermore, half of the rejected targets experi-enced value losses over the fourteen-month period. Since a large part of the initial value gain is eroded, at least part of the merger benefits are likely to be unique to the merger (and allocational in the Grossman–Hart sense). However, partial erosion suggests that some part of the antici-pated merger benefits are not unique—either because the benefits are acquisitional or because other companies are expected subsequently to bid for the target.

We have argued that erosion of value gains in Commission rejections is a sign that the perceived benefits are unique to merging and that those benefits derive from changes in real resource allocation. Evidence on value changes in failed bids provides an interesting comparison. It would be logical for managers and shareholders to terminate merger plans if an alternative to the proposed merger provided a superior means of reaping the merger benefits. In such a case, despite the failed bid, we would not expect an erosion of value.

Studying failed bids in the US, Bradley, Desai, and Kim (1983) conclude that targets in unsuccessful bids do not show an erosion of value when the bid fails; however, the result holds only when the target is acquired by another bidder. Bradley *et al.* conclude that such a pattern implies that merger benefits are unique to merging but not necessarily unique to a specific merger. In cases when the target is not subsequently taken over (about one-quarter of the US sample), all value gains are eroded within two to four years following the bid.

Though limited, UK evidence also shows a persistence of value gains in failed bids generally. For a sample of 60 failed bids supplied to us by an investment banking house (for the period 1981–4), we found no erosion of initial value gains in the ten months following the bid. We did not, however, trace whether a firm was subsequently acquired. Indeed, part of our sample is too recent to test for a subsequent acquisition.

Commission rejections appear different from failed bids generally, supporting the notion that in Commission rejections, part of the merger benefits are more likely to be unique to the particular merger.

Our results suggest that mergers referred to the Commission are anticipated to be value-creating to shareholders, with essentially all gains accruing to target shareholders. For Commission acceptances, the Commission imposes costs on shareholders in terms of time delays and value reductions due to uncertainty about the final disposition of the case.

When a favourable report is released, however, shareholders ultimately reap value gains comparable to those in successful mergers generally. In contrast, Commission rejections lead to erosion of part of the value gains estimated around the initial bid. This value erosion is different from the pattern for failed bids generally, which suggests that many of the merger benefits anticipated in Commission rejections require a merger and are not captured by independent action on the part of the target. This would be consistent with mergers motivated by planned reallocations of real resources, such as exercise of market power or achievement of economies of scale. What is clear is that Commission rejections impose costs to shareholders in the form of forgone benefits. This is an expected outcome if Commission rejections are based on neo-classical analysis of the effects of anti-competitive behaviour.

Indeed, there is some evidence that the Monopolies Commission had some limited success in eroding the dominance of some companies that were investigated in the period 1959–73 and became subjects of dominant firm or 'complex monopoly' reports (see Shaw and Simpson (1986)). Such an erosion of market position presumably resulted in losses to shareholders. It is beyond the scope of this chapter to measure the net benefits to the public resulting from Commission actions.

4. PUBLIC POLICY TOWARDS MERGERS

The results of the previous section of this chapter suggest that the current policy of investigating mergers is costly to at least one party—the shareholders. Of course the benefit of the Commission's actions is the deterrence of increased market power which certain mergers would produce. Over and above the costs isolated in our empirical section, there may be additional costs to the economy in general, purely because of the possibility of an investigation. The source of the costs is that an investigation reduces the incentive for bidders to gather and process information about prospective acquisitions, if the possibility of investigation increases the likelihood that private information collected by the bidder will be revealed to other potential bidders.

Furthermore, the delays accompanying an investigation (regardless of the outcome) may permit other companies to become bidders, thereby reducing the prospective profits of first processing the information. Such free-rider problems will discourage mergers where the benefits of the merger are either informational or require resource reallocations (for example, the target management is inefficient) not unique to one bidder. The potential for such free-rider problems may be large since share price evidence in both the US and UK suggests that merger benefits are usually not unique to one bidder.

However, due to the relatively small number of investigations by the Commission and the evidence presented here suggesting that Commission referrals are more likely to involve some benefits unique to the merging firms, current Commission activity is not likely to create large disincentives for gathering information.

Drastic changes in the Commission's mandate may, however, lead to such disincentives. Concerns about the levels of merger activity are widespread and are not simply confined to those of market power. Some politicians have suggested a much stronger investigative role for the Commission, where the onus of proof that merger benefits exist would fall upon the bidder. If a new policy were implemented which changed the criteria for referral and increased the number of investigations, the incentives of bidders to gather and process information could be much reduced. Thus, some mergers which are profitable to shareholders and possibly to the economy would not take place.

In this section, we describe some of the wider concerns expressed about the level and motivation of merger activity. We try to trace possible malfunctions in markets (financial or managerial) which form the basis of these concerns, with the objective of finding institutional solutions. Such solutions may be preferable to a more wide-ranging regulatory role for the Commission envisaged by some parties, where the prospect of investigation may inhibit worthwhile mergers.

The Merger Market when Financial and Managerial Labour Markets are Well Functioning

If managerial labour markets are well functioning, managers will be motivated (by both pecuniary and non-pecuniary benefits) to work in shareholder interests. Further, in such a sublime state, equity market prices will give unbiased estimates of value gains to shareholders. As a result, mergers would only be pursued by management if they were value-creating to shareholders. Multiple bidders might compete for a target firm, but we would not expect to observe target management opposing value-creating bids.

In such a stylized world, there would still be concerns about merger activity. Shareholder gains in a merger could be a direct result of those anti-competitive effects which raise product prices and distort resource allocation. Since mergers could also be motivated by cost-reducing measures, there might also be concerns about effects on non-shareholder interest groups regarding lost jobs or stranded customers or suppliers. Such non-shareholder concerns might be broadened to include regional issues of concerns about the aggregate concentration of economic power and its effects on the political process.

It is precisely these sorts of concerns that are appropriately dealt with by a body such as the Commission, which applies a social calculus to weigh costs of merger. It has responsibility to assess anti-competitive effects as well as to weigh factors such as employment or regional concerns. However, the case for the Commission's giving high weight to job losses as a reason for obstructing a take-over may be limited. Given international competition, attempts for short-term job security may come at long-term costs of wholesale employment loss if British industry were supplanted by foreign competitors. It is perhaps for this reason that so few mergers have been prohibited on these grounds.[5]

[5] A suggestion often made as a means of addressing non-shareholder interest is to make managers responsible to a board of directors that includes representatives of various

Certainly in the 1960s, there was a great concern that mergers would increase the rate of concentration and thereby reduce competition (see Opie (1982)). Such concerns led in the UK to the passage of the 1965 Monopolies and Mergers Act. There were similar concerns in the US. However, existing legislation and the size of the resulting institutions were simply not designed to act as a 'public conscience' for aggregate merger activity. Moreover, in recent years, governments in both countries have been more pro-business and less interventionist than have previous administrations.

Despite recent increases in the number of Commission referrals and investigations, it is probable that neither the Monopolies and Mergers Commission in the UK nor the Federal Trade Commission and Justice Department in the US have significantly dented the merger boom in recent years. Greater international competition has not only reduced the fears of increased concentration, but has sustained the impression that UK firms must grow larger if they are to compete internationally.

The previous discussion does not imply complacency over mergers and competition. Rather, it simply recognizes that much stronger anti-competitive legislation against mergers would be unlikely to reduce the level of merger activity substantially.

Implications for Policy when Financial Markets are not Well Functioning

The *Financial Times* (3 July 1986) has stated that 'Takeover bids and bull markets go hand in hand'. This is a controversial proposition since there is some empirical evidence that the level of merger activity is not correlated with stock prices (see Geroski (1984)). However, both practitioners and academics remain unconvinced, if not sceptical, about the lack of a relationship. We discuss in this section some theories about how financial markets may motivate mergers and what concerns this motivation may give rise to.

One model, described by King (1986), suggests that merger activity has historically been correlated with stock market prices due to a tax-induced distortion in the pricing of financial assets. King claims that this distortion arises from the extra tax burden on corporate income compared with personal income, a burden that increases with rising corporate profits and resulting bull markets. However, the Finance Act of 1984 has reduced this tax wedge in the imputation system. In effect, the 1987 corporate tax rate of 35 per cent and the income tax rate (for standard rate taxpayers) of 27 per cent imply that the additional tax burden on corporate income

constituencies including employees. Effective working of such a scheme has difficulties, however, since small board representation may have little ultimate effect if the non-shareholder interest is always outvoted.

is now 8 per cent only. As a result, King's argument predicts that merger booms are a thing of the past, at least those motivated by tax distortions in financial markets. In this respect, the source of a market malfunction has been removed.[6]

A second source of market malfunction will occur if markets mis-price equities. If that mis-pricing provides an incentive to merge, then it is a matter of public concern, since such a malfunction would disrupt the role of mergers in allocating resources. If a significant proportion of mergers were motivated by inefficiencies in the capital market, then very different regulatory policies from those charged to the Commission would be sought.

Mis-pricing may occur because it may be necessary for management to retain valuable information on the economic value of real assets if its release to shareholders would result in a deterioration of the company's competitive position (see Myers and Majluf (1984) for a discussion). If some equities are overpriced, this may provide the management of those companies with an incentive to finance acquisitions of properly priced companies with their overpriced equity. Indeed, the opportunities to acquire may encourage management or its agent to release information which would lead to overpricing. Until recently, UK rules have severely restricted the sale of equity to anyone other than existing shareholders, and thus the only method of selling equity to external or new share-holders was through an acquisition.[7] Shareholders of the prospective acquisition may not recognize the overpricing, if they cannot distinguish between equity-financed mergers motivated by mis-pricing and those motivated by, say, capital structure reasons.

Low-cost remedies for such mis-pricing are difficult to construct. One drastic one would be to force companies to finance mergers with cash only. If companies did not have sufficient liquidity, they would have to issue equity to their shareholders. To the extent that current shareholders purchased new equity, there would no longer be an incentive to issue overpriced equity to benefit existing shareholders. Further, such a market discipline would require shareholders to vote with their cash. There is an

[6] We note that King's argument depends on strong assumptions about the pricing of assets in the corporate and non-corporate sectors. For example, King assumes companies cannot be liquidated and reincorporated on a regular basis to reduce the burden of corporate taxes. Important additional assumptions are also required, and we refer the interested reader to the original paper.

[7] Even though UK companies may now issue new equity to shareholders (via, say, a placing) this may not remove entirely the incentives to acquire to capitalize on overpriced equity. First, such fund-raising activities require a motive, and the issuing management could hardly declare the motive to be 'to sell overpriced equity'. Second, higher levels of corporate income may make it more profitable to acquire assets already in the corporate sector (via merger) than to raise cash to purchase newly produced assets or financial assets (see King (1986)).

impression gained from some market participants that shareholders have a smaller incentive to express disapproval when management is using internally generated funds. However, such a new measure would add to the transaction costs of merging.

Mis-pricing may also create incentives for take-over based on under-pricing of potential targets. Bidders may be performing the role of arbit-rageurs buying up underpriced securities. If such take-overs are 'acquisitional' in the Grossman–Hart sense and provide incentives for gathering and processing information, such mergers may provide benefits in the form of superior information flows to financial markets. The Grossman–Hart argument depends, however, on financial markets' prop-erly pricing securities, given the information available. If financial mar-kets are not efficient in pricing equities, take-overs of 'underpriced' securities may well produce undesirable effects. The management of would-be targets may forgo profitable investment opportunities or cut research and development if it is perceived that the market does not properly price such opportunities. If financial markets were well function-ing, management time devoted to mergers may be well spent, but if there is substantial mis-pricing, mergers (and attempts to avoid take-over) may lead to dissipation of long-term economic benefits.

Remedies for various sources of mis-pricing are beyond the scope of this chapter.[8] They are certainly made more difficult by the lack of theory as to why such mis-pricing should occur and the lack of empirical evi-dence of its sign and size.

Our final concern about the operation of the financial market concerns the costs of transactions incurred in the merger process. Kay (1986) has estimated that the annual fees paid to third parties in the merging process might be £500 million. The DTI data suggest that the value of acquisi-tions in 1985 is about £7 billion. Simple arithmetic therefore suggests that the costs of merging may average about 7 per cent of acquisition value; and this excludes the cost of management time expended by the merging parties. Some examples of costs incurred in particular mergers suggest that Kay's figure may be conservative for 1986. Argyll's unsuccessful bid

---

[8] One possible remedy is to introduce rules and laws that delay the speed of take-over, the rationale being that such procedures give financial markets more time to digest impor-tant information. However, we have already referred to the disincentive effects of delays. A more drastic step, proposed by some in the US, would be to change the traditional link between share ownership and voting rights, for example, by requiring a shareholder to have owned shares for a certain period of time before voting rights can be exercised. The intent of such measures, at least in part, is to delegate authority to those shareholders with 'long-term' horizons. The assumption is that financial markets are influenced too much by short-term factors and too little by the long term. As a result, management may have incentives to take measures which increase reported profits at the expense of longer-term profitability. The difficulty with an approach that limits voting rights is that it may also insulate current management from desirable financial market discipline.

for Distillers may have resulted in £47 million in fees, with 75 per cent being paid for underwriting fees for the separate bids. Some of these costs (£13.9 million) were offset by profits on the sale of Argyll's share stake, but this should not be used to justify the transaction costs. In another contested take-over, Dixons spent £12 million in its unsuccessful bid for Woolworths, while the latter spent £20 million in repulsing the bid. (All these figures are taken from the *Financial Times*.)

The question as to whether these costs are excessive depends upon several considerations. The most important is, what alternatives are there to merging as a way of obtaining the benefits that would arise? If many of these bids are simply vehicles for removing weak and inefficient management, then it seems very expensive to spend millions or even tens of millions to remove the chairman or part of the board of directors. It is like buying an entire football team when only one player is wanted.

We do, however, have several cautions regarding the previous argument. First, the little evidence we have suggests that a large part of these transaction costs occur in hostile bids which account for only a small fraction of acquisition activity. Second, the transactions costs we have described consist of two very different kinds of costs. One, such as advertising and fees to merchant banks for managing the take-over process, are pure costs to the economy as well as to the company. However, underwriting fees which may account for a large proportion of total costs are of a very different nature. Underwriting fees are made for the purchase of short-term financial assets (they are 'side-bets' on the future price of the acquiring company's stock made between underwriter and company). Such fees should not be classified as costs to the system; rather, they consist of the purchase of insurance which changes the risk borne by the company.[9] If these risks are properly priced, then they are no more of a cost to society than the purchase of insurance against fire risk. It is the fire risk that is the source of the cost, not the insurance. In this respect, the estimate of £500 million attributed to the cost of merging may be an excessive estimate of the costs to the system of the merging process. It could certainly be undesirable to inhibit merger activity in general because of these high costs, if most are incurred in only a few hostile bids.

Internal versus External Disciplines on Managers: Alternatives to Acquisitions

Many authors, for example Mueller (1969), have questioned the ability of shareholders to monitor and control the conduct of management. They

[9] The cost of underwriting has been analysed as the purchase of a put option by the company from the underwriter. Marsh (1980) has raised questions as to whether underwriting fees have been properly priced.

have argued that, as a result, management is able to follow policies that maximize the wealth and status of the managers rather than that of the shareholders.[10] According to this view, many take-overs would dissipate shareholder wealth as acquiring firm managements overbid for targets. However, the weight of US and UK evidence (see Franks and Harris (1989), Jensen and Ruback (1983)) would not support this view.

Starting from similar concerns about shareholders' monitoring of managers, Grossman and Hart (1981) provide a role for the acquisitions market in disciplining management. As described earlier, they argue that where share ownership is widely dispersed, it does not pay individual shareholders to bear the costs of monitoring and gathering information in order to increase the efficiency of management. By separating (and dispersing) ownership and control, a free-rider problem has been created. All shareholders share the benefits if one shareholder disciplines management, but that one shareholder is forced to bear all the costs of so doing. Thus, acquisitions play a pivotal role in the market for corporate control.

What are the alternatives to acquisitions as a disciplining process? One way would be for shareholders to elect a body of professionals to represent them, whose sole purpose would be to monitor the performance of management. In another form, this is surely part of the role of the non-executive director, except that in the UK those directors are usually appointed by, and are responsible to, executive management. It may be that non-executive directors should be appointed by nominating committees directly representing shareholder interests. This form of appointment has been increasingly adopted in the US. The monitoring role performed by non-executive directors does overcome the free-rider problems described earlier; all shareholders now pay for their information processing costs.

The important role played by non-executive directors has been widely discussed in the changes in senior management brought about in companies such as Beechams, STC, and Thorn-EMI. In the US, the Chairman and Chief Executive of Alleghany International recently resigned after public criticism described him as an extravagant and careless executive. An Alleghany shareholder filed a class action lawsuit against the company's directors charging them with 'waste of corporate assets and grossly improper business decisions'. It is of some interest that there are a number of well-known non-executive directors on the Alleghany board. It could be argued that the presence of such directors hastened the disclosures and ultimately the change in top management; alternatively, it may be said that the presence of those non-executive directors did not restrain top management from an apparently excessive lifestyle. It may be that the

[10]   These agency costs have been analysed in a more formal setting by Jensen and Meckling (1976).

role and duties of the non-executive directors should be m
defined, just as is the role of the external auditor. The quest'
however, as to whether the role should be defined by legal a_{pr}
institutions acting collectively, or on a company-by-company basis.

An alternative suggestion to the appointment of non-executive directors
would be for institutions to play a more active role in changing the management of a company. The free-rider problem could be mitigated if institutions formed shareholder groups which would investigate companies
that appear to stumble and falter. As a result, they would play a more
prominent role in the election of directors at shareholder meetings. This
is an interesting alternative, but it requires co-operation among otherwise
competing financial institutions. Furthermore, the skills of portfolio managers may not be suitable for pronouncing on the fitness of incumbent
management. It may be that a prerequisite for more active institutional
shareholders is a somewhat differently educated portfolio manager.[11] As a
result, we suspect that increasing and strengthening the role of the non-
executive director would prove to be the preferred option.

5. CONCLUSION

In this chapter, we have analysed the costs to shareholders that result
from Commission investigations. We show that Commission rejections
lead to substantial erosion of value gains that were capitalized at the bid
date, suggesting that the prospective shareholder benefits involved some
reallocations of real resources unique to merging. The neo-classical economic argument is that the costs of such forgone shareholder benefits are
more than offset by the Commission's deterrence of increased market
power. We suggest that Commission investigations may introduce further
costs in terms of reduced incentives of prospective bidders to investigate
inefficiently run companies. Since the number of companies investigated
by the Commission is small, such disincentives should be similarly small.
However, a much wider role in merger regulation, envisaged by some,
could alter the size of these disincentives.

Concerns about mergers have substantially increased, rising with the
level of merger activity, and these concerns go well beyond the types of
anti-competitive behaviour which may be deterred by the Commission.
As a result, we have examined potential sources of those concerns and

---

[11] Direct stockholder interest may not be the only answer to a more efficient managerial
labour market. It is important that managers' compensation provides an appropriate incentive structure. Therefore, managerial compensation plans should be related more directly to
the profitability of the organization. However, compensation schemes on their own will not
be sufficient if there is little provision for the removal of inadequate management.

158 Julian Franks and Robert Harris

described institutional changes that may be appropriate. The problem is to find possible sources of market malfunction and, where possible, correct them rather than to turn immediately to governmental mechanisms for counterbalancing such malfunctions.

Appendix 3.1.
Estimation of value gains

To implement our measure of value gain, for any company j we construct 'abnormal returns' calculated as:

$$AR_{jt} = R_{jt} - C_{jt}$$

where R_{jt} is the realized return in month t (dividends plus capital gains) and C_{jt} is the control return. These abnormal returns are estimates of value gains. To focus on the effects of a particular event, we define time relative to an event date. For example, $t = 0$ can be defined as the bid month, the month of referral, or the reporting month. Methods of estimating control returns have been widely studied in the finance literature. Here we use the so-called market model where control returns are defined as:

$$C_{jt} = \alpha_j + \beta_j\, RM_t$$

where RM_t is the return on the equally weighted index of all stocks covered in LSPD and α and β are parameters estimated by the regressing R_{jt} on RM_t for the sixty-month period beginning at $t = -71$. The market model thus controls for general market movements, adjusting for both company risk (β) and the company's performance over and above the market (α) prior to the event being studied. Brown and Warner (1980, 1985) provide extensive discussions of 'event study' methodology. For a more complete discussion as applied to mergers, see Franks and Harris (1989). Average values for target firms are $\alpha = 0.004$ and $\beta = 0.93$. For bidding firms, the average values are 0.006 and 0.99 respectively.

We also test the sensitivity of our results to two alternative methods. The first controls only for market movements ($C_{jt} = RM_t$) for all companies. The second is an empirical adaptation of the capital asset pricing model as described in Franks and Harris (1989). Our conclusions are not materially affected by the choice of model. We use continuously compounded (log) returns in all cases.

To assess returns for a portfolio of companies (for example, target firms when there is a Commission rejection) over a number of months, we calculated company-specific, multi-period returns by summing AR_{jt} over time. These returns are then averaged across companies into portfolio cumulative returns ($PCAR$) defined as:

$$PCAR_t = \frac{1}{n} \sum_{j=1}^{n} \sum_{i=t_b}^{t} AR_{jt}$$

where n is the number of companies in the portfolio ($j = 1, \ldots, n$), and the cumulation process begins at time t_b and includes those monthly abnormal returns that are observed up to and including month t. These portfolio returns ($PCAR_t$) thus measure the average excess (or short-fall) in shareholder returns relative to the market model bench-mark, which estimates what shareholder returns would have been if the company's returns had maintained their normal return relationship to equity markets in general.

We have considered two statistical tests for the significance of $PCAR_t$. The first uses a t-statistic calculated as $T = PCAR_t/s$ where s is calculated as

$$\{\sqrt{(t_b - t + 1)}\}\ SD$$

and SD is the standard deviation of one-month $PCARs$ for a time period assumed to be unaffected by merger (in this case the period used to estimate the market model). The second significance test is non-parametric and uses the percentage of the multi-period, company-specific returns that are positive. For a detailed discussion of these and other statistical tests, see Franks and Harris (1989) and the references therein. Significance levels in the text (indicated by an asterisk) are determined using the t-statistic (two-tailed tests for 95 per cent confidence level).

To test the significance of differences between value gains for different groups of companies, we use a t-statistic calculated as

$$(M_1 - M_2) / \sqrt{(\sigma_1^2 + \sigma_2^2)}$$

where M denotes a cell mean, subscripts 1 and 2 the two portfolios, and s is defined as above.

In ten cases, bid and referral months coincided. This would have the effect of biasing downwards our estimate of gains at the bid date (since some bid month returns would also contain negative reactions to referrals) and biasing downwards in absolute value our estimate of losses at the referral date. Where possible, we estimated the effects of such contamination. The losses at referral date were above 10 to 11 per cent for each of the three categories of referrals, and gains at the bid date increased only modestly. The adjustment thus changed none of our basic conclusions.

REFERENCES

Barnes, P. A. (1984), 'The effect of a merger on the share price of the attacker, revisited', *Accounting and Business Research*, **15**, 45–9.

Bradley, M., Desai, A., and Kim, E. (1983), 'The rationale behind interfirm tender offer: information or synergy', *Journal of Financial Economics*, **11**, 183–206.

Brown, S. J., and Warner, J. B. (1980), 'Measuring security price performance, *Journal of Financial Economics*, **8**, 205–58.

—— —— (1985), 'Using daily stock returns: the case of event studies', *Journal of Financial Economics*, **14**, 3–31.

Cosh, A. D., Hughes, A., and Singh, A. (1980), 'The causes and effects of takeovers in the UK: an empirical investigation for the late 1960s at the micro-economic level', in D. C. Mueller (ed.), *The Determinants and Effects of Mergers*, Cambridge, Mass.: Oelschlager, Gunn and Hain.

Dodds, J. C., and Quek, J. P. (1985), 'Effect of mergers on the share price movement of the acquiring firms: a UK study', *Journal of Business Finance and Accounting*, **12**, 285–96.

Firth, M. (1979), 'The profitability of takeovers and mergers', *Economic Journal*, **89**, 316–28.

—— (1980), 'Takeovers, shareholder returns and the theory of the firm', *Quarterly Journal of Economics*, **94**, 235–60.

Franks, J. R., Broyles, J. E., and Hecht, M. J. (1977), 'An industry study of the profitability of mergers in the United Kingdom', *Journal of Finance*, **32**, 1513–25.

—— and Harris, R. S. (1989), 'Shareholder wealth effects of corporate takeovers: the UK experience, 1955–1985', *Journal of Financial Economics*, August, 225–49.

—— —— and Mayer, C. (1988), 'The role of medium of exchange in the US and the UK', in A. J. Auerbach (ed.), *Corporate Takeovers: Causes and Consequences*, National Bureau of Economic Research, Chicago: University of Chicago Press.

Geroski, P. A. (1984), 'On the relationship between aggregate merger activity and the stock market', *European Economic Review*, **25**, 223–33.

Grossman, S. J., and Hart, O. D. (1981), 'The allocational role of takeover bids in situations of asymmetric information', *Journal of Finance*, Papers and Proceedings, **36**, 253–70.

Jensen, M. C., and Meckling, W. H. (1976), 'Theory of the firm: managerial behaviour, agency costs and ownership structure', *Journal of Financial Economics*, **3**, 305–60.

—— and Ruback, R. S. (1983), 'The market for corporate control: the scientific evidence, *Journal of Financial Economics*, **11**, 5–50.

Kay, J. A. (1976), 'Accountants, too, could be happy in a golden age: the accountant's rate of return and the internal rate of return', *Oxford Economic Papers*, **28**, 447–60.

—— (1986), 'The role of mergers', IFS Working Paper 94, July.

King, M. A. (1986), 'Takeovers, taxes and the stock market', mimeo, London School of Economics.

Marsh, P. (1980), 'Valuation of underwriting agreements for UK rights issues', *Journal of Finance*, **35**, 693–716.

Meeks, G. (1977), *Disappointing Marriage: A Study of the Gains from Merger*, Cambridge: Cambridge University Press.

Mueller, D. C. (1969), 'A theory of conglomerate mergers', *Quarterly Journal of Economics*, **83**, 643–59.

Myers, S., and Majluf, N. (1984), 'Corporate financing and investment decisions when firms have information that investors do not have', *Journal of Financial Economics*, **13**, 187–221.

Office of Fair Trading (1985), *Mergers: A Guide to the Procedures under the Fair Trading Act 1973*, London: HMSO.

Opie, R. (1982), 'Merger policy in the United Kingdom', in K. J. Hopt (ed.), *European Merger Control: Legal and Economic Analyses on Multinational Enterprises*, volume 1, Berlin: Walter de Gruyter.

Shaw, R., and Simpson, P. (1986), 'The persistence of monopoly: an investigation of the effectiveness of the UK Monopolies Commission', *Journal of Industrial Economics*, **34**, 355–72.

Singh, A. (1971), *Takeovers: Their Relevance to the Stock Market and the Theory of the Firm*, Cambridge: Cambridge University Press.

—— (1975), 'Takeovers, economic "natural selection", and the theory of the firm: evidence from the post-war UK experience', *Economic Journal*, **85**, 497–515.

Solomon, E., and Laya, J. (1967), 'Measurement of company profitability: some systematic errors in accounting rate of return', in A. A. Robichek (ed.), *Financial Research and Management Decisions*, New York: John Wiley.

Summers, L. H. (1986), 'Does the stock market rationally reflect fundamental values?', *Journal of Finance*, **41**, 591–601.

4

European Capital Markets and Corporate Control

JULIAN FRANKS* AND COLIN MAYER†

1. INTRODUCTION

This chapter is about capital markets and corporate control. It is concerned with the way in which capital markets exert control over the management and operations of firms. Corporate control is generally associated with take-overs. In the UK and the US take-overs are regarded as a central function of stock markets. The take-over process acts as a discipline on firms allowing control to be transferred from inefficient to efficient management and encouraging a convergence of interests between management and shareholders.

Elsewhere in Europe, less emphasis is placed on the role of take-overs in changing corporate control. Stock markets are often much smaller and their role is not perceived as being one of disciplining management. Instead, banks, families, and sometimes the State have controlling shareholdings that impede the take-over process. There are therefore different methods of changing corporate control in Europe.

The relation between capital markets and corporate control is of particular significance to Europe. There are pronounced cultural differences regarding the control of firms. Hostile take-overs are anathema in several countries and the prospect of them becoming more commonplace is regarded with little relish. However, it is widely thought that the integration of capital markets is likely to see UK-style securities markets and take-overs dominate continental European systems.

This development is being encouraged by regulatory changes being proposed by the European Commission. These changes will have the effect of

* National Westminster Bank Professor of Finance at the London Business School.
† Professor of Economics and Finance at Warwick Business School.

This chapter is based on a paper entitled 'Capital markets and corporate control: a study of France, Germany and the UK' which was published in *Economic Policy*, No. 10, Spring 1990. We are grateful to Nick Carrick, Myriam Soria, and Theodore Schofner for assistance in the revision of this chapter. Further acknowledgements can be found in the original paper.
This chapter is part of an ESRC-funded project, No. W102251003, on Capital Markets, Corporate Governance, and the Market for Corporate Control.

introducing take-over rules in Europe similar to the UK's Takeover Code. There will be provisions relating to disclosure of share interests, equality of treatment of shareholders, requirements to make full bids once certain shareholdings have been exceeded, and timetables for bids. The objective of this regulation is to establish common rules for effecting take-overs.

Longer-term goals are still more far-reaching. The European Commission regards competition in the market for corporate control as an extension of competition in product, labour, and capital markets. Regulatory and institutional impediments to the take-over process are perceived to be a distortion of the competitive process and a violation of the principle of level playing-fields. The dictum that companies benefit from being exposed to take-over threats receives a large measure of support.

Is this correct? Should an extension of the take-over process from the UK to continental Europe be welcomed? Is harmonization of take-over codes desirable? What is the implication of harmonization for the operation of different countries' financial systems?

This chapter compares the relation between capital markets and corporate control in France, Germany, and the UK. Its primary focus is the relation between ownership and control changes. It begins in Section 2 by documenting the level of take-over activity and controlling ownership changes in the three countries. It is the first attempt of which we are aware to evaluate the international comparability of take-over data.

The results point to differences in the level of take-overs and controlling share stakes across countries. However, the main difference that emerges is not so much one of scale as of form—the extent to which take-overs are contested. Section 3 reports the level of executive control changes in a comprehensive sample of contested bids over £10 million in the UK in 1986 and a matched sample of uncontested bids in the same year. It finds that the effects of the two classes of take-over on executive control are quite different.

Take-overs are not the only form of ownership change. Buy-outs and buy-ins have become prominent over the last few years and Section 4 compares the level of buy-in and buy-out activity in the UK with that in the other two countries. Again it finds significant differences. Section 4 also records the results of a press search of reported executive dismissals in the three countries over the first six months of 1988. It points to a higher level of executive changes in the UK than elsewhere. Equally interestingly, a substantial proportion of these changes are not associated with take-overs. Instead, they are often the product of boardroom and shareholder disputes.

There is an important caveat to this. A study of three cases of corporate restructurings in Germany finds a high level of executive changes. Control changes do occur in response to corporate failures in Germany. However, they may be more limited at other times than in the UK.

The most obvious explanation for these differences is regulation. Company law, competition policy, stock exchange rules, and labour law all bear on the extent to which ownership and control changes occur. Section 5 considers differences in relevant national regulations; it focuses on regulations pertaining to the rights of employees, managers, and shareholders. The differences are illustrated in Appendix 4.1 with a case study of control changes in each of the three countries.

Regulation can explain much of the difference in control and ownership changes across countries. The significance of regulation depends on the extent to which it interferes with the process by which poor managerial performance (what this chapter terms *managerial failure*) is corrected. Jensen (1989) argues that regulation in the US created a passive investor class. The Glass-Steagall Act of 1934 prevented banks from taking equity positions in other companies and thereby restrained their involvement in corporate activities. According to this view, the golden age of the active investor was destroyed by government edict. Hostile take-overs were a response to those regulatory restrictions.

According to Jensen, regulation has interfered with the process of correcting managerial failure. There is an alternative view, namely that regulation, corporate control, and the structure of capital markets all reflect more fundamental considerations. These concern the nature of the contractual and implicit relations between different parties to a firm, in particular investors, managers, and employees. We argue that the existence of take-overs has implications not only for the correction of managerial failure but also for the types of contracts that can be sustained.

The advantage of take-overs is that they assist in the correction of certain classes of managerial failure that are otherwise difficult to rectify. Section 6 contrasts different forms of managerial failure, and argues that take-overs may be necessary to correct some of them. To that extent, a UK market for corporate control may have advantages over Continental systems where family, bank, or State control is widespread.

On the other hand, take-overs undermine contractual relations between investors, managers, and employees. Long-term contracts are hard to sustain and reputations for maintaining informal arrangements easy to extinguish. As a consequence, managers and employees may be denied the benefits of their firm-specific investments by changes in ownership. Faced with this risk, employees may be unwilling to incur costs of investment in firm-specific training and managers may be unwilling to forgo current earnings for long-term R & D projects.

Financial markets in which take-overs are prevalent may therefore suffer from 'short-termism'—an inability to sustain long-term investments. Short-termism may not be so much a product of the mis-pricing of assets, as has frequently been suggested, but more a reflection of contractual failures in securities markets in part brought on by the take-over process. According to this view, short-termism is a feature of investments in firm-specific assets that have a low resale value outside the firm. Thus it will be less prevalent in the development of oil fields and property sites than in R & D and training.

One piece of evidence in favour of this proposition comes from an examination of the behaviour of the three cases of corporate restructuring mentioned above. Each displays a rather striking characteristic by UK standards: an increase in R & D and the maintenance of investment expenditures in the face of acute financial distress.

The conclusion of the chapter is that there is a trade-off between different methods of correcting managerial failure. Take-overs may result in a higher level of managerial correction but only at the expense of long-term investment. Therefore, there can be no presumption that the UK take-over market is superior to the bank-dominated capital market of Germany. If so, as Section 7 concludes, without strong empirical evidence, proposals to harmonize on a UK-style market for corporate control may be premature.

2. TAKE-OVERS AND PURCHASES OF SHARE STAKES IN FRANCE, GERMANY, AND THE UK

This section examines levels of ownership changes associated with purchases of shares in France, Germany, and the UK. Share purchases may involve full or partial acquisitions of issued capital. UK figures record both full take-overs and majority stakes of more than 50 per cent of issued capital. However, majority stakes are rare in the UK because of take-over code rules compelling buyers to make full bids when shareholdings reach 30 per cent. Tender offers are conditional on acceptance by 90 per cent of shareholdings. This level is chosen so that any shares not tendered may be compulsorily acquired under section 209 of the Companies Act. In contrast, French and German statistics include purchases of minority as well as majority stakes. Full acquisitions of company shares are relatively uncommon.

Table 4.1 reports domestic and foreign take-overs by UK firms over the period 1969 to 1988 as recorded by the Department of Trade and Industry (DTI). A commercial organization, AMDATA, reports a higher level of take-over activity of 503, 814, and 1,277 bids in 1985, 1986, and

1987 respectively. The difference between the two data sources is in part explained by the exclusion of take-overs in the financial sector in the DTI data and in part by a larger number of bids for private firms in AMDATA.[1]

Table 4.1 confirms the large waves in take-over activity that have been previously noted by others.[2] According to the DTI, at both its peaks in 1972 and 1988, take-overs amounted to around 4 per cent of the capital stock of the UK corporate sector measured at either replacement cost or market value. While there has been substantial growth in take-over activity over the last five years, there were actually fewer transactions during this period than the previous wave from 1969 to 1973. The rise in values can be attributed to a small number of large acquisitions; for example, in 1988 the largest five take-overs accounted for more than one-third of the annual value of take-over activity. On average over the entire twenty-year period, take-overs amounted to 1.6 per cent of the replacement cost and 2 per cent of the market value of the UK capital stock.

Table 4.2 reports the number of partial and full acquisitions of German companies and purchases of overseas companies by German firms as recorded by the Federal Cartel Office. There are no data on values. To improve comparability with UK data, purchases of assets (as distinct from shares) and joint ventures, both of which are included in the Federal Cartel Office figures, have been excluded. Joint ventures are shown separately in column 4.

Column 1 of Tables 4.1 and 4.2 are the most comparable estimates of control changes in the UK and Germany. According to these, the number of partial and full German acquisitions in 1988 was about two-thirds of that in the UK. However, comparability is impaired by the inclusion of overseas acquisitions in the German numbers. It is estimated that these

[1] The AMDATA figures are broken down as follows:

Bids	1985	1986	1987
Public	92	155	136
Private	407	639	1,124
Foreign	4	20	17
TOTAL	503	814	1,277

Another source of data on public bids is delistings from the London stock market. Delistings attributable to take-overs were as follows: 58 in 1985; 178 in 1986; and 165 in 1987 (figures are taken from the London Share Price Data Bank). With the exception of 1985, there is a close association between AMDATA and stock market delistings. Some of the discrepancy in 1985 may be due to the fact that delistings are recorded in the year of consummation not the announcement of bids. Private bids account for 407, 639, and 1,124 bids in 1985, 1986, and 1987 respectively. Foreign bids amounted to 4, 20 and 17 bids in the three years. In all cases, data reported refer to completed bids and exclude unsuccessful bids.

[2] See e.g. King (1989).

Table 4.1 Take-overs of UK companies, 1969–1988

Year	Number[a,b]	Value[c] (£bn)	Value as[d] a proportion of replacement cost of capital stock (%)	Value as[e] a proportion of market capitalization of securities (%)
1969	744	0.97	2.8	2.0
1970	614	1.00	2.9	2.3
1971	620	0.74	1.7	1.8
1972	938	2.35	4.5	3.7
1973	951	1.06	1.6	1.8
1974	367	0.46	0.6	0.8
1975	200	0.22	0.2	0.6
1976	242	0.35	0.3	0.7
1977	372	0.73	0.6	1.3
1978	441	0.98	0.7	1.5
1979	417	1.47	0.8	1.7
1980	368	1.26	0.6	1.7
1981	327	0.88	0.4	0.9
1982	299	1.40	0.6	1.3
1983	305	1.91	0.8	1.4
1984	398	4.35	1.7	2.4
1985	340	6.30	2.2	2.8
1986	537	12.13	3.9	4.0
1987	905	11.28	3.4	2.7
1988	937	16.87		4.2

[a] All completed domestic mergers and acquisitions. *Source*: Department of Trade and Industry, *Business Monitor MQ7*, 1989. But see note d.

[b] An alternative source of information on acquisitions in the UK is *Acquisitions Monthly* (AM Data):

Year	Number	Value (£bn)
1984	187	3.98
1985	495	7.62
1986	794	15.73
1987	1,260	18.10
1988	1,465	15.84

[c] Figures represent the market value of the consideration paid by the bidder which represent the value of the equity and the publicly traded debt instruments.

[d] This is the replacement cost capital stock of the total UK corporate sector. *Source*: CSO, National Accounts.

[e] The securities include equities, preference, and marketable debt. Bank borrowings are not included, thereby overstating the measure as a proportion of firms' assets.

Table 4.2 Partial and full acquisitions of German companies[a]

Year	(1) Partial and full acquisitions	(2) Majority stakes[b]	(3) = (1) − (2) 100% acquisitions and minority stakes[c,d]	(4) Joint ventures
1980	287	205	82	161
1981	325	237	88	129
1982	261	181	80	183
1983	217	152	65	156
1984	279	202	77	167
1985	372	275	97	178
1986	430	326	104	200
1987	481	357	124	195
1988	616	451	165	283

[a] Includes purchases of German companies and German acquisition of overseas companies.

[b] Majority means in excess of 50%.

[c] Overseas transactions involving joint ventures, majority stakes, and take-overs amount to 8% of the aggregate.

[d] Minority means greater than 25% and less than 50%.

Source: Federal Cartel Office.

account for 18 per cent of total German acquisitions. Furthermore, the data also include minority stakes of between 25 and 50 per cent of the target's capital.

Of more significance than differences in *numbers* are differences in *form* of take-overs in the two countries. First, there are few *full* acquisitions in Germany. Most transactions are purchases of majority stakes rather than full acquisitions. Second, and still more significantly, there have been few overtly *hostile* take-overs.[3] A higher proportion of mergers in Germany appear to be associated with economies of scale considerations than executive control changes. The fact that the German authorities treat joint ventures on a par with mergers is indicative of the function that mergers are seen as performing in Germany.

Table 4.3 reports data on partial and full acquisitions of French firms. In Panel A the number and value of domestic transactions are given for six years from 1983 to 1988. These statistics include management buy-outs, divestments, new issues of shares for assets, assets bought in bankruptcy, and spin-offs and so are not directly comparable with the UK.

---

[3] By hostile we mean a bid opposed by the target's management. The Flick Brothers' acquisition of Feldmuehle-Nobel in 1989 is the first example of a hostile acquisition in Germany. This is discussed in Section 5 and Appendix 4.1.

Table 4.3 Partial and full acquisitions of French companies

A. Number and value of domestic transactions

Year	Number of domestic transactions	Value of domestic mergers (£bn)[a]
1983	161	
1984	155	
1985	234	2.63
1986	249	4.76
1987	719	10.44
1988	825	17.96

B. Breakdown of transactions in 1988[b]

	Total	Listed		Unlisted		
		Merger[c]	Purchase of controlling stake[d]	Merger[c]	Purchase of stake[e]	Minority stake in listed companies
Number	537	6	41	25	465	159
Value (£bn)	7.56	0.43	0.99	0.81	5.33	7.54

[a] Exchange rate (for 1988) is 10.4 FF to £1.

[b] Total excludes from aggregate figures from the Panel above partial or full acquisition of overseas companies, divestments, MBOs, new issue of shares for assets, assets bought in bankruptcy, and spin-offs. Acquisition of shares in other companies will be included if accumulated stake is greater than 10% of share capital, or less if the company is very large with a highly diffuse share ownership.

[c] 100% ownership of target's share capital with fiscal integration.

[d] Transaction is included if accumulated stake exceeds 50%.

[e] A stake maybe acquired by a tender offer for cash, a share exchange, or purchases on the open market.

Source: PF Publications.

Only for 1988 is it possible to disaggregate the figures to obtain comparability; this is shown in Panel B. The total volume and value figures of 537 and £7.56 billion include majority stakes (above 50 per cent) and full acquisitions of listed companies. In addition, they include all stakes of 10 per cent and above in unlisted companies. For purposes of comparison, minority stakes (between 10 per cent and 50 per cent) in listed companies are shown as a separate statistic. Although it is not possible to calculate aggregate acquisition activity as a proportion of replacement cost capital stock, Bavay and Beau (1988) estimate that it amounted to 1.8 per cent of the historic cost value of a sample of companies.

This exercise has illustrated how sensitive international comparisons of acquisition activity are to definitions of a take-over. If acquisitions are defined as the purchase of majority stakes and full take-overs, then UK activity was well above that of France and Germany in 1988:[4]

	UK	France	Germany
Number	937	537	534
Value (£bn)	16.9	7.4	—

German figures for 1988 have been adjusted to exclude minority stakes of between 25 and 50 per cent.

Table 4.4 reports cross-border acquisitions for the three countries. The data show a large and increasing level of activity. In 1988 the three countries together bought 1,319 targets, of which 525 firms were in North America. During 1987 and 1988, the UK was a net purchaser of overseas firms, Germany a net seller of domestic firms, and France was approximately in balance in 1987 and a net purchaser in 1988. While the UK has predominantly bought North American firms, German and French firms have acquired European firms.

Table 4.4 Cross-border take-overs for the UK, Germany, and France

Year	UK			Germany			France		
	Total	North America	Europe	Total	North America	Europe	Total	North America[a]	Europe[b]
Sellers									
1987	138	32	83	269	54	190	178	43	127
1988	230	40	155	360	83	250	235	51	170
Buyers									
1987	427	256	156	137	43	85	194	58	133
1988	767	390	260	180	53	109	372	82	277

[a] Citibank reports 61 US acquisitions by French companies for 1988 and 60 for 1987.
[b] Citibank reports 130 EC acquisitions by French companies for 1988 and 97 for 1987.

Source: *Acquisitions Monthly*, May 1988 and 1989.

However, the most important distinction between the three countries lies in the *nature* not the level of take-over activity. In the UK there is an active market in hostile take-overs. In France and Germany there have until very recently been no reported cases of hostile acquisitions. Over the last few years a number of hostile bids have been launched in France and, according to some commentators, these are set to increase in the

---

[4] The French data include minority stakes of unlisted companies and the German data include overseas purchases. If overseas purchases are excluded, the number of German transactions is estimated to be around 440.

future. It is much more questionable whether hostile acquisitions will emerge to any significant degree in Germany in the immediate future. As Section 5 describes, there are more serious regulatory and institutional impediments to hostile take-overs in Germany than in France.

The significance of this distinction between hostile and friendly acquisitions is that the control change associated with the different forms of take-over may be very different. The next section describes how hostile take-overs are associated with a much higher level of managerial dismissal in the UK than agreed mergers.

3. TAKE-OVERS AND EXECUTIVE CHANGES IN THE UK

This section examines the association of take-overs with executive control changes in the UK. It describes the results of a study of 40 take-overs that occurred in the UK in 1986. The study distinguishes between contested and uncontested bids. A contested bid is defined here as one that is not recommended by the management of the target firm on first approach by the bidder, irrespective of whether it was eventually recommended. An uncontested bid is accepted by management on first approach by the bidder.

In 1986 there were 20 contested bids in the UK for companies valued at over £10 million (excluding those for investment trusts). This compares with a total of 537 take-overs so that by number contested bids accounted for just 4 per cent of all take-overs. However, contested take-overs tend to involve large companies so that by value they amounted to 19 per cent of total take-over activity in 1986.

All the target firms of contested bids were publicly traded and in general only listed firms are vulnerable to hostile bids. It is therefore more informative to consider contested bids in relation to listed take-overs. There were 180 take-overs of publicly listed firms in 1986; contested bids therefore accounted for over 10 per cent. Furthermore, there were 31 contested bids that were launched in 1986 but failed to be completed. In total, contested bids represented nearly 25 per cent of take-overs of listed firms (25 out of 211 take-overs).

The 20 contested bids were matched with a sample of 20 uncontested bids. The total value of both groups was about £2 billion so the average size of both samples was of the order of £100 million.

A search of company accounts and stock exchange records was performed for the following information:

1. The number of main board directors of the target, including the number of non-executive directors.

2. The number of directors who resigned after the acquisition. Resignations were recorded by whether they occurred within one month, one year, or two years of the acquisition.
3. Whether the chairman was executive or non-executive and whether the chairman resigned.
4. Whether there were any promotions from the target to the main board of the bidder.
5. Whether there were any asset disposals. These were classified as being zero, small (if they were less than 10 per cent of the bid value), or large.
6. Whether there was any significant reorganization or rationalization.

Telephone interviews were conducted with 29 firms to corroborate or supplement the information collected from published sources.

There were 155 resignations of directors of target companies, representing 56 per cent of the total size of boards of target companies before acquisition. The rate of resignation was much higher in contested than in uncontested bids: 71 per cent of directors of target firms resigned after a contested bid, 39 per cent after an uncontested bid. The difference is even more striking if the comparison is confined to executive directors: the rates were 64 and 24 per cent for contested and uncontested bids respectively.

The basic question that arises is whether take-overs are associated with changes in managerial control. Two criteria have been used to determine whether there was a change in control:

1. The executive chairman resigned *or* there were no promotions of directors from the target to the main board of the bidder.
2. The executive chairman resigned *and* there were no promotions of directors from the target to the main board of the bidder.

Table 4.5 reports that on the basis of criterion (1) control changes took place in 85 per cent of contested take-overs as against 50 per cent of uncontested take-overs. Numbers are obviously lower using criterion (2) but the large differences between contested and uncontested bids remain. A similar pattern emerges in relation to value as well as number of acquired firms. Asset sales and reorganizations were also greater after contested take-overs. Large asset sales occurred in 10 contested take-overs compared with 4 in uncontested take-overs. Significant rationalization occurred in 14 contested and 4 uncontested take-overs. In any analysis of control changes associated with take-over, it should be remembered that the level of control changes in uncontested bids may have been influenced by the very existence of hostile bids, and their impact on the boardroom.

Table 4.5 Board changes consequent on successful take-overs in the UK in 1986: recommended and non-recommended bids

Analysis of take-overs by number

Bid type	Total deals	Control changes			
		Criterion (1)[a]		Criterion (2)[b]	
		No.	%	No.	%
Recommended	20	10	50	3	15
Not recommended	20	17	85	11	55
Total	40	27	68	14	35

Analysis of take-overs by value

Bid type	Total deal value (£m.)	Control changes			
		Criterion (1)[a]		Criterion (2)[b]	
		Value (£m.)	%	Value	%
Recommended	1,815	597	33	243	13
Not recommended	2,314	2,075	90	1,334	58
Total	4,129	2,672	65	1,577	38

[a] Executive chairman resigns *or* no promotion of any director of target to the main board of bidder.
[b] Executive chairman resigns *and* no promotion of any director of target to the main board of bidder.

4. OTHER FORMS OF OWNERSHIP AND CONTROL CHANGE IN FRANCE, GERMANY, AND THE UK

Take-overs are just one form of ownership change. Recently there has been a rapid increase in management buy-outs, management buy-ins, and spin-offs. Management buy-outs involve purchases of a company in whole or in part by the incumbent management. Management buy-ins are purchases of a firm by a new incoming management. Spin-offs are sales of subsidiaries between companies.

Table 4.6 reports data on buy-outs, buy-ins, and spin-offs in the UK. The growth in buy-outs and buy-ins has been particularly pronounced. At the beginning of the decade, they were virtually unknown in the UK. By 1988 they amounted to half by number and nearly one-third by value of take-over activity. While the number of spin-offs has not increased quite so dramatically, there has been a sharp increase in value so that by 1988 the value of buy-outs, buy-ins, and spin-offs together amounted to three-fifths of take-over activity. Table 4.6 shows that buy-out activity in the UK has been appreciably in excess of that in France or Germany. The clear result to emerge from this and the previous section is that there are more controlling ownership changes in the UK than in France or Germany. Following the analysis of take-overs in the previous section, the question then arises as to whether these are associated with higher levels of executive control changes.

Table 4.6 Buy-outs, buy-ins, and sales of subsidiaries in UK, France, and Germany

Year	Buy-outs		Buy-ins		Sales of subsidiaries between companies	
	No.	Value (£m.)	No.	Value (£m.)	No.	Value (£m.)
UK						
1979	18	14	—	—	117	186
1980	36	28	—	—	101	210
1981	145	193	—	—	125	262
1982	238	348	8	315	164	804
1983	233	364	8	8	142	436
1984	238	403	5	3	170	1,121
1985	261	1,141	29	39	134	792
1986	313	1,188	49	297	159	2,810
1987	345	3,220	89	307	220	4,086
1988	373	3,717	94	1,226	287	5,253
Buy-outs and buy-ins (1988)						
France	100 [a]					
Germany	30 [b]					

[a] Includes five deals over £25m.
[b] Includes one deal over £25m.

Source: CMBOR, an independent research centre founded by Touche Ross and Barclays Development Capital Ltd at the University of Nottingham, 1989.

To address this question, an analysis was made of executive changes in the three countries during the first six months of 1988. A search was made for references to executive retirements, resignations, replacements, and dismissals, using a computer-based press report service called Textline. This accesses major national newspapers, specialized business and trade newspapers, and journals in the three countries. Information was collected on:

1. *The rank of the executive involved.* While the search related to *all* cases of executive changes, only those involving chief executives, chairmen or presidents are reported below.[5]
2. *Whether the change was an involuntary resignation or a voluntary retirement or resignation.* Only cases of involuntary resignation are reported below.
3. *The event giving rise to the change in the executive.* This is recorded as (*a*) a boardroom dispute, (*b*) a take-over, (*c*) a shareholder dispute, (*d*) financial distress, (*e*) an individual being found unsuited to his or her function, or (*f*) other.
4. *The party initiating the change.* This is classified as (*a*) initiated internally, (*b*) a corporate shareholder, (*c*) private shareholders, (*d*) an institutional shareholder, (*e*) a bank, or (*f*) other.

Table 4.7 reports 55 cases of involuntary resignation of chief executives or chairmen of UK boards over the six months from January to June 1988. One striking result to emerge is how many are associated with events other than take-overs. The largest single category of event leading to a resignation was a 'boardroom dispute'. Boardroom and shareholder disputes together accounted for half the reported cases of executive changes. Financial distress or managerial incompetence were cited in less than one-sixth of cases.

Corresponding to the large number of boardroom disputes, executive changes were most frequently initiated internally, perhaps because management failure is first revealed by other boardroom members (see Weisbach (1988)). Corporate shareholders were the next most important party initiating executive changes, often, but not always, associated with take-overs. There were no reported cases of institutional or bank involvement in involuntary executive changes, although non-executive directors may have been used to implement changes proposed by institutional shareholders.

There is therefore a high level of involuntary executive change in the UK, much of which is not directly associated with take-overs. In comparison, there is a very low rate of dismissal in France and Germany. Textline reports only four cases in France and three in Germany. Furthermore, the changes reported in Germany were associated with political or commercial scandals. However, care has to be taken in interpreting these data. Inadequate coverage of published sources in France and Germany by Textline, and poor disclosure may be factors contributing to the low recorded rate of dismissals.

Three checks were performed on the reliability of the results reported.

---

[5] The reason for this is that the study is concerned with the interaction between capital markets and corporations not the internal operations of firms.

Table 4.7. Chief Executive dismissals in the UK during the six-month period
ending June 1988

Event causing dismissals[a,b]

Total	Boardroom dispute	Boardroom take-over	Shareholder dispute	Financial distress	Not suitable for job	Other[f]
55	18	14	9	5	4	5

Parties initiating dismissals

Total	Initiated internally[c]	Corporate shareholders	Initiated externally by	
			Private shareholders[d]	Other[e]
55	26	15	10	4

   [a] Includes dismissal of vice-chairmen, vice-presidents, and chairmen who are also chief executives.

   [b] Involuntary dismissals include: voluntary resignations and retirements; demotions; and involuntary internal movements.

   [c] Internal moves generally initiated by chief executive or the board.

   [d] Private shareholdings may include coalitions.

   [e] Other includes creditors other than banking regulatory organizations, associate companies, and employees.

   [f] Other includes resignations due to political scandals, and cases where cause could not be established.

Source: Reuter's Textline (extracts from newspapers and trade journals).

First, data were collected from Textline on dismissals in Germany over another six-month period beginning January 1989. The level of dismissal for these months totalled seven, slightly higher than the earlier period. Furthermore, a smaller proportion of dismissals was associated with 'scandals' than over the earlier period. Second, another news reporting service in Germany (SVP) was used to collect references to executive dismissals over the period January to June 1989. This reported twice as many dismissals as Textline. In addition, the degree of overlap between the two data sources was low. This suggests that the data do indeed have to be treated with caution and that the level of executive replacement may well be higher than that recorded by Textline.

   A third approach examined executive changes in three German companies involved in corporate restructurings during the 1980s. The three companies were AEG, Bayer, and MAN. Table 4.8 reports changes to their managerial and supervisory boards. All three firms display a high rate of turnover in the managerial board. For example, in 1984, the chairman of the management board of Bayer resigned in response to a dramatic fall in profits and a cut in dividends. Subsequently, he succeeded

Table 4.8. Resignations (−)[a] and additions (+) of members of the supervisory board and the board of management of three German companies: Bayer, AEG, and MAN

Year	Board of management									Supervisory board								
	Bayer			AEG			MAN			Bayer			AEG			MAN		
	−	+	Total	−	+	Total	−	+	Total	−	+	Total	−	+	Total	−	+	Total
1980	n.a.	n.a.	n.a.	n.a.	n.a.	n.a.	n.a.	n.a.	n.a.	n.a.	n.a.	n.a.	3[b]	5	24	n.a.	n.a.	n.a.
1981	0	0	14	3[b]	6	8	0	0	3	1	0	21	0	1	22	n.a.	n.a.	n.a.
1982	0	1	15	3	2[c]	7[g]	0	0	3	4	0	20	5	3	23	0	0	20
1983	1[d]	1	14	1	1[e]	7	n.a.	n.a.	n.a.	1	1	20	6	7	26	n.a.	n.a.	n.a.
1984	2[b]	1	12	0	0	7	2	2	4	3	1	21	3[b]	2	22	3	3	21
1985	0	2	14	0	1[f]	9	0	0	2	1	0	21	1	1	22	0	0	21
1986	4	2	12	0	1	10	0	4	6	0	0	21	2[b]	1	21	3	3	24
1987	3	0	9	1	1[e]	10[g]	0	2	8	7	7	21	0	1	20	1	1	21
1988	1	1	9	16	1[h]	10[g]	1	1	8	1	2	21	6[i]	5	26	7	8	28
1989	0	0	9	4	0[j]	11[g]	0	0	8	2	2	21	4	4	24	0	1	21
TOTAL	11	7		13	13		3	9		20	14		30	30		14	16	

[a] There were no deaths.
[b] Includes chairman.
[c] Deputy chairman resigned for health reasons, new finance director and new controller. In addition, 3 new general managers (not included in figures).
[d] Moved to supervisory board.
[e] Promotion.
[f] 2 new senior executives appointed (not included in figures).
[g] 1 or 2 deputy members are not included.
[h] 3 new senior executives (not included in figures).
[i] Includes deputy chairman.
[j] 1 promotion, 1 new senior executive.

Source: Adapted from Schofner (1990).

the chairman of the supervisory board, who resigned on the grounds of ill health. During 1986–7, seven of the twelve board members resigned so as to form a board 'with a greater policy focus' (1983, Annual Report). In AEG, six of the eight members of the management board resigned in 1981–2, including the chairman, following severe losses and a failure of the first restructuring plan.

The level of resignations on the supervisory board is also high. In 1987–8, almost a third of the board resigned in each of the three companies. This may appear surprising in light of evidence from Gerum, Steinmann, and Fees (1988) that 86 per cent of supervisory boards meet only twice a year and might not therefore be expected to be held responsible for managerial failure at the executive level. Similarly, Edwards and Fischer (1990) claim that 'it is not altogether clear that supervisory boards in Germany are able to monitor managements particularly closely'.

In sum, the evidence from press reports is suggestive of a significantly higher level of executive dismissal in the UK than in Germany and France. Furthermore, executive dismissals in the UK are not restricted to take-overs. However, the three case studies reveal that executive dismissals do at least occur in Germany in response to corporate failure.

This section raises two substantive questions: (1) why are there differences in levels and forms of ownership and control changes between countries, and (2) what are their effects? The next section considers one possible explanation for the differences; Section 6 examines their effects.

5. REGULATORY AND INSTITUTIONAL IMPEDIMENTS TO CORPORATE RESTRUCTURING

This section[6] examines the regulatory and non-regulatory impediments to corporate restructuring in France, Germany, and the UK. It focuses on those factors influencing changes in ownership associated with corporate restructurings. There are two relevant considerations: (1) those factors that impede the transfer of ownership, for example, limitations on transfers of shares, cross-shareholdings of corporations, and shareholdings by banks, and (2) those that dilute control arising from transfer of ownership, for example, rights of employees, limitations on the voting rights of shareholders, and restrictions on the extent to which management can be replaced.

The section begins with regulation. It considers regulatory rules per-

---

[6] Much of the data in this section come from a report by Coopers & Lybrand (1989) for the Department of Trade and Industry, entitled *The Barriers to Takeovers in the European Community*.

taining to three groups of individuals in turn: employees, managers, and shareholders. It then discusses institutional influences coming from the role of banks, cross-shareholdings, and the government.

Regulation relating to employees. There are marked differences in the degree to which French, German, and British laws confer rights on employees and their representatives (Table 4.9). *In France*, employees, trade unions, and workers' councils have the right to be consulted about a range of corporate activities but do not possess a right of veto. *In Germany*, representatives of employees and trade unions have 50 per cent of seats on the supervisory boards of stock corporations (AGs) with more than 2,000 employees. In addition, workers' councils have rights relating to terms of employment and dismissal. *In the UK*, companies are free to consult and involve employees in corporate activities as they see fit but are not required to do so. Therefore, employee rights are considerably greater in Germany than in France, which in turn are greater than those in Britain.

Table 4.9. Rights of employees relevant to the control of French and German corporations

France	Germany
Two employee representatives may attend board meetings but have no voting powers	50% representation on supervisory boards of AGs with more than 2,000 employees. 33% representation on AGs with less than 2,000 employees
Trade unions do not have to be consulted about a merger but in companies with more than 50 employees they can attend meetings between employers and employees	Trade unions are entitled to supervisory board positions
Workers' councils are informed about bids but have no power to block them	Workers' councils have rights regarding working hours, holidays, salaries, hirings and dismissals

Regulation relating to managers. Managers can also enjoy a high degree of protection (Table 4.10). *In Germany*, the board of managing directors (the *Vorstand*) is appointed by the supervisory board. Their term of employment usually extends for five years and dismissal can occur in the intervening period only if there has been a clear breach of duty. Bearing in mind that 50 per cent of seats on the supervisory board are held by employees who may support existing management, the impediments to wresting control from management are formidable. Furthermore,

Table 4.10. Rights of management relevant to the control of French and German corporations

France	Germany
Shareholders have the power to elect and dismiss management with a 50% majority of the voting rights	Removal of members of the supervisory board requires approval of 75% of shareholders
	The board of managing directors which is elected by the supervisory board, is appointed for a fixed term of up to 5 years. They can only be removed for 'good causes' during their term of office

members of the supervisory board (the *Aufsichtsrat*) can only be replaced with a 75 per cent vote of shareholders. *In France*, management can be dismissed by a majority vote of shareholders. *In the UK*, board members can be replaced by the chief executive or by controlling shareholders, possibly after payment of compensation.

Regulation relating to shareholders. While employee and management rights are limited in *France*, French companies are able to place serious restrictions on the transfer of shares and voting rights of shareholders. Companies can limit share transfers by contract or articles of association (Table 4.11). Certain classes of shareholders can enjoy privileged voting rights, others have no voting rights at all. Restrictions are also observed, but not quite so extensively, *in Germany*. The case study of Feldmuehle Nobel in Appendix 4.1 exemplifies how restrictions have been used in Germany to reduce the threat of take-overs. For example, Feldmuehle Nobel changed the articles of association limiting the voting rights of any one shareholder to 5 per cent of the share capital.

Institutional influences. Much of the protection that firms have enjoyed in France and Germany reflects institutional rather than regulatory factors (Table 4.12). In particular *in Germany*, banks are significant shareholders in their own right in German corporations. Still more significantly, German banks have been able to exert control through the voting rights conferred on them by custody of bearer shares of individual investors who have surrendered their proxies. Bank representatives sit on the supervisory boards of stock corporations, sometimes in the capacity of chairman of the board. There is much discussion in Germany about the extent to which banks can and do exert power over corporations. However, it would seem that one important effect of bank control is to protect firms from interference from external parties, in particular from

Table 4.11. Rights of shareholders relevant to the control of French and German corporations

France	Germany
Transferability of shares	
Listed companies may limit transferability of shares by contract or articles of incorporation	There is no barrier to transfer of shares in an AG
Transferability may also be limited by establishing private companies that hold a group of shareholders' shares in a GmbH but not in an AG	Consent of the company is private often required for the transfer of equity
Voting rights	
Shareholders that have held shares for a specified period (for example, 2 to 4 years) may be entitled to double votes	AGs can issue non-voting shares up to an amount equal to that of all the voting shares issued
Up to 25% of capital can, under certain circumstances, be issued as non-voting preferred equity	AGs can limit the voting power of an individual shareholder irrespective of the number of shares held
Up to 25% of capital may be issued as investment certificates that can only be transferred to holders of other investment certificates	

hostile take-overs.[7] In the case of Feldmuehle Nobel, Deutsche Bank is said to have controlled the votes of about 55 per cent of the share capital and played a decisive role in rejecting a hostile take-over bid.

In both *France and Germany*, mutual cross-shareholdings between corporations are permitted and commonplace. There is an implicit agreement that cross-shareholdings are not used to launch unwelcome take-overs; on the contrary, as the Navigation Mixte case in Appendix 4.1 illustrates, they can be used to frustrate take-overs. Some of the restrictions on transfers of control in France come from involvement of the government. The French government has traditionally been a substantial shareholder in French corporations. While several firms have been privatized over the last few years, the *noyau dur* (hardcore shareholding) has often limited the external control that investors have been able to exert in these firms. In other cases, it is thought that the French government has delayed take-overs by foreign firms while a 'French solution' has been sought.

[7] For a much more extensive discussion of this see Edwards and Fischer (1990).

Table 4.12. Institutional influences on the control of French and German corporations

France	Germany
Non-banks	
Companies can take cross-shareholdings up to a limit of 10%. Subsidiaries may own up to 10%	Companies can take cross-shareholdings subject to a limitation of 25% of the voting rights associated with those shareholdings irrespective of their size
Concert parties that hold more than 33% of a company's equity are required to launch full take-overs	
Government	*Banks*
The French Government has influenced the shareholdings of privatized corporations	Banks have significant shareholdings in other corporations
It has delayed and impeded take-overs that have been deemed to be against the national interest	Banks also exercise power through the voting rights associated with the custody of the bearer shares of private investors.
	Banks sit on the supervisory boards of AGs. In some cases their representative is chairman of the board

The Navigation Mixte case illustrates how the French government can at its discretion determine whether there is evidence for the existence of concert parties.

To summarize, the level and form of impediments to corporate restructurings differ appreciably between the three countries. Essentially, three classes of institutional and regulatory arrangements have been identified: free markets in ownership and control; limitations on the transfer of ownership; and restrictions on shareholders' rights of control. The UK imposes few impediments to the free transfer of both ownership and control. In France, there are few impediments to shareholder control but there are barriers to the transfer of ownership resulting from limitations on the transferability of shares, concentrations of voting rights, and the intervention of the government. In Germany, limitations on transferability of ownership are less pronounced. However, the transfer of control is restricted by rights of workers and managers, and power of the banks.

The primary distinction between countries' capital markets comes from the degree of association between property and control rights. A basic premiss of the UK capital market is that investors should have the right to determine how their property is employed and controlled. The restructuring of the Imperial Group following its acquisition by Hanson Trust, as described in Appendix 4.1, exemplifies the extent to which acquiring firms can exert control over their targets. Superficially, this suggests that the UK system is less interventionist than others in not imposing employee or managerial rights on firms but instead allowing firms to choose the degree of protection that they offer. In fact, the UK imposes impediments of a different nature. The Stock Exchange has discouraged the use of discriminatory voting rights as a means of limiting transfers of control. The Takeover Code discourages the accumulation of cross-shareholdings as a method of preventing transfers of ownership. Insider-trading laws discourage privileged access to information as part of the process of direct investor control.

The rationale behind these rules and regulations is the promotion of securities markets. Equal access to information and protection of small investors from exploitation by dominant shareholders are regarded as central to that process. Thus, in relation to other countries, UK regulation (including company law, Stock Exchange rules, and the Takeover Panel), has emphasized the rights of minority investors rather than those of management and employees.

Regulation may go a long way towards explaining patterns of ownership and control changes in different countries. In the UK, stock exchange and take-over codes have discouraged direct investor involvement in corporate control, for example by limiting share stakes that can be accumulated without requiring full take-over bids to be made. Instead, comparatively free markets in corporate control have encouraged the use of take-overs and other forms of ownership change as methods of correcting managerial failure. The case study of the Imperial Group illustrates how the UK Takeover Code limits share stakes and promotes markets in corporate control. In France and Germany, impediments to direct investor control have been less serious and restrictions on transfers of ownership and control more pronounced.

The relevance of these regulatory provisions for corporate performance depends on the degree of substitutability between alternative forms of restructuring. If substitutability is high, then impediments to one form encourage the use of another at little cost to corporate performance. On the other hand, if different forms of restructuring fulfil different functions, costs of regulation may be high. The next section suggests a reason why substitutability may be low. Furthermore, it points to regulation as being a manifestation of more fundamental characteristics of financial markets.

6. CAPITAL MARKETS AND CONTRACTUAL RELATIONS

The empirical analysis has emphasized the association between ownership and control changes. Take-overs, management buy-outs, and buy-ins involve ownership changes. In a take-over, there is a transfer of ownership from acquired to acquiring shareholders. In buy-outs, the transfer is either from investor to management, which is typically the case in the US, or from a parent to a more junior management, which is more common in the UK. In buy-ins, the transfer is from existing investors and senior management to the incoming management. In contrast, in interventions initiated by a bank, supervisory board, or non-executive directors, there may be a change in control without any change in ownership.

What is the significance of changes in ownership? In principle, ownership changes should allow assets to be employed in their most productive activity. Take-overs, buy-outs, and buy-ins permit those who attribute the highest value to running a corporation to take control. They essentially subject firms to continuous auctions and thereby automatically elicit the greatest returns for investors. Ownership changes are an effective and efficient method of correcting managerial failure. They ensure that only those who are able to achieve the highest level of productivity and lowest costs of production remain in control and thereby encourage 'productive efficiency'.

However, care is required in defining the term managerial failure. There are three distinct forms that it can take (see Table 4.13). The first is the most readily recognizable: poor *ex post* performance by management. Management may have failed to meet its contractual obligations through being negligent, incompetent, or dishonest. These are described as *absolute failures*. Few would deny that they are valid grounds for managerial correction.

Table 4.13. Managerial failure and correction

Type of failure	Example of failure	Form of correction
Ex post absolute failure	Negligence, incompetence, and dishonesty	Contracts
Ex post relative failure	Inferior performance to other managers or changing market conditions requiring new management	Contracts and ownership changes
Ex ante failure	Differences in expectations about investment and managerial ability	Changes in ownership

Somewhat less clear-cut is the case where there has been no contractual failure but performance has not been equal to that which might reasonably have been expected or which others have achieved. This may reflect changing populations of managers, for example the emergence of new generations of managers, or changing technologies and markets that make a new class of individuals better suited to manage. Buy-outs in the UK are frequently motivated by a belief that performance of a subsidiary has been below its potential. This is termed *relative failure*.

There is a third set of circumstances in which changes in control may occur. These result not from an *ex post* failure in the sense just mentioned but where there are *ex ante* differences in expectations. In the absence of complete markets, investors and managers may not agree on the policies that firms should pursue. Expectations may differ on two accounts. First, investors may have different views about the prospects of particular investments. Secondly, they may have different views about the ability of managers. Views may change over time and the relative bargaining positions of investors may alter. Coalitions between different managers will form and the relative bargaining position of coalitions will fluctuate. As it does, control will shift between different parties and boardroom changes and take-overs may occur.

Contractual arrangements are used to avoid absolute failure: manifest incompetence, negligence, or dishonesty are generally grounds for dismissal. It is harder but not necessarily impossible to write contracts that correct for relative failure. Fund managers are often judged on the basis of their performance relative to that of others or relative to a general measure of performance such as a stock market index. Managers may be evaluated on their ability to sustain dividends at levels commensurate with those in other firms. Yardsticks are sometimes used to regulate utilities and other firms that can exert monopoly power.

Some forms of relative failure are difficult to correct because contracts are only enforceable if they specify precise conditions for judging relative performance. Contracts are still worse suited to the correction of *ex ante* failure. Changes in ownership permit control to be transferred to those with the highest *ex ante* valuations. In the absence of clear evidence of *ex post* failure it is difficult to write contracts that have the same effect. For example, it is impossible to conceive of a contract that could have achieved the same outcome as the take-over of the Imperial Group by Hanson. Such a contract would have required the existing management to commit itself contractually to dispose of assets at prices that Hanson claimed it could achieve.

Another example is provided by the problems that the banks have had in their lending to Eurotunnel in specifying performance contracts. *Ex ante*, the banks attempted to include covenants that specified the timetable for construction. *Ex post*, it has proved difficult to establish the exact causes of delays in construction and in particular whether the failures lie with the management of Eurotunnel, the construction consortium, or simply result from bad luck. Providing better management can be identified it may be much easier to put Eurotunnel up for auction by take-over, rather than trying to dismiss the existing managers by proving contractual failure.

In a compendium paper, Franks and Mayer (1991) attempt to discriminate between these alternative motives for take-overs. We take a sample of recommended and contested bids in 1985 and 1986, which includes the sample in Table 4.5, and examine the financial and real performance of target firms in the two years prior to the announcement of an acquisition. If contested bids are associated with the correction of *ex post* managerial failure, then target firms should display abnormally poor performance prior to the bid. Financial performance is measured by abnormal share price returns relative to a market index. Real performance is measured by frequency of declines in employment and sales. Table 4.14 summarizes results for one year before the acquisition.

Table 4.14. A comparison of financial and real performance of target firms in recommended and rejected bids one year before a bid

Performance	Recommended bids		Rejected but successful bids	
	No.	%	No.	%
Abnormal share price performance	35	8	35	–5
With declines in employment	28	50	30	50
With declines in sales	30	20	31	32

Source: Franks and Mayer (1991).

Target firms that resist bids display worse financial performance in the year preceding the bid and more instances of declines in sales. However, the difference between the two groups of firms is not statistically significant at the 5 per cent level. Furthermore, there is no difference in frequency of employment declines. There is therefore little evidence of differences in *ex post* performance prior to acquisition of accepted and rejected bids. However, there is evidence of differences in *ex ante* expectations. First, bid premia in the month of the announcement of bids that are rejected by incumbent management are significantly in excess of those that are accepted. Franks and Mayer (1991) report bid premia of 28 per cent in rejected but successful bids as against 19 per cent in accepted bids. The difference is statistically significant (t-statistic = 1.96).

Secondly, the level of control changes is much greater in rejected than accepted bids: the rate of replacement of executives in rejected bids was 65 per cent as against 47 per cent in accepted bids, as reported by Franks and Mayer (1991). Thirdly, the level of asset disposals is higher in rejected than in accepted bids: there were large asset disposals in 46 per cent of our sample of rejected bids but only 17 per cent in accepted bids.

There is therefore evidence of hostility being associated with *ex ante* differences in expectation but not *ex post* failure. Changes in ownership thus allow control changes to occur in circumstances in which they would otherwise not be possible. Some changes involve desirable corrections of *ex ante* failure, i.e. the substitution of more suitable management for future activities. For example, it might quite justifiably be expected that, even if past performance has been quite acceptable, managerial changes are required to cope with a more international environment of integrated European markets. On this basis, the higher level of control changes in the UK reported in Section 4 should be associated with superior corporate performance. However, other changes may be the outcome of power struggles that have more to do with coalition formation and access to financial resources than corporate performance.

There is a still more fundamental respect in which changes in ownership may be undesirable. It was noted above that correction of *ex ante* failure is associated with incomplete markets. Were markets complete, including the managerial labour market, then differences in expectations would not be of significance—changes in policy associated with changes in ownership would be irrelevant. The question then arises as to how changes in ownership affect relations between different parties where contracts are incomplete. The first point to note is that changes in ownership may themselves contribute to contract incompleteness. In general, contracts between existing owners and employees remain in force when ownership changes. New owners are bound by contracts that old owners previously signed with their employees regarding, for example, periods of employment and pensions. However, it is difficult to require future owners to abide by terms of employment that are not part of current agreements between owners and employees. For example, it is not possible to compel future owners to pay compensation in the event of redundancy or dismissal due to a take-over unless existing owners are bound by a similar obligation. There are good reasons why existing owners may be unwilling to tie themselves in this way: the payment of large compensation when a company is in difficulties and is seeking a white knight may prove an obstacle to the company's survival. The implication is that employers are unable to offer their employees safeguards against changes in control without themselves accepting burdensome obligations. Furthermore, attempts to introduce such contracts in the face of a take-over threat may well be deemed not to be part of normal business conduct and therefore *ultra vires*. Thus when firms want to introduce contracts to protect employees they may be unenforceable and where they are enforceable they may well be undesirable.

Section 5 noted that regulation conferred considerable protection on employees and managers in France and Germany. In the absence of regulation or complete contracting, protection of stakeholders relies on implicit understandings between employees, employers, and investors. *Inter alia*, these implicit understandings relate to periods of employment, promotion, and other conditions of employment. They are sustained by the desire of different parties to maintain reputations. For example, abrogating implicit contracts to retain employees may make future employment more expensive by raising wage demands of employees who require compensation for increased risk of involuntary redundancy. Likewise, in the absence of clear *ex post* failure, institutions may be unwilling to replace management for fear of blackening their reputations as investors and thereby losing potential custom from firms. This may well explain the unwillingness of German banks to accept hostile acquisitions of their corporate customers.

Changes in ownership undermine the ability of firms to sustain a reputation for long-term relationships. Employees are unable to impose penalties on the now departed owners and the new owners may have very different reputations to sustain from those of the old. What comfort can the management of a potential target draw from knowing that Hanson has a reputation to sustain to investors for engaging in frequent asset disposals? Changes in ownership reduce the set of implicit agreements that can be sustained between different parties to a firm. Furthermore, as noted above, the range of explicit contracts that are enforceable in the face of ownership changes is limited so that, in total, take-overs shrink the set of feasible arrangements between employees, employers, and their owners.

As Schleifer and Summers (1988) have noted there are two consequences of such 'breaches of trust'. First, wealth transfers between different stakeholders can occur: at least some of the observed gains that shareholders have enjoyed around the time of acquisitions may have been at the expense of employees. Second, *ex ante* incentives to invest are affected by risks of *ex post* expropriation. The possibility that managers and employees may be denied the benefits of their firm-specific investments by changes in ownership may discourage them from engaging in these investments in the first place. For example, employees may be unwilling to incur the costs of firm-specific training in the absence of assurance that benefits will accrue to them. If formal and informal contractual arrangements between employees, employers, and their owners are inadequate, there will be insufficient investment by firms and their employees and too much emphasis on investments of a general rather than a firm-specific nature. Investment in long-term training may therefore be discouraged. Likewise, investment in R & D and other long-term projects that reward managers on the basis of performance may require long-term contracts to provide adequate incentives.

There is therefore a trade-off between the flexibility of ownership changes in correcting relative and *ex ante* failure and limitations on the contractual arrangements that can be sustained between different parties to a firm. Furthermore, the significance of take-overs in this comparison may be much greater than the numbers and values cited in Section 2 suggest. The mere threat of take-over may, on the one hand, be sufficient to encourage good performance by managers and employees. On the other hand, it may also be enough to discourage employees and managers from committing themselves adequately to firm-specific investments.

There is some evidence that these considerations may be of real significance. The three case studies of German corporate restructurings discussed in Section 4 point to a marked difference between countries in the response of corporations and investors to financial distress. Table 4.15 describes the nature of the restructurings and the financial performance of the firms during the period. Two of the companies suffered large decline in earnings and the third, AEG, made large losses and went in bankruptcy. All three cut or omitted their dividends. Sales of assets, the creation of new joint ventures, closures, and redundancies characterized all three restructurings. In addition, the restructuring continued for some length of time: eight years in the case of AEG, and five years for Bayer. For MAN, the restructuring was initiated by the two major shareholders, Commerzbank and Alliance. They also initiated changes to the board. By the end of the restructuring all three companies were profitable, with dividends restored to the highest level in the ten-year period.

In Appendix 4.2, a time series of earnings and expenditures for the three companies is reported for the period 1980–9. There are two striking features of this series. First, despite the extensive restructuring and financial constraints, spending on R & D remained high. For example, Bayer's spending exceeded earnings throughout the period, and rose in nominal terms even when earnings declined. Similarly, AEG's spending was greater than earnings, although it was reduced in two out of the ten years. Figures are not available for MAN but company reports suggest it was increased significantly in 1982 even when earnings fell.

Secondly, while capital spending was reduced by all three firms, reductions were much smaller than the decline in earnings. Even when AEG's

Table 4.15. Financial performance and restructuring programme of three German companies

	AEG	Bayer	MAN
Financial performance			
Earnings	Losses 1979, 1980, 1982 +	Collapse in 1981–2	Large decline in 1982. Losses 1983–4
Dividends	No dividends: 1980–7	Cut in dividend in 1982 (restored in 1983)	Dividend cut in 1983 and 1984. Fully restored only by 1989
Restructuring of business activities			
R & D spending	Reductions in 1982–3 and increases in 1984–8	R & D increased every year	R & D increased 1982
Training	Increased in 1983	No entry for training	No entry for training
Capital spending	Fell in 1982–3. Rising in all subsequent years	Fell by 25% in 1980–5. Rose significantly thereafter	Increased sharply 1983
Closures, sales of assets	Significant	Significant in 1981–4	Significant
Joint ventures	New joint ventures	Some discontinued, others created	New joint ventures
Aspects of restructuring	First restructuring plan failed (1982). Restructuring during 1980–8	Restructuring of board—reduction in numbers, new type of directors, greater policy focus. Restructuring continues through 1981–5	Major shareholders (Commerzbank and Alliance) initiated restructuring and board changes
Outcome	Bankrupt in 1982, and subsequently acquired by Daimler-Benz. Profitable and dividends recommended in 1988	By 1989 highly profitable and rising dividends	Profitable and dividends increased to beyond pre-crisis levels

Source: Adapted from Schofner (1990).

earnings collapsed, capital spending was reduced by less than 25 per cent. Similarly, in the case of MAN spending was reduced significantly in only one year even though the company reported profits in just two years.

7. CONCLUSIONS

This chapter has documented significant differences between countries in forms of ownership and control changes. Hostile take-overs, buy-outs, and buy-ins are higher in the UK than in France or Germany. Levels of executive dismissal are also higher in the UK.

The chapter has suggested that these observations reflect fundamental features of different countries' capital markets. The UK system is directed towards the promotion of markets. As part of that process, close links between investors and firms are discouraged by laws relating to insider dealing and the exploitation of minority shareholders. In particular, arrangements that limit transferability of ownership and control are restricted by stock exchange and take-over codes. With limited direct investor involvement and with few impediments to transfers of ownership and control, the correction of managerial failure in the UK would be expected to be associated with changes in ownership. Evidence from a sample of take-overs confirms that prediction, even though control changes stem from other sources as well.

In contrast, in France and Germany, far less emphasis has traditionally been placed on the operation of markets. Limitations on transfers of ownership and control are therefore not discouraged and indeed are widely observed. The chapter has suggested a difference between France and Germany, with limitations on transfer of ownership being more significant in France and limitations on transfer of control being more in evidence in Germany. But in both cases, the effect is to diminish the association of corrections of managerial control with changes in ownership. This is reflected in a relatively low incidence of hostile take-overs, buy-outs, and buy-ins. Furthermore the overall level of executive dismissal is apparently relatively low in both France and Germany.

The advantage of the UK approach is that it permits the correction of *ex ante* managerial failure. The drawback is that it undermines the implementation of informal implicit agreements. It may also complicate the writing of formal contracts. In the absence of complete contracts the allocation of rights between different stakeholders is of considerable importance. The rights that are conferred on employees and managers in the event of take-overs are limited in the UK but considerable in Germany. If complete contracting is not feasible and the rights of employees and managers are limited then in the presence of hostile take-overs it may not be possible to provide managers and employees with adequate incentives to engage in long-term investment. As a consequence, investment in R & D and training may suffer.

In this regard, the case for harmonization across members of the European Community is open to serious question. There is a trade-off between correcting managerial failure and promoting investment. Where the balance lies will depend on the circumstances of individual firms and economies. Fast-growing firms or economies will opt for arrangements that promote dynamic over static efficiency. More mature firms and economies will emphasize the advantages of corporate efficiency.[8]

Furthermore, there are important interrelations in the liberalization of different markets. Increased competition in product markets through, for example, eliminating barriers to trade, acts as a spur to efficiency by raising the risk of absolute failure. The need for correction through markets for corporate control may thereby be diminished.

Looking forward, the differing pattern of restrictions on markets in corporate control implies that the durability of existing arrangements is likely to vary appreciably across countries. The impediments to transfers of control, if not ownership, would appear to be more deep-rooted in Germany than in France. It is not difficult to imagine that firms that have in the past appeared immune to external control in France will in the not-too-distant future be subject to the 'discipline' of the market for corporate control. More fundamental changes to regulations and relations, however, will be required before this is likely to occur in Germany.

The observation that one form of restructuring may lead to more of another has important implications for the extension of hostile acquisitions from the UK to the Continent. Not only will continental Europe be subject to an unfamiliar (and apparently unwelcome) form of restructuring but also, in the process, the stable relations that have existed between investor and firm may be extinguished. Take-overs could therefore be a catalyst for much greater change in European corporate arrangements.

---

[8] The Commission views free markets in corporate ownership as an adjunct to free product and capital markets: they allow firms access to what might otherwise be protected markets. But that analogy is incorrect: economic theory does not suggest that competition in markets for corporate control is a substitute for competition in product markets. Instead, corporate control is concerned with the promotion of corporate efficiency, and in that regard there is no clear merit of one system over another.

Appendix 4.1.
Three Case Studies of Ownership and Control Changes

The influence of regulatory and institutional considerations is illustrated in this appendix with a case study of a hostile acquisition in each of France, Germany, and the UK.

1. France: Navigation Mixte

Navigation Mixte is a highly diversified group, with a substantial presence in insurance. The company is publicly owned with its shares being held principally by banks, finance houses, and insurance companies.

The first sign of take-over activity came when the state-owned insurer Assurances Generales de France increased its holding from below 5 per cent to over 7 per cent, describing this as a defensive measure to counter stake-building by another shareholder. This was followed by the announcement by Navigation Mixte that the West German insurer Allianz AG had agreed to purchase 50 per cent of Mixte's insurance assets for FF 6.5 billion and to take a 5 per cent share of its capital. It also became known that Paribas was the other stakeholder and had increased its stake in Navigation Mixte, from 1.8 per cent to about 10 per cent. Mixte responded defensively by buying, with the help of its allies, into Paribas.

On 23 October 1989 the French stock exchange association, the Société des Bourses Françaises (SBF), announced that Paribas, which had by then accumulated a stake of 18.7 per cent in Navigation Mixte, had applied to make a cash offer, with an equity alternative, for two-thirds of the company's capital.[9] This bid valued the target at just over FF 22 billion. Michel Francois-Poncet, chairman of Paribas, stated that there would be no sales of Mixte assets if the bid succeeded, and that the bank would respect the sale agreement between Navigation Mixte and Allianz.

To counter the Paribas attack, Mixte chairman Marc Fournier asked for permission from the Finance Ministry to raise his stake in Paribas to over 10 per cent. Approval is required to take a stake above this threshold in any one of the recently privatized banking groups, the restriction having been introduced to ensure that these companies retained their independence. Independence was further enhanced by distributing their capital among a large number of shareholders. Thus Mixte already had a stake in Paribas prior to the bid, and Paribas was

---

[9] New laws dictate that once a company controls one-third of its take-over target, it must bid for the remaining two-thirds.

accused by Mixte of 'dubious' professional ethics in launching a hostile take-over bid against one of its own core group of shareholders.

On 26 October the Paribas bid was cleared by the SBF. Then on 2 November the French Finance Minister, Pierre Beregovoy, gave permission for Navigation Mixte to raise its stake in Paribas above the 10 per cent threshold. The Finance Ministry also said that if one or more shareholders acting in concert (other than Paribas) took a stake of over 20 per cent in Mixte, the authorization would have to be re-examined. Under French take-over rules, concert parties must reveal any accords at the beginning of a take-over battle and any organized defence must entail a counter-bid. These terms of approval thus threw into doubt Fournier's main line of defence, namely the consolidation of his core of friendly shareholders. Among these were Allianz, which later announced that it had received the approval of the supervisory authorities to take its stake in Mixte from about 5 per cent to between 20 and 33.3 per cent, Framatome, Credit Lyonnais, and Société Général, which raised their stakes gradually to 7 per cent, 6.33 per cent, and 5.2 per cent, respectively.

On 8 November Paribas revised its bid to acquire 100 per cent instead of two-thirds of the capital of Navigation Mixte, the other conditions of its cash or shares offer remaining the same. This new bid, which was cleared by the SBF, valued the whole of Mixte at FF 25.6 billion.

On 13 November the SBF said that, 'given the information to hand', the recent purchases of shares in Mixte by Société Général, Credit Lyonnais, Framatome, and Allianz AG did not constitute a concerted action. This verdict took into consideration declarations by some of the groups that their purchases had been made independently, and also the small sizes of the purchases relative to stakes held previously. The judgement added that even if the four groups had been acting in concert their purchases would not have been enough to take their holdings above the level at which a counter-bid for Mixte would have been required.[10] Yet Fournier continued to claim that, with the support of other shareholders whose identities were not disclosed, his allies held close to 50 per cent of Mixte's capital; still no concert action was announced.

On 17 November the French construction group Bouygues announced that it had bought 3.9 per cent of Mixte's shares. Although it denied acting in concert with Fournier, Bouygues was known to be close to one of Fournier's strongest supporters, Credit Lyonnais, which held 12.5 per cent of its capital. Paribas said it had reason to believe that Bouygues's purchase was contrary to French stock exchange regulations, which stipulate that opposition to a take-over bid must take the form of a counter-bid. The bank felt there was also evidence to suggest that the price of Mixte shares was being maintained at a level slightly above the bid price to hinder Paribas buying additional shares in the market. It called on the authorities to intervene.

The French Finance Minister appeared to share Paribas's scepticism over the claims by Mixte's allies that they were not colluding. He wrote to the chairmen of Credit Lyonnais, Société Général, Bouygues, Framatome, and Allianz reminding

---

[10] Mixte's known allies were said to account for 28.7% of its capital, and 29.4% of the voting rights.

them that they were obliged to launch a full take-over bid once the 33 per cent threshold had been reached. All five companies, except Bouygues, were represented on Mixte's board, had voted to reject Paribas's bid, and had been active buyers of Mixte stock in the market.

On 24 November the stock exchange announced that Paribas had accumulated 21.1 per cent of the capital of Navigation Mixte, just 2.4 per cent more than when its bid was announced. Although the deadline for a formal increase in the offer had passed, on 27 November Paribas was able to increase its offer by taking advantage of the take-over rule which stipulates that the buying of shares by the initiator of a bid at more than 2 per cent above its offer price triggers an automatic increase in that offer price. The closing date for the offer was extended by one day to 30 November. The bank said that there was 'blatant evidence' that the market had been manipulated by Mixte's allies: Mixte's share price had been quoted slightly above Paribas's offer of FF 1,850 ever since the bid had been launched, and following purchases by Paribas at the new price of FF 1,887 Mixte shares were immediately quoted at FF 1,888. An inquiry has been launched to investigate this claim.

Latest reports indicate that Paribas has received just less than 40 per cent in acceptances, and the bank now has to decide whether to accept the shares offered or allow the bid to lapse.

The case illustrates the role of corporate crossholdings and informal coalitions in frustrating a bid, and the discretion the authorities have in applying the take-over rules. It is likely that in the UK, Mixte's allies would have been viewed as acting in concert and would have been forced to make their own bid.

2. Germany: Feldmuehle Nobel AG

This is the only recorded case of a hostile acquisition in Germany. Feldmuehle Nobel AG was formed when Deutsche Bank acquired the industrial assets of Flick Industrieverwaltung in 1985, prior to it being floated in April 1986. The flotation was unique because (1) it was the largest recorded new issue (£703 million), (2) it was the first time 100 per cent of a company's share capital had been offered via a new issue, and (3) unlike many other issues, the shares were ordinary voting as opposed to non-voting preference shares.

In 1988, because of their stated dissatisfaction with the management of Feldmuehle Nobel, Friedrich and Gert Flick (nephews of the Friedrich Flick who sold the original company to Deutsche Bank) made an unsuccessful tender offer for 51 per cent of the shares. In the face of this and other bid speculation, the management recommended a restriction of any individual investor's voting rights to 5 per cent, irrespective of the number of shares held. Since Deutsche Bank, which was opposed to hostile take-overs, held proxy voting rights for what was thought to be about 55 per cent of Feldmuehle's equity, the resolution was passed with the required 50 per cent majority at the Annual General Meeting. The restriction, however, did not limit a bank's use of the voting block arising from its role as custodian of other investors' shares.

In 1989, a shareholder group led by the two Flick brothers sold a secretly accumulated 40 per cent stake in the company to Veba AG. The use of an investor coalition avoided the rule that requires disclosure of individual interests in excess of 25 per cent, and overcame the 5 per cent voting restriction by spreading the 40 per cent stake over seven individual investors. The acquisition by Veba was approved by the Federal Cartel Office, whose permission was required for purchases of stakes in excess of 25 per cent. With other purchases Veba currently owns 50 per cent of the company.

The rules that permit individual investors to accumulate stakes of up to 25 per cent without disclosure, and the absence of restrictions on the activities of investors working in concert, contrast with those of the UK. In the UK, company law requires disclosure of holdings in excess of 3 per cent, and the Takeover Panel prevents the circumvention of these restrictions through the use of coalitions.

In an attempt to avoid a hostile take-over, a German firm can restrict voting rights if shareholders' agreement is obtained. Banks play an important role in such decisions because they may wield the proxy votes of shares held in their custody. They can use their block vote to pass the resolution, but that block vote is not subsequently affected, since the shares are not owned by the banks. Also, custodianship enables them to monitor changes in ownership and stake-building and use that information to influence the outcome of a bid. The result is that banks are able to obstruct or accelerate the development of contested bids.

3. The UK: Imperial Group

On 2 December 1985 the Imperial Group and United Biscuits announced a merger based on an exchange of shares. On 6 December 1985 Hanson Trust made a share exchange offer for the Imperial Group, valuing it at £1.8 billion. This offer was strongly rejected by the Imperial management, which urged shareholders to accept the favoured merger with United Biscuits.

On 12 February it was announced that the Imperial–United Biscuits merger was to be referred to the Monopolies and Mergers Commission (MMC) for investigation on the grounds that together the Imperial Group and United Biscuit would control 30 per cent of the UK crisps market and 48 per cent of the snack market. United Biscuits and the Imperial Group criticized the government's decision, but as a result they abandoned their merger plans. Hanson's bid for Imperial was not referred.

On 17 February Hanson increased its bid to £2.32 billion, but simultaneously United Biscuit announced a competing bid of £2.56 billion, the largest bid then recorded. To avoid another referral to the MMC, the Imperial Group made a conditional sale of their major crisp brand ('Golden Wonder') for £54 million. This price was viewed by observers as being on the low side. During the course of the offers Hanson purchased 14.1 per cent and United Biscuits 14.9 per cent of Imperial's share capital in the open market. The maximum a bidder can purchase without providing a cash alternative is 15 per cent. Hanson's bid was successful and was declared unconditional after receiving acceptances of more than 50 per cent of Imperial's shares.

The change in ownership brought an immediate change in managerial control. The chairman and chief executive of Imperial, Mr Geoffrey Kent, resigned within a month of the offer going unconditional, taking with him compensation rumoured to be about £1 million. The five non-executive directors resigned immediately and three other executive directors resigned soon after.

Within two years Hanson had raised £2.05 billion through the sale of Imperial assets, including the Courage brewery and its public houses (£1.4 billion), hotel and restaurant interests (£190 million), Golden Wonder (£87 million), Findlays (£17 million), and Ross Young (£335 million). The retained businesses generated pre-tax profits of £170 million in 1987 for a net acquisition price of £550 million.

This case study provides a good example of how the Takeover Code promotes a market in corporate control and how UK company law provides a successful bidder with unfettered control over the target's board and assets. This is important for take-overs motivated by anticipation of profits on sales of assets, as in the Imperial Group case.

Appendix 4.2.

Time Series of Expenditures and Income for 1980–1989 for three German companies: Bayer, AEG, and MAN.

Year	Earnings (DM m.)	Dividends (DM)	Capital expenditure (DM m.)	Personnel expenditure[a] (DM m.)	R & D (DM m.)
Bayer					
1980	730	7.0	2,659	8,637	1,241
1981	517	7.0	2,539	9,550	1,406
1982	64	4.0	2,058	10,169	1,550
1983	754	7.0	1,872	10,759	1,694
1984	1,174	9.0	1,842	11,621	1,956
1985	1,436	10.0	2,058	12,303	2,134
1986	1,354	10.0	2,408	11,315	2,159
1987	1,544	11.0	2,565	11,833	2,343
1988	1,909	12.0	3,145	12,616	2,460
1989	2,116	13.0	3,447	13,228	2,695
AEG					
1980	(247)	0.00	499	5,567	996
1981	24	0.00	516	5,424	1,010
1982	(85)	0.00	362	4,494	843
1983	37	0.00	383	3,802	741
1984	398[b]	0.00	407	3,694	791
1985	0	0.00	418	3,809	852
1986	0	0.00	701	4,095	900
1987	0	0.00	633	4,383	929
1988	27	2.40	651	5,013	1,090
1989	275	2.50	720	4,502	787
MAN					
1980	121	7.00	562	3,708	n.a.
1981	117	7.00	599	4,025	n.a.
1982	64	7.00	651	4,222	n.a.
1983	(84)	5.00	687	3,088	n.a.
1984	(59)	3.00	537	2,999	n.a.
1985	503	5.50	340	3,138	n.a.
1986	122	5.50	486	3,222	n.a.

Year	Earnings (DM m.)	Dividends (DM)	Capital expenditure (DM m.)	Personnel expenditure[a] (DM m.)	R & D (DM m.)
MAN (*cont.*)					
1987	135	5.50	698	3,887	n.a.
1988	202	6.50	795	4,080	400
1989	254	8.00	889	4,177	415

[a] Incl. pension expenses.
[b] Resulting from ordinary income.

REFERENCES

Bavay, F., and Beau, D. (1988), 'L'Efficacité des strategies' de croissance externe: l'experience de l'industrie Française', *Banque de France*.

Coopers & Lybrand (1989), *The Barriers to Takeovers in the European Community*, Department of Trade and Industry, London: HMSO.

Edwards, J., and Fischer, K. (1990), 'Banks, finance and investment in West Germany since 1970', mimeo, University of Cambridge, St John's College, and University of Bonn.

Franks, J., and Mayer, C. (1991), 'Hostile takeovers and the correction of managerial failure', London Business School Working Paper.

Gerum, E., Steinmann, H., and Fees, W. (1988), *Der Mitbestimmte Aufsichtrat—Eire Empirische Untersuchung*, Stuttgart: Poeschel Verlag.

Jensen, M. C. (1989), 'Eclipse of the public corporation', *Harvard Business Review*, No. 5.

King, M. A. (1989), 'Takeover activity in the United Kingdom', in J. A. Fairburn and J. A. Kay (eds.), *Mergers and Merger Policy*, Oxford: Oxford University Press.

Schofner, T., (1990) 'The correction of managerial failure in Germany: three case studies', London Business School.

Schleifer, A., and Summers, L. H. (1988), 'Breach of trust in hostile takeovers', in A. J. Auerbach (ed.), *Corporate Take-overs: Causes and Consequences*, Chicago: National Bureau of Economic Research.

Weisbach, M. (1988), 'Outside directors and CEO turnover', *Journal of Financial Economics*, **20**, 431–60.

5

Corporate Governance, Take-overs, and the Role of the Non-executive Director

EVAN DAVIS* and JOHN KAY†

IMAGINE a system of government in which there are annual elections, but these are almost never contested. Whenever they are, the incumbent government wins by an overwhelming majority. All the information about the state of the nation which the voters receive is controlled and distributed by the government and is glossy and self-congratulatory in tone. Changes in the senior leadership do take place, normally through an orderly process of retirement in which the incumbent leaders select and groom their successors. Occasionally there is more violent change. Sometimes this takes the form of an internal *coup d'état*. Or it may occur as a result of the intervention of the hostile government of another state. This is not a description of Eastern Europe before perestroika and glasnost. It is a description of the system by which public companies in Britain are controlled and governed.

The government of corporations in Britain today suffers from the absence of an effective mechanism for making senior managers, who in the main no longer hold significant equity stakes in their companies, accountable to anyone. A theoretical structure exists, through the election of boards by shareholders and the appointment of executives by the elected board, but in practice it is defunct. Of course, many companies are well run and perhaps then this lack of external accountability does not matter. It does matter where the competence of the incumbent management is more doubtful, where there is a potential conflict of interest between senior managers and other stakeholders in the business (as, for example, over executive remuneration, defence against hostile take-over, or the company's own diversification), or where a strategic change of

* Economics Correspondent at the BBC. Evan Davies was a Research Fellow at the Centre for Business Strategy at the London Business School when this chapter was written.
† Chairman of London Economics and Professor of Economics at the London Business School.

The authors have enjoyed extensive and helpful discussions with Stanley Wright on the topics covered in this chapter. While he shares many of the views expressed herein, he takes no responsibility for their presentation here. They are also grateful to Filippo dell'Osso for compiling Table 5.3.

direction is required which incumbent management may find difficult to perceive, or to implement. The inability of the present system to cope well in these situations is damaging in the long term to both the reputation and the performance of the corporate sector.

At the same time, there is an excessive concentration on mergers and deal-making. Strategic management is increasingly seen as the construction and management of a portfolio of businesses, akin to the construction and management of a portfolio of shares. Good management lies in making good deals, rather than improving the underlying performance of the business through organic growth. Those who do concentrate on these real, rather than financial, objectives find their freedom of action seriously restricted by the threat of hostile take-over. The financial services industry has a strong vested interest in encouraging this perspective. The result is that much managerial effort is devoted to issues which are essentially peripheral to the better organization of production and distribution, and of marginal value to the economy taken as a whole.

These problems of corporate governance and of excessive take-over activity are increasingly recognized, and much of the concern that has developed has generated a number of proposals, frequently for establishing alternative, more institutional means of control—such as revitalizing the non-executive director or creating 'supervisory boards'—and for protecting managers from attack by hostile predators.

These proposals imply that take-overs are undesirable and interfere with management's ability to plan and develop long-term relationships, but that before removing the take-over system, some other means of making managers accountable to their shareholders is necessary. If implemented in the UK or USA, they would result in a system of corporate government more akin to that of continental Europe.

Pitched against this strand of thinking is what can be described as a more *laissez-faire* view: regulatory failures are in most cases more severe than market failures; companies should sort out their own structure of internal relationships; hostile take-overs are an important way of ensuring that managers face the right incentives to represent their shareholders' interests. This outlook has led the current UK administration to adopt a permissive attitude to the take-over process, allowing almost any bid that has no implications for competition to proceed unhindered by the public interest considerations of the Monopolies and Mergers Commission. This approach was informally codified in the 'Tebbit Guide-lines' in 1984.

We believe each of these views is partly, but only partly, correct. The take-over mechanism is an appropriate, if rather expensive, part of a capitalist economy, and one which would work better with an improved system of corporate governance. But the take-over mechanism as it exists does not solve the problem of managers undermining the value that belongs to their shareholders; it is, in fact, the primary means by which they divert value to their own use. We agree that the non-executive director is an important means of achieving management accountability; but if that function is to be performed effectively we believe the functions of the non-executive need far clearer definition.

1. THE PROBLEM OF MANAGEMENT ACCOUNTABILITY

The view that managers need to be controlled derives from the existence of two different problems of management accountability. The first is based on the general human observation that people make self-interested decisions, often assuaging any guilt they might be inclined to feel by persuading themselves that their actions are in accord with the general good. Managers and shareholders do not always have coincident interests—for example in the setting of remuneration—and in order to get them to make decisions for the shareholders, managers have to be furnished with the right incentives or lose the power to make decisions in areas characterized by conflict.

The second problem is that of management competence. Managers may be acting with integrity, and there may be no conflict of interest, but the managers in charge may not be the best able to do the job. We need some process by which good managers can drive out the bad.[1]

Both these problems, whose importance is largely underestimated by managers themselves, were notably present in the 1980s. The extent to which managers in the UK exploited a favourable political climate to reward themselves for what they themselves judged as their good work is documented in Table 5.1. Table 5.1 does not even reflect the contribution of stock options to executive remuneration, which has been very substantial in many cases.

In other cases, managers have formalized their claim to the assets of the company by purchasing them in a buy-out. They sell the shareholders' belongings to themselves on the shareholders' behalf at prices that would be too low if the company was being managed to the best ability of the manager.

Incompetence is a problem even where conflicts of interest do not arise. There has to be some mechanism for placing effective stewards in charge of poorly managed concerns. But in the absence of any effective system of corporate governance, this is very hard. The case of Distillers does as

---

[1] This account still leaves a third problem, labelled *ex ante* managerial failure by Franks and Mayer (1990), in which there are different views as to the future potential of a company without any necessary implication that it has been mismanaged in the past, or that wilful neglect has occurred. This is covered in Section 2.

Table 5.1. Chief executive pay in large UK firms

Date	Minimum turnover of firms included in sample[a] (£b)	Chief exec's salary & bonuses (£000s)	Rise between dates (%)	Rise in average earnings over same period (%)
Oct. 1981	1.1	110.3		
Oct. 1985	1.3	128.2	16.2	5.9
Oct. 1986	1.7	152.5	19.0	8.3
Oct. 1987	1.7	205.0	34.4	8.0
July 1988	1.8	240.0	17.0	8.3
July 1989	2.0	329.5	37.0	8.7

[a] Part of the increase in salary can be attributed to the changing composition of the sample.

Source: Office of Manpower Economics, 'Survey of Top Salaries in the Private Sector', *Employment Gazette*.

much to demonstrate this as any other. Formed in 1926 by the merger of all the leading Scotch whisky producers, it was always a loosely integrated company. Its output, spirits, traditionally were sold through wine merchants and publicans, but in the 1950s and 1960s, wine merchants lost their share of the retail trade in spirits to specialist cut-price liquor stores and supermarkets, while concentration in the brewing industry encouraged the major brewers to use the outlets they had acquired to sponsor their own brands of spirits. Distillers did not respond to these developments and as a result, the company lost its leadership in both these markets, as it did at the same time in its major export markets. The decline of the company was accelerated by two specific disasters. First, in seeking to diversify from its base, it selected pharmaceuticals as an area for expansion, and secured UK marketing rights to thalidomide. Secondly, the company's attempts to restrict parallel export of its whisky was attacked under Article 85 of the Treaty of Rome, and it responded to this by withdrawing several brands, including Johnny Walker, its best seller, from the UK market. By the mid-1980s, the company's once dominant market share in the UK had declined to under 20 per cent.

The sustained mismanagement of Distillers over several decades had significant consequences not only for its shareholders, but for employees, for the regional economy of Scotland—it was the largest company based there—and for UK exports. There was persistent City dissatisfaction with the company, and there is evidence of a number of expressions of concern by institutional shareholders to the management of the company, which were not, in the main, well received.

How a change of management can be orchestrated in a company like this, with the existence of many disparate and uninformed shareholders, and a concentrated well-informed board, is hard to see other than through some powerful and effective system of corporate governance. Certainly no such system existed until the mid-1980s, when a well-publicized and costly solution emerged. The result was the necessary improvement in performance, but we do not believe that anyone would regard the process by which that was achieved as one which reflects an appropriate system of governance.

2. TAKE-OVER AND CORPORATE GOVERNANCE

With the exception of some merger and acquisition departments in merchant banks, most would agree that there was too much take-over activity in the 1980s. This is a view shared as much by managers in industry as left-wing critics of the capitalist system. The perception of those taking these positions is that an active take-over market engenders the belief that the role of management is that of managing a portfolio of companies; and that this in turn replaces long-term corporate development with the short-term attitude that when things go wrong you can cut and run.[2] The take-over process also has a disturbingly contagious effect, with many executives apparently believing that if they are not seen to be joining in, they become more vulnerable to its effects. Certainly, the idea that the take-overs serve well is, prima facie, belied by the fact that the level of hostile take-over activity and post-war economic performance are perfectly inversely related among the 'Group of Five' nations (Bannock (1990)).

One easy response to this problem would be to throw sand into the take-over mechanism to slow it down or grind it to a halt, and the most commonly suggested method of doing this is to provide more protection for the managers of firms under attack, particularly in hostile bids. John Plender, for example (IPPR (1990)) has argued for the tougher application of competition policy to deter contested bids, and says:

And if, in a world where bankers have such a powerful incentive to put companies into play, the restraint proves inadequate, this broad change in competition policy could be buttressed by specific regulatory measures designed to give incumbent management a fair chance against more determined predators.

---

[2] For example, articulate criticisms of take-over as it currently operates can be found in Schleifer and Summers (1988) and Sykes (1990).

The idea that managers should be protected from unwelcome bids is also, not surprisingly, often propagated by managers themselves. It is, however, a curious solution to the problem, for as Table 5.2 shows, it is actually the shareholders in companies which are taken over who derive large benefits from these deals. It is, indeed, shareholders in the companies who do the taking over who might have reason to complain. On average, they gain almost nothing at all out of acquisitions, and in a large minority of cases they lose out from it. This is not surprising: with bid premiums of about 40 per cent, shareholders have companies bought on their behalf at prices well in excess of those they would have needed to pay if they had bought them for themselves. The market believes that synergies and other benefits of combining firms will not yield returns large enough to compensate for the difference; and evidence on the profitability of companies subsequent to acquisition suggests that that market view is generally right (see Hughes (1989) for a survey).

Table 5.2. Impact of acquisitions on the share price of companies involved[a]

	Average value changes		Percentage of firms with value increases	
	Month of bid (%)	Six months around bid (−4 to +1) (%)	Month of bid	Six months around bid
Acquiree	22	30	86	85
Acquirer	1	7	50	65

[a] Franks and Harris report that on average the acquirer is 7 to 8 times as large as the acquiree, based on market value of equity; thus, a direct comparison of percentage value gains does not give a full picture of the split of value gains. They show, however, that value gains still go largely to the acquiree after controlling for the relative size of merging firms.
Source: Franks and Harris (1989).

The fact that managers spend their shareholders' money on take-overs of dubious value, and that other managers oppose take-overs that generally could be expected to benefit their shareholders, suggests that take-over is an area of conflict of interest between managers and shareholders. The take-over problem then, is not one of innocent companies being taken over; it is one of innocent shareholders unwittingly taking over companies in which they have no real interest. This is a view of the take-over mechanism that many find paradoxical. Few people worried about the Nestlé take-over of Rowntree on the grounds that it was not good value for the Nestlé shareholders, and few would have done so even if the

Nestlé shareholders had not been Swiss. The fact that it yielded the English owners of Rowntree—mostly pensioners and future pensioners—about a billion pounds more than anyone in the UK had ever supposed it was worth (and, for that matter, than there is reason to think it was worth) was a fact that hardly entered the wide public discussion of the merger.

What does the view that take-over is a problem on the acquirer's side rather than the acquiree's imply for policy? All deals derive from the fact that the participants place a different value on the assets in question and the appropriate policy depends on the particular source of that difference. Three main cases arise.

The first class of deals are those where the different value derives from the fact that the company is worth more in one party's hands than another. In these cases, it is quite clear that it is usually appropriate to allow deals to proceed unless the benefits derive from the suppression of competition—indeed, not only to allow them to proceed, but to ease their passage. A well-functioning market in corporate control is beneficial to economic development in these situations.

The second class of deals are those where one party has simply made a mistake over the potential value of the company in question. One group believes that it is worth more than the other because it is inherently more optimistic than the other. Over the mid-1980s a surge in acquisitions activity, mostly financed by imprudent bank lending, highlighted the damage that can be done by reckless and optimistic predators with more money than management talent. The story of Robert Campeau, who wielded several billion dollars' worth of damage before the banks realized he was not fit to manage prestige department stores (Loomis (1990)), was but the most extreme example. It is not hard to find UK corporate stars whose popularity in the City allowed them to embark on take-over sprees in which they destroyed not only their targets, but themselves in the bargain: Coloroll and British and Commonwealth come to mind.

But while these mistakes are costly and destructive, it is also the case that they are self-correcting. They are financed by banks who tend to spot the error of their ways—albeit too late—and if the banks do not spot them early enough, the companies are usually not around long enough to continue wielding damage. It would be difficult for a process of regulation or vetting of mergers to screen the sensible mergers that occur—some of which might be daring and ambitious—from the reckless ones. As in other areas of regulation, the existence of imperfect behaviour by agents should not be sufficient to generate regulation if there are no conflicts of private and public interest, and to use the Monopolies and Mergers Commission to do so would benefit no one. In these cases, it really does seem best to leave the decision to those willing to put their money behind their judgement. Of course, sometimes groups with money will make mistakes—sometimes at a very large cost—but it is hard to see why, on average, they are likely to make more mistakes than regulators with precious little business experience, and with no financial incentive to get the answer right.

The third, and perhaps the most common, mergers are those that are a mistake not because there is some serious business misjudgement, but because the incentives of the decision-makers are inconsistent with the desires of those whose money they are spending. It is in these cases—where take-over is financed by shareholders but serve the goals of management—that it is hard to identify any effective self-correcting mechanism, for few shareholders have the interest, the power, or the incentive to monitor their company's performance very closely. So, the tendency is for ambitious managers to pursue strategic goals which the shareholders could themselves pursue more cheaply without their managers being involved. The fact that it is not their money that is staked on the deal imposes too few incentives on the manager to ensure that the strategic move is right from the shareholders point of view—and in these cases it is the shareholders' perspective, not the manager's one, which coincides with the interests of the economy at large. These cases provide a strong reason for removing these decisions from the managers suffering from a conflict of interest into the hands of those who are most affected by them.

So take-over has an important but ambiguous role in the process of corporate governance. On the one hand—as the Distillers case showed—it does provide an effective method of last resort for replacing incompetent management. The mere existence of this option can be important in generating changes in managers without the need for resorting to that method. While take-over is beneficial in dealing with these sorts of problems of management accountability, however, it simultaneously exacerbates the problem of conflicts of interest. Managers enjoy acquisition activity, and are frequently rewarded by it in terms of remuneration, power, and prestige. All these rewards can accrue to executives, even when there are negative returns to shareholders.

From the point of view of corporate governance, then, there are three major problems with take-over as it now operates. First, it is too easy for managers to spend shareholders' money without their permission. It should be made more difficult. On top of this, take-over does still not provide a very effective solution to the other problems of conflict of interest. Excessive managerial remuneration, for example, is unlikely to be on such a scale as to prompt a hostile bid, but the fact that managers will not do unlimited damage to the company is not to say that they should not face accountability.

Thirdly, there is still the sheer difficulty of changing management through take-over. In order to change control, there has to be a change in ownership. Yet, many shareholders may not want to sell their shares, or may be happy to keep shares in the newly controlled company. Indeed, some shareholders might hang on to their shares while nevertheless hoping that the others will sell and control of the firm will change. It would be perfectly rational for everyone to adopt this posture, and for control not to change at all despite unanimous agreement that it should (Grossman and Hart (1980)). It certainly seems odd that shareholders should not be able to orchestrate a change in management other than through selling their shares, or through buying everyone elses'.[3]

These deficiencies in the take-over system suggest that, as the popular debate has concluded, there is room for institutional change of some sort to make take-over less frequent.

3. THE ROLE OF THE NON-EXECUTIVE DIRECTOR

Most discussion of corporate governance stresses the role of the non-executive director. If we ask who non-executive directors generally are, Table 5.3 and the box on page 210 provide some guidance. The majority of non-executive directors are people who are, or recently have been, senior executives in other commercial and industrial companies. The second largest category are those with experience of government, either as politicians or civil servants. This is particularly common in companies which themselves have extensive dealings with government, either because government buys their products or where regulation is important. A small group of non-executives have a background in finance, usually as executives in a merchant bank or stockbroking firm. There are only a few non-executive directors of major UK companies whose principal experience is in professional practice—such as law or accountancy—or in education or the media.

Non-executives have three functions in practice—as consultants, as monitors, and as decision-makers. The non-executive acts as adviser to executive management, and this part of the role is the one most often stressed by companies themselves. For example, in its annual report, British Telecom argues of its non-executive directors: 'Each brings a particular expertise to the board to complement the expertise of executive

---

[3] The Isosceles take-over of Gateway provided a paradoxical illustration of these problems. Certain shareholders instituted a change in management, not through an annual general meeting, but through a purchase of control. In the debate and contest that followed, those who agreed with the Isosceles plans ended up with no stake in the company, while those who did not still had a large share.

Table 5.3. The principal occupation of non-executive directors[a]

Main occupation (or recent occupation if retired)	No. in sample	Proportion in sample (%, rounded)
Executive director/chairman	209	62
Government (politician or civil servant)	49	14
Financial sector position	21	6
Professional career	20	6
Other	36	11
TOTAL	335	100
Unclassified	13	

[a] Data for this table were compiled by analysis of the annual reports of private sector quoted companies in the top 100 of the *Times* 1,000 Index (some 74 companies). Biographical information was obtained from the companies' annual reports and *Who's Who*. Some categorizations were subjective. People who held more than one non-executive post in the sample of companies are counted more than once.

Source: Centre for Business Strategy analysis.

colleagues. Collectively they help to ensure that board decisions are taken from a suitably broad perspective.' There is no reason why someone need be a director of a company to perform this function, and almost all firms have advisers and consultants who are not directors of the company. It is unusual, however, for companies to have advisers who are currently in executive posts in other firms, unless they take the role of non-executive director. This seems to be no more than a convention.

The non-executive director also acts as monitor of the performance of executive management. This is a function stressed, not surprisingly, by the Association of British Insurers (ABI (1990)), which argues that: 'While all directors have a duty to monitor the performance of a company, the non-executive directors should acknowledge a duty to monitor the performance of the executive directors, and to report to the shareholders if they are not satisfied after reasonable efforts have been made by them to remedy the causes of their dissatisfaction.' But the legal role of the non-executive director is that of decision-maker. British law recognizes no distinction between executive and non-executive directors. Both categories are equal members of a unitary board, and both share, at least in principle, the increasingly onerous responsibilities for the behaviour of the company and its consequences, which are associated with company directorship.

So non-executives have responsibilities as advisers, as decision-makers and as monitors; yet it is apparent that there are serious incompatibilities

Who Are Britain's Non-executive Directors?

A survey of Britain's Top 100 companies reveals that, on average, a large British company will have about five non-executive directors on the board, with an average age of just over 60 years. Non-executives are overwhelmingly British and male.

As illustrated in Table 5.3, the main occupation of 62 per cent of the non-executive directors surveyed is, or has been, as an executive director or chairman of another, usually British, company. About a tenth of these are former executives of their own board. Among the rest there is a smattering of financial, professional, and government personnel, and the remainder include academics, media personalities, nobility, and the wives of former Tory Cabinet ministers.

Although many British companies have recently made a point of selecting women or foreign citizens as non-executive directors, these are still a small minority. Only 4 per cent of non-executives are women, and suitable women are in demand. About one non-executive director in nine is a foreign national.

Companies have an average of 4.6 non-executives, but this is a number that varies between 1 for Great Universal Stores and 10 for Tate and Lyle. There is some evidence of occupational clustering on boards with, for example, three of the five independent directors of Shell Transport & Trading in the 'government' category.

It is hard to estimate accurately the number of other non-executive positions that each non-executive has. It appears that about half the independent directors also hold non-executive positions on the boards of either one or two other companies. About 10 per cent hold three or four posts, and a large minority hold five or more non-executive directorships, with one or two people, such as Sir David Nicolson, sitting on as many as eight boards.

among these functions. There is a clear distinction between the role of the adviser who provides input into a decision based on specific, if necessarily limited, expertise and perspective, and those who make the decision. It is also obvious that one cannot both make decisions and assess the performance of those who do. It is the inconsistency of these functions which makes the non-executive directorship a weak institution in practice, and explains why many conscientious non-executive directors find the job an unsatisfactory one. It is not in any way to demean these individuals to observe that Norman Tebbit's contribution to the evolution of British Telecom's international strategy cannot be of the same kind as that of the company's executive management; or that Sir Michael Palliser's responsibility for the direction of Shell's exploration programme is not equal to that of its managing director. It is simply a statement of obvious fact, and to appear to deny it is to obscure the true role of the non-executive director. As shareholders in British Telecom and in Shell, we would be pleased to think that these individuals were making their advice available to the Board in their areas of expertise; and we would also be glad to have them as independent assessors of the performance of executive management. We would be unhappy if they were substantive decision-makers on operating issues which were outside these areas of expertise, and we do not believe that, whatever the theoretical legal position, this is in fact their role.

Yet the blending of these functions diminishes the ability of the non-executive to perform any of them. Events of the following kind will, we believe, be familiar to almost anyone who has experience as a non-executive director. Executive management bring to the Board a proposal, based on extensive analysis, to which they are strongly committed. The non-executive director has reservations which are partly, but not completely, answered. On this basis he acquiesces in the decision to go ahead. The proposal is implemented and is not successful. The non-executive feels that some reorganization of personnel and procedure is an appropriate response. But the view of management is that the failure of the initiative could not reasonably have been anticipated and they point to the full discussion, and subsequent agreement, of the Board which preceded it.

We do not believe it is right, except in extreme cases, to suggest that the non-executive should have pressed his reservations to outright opposition. By the nature of his role, he is less well informed about the issues and, more importantly, by asserting his authority on the issue he undermines the real responsibility of executive management for the conduct of the business. That means that the advisory role is inhibited by the responsibilities of directorship. There is a substantial difference between rejecting the advice of a consultant and outvoting a director, and all parties know this. But it is equally inconsistent with the conduct of a unitary board for a director to blame others for a decision in which he has, both practically and formally, shared. The non-executive's capacity to act as monitor is necessarily limited by the requirement that he share responsibility for the company's affairs on an equal basis with those he monitors.

While it is easy to enjoy the free lunch and remain unconcerned about these issues, it is the lack of clarity about function, and the conflicts inherent in the multiple functions which there are, which makes it impossible to leave all forms of corporate governance in the hands of the non-executive director. We believe it is clear that the primary role is that of monitor, not consultant or decision-maker. Decision-making is the responsibility of executive management, and there are plenty of other mechanisms by which executive managers can secure external advice. The role which is not fulfilled in other ways—and the role which it is most appropriate for non-executives to play—is that of supervising the performance of executive managers. For them to act also as advisers on executive decisions, far less to share responsibility for the company's principal decisions, is necessarily to limit their effectiveness in that role.

The operation of such a role is demonstrated in the case of Dennis Stevenson, who led a non-executive coup against Tony Berry, the chairman and chief executive of Blue Arrow. Dissatisfied, with good cause, with the company's performance and management style, Stevenson determined to promote change and, denied access to company resources, invested thousands of pounds of his personal funds in obtaining independent legal and financial advice to fight his corner; a corner which he eventually won. The case stands out because it is exceptional. Stevenson's boardroom colleagues made clear that the proper course of action for him to take was to resign, and if the function of the non-executive is to advise that must be true, since advice could not effectively be tendered in these circumstances.

Yet if a primary function of non-executive directors is to monitor, it is clear that both the mechanism by which they are chosen and the results of that mechanism are quite inappropriate for that purpose. Non-executives are usually company executives themselves, sharing the culture of those they monitor. Or they are people with too little business experience to be effective protectors of shareholder rights. The most natural group among which to look for monitors with independence, standing, and experience—professional advisers, the group from which Dennis Stevenson was drawn—is precisely that which is markedly under-represented in the ranks of non-executive directors. Non-executives are in general picked by the executives, owe their salary to the executives, and commonly share social and other business connections with the executives. They rely on executives for information and advice, and their principal duties are carried out in the presence of the executives. It is hardly surprising that changes in executive management are more frequently the product of expensive, external action through take-over than consequences of the activities of non-executive directors.

If our view of the proper role of the non-executive is correct, it carries strong implications for company practice, and probably company law. On the one hand, it points to a range of issues on which the non-executive voice should be decisive—such as executive remuneration, response to take-over, and most importantly, on the appointment of executive management. These are areas where the monitor is in a better position to make a decision than the executive. On the other, it points to a range of issues on which the non-executive voice should be a quiet one, if heard at all—those concerned with the operating tactics and strategy of the business. In these, it is clear that the expertise lies with the executive, and in as far as there is disagreement between them, it is the executive who should decide. Indeed, if we believed the monitor could decide on the basis of far more limited information and relevant experience, we would do well to employ the monitor as an executive. Of course, executive management should be free to consult non-executives in these matters—as they are free to take other advice—but it should be clear that this does not diffuse, or reduce, their own responsibility for the consequences of their actions. All this does no more than spell out, and push to a logical conclusion, what is already practice in most companies which make thoughtful use of non-executive directors.

Unfortunately, this view is difficult to reconcile with the notion of the unitary board, since it allocates distinct, and largely disjoint, areas of responsibility to executives and non-executives. Whether provision for these different roles is best made through the mechanism of the supervisory board—most large companies already have distinct executive meetings—or through legal recognition of the position of the non-executive director is a secondary matter. Certainly, the current absence of such recognition is one aspect of the present ambiguity in the role of the non-executive; and it is not sensible to impose on non-executives legal responsibilities which it is not realistic to expect a part-time director, largely dependent on executive management for knowledge of the day-to-day operations of the business, to be able to discharge.

It further follows that the initiative in the appointment of non-executives should rest, not with executive management, but with shareholders, which in practice means the large investment institutions. This is not an issue on which there is any divergence of interest between shareholders, and institutional shareholders can represent the rest well enough. If the primary role of the non-executive is that of monitor, then people should not appoint their own monitors. Asked to vouch for their own character, the crook appoints another crook and the honest man appoints a friend; in neither case is the resulting character reference worth much. That is not to say that the relationship between executive and non-executive should be an abrasive one or that a good non-executive would not expect to establish friendly working relationships with creative management; but it is to say that if the relationship is invariably a friendly one it does not serve its function.

And we have to recognize that human nature tends to create personal relationships which undermine the monitoring function. This is the phenomenon of regulatory capture—the monitor and the manager have an entirely appropriate inclination to work out together what needs doing, and to agree on it, and ultimately to start to blur their divergent roles and obligations. As Gilson and Kraakman (1990) have observed, this can lead to further regress in which a monitor is needed to check on the monitor. Yet the non-executive's incentives to pursue a quiet life, rather than to argue over issues of conflict and competence, is very strong. The Stevenson route is a costly one, in time, money, emotion, and perhaps even in reputation, particularly if, as would normally now be the case, the non-executive is unsuccessful in securing the outcome he seeks. It is necessary that the non-executive's own reputation should be substantively dependent on the effectiveness with which he performs his monitoring role and this, in turn, has implications for who it is that should be non-executives. It tells against those who are retired; it tells against—again—those who hold executive positions in other large companies; it points—again—towards professional advisers. We are attracted by Gilson and Kraakman's proposal that there should be a new breed of professional non-executive director—not only independent of the executives, but also *dependent* on the shareholders—whose primary responsibility is to perform that function for several companies, and whose continued reputation in that role depends on the effectiveness with which they are judged to have performed the monitoring function.

4. CONCLUSION

There are two approaches to making managers accountable. The first is to look at the results of their work and to assess them by the performance of the firm. This avoids interference in the process of decision-making, judging them against some set standard after a period of time has elapsed. In this case, managerial punishment or reward depends on how well the company does, with perhaps only a tenuous regard for whether the managers are themselves responsible for that performance.

It is clear that the take-over mechanism, like the system of indirect democracy in Britain and most of the West, falls into this category. No one interferes with the decision-making process, but if your decisions have not performed well, you will lose your job eventually.

The second approach, more like the one that operates in referendum-based Swiss cantons, is to monitor the decisions themselves—to appoint someone to stand next to the manager, looking at what he does and deciding whether the decisions are sensible. This can be done on a weekly, monthly, annual, or longer basis. This sort of structure is presumably what was intended in the design of a non-executive presence on the board.

These two approaches can respectively be characterized as market or regulatory. However the first is put into practice, it is a market-influenced approach because it operates through incentives, rather than dictat, and at no stage does anyone have to judge the decisions of the decision-maker. The idea is not to judge the decisions, but to look at their effect. In principle, the information needed is not what the decisions were, but what the performance of the company has been. The second is a bureaucratic solution to the problem, and shares with bureaucratic solutions in general the features that it does not act on the incentives of the agents, it rather limits their power, and secondly, that it relies on the good judgement of the monitor in order to come up with good decisions.

Our view is that as long as there are effective means for appointing and firing managers, and as long as they do not suffer from conflicts of interest, the market approach is best. To ensure that these two conditions hold, however, monitors are needed: they can lubricate the appointments' process; and they can make decisions—such as what salary managers should be paid—which managers are singularly unqualified to make.

If there is to be some role for a corporate monitor, the non-executive director appears to be ideal for the purpose. And this is reflected in the proposals emerging for the non-executive role. The arguments we have presented here provide a rationale for these and other proposals. They also suggest that there is little point in merely going half way down the road to independent non-executives. The two components to the process of successful monitoring are that the monitor is independent of those being monitored, and that the monitor does not bear any responsibility for the decisions being monitored. The two measures together are worth more than the sum of the two on their own. Eradicating the notion that there should be a unitary board with collective responsibility for decisions is a precondition to giving the independent directors a useful presence on the board. And understanding that the non-executive directors are there to facilitate changes in management without the need for a take-over in cases where this is desirable is an important step in the process of reducing the significance of the take-over mechanism in controlling our economy. Reform of the take-over process itself will then no longer be an issue.

REFERENCES

ABI (1990), 'The role and duties of directors—a discussion paper', Association of British Insurers, London.

Bannock, G. (1990), 'The takeover boom: an international and historical perspective', Papers Prepared for the Inquiry into Corporate Takeovers in the United Kingdom, No. 2, The David Hume Institute, Edinburgh.

Franks, J., and Harris, R. (1989), 'Shareholder wealth effects of UK takeovers: implications for merger policy', in J. A. Fairburn and J. A. Kay (eds.), *Mergers and Merger Policy*, Oxford: Oxford University Press

—— and Mayer, C. (1990), 'Capital markets and corporate control: a study of France, Germany and the UK', *Economic Policy*, April, 191–231.

Gilson, R. J., and Kraakman, R. (1990), 'Reinventing the outside director: an agenda for institutional investors', Presented at the Salomon Brothers Center and Rutgers Center Conference on *The Fiduciary Responsibilities of Institutional Investors*, June.

Grossman, S., and Hart, O. (1980) 'Takeover bids, the free rider problem and the theory of the corporation', *Bell Journal of Economics*, Spring. 42–64.

Hughes, A. (1989), 'The impact of merger: a survey of empirical evidence for the UK', in J. A. Fairburn and J. A. Kay (eds.), *Mergers and Merger Policy*, Oxford: Oxford University Press

IPPR (1990), *Takeovers and Short termism in the UK*, Institute for Public Policy Research, Industrial Policy Paper No. 3 by Andy Cosh, Alan Hughes, Ajit Singh, James Carty, and John Plender.

Loomis, C., (1990), 'The biggest, looniest deal ever', *Fortune*, 18 June, 42–52.

Schleifer, A., and Summers, L. H. (1988), 'Breach of trust in hostile takeovers', in A. J. Auerbach (ed.), *Corporate Takeovers: Causes and Consequences*, National Bureau of Economic Research, Chicago.

Sykes, Allen (1990), 'Corporate takeovers—the need for fundamental rethinking', Papers Prepared for the Inquiry into Corporate Takeovers in the United Kingdom, No. 9, The David Hume Institute, Edinburgh.

6

The Empirical Analysis of Market Structure and Performance

JAMES FAIRBURN* and PAUL GEROSKI†

1. INTRODUCTION

In evaluating any horizontal merger, a central concern is the likely effect of that merger on industry performance. Although many performance criteria might be thought relevant—level of costs and efficiency, standards of inventiveness and innovation—much attention is typically given to the apparently more direct and tractable effects on prices and thence profits. Will the reduction of competition arising from the merging of competing firms, and the corresponding changes in the concentration of sales within an industry, elevate prices over costs and thus increase profits?

A potentially fruitful approach to this question is to consider the past performance of a range of industries which differ in their configuration of firms and in other attributes, and to isolate and measure the general effect on observed prices or profits of varying levels of sales concentration. Research of this type is the subject of this chapter.

The chapter is structured as follows. In Section 2 we set out the common framework of this type of analysis, which is known in the industrial economics literature as the 'structure-conduct-performance' paradigm, and we examine and assess the British evidence. Dissatisfaction with this basic approach has led in recent years to a number of modifications to and developments of the underlying framework, which are discussed in Section 3. Although as yet subject to only limited empirical testing for Britain, these new approaches nevertheless offer a number of insights into industry performance. Section 4 contains our conclusions.

* Lecturer in Economics at the University of Sussex.
† Professor of Economics at the London Business School.

This chapter first appeared in J. A. Fairburn and J. A. Kay (eds.), *Mergers and Merger Policy*, Oxford: Oxford University Press, 1989.

2. STRUCTURE, CONDUCT, AND PERFORMANCE

Analysis of inter-industry variations in performance commenced with the work of Bain in the 1940s and 1950s, and the essence of the 'structure–conduct–performance' approach was also established by him. The approach views the structure of the industry, or 'market structure', as the major exogenous variable of interest, determining the extent to which firms in a particular industry are able to achieve a long-term elevation of prices over marginal costs, and therefore earn persistently high returns. The manner in which structure affects performance is through its effect on firms' behaviour or 'conduct', i.e. the ways they interact with each other and the way in which prices and output levels are chosen. The basic 'structuralist' hypothesis that structure is the important determinant of performance follows from the view that the range of conduct it is possible to observe in an industry with a given structure is extremely limited. Hence structure determines conduct, and performance follows directly from this. Indeed, in much of the literature we are to discuss, conduct is suppressed almost entirely, and little is lost by concentrating one's attention on the structure–performance link alone.[1]

Of the many possible 'structural' characteristics of industries, that which has been the subject of most persistent attention is the level of industry concentration. Concentration indices are summary measures of the number of firms within an industry and the distribution of their sizes.[2] The most widely used index in both official statistics and empirical work is the k-firm concentration ratio, which gives the proportion of industry sales accounted for by the largest k firms. (The 5-firm concentration ratio, CR5, is most commonly available in the UK.) Much recent work has, however, favoured the Hirshmann–Herfindahl index, the sum of squared individual market shares for all firms in the industry. The attributes of an industry captured by concentration indices are generally thought to characterize the extent to which it will be able to raise prices.

[1] A classic exposition of the basic structuralist view is given in Bain's (1959) textbook. Scherer's more recent text (1980) argues that a range of possible behavioural patterns can in principle be observed in markets with a given structure. In more modern work—see Waterson (1984)—prime attention is given to conduct and the structure–performance link down-traded. For arguments that question the exogeneity of market structure to pricing decisions, see Clarke and Davies (1982), Geroski (1982a), and Donsimoni, Geroski, and Jacquemin (1985).

[2] There is a large literature on the properties that a concentration index should embody and on the relative merits of those available, see e.g. Hart (1975), Hannah and Kay (1977), and Davies (1979). (For discussion of the impact of merger on concentration, see Hughes (1989).) Many of the indices are highly correlated, suggesting that as an empirical matter the choice between them may be of little consequence. For alternative approaches stressing the importance of making the correct choice, see Schmalensee (1977), Kwoka (1979, 1981), and Geroski (1983).

Thus, an industry with relatively few firms, or one with several firms much larger than the remainder, is generally thought more likely than a relatively unconcentrated industry to achieve high prices in equilibrium. This outcome does not depend on firms making a collusive agreement, and hence is sometimes termed 'tacit' collusion. However, it may be that the probability of overt collusion does additionally increase with increasing concentration, a factor which, if true, will strengthen the observed relationship between concentration and profits.

Testing the basic structuralist hypothesis has taken the form of looking for a systematic and stable positive association between average industry price–cost margins or rates of return on capital, and levels of industry concentration. However, Bain (1956) argued that in examining the concentration–profits relationship, one must hold constant industry cost and demand conditions, and make allowance for the condition of entry into the industry.[3]

Bain's own approach was to examine individual industries in detail, and make a necessarily subjective assessment of the height of individual and overall barriers to entry. Following the influential paper of Comanor and Wilson (1967), the far more common approach has been to find statistical proxies for entry barriers. Thus one can derive estimates of the minimum efficient scale (the importance of economies of scale in relation to the size of the industry) from the actual scale of operation of existing firms, and one can take the industry advertising–sales ratio as a proxy for product differentiation advantages. Such proxies are then added to measures of concentration in regressions explaining profits, together with additional conditioning variables, such as the growth of industry sales, the level of imports, etc. Entry barriers normally seem to exert a positive influence on profits, with a significant positive correlation almost invariably being observed between advertising intensity and profit margins.[4]

Following Bain's first study (1951), this type of exercise has formed the basis of a huge number of studies covering a number of different countries.[5] Most researchers have detected a positive correlation between

[3] In addition to using proxies for entry barriers to explain profitability, it is also possible to use them in the explanation of actual rates of entry. For a survey of models of this type, see Geroski and Masson (1987).

[4] This finding has attracted considerable controversy. There are questions of whether current advertising expenditure or the accumulated stock of advertising capital is appropriate, and whether the positive coefficient reflects a barrier to entry. See Comanor and Wilson (1979) for a survey. There are also reasons to expect advertising expenditures to be determined by concentration (Waterson (1984, ch. 7), so that it would be inappropriate to regard advertising as an exogenous determinant of profits. However, simultaneous equations models suggest that it can in fact be taken as exogenous for the purposes of estimation (Strickland and Weiss (1976), Geroski (1982b), Martin (1979, 1980)). We return to this below.

[5] Surveys of the literature include Weiss (1974), Scherer (1980, ch. 9), and Schmalensee (1989). The studies covered often involve modifications we discuss in the remainder of this section.

industry concentration and average industry returns. However, the relationship is typically rather weak, and is often estimated with a fair amount of imprecision. Although dwarfed by research on the USA, there have now been some fourteen published studies relating to the British manufacturing sector. We have chosen to focus on the more recent studies, which have examined the period from 1968 onward.[6]

The most common specification of the structure–performance model is an equation which is linear in the relevant variables or, less frequently, linear in their logs. Hart and Morgan (1977) produced results for this model on a sample of 113 MLH (3-digit) Census of Production industries for 1968. Their first step was to carry out a log-linear regression of their chosen measure of profits, the ratio of gross profit to value added, on a constant term and the 5-firm concentration ratio. This yielded a positive, significant relationship, which implied that a 10 per cent rise in concentration would be associated with a 1 per cent increase in industry profits. However, less than 10 per cent of the variation in industry profits was explained in this way. Further variables were then added: the import–sales ratio (MS), a measure of the efficient scale of operation in the industry (MED), the growth of industry sales (G), the advertising–sales ratio (AS), and a proxy for the capital–labour ratio (KL), AS and MED are fairly common proxies for the product differentiation and economies of scale entry barriers identified by Bain. A variable such as KL is often added to correct for the fact that the profits variable does not include the cost of capital, which varies with capital requirements across industries. Finally, measures of growth and imports are often added as conditioning variables to reflect disruptions caused to the concentration–profits relationship by rapid growth in demand (and the consequent need for capacity adjustment) or by the influx of imports. Equation 1 shows the results of these extensions.

Equation 1

(Equation 5 from Table 1, Hart and Morgan (1977), p. 183)

$$PCM = \text{constant} + 0.0021\ CR5 + 0.1562\ KL + 0.0397\ G + 0.0746\ AS$$
$$\phantom{PCM = \text{constant} + 0.0021\ CR5 + 0.1562\ KL + }{}^{**}{}^{**}$$

$$- 0.0047\ MED + 0.0285\ MS.$$

[6] The earlier studies excluded from consideration are Shepherd (1972), who found an insignificant positive profits–concentration relationship for 1958 and 1963; Phillips (1972), who revealed a significant positive relationship for 1951; Holtermann (1973), with an insignificantly negative relationship for 1963; and Khalilzadeh-Shirazi (1974) with an insignificantly positive relationship for the same year. Caves, Khalilzadeh-Shirazi, and Porter (1975) present modifications of the latter study which lead to a significant positive relationship. The studies are reviewed, and their specifications and data discussed, in Hart and Morgan (1977).

n = 113;
R^2 = 0.432;
** indicates significant at 5% level;
PCM log of gross profit as share of value added (value added minus employee compensation all divided by value added);
CR5 log of 5-firm employment concentration ratio;
KL log of ratio of gross capital expenditure to labour;
G log of proportionate change in money sales;
AS log of ratio of advertising to sales;
MED log of median size of enterprise by employment;
MS log of ratio to imports to domestically produced sales.

Advertising intensity and the capital–labour ratio are positive and significant, but the remaining variables are not significant, and MED and MS have unexpected signs. The non-significant coefficient on concentration would appear to be due to the inclusion of the capital–labour ratio, which is collinear with concentration. Introduction of KL dramatically lowered the coefficient on CR5. Hence, one can only conclude that highly concentrated, capital-intensive industries earn relatively high profits, *ceteris paribus*.[7] The problem of multicollinearity makes it difficult to isolate the effects of each variable on profits and is common in these studies, particularly with the concentration and minimum efficient scale measures.

More recently, Clarke (1984) has applied a similar model specification to the period 1970–6. Using the 7-year panel data at his disposal, Clarke derived the level, trend, and variance of profits in each industry, and examined relationships involving each of these measures. (We focus on the approach comparable to Hart and Morgan.) Clarke began by regressing the level of profits against dummy variables for a number of different industrial sectors, a procedure which explained approximately 60 per cent of the inter-industry variation in profits, with significant positive coefficients for the food and drink, and chemicals sectors. Further variables were then added, and a typical result is shown as Equation 2.

Equation 2

(Equation 8 from Table 1a, Clarke (1984) p. 61)

PCM = 45.8 − 0.06 CR5 + 0.52 AS + 3.40 KS + 0.012 G
    (22.0) (1.55)   (3.02)   (2.81)   (1.84)
    + 0.05 MS + Sectoral dummies.
    (1.22)

---

[7] Hart and Morgan also tried replacing the concentration ratio simply with the number of enterprises as an indicator of the degree of competition. The variable attracted the expected negative coefficient, which was significant despite the inclusion of the other variables.

n = 105;
R^2 = 0.666;
t-statistics in parentheses;
PCM measure of average profit margin (net output minus wages and
   salaries divided by net output, expressed as percentage), 1970–6;
CR5 5-firm employment concentration ratio for 1970;
AS   advertising expenditures divided by value added, 1968;
KS   net assets at order level, allocated to industries on basis of propor-
     tions of total capital expenditures, then deflated by value added,
     1970;
G market growth in sales, 1970–6;
MS   import–sales ratio as percentage, 1970.

The findings of central interest here are that concentration appeared to
have only a negative and insignificant relationship with profits, and that
only advertising intensity and capital intensity were significant. Noting
the significance of capital intensity, and comparing these results with
those of Hart and Morgan, leads one to suspect that capital intensity
(and perhaps the industry dummies) may to some extent obscure the relationship between profits and concentration. The results did, however,
prove robust to alternate specifications, including ones where advertising
and capital expenditures were netted out of profits, and advertising and
capital intensities omitted from the equation.[8]

One clearly interesting feature of a relatively small, open economy like
Britain is that profits are likely to be affected by trade. Consideration of
this topic has been somewhat peripheral in the studies covered so far, and
import variables have perversely attracted positive (though not
significant) coefficients. By contrast, Lyons (1981) derived a more precise
theoretical relationship between profits and import intensity, and estimated this on a sample of 118 MLH industries for 1968. Equation 3 is
one of his estimated equations.

Equation 3

(Equation R5 from Lyons (1981), p. 291)
$$PCM = - 0.017 + 0.180\,H + 0.154\,DDM + 0.136\,XS$$
        (0.43)   (1.93)   (3.69)   (3.68)
$$+ 1.06\,AS + 0.050\,HET.$$
        (4.60)   (2.96)

---

[8] Clarke also found that the variation in profits was positively associated with concentration, thus rejecting the hypothesis that slightly lower profit rates in concentrated industries
might be compensated for by less profit variation.

n = 118;
R^2 = 0.3123;
t-statistics in parentheses;
PCM   value added less wages and salaries divided by sales, 1968;
H Herfindahl index by employment for domestic production;
DDM domestic industry's share of the domestic market (production less exports plus imports);
XS   proportion of domestic production which is exported;
AS   advertising–sales ratio;
HET   imports plus exports less the difference between them, all divided by imports plus exports (see text).

A significant negative impact of imports on profitability is shown by the coefficient on domestic industry's share of home sales (DDM), which of course falls as imports rise. Product differentiation was proxied by the conventional advertising–sales ratio and more interestingly by a measure of the heterogeneity of traded goods (HET). This measure was derived from the assumption that if an industry both imports and exports goods, those goods are likely to be differentiated. Equally, if goods are differentiated, they are likely to be less directly competitive with home production, and will therefore exert less of a discipline on pricing and profits. Both AS and HET attract significant positive coefficients as hypothesized. More important for our purposes is that the chosen measure of concentration, the Herfindahl index, is significant.[9] Note that Lyons does not include capital intensity or minimum efficient scale, which, as we have seen, have obscured the concentration–profits relationship.

A question which arises with the models discussed thus far is whether estimating just a single equation will yield consistent and unbiased estimates of the coefficients of interest, particularly the coefficient on concentration. Can concentration and the other explanatory variables reasonably be taken as exogenous? The fear that they cannot has led researchers elsewhere to estimate simultaneous equations systems, in which, for example, concentration, advertising intensity, and profitability are simultaneously determined by the exogenous variables. Indeed, several models with a very large number of equations have been estimated.[10]

Clearly there are good reasons to suspect that many of the right-hand

[9] In previous work on the traded sector, Hitiris (1978) had similarly found that modelling the effects of trade variables—in his case, the degree of protection of home production—led to a significant positive concentration–profits relationship for 1963 and 1968, for smaller samples of industries of around 40 observations. Following criticism of his original work, new estimation suggested a significant positive relationship for 1963 which collapsed in 1968. See Lyons, Kitchen, and Hitiris (1979).

[10] Caves, Porter, Spence, and Scott (1980) is an example, which contains a good discussion of this way of modelling structure and performance.

side variables are endogenous. First, high profitability is likely to attract new entry (thus affecting concentration) and imports, as well as itself being explained by concentration, imports, etc. Second, several variables are likely to be the simultaneous result of firms maximizing profits through the contemporaneous choice of advertising expenditures, capital stocks, and output levels. A natural procedure to follow is then to test for exogeneity, and this is done by Geroski (1982b). Using techniques which fortunately do not require that all the equations in the system be fully specified, he concluded that the variables which are most probably endogenous are imports and exports. His results suggest that the estimated effect of import competition on profits is biased down when imports are erroneously assumed to be exogenous, i.e. taking imports to be exogenous when they are in fact endogenous understates their effect on profits. However, as with other work in this area, the estimates of simultaneous and single equation models appear to be generally similar.

Some dissatisfaction with the simple linear models used in the literature has arisen from the feeling that they lack a solid theoretical formulation. This defect was remedied by Cowling and Waterson (1976), who showed that the price–cost margin was proportional to the Herfindahl index and to a conjectural variation term, and inversely proportional to the industry elasticity of demand. The conjectural variation term captures the extent to which firms think that competitors will react to their output changes, and therefore describes the type of equilibrium in the industry. Estimation of this relationship is hampered by the lack of good estimates of industry demand elasticities at the correct level of aggregation. As a way round this, the authors proposed taking ratios of the relationships at different points in time. Assuming elasticities of demand and the conjectural variation term to be constant over time, one can then obtain an estimate of the association between changes in concentration and changes in price–cost margins. Cowling and Waterson also anticipated that the degree of collusion would increase with concentration, and to capture this specified a log-linear form for the equation linking price–cost margins to the Herfindahl index. The relationship was then estimated for 94 industries using data from 1968, 1963, and 1958. No other entry barrier variables could be included due to the paucity of data, but a unionization variable and a durable goods dummy were included. (This had little impact.) The result is given as Equation 4, which shows a positive and significant relationship between margins and concentration.[11,12]

[11] Hart and Morgan (1977) were unable to replicate this result, finding no significant relationship with a smaller sample of industries which they considered to be comparable over the same period.

[12] Waterson (1980) used the same procedure when examining the effect of concentration at successive stages of production, and again found a significant and positive relationship between (seller) concentration and margins. The coefficients on margins in this and the

Equation 4

(Equation 3 from Table 1, Cowling and Waterson (1976) p. 272)

$$\log (PCM_{68}/PCM_{63}) = 0.0333 + 0.2957 \log (H_{63}/H_{58})$$
$$\quad\quad\quad\quad (0.683) \quad (2.942)$$
$$\quad\quad\quad\quad + 0.4985 \log (TU_{63}/TU_{58}) + 0.0344 \; DG.$$
$$\quad\quad\quad\quad (1.480) \quad\quad\quad\quad\quad\quad (0.619)$$

$n = 94;$
$R^2 = 0.096;$
t-statistics in parentheses;
PCM value added minus wages and salaries divided by sales revenue;
H Herfindahl index;
TU   proportion of total employees who are union members;
DG   dummy variable with value 1 in industries producing durable goods, 0 otherwise.

The studies reviewed so far typically find only rather weak relationships between concentration and profits. One reason for this is that the usual assumption of a linear relationship might be erroneous. In his original study, Bain argued that the important variation in market structure 'is not between industries of oligopolistic and atomistic structure, but between the more highly concentrated oligopolies and all other industries' (1951, p. 194). This idea translates into what has become known as the critical concentration ratio hypothesis. When concentration in an industry exceeds some critical level, profits will be increased, whereas if concentration lies below that level, a competitive pricing outcome will be observed. Bain found such a break to occur when the 8-firm concentration ratio exceeded 70 per cent. In general, modifications of the basic structuralist hypothesis of this type have had some success in yielding a more comprehensive description of the data, and revealing a stronger, though more complex, profits–concentration relationship than suggested by linear regressions.[13] Cowling and Waterson, as just noted, chose a log-linear specification to capture any change in the coefficient on concentration, induced by a changing propensity to collude, as concentration levels altered.

Geroski (1981) was led by similar concerns to build up the relationship from the data, rather than imposing on the data any specific linear or

earlier paper do suggest perversely that the degree of collusion falls with rising concentration. However, Dickson (1982) has shown that when a conjectural elasticity is used, collusion as now defined does indeed seem to increase with concentration.

[13] White (1976) is a well-known example of this type of work. It is, of course, possible to posit a more complex formulation than a single break in the relationship. Indeed, Bradburd and Over (1982) suggest two critical thresholds according to whether concentration is rising or falling.

non-linear functional form. He followed a number of approaches to this issue, the preferred one being to insert a series of dummy variables for different concentration levels.[14] The resulting equation, Equation 5 below, also included a concentration–growth interaction term to examine whether industry growth tended to weaken the concentration–profits relationship in addition to increasing profits directly as previous studies had found. Geroski discovered that margins rose gently with the 5-firm concentration ratio up to a level of 35 per cent, then stayed roughly constant to 75 per cent, fell sharply to 85 per cent, and rose sharply thereafter. It was also observed that the concentration–profits relationship was weaker in fast-growth industries (as hypothesized) and in advertising-intensive industries. Unlike earlier studies, inclusion of a capital intensity variable did not completely obscure the effect of concentration, although the effect was weakened.

Equation 5

(Equation 5 from Table 1, Geroski (1981) p. 283)

$$PCM = 0.186 - 0.528\ CR5 + 0.359\ Z1 + 0.473\ Z2$$
$$(4.03)\quad(1.12)\qquad(0.897)\qquad(1.14)$$
$$+\ 0.515\ Z3 + 0.780\ C8 + 0.565\ C15 + 0.604\ C19$$
$$(1.17)\qquad(1.80)\qquad(1.27)\qquad(1.33)$$
$$+\ 0.634\ C20 + 0.130\ G - 0.156\ G.CR5 + 0.241\ AS$$
$$(1.48)\qquad(2.49)\quad(2.01)\qquad(2.41)$$
$$-\ 0.292\ AS.CR5 + 0.001\ KS + 0.063\ XS - 0.0102\ MS + 0.095\ DV.$$
$$(1.48)\qquad(0.066)\quad(1.02)\qquad(1.52)\qquad(0.731)$$

n = 52;
R^2 = 0.459;
t-statistics in parentheses;
PCM gross output less wages and salaries divided by gross output, 1968;
CR5 5-firm sales concentration ratio, 1968;
G average industry sales growth rate, 1963–8;
AS   advertising expenditures divided by sales, 1968;
KS   capital stock divided by sales, 1968;
XS   exports divided by industry sales, 1968;
MS   imports divided by industry sales, 1968;
DV   Berry index of diversification, 1968.

Remaining terms are dummies for particular intervals of CR5. Twenty equal-sized intervals constructed, C1 = 0.00 to 0.05, C2 = 0.05 to 0.10,

---

[14] This is a generalization of the critical concentration ratio, allowing the data to reveal a number of thresholds and discontinuities.

etc. Four intervals then omitted due to missing observations and to avoid perfect collinearity, and remaining 16 grouped into 7 classes:
Z1 = C4 + C5 + C6; Z2 = C7 + C9;
Z3 = C10 + C11 + C12 + C13 + C14 + C16 + C17; C8; C15; C19; C20.

The studies described above have each used data at industry level drawn from the official Census of Production. One of the problems with such data is the paucity of information on the level of industry costs, particularly the costs of capital. In an attempt to circumvent this problem, Nickell and Metcalf (1978) examined a sample of products which were available as both proprietary brands and supermarket own-brands. They hypothesized that own-brand prices were linked directly to costs, and used the ratio of own-brand prices to proprietary prices as their (inverse) measure of margins. The data were obtained simply by perusing the supermarket shelves. The cost–price ratio was then regressed against market structure variables at the product group level (where the concentration ratio was used) and at the MLH level (where the Herfindahl index was also available). As hypothesized, a negative relationship with concentration was obtained, suggesting that proprietary brands are relatively more expensive at higher concentration levels. The relationship was generally statistically significant, and a significant relationship with advertising was also observed. An example is given as Equation 6.

Equation 6

(Equation 6 from Table 1, Nickell and Metcalf (1978) p. 264)

$$Po/Pp = 1.01 - 0.206\ CR5 - 1.28\ AS + 0.062\ G$$
$$(14.8)\ (2.93)(3.66)(1.30)$$
$$-\ 0.044\ B +\ 0.022\ MES - 0.062\ NF.$$
$$(0.93)(2.02)(2.43)$$

n = 29;
R^2 = 0.564;

t-statistics in parentheses;

Po/Pp ratio of own-brand to proprietary brand prices, 1976;
CR5 5-firm concentration ratio at product group level, 1968;
AS advertising expenditure as percentage of sales, 1975–6;
G 5-year growth in sales, 1963–8;
B average size of all establishments in MLH employing over 25 people, value added, 1968 (proxy for absolute cost barrier to entry);
MES minimum efficient scale as a percentage of industry size;
NF non-food industry dummy variable.

Although these various studies provide some support for a positive correlation between industry profits and concentration, there remains the important question of interpretation. According to the traditional view, market structure determines profits through its effects on pricing behaviour. This may be labelled the 'market power' hypothesis. An alternative explanation of the same correlation is associated with Demsetz (1973, 1974). This 'efficiency' hypothesis suggests that relatively efficient firms will tend to achieve large market shares and high profits. One would still observe a positive correlation between concentration and profits, but the interpretation placed on it would be different and considerably less malign.[15]

There is no reason to prefer either the market power or the efficiency hypothesis on purely theoretical grounds, and attention has consequently turned to empirical work. Initial research, including Demsetz's own, centred on the reasoning that if the efficiency hypothesis were true, one would expect to observe a positive relationship between firms' market shares and their levels of profitability within concentrated industries. By contrast, the advantages of market power were thought to benefit all members of an industry, and thus no intra-industry relationship of this kind would be expected. Some support for these observations was found with US data.

Tests of the efficiency hypothesis on British data have recently been undertaken by Clarke, Davies, and Waterson (1984). The authors first examined the price–cost margins of large and small firms, and found no significant difference between them either in industries of above-average or in industries of below-average concentration.[16] If anything, small firms' margins were somewhat higher than large firms' margins. This clearly offered no support for the Demsetz view. They then developed a more detailed model, which involved regressing individual firms' price–cost margins on their market shares within each industry, and examining the slope of the fitted relationship. A steep slope would favour the efficiency viewpoint, a flat slope the collusion interpretation. Using data derived from the Census of Production size–class distributions and pooled for the years 1971–7, Clarke, Davies, and Waterson examined this relationship for 104 industries. Their first conclusion was that only 29 industries showed a positive linear relationship, which meant that only this minority of the sample fell into a pattern amenable to discriminating between the two hypotheses. In 13 further cases, economies of scale appeared to be the factor making any distinction impossible, and in the remainder the complications were perhaps caused by the effects of product differentiation. For the 29 industries consistent with the model, their

---

[15] However, even if true, the limited diffusion of efficient techniques is clearly suboptimal.

[16] On one measure, small firms' margins were higher in industries of above-average concentration, suggesting a collusive effect.

measure of collusion could be recovered. A spread of results was observed: in some cases it was high, but in others low, leaving a role for efficiency. The estimates of the degree of collusion were then regressed against measures of concentration for these 29 industries, and the positive and significant relationships found were taken as further support for the collusion hypothesis.[17] Overall, then, one can reject the extreme Demsetz view that efficiency is all, but retain some role for efficiency in explaining the profits–concentration relationship.

The market power or efficiency dispute has also become associated with another line of research in industrial economics, which compares inter-industry and intra-industry variation in profits. The traditional story here is that all firms in an industry gain from output restriction and the conse-quent rise in product price. Thus high levels of concentration identify broad pools of excess profits across industries. An alternative is that the larger firms may be sufficiently insulated from their smaller rivals that in restricting output only they attain higher profits. In this scenario, high levels of concentration identify only narrow pockets of market power. To discriminate between the two, one might therefore wish to explore the relationship between market share and profitability. Although this approach shares with the Demsetz approach the desire to look within industries, it is more concerned with the distribution of profits within the industry than with the origin of those profits in terms of collusion or efficiency.

A number of studies for the USA have followed this approach.[18] The authors have examined the variation in firms' profits, and have discov-ered that the firm's market share is an apparently far more important determinant of its profits than is the level of concentration in industries where it operates. Although market shares and concentration are inter-related, these results would seem to describe the distribution of gains within an industry, leading one to the conclusion that it is the larger firms which derive most of the benefits. The 'shared asset' of monopoly power is not shared very evenly within industries.

Utton (1986) has conducted some intra-industry analysis on British data. Using a sample of about 50 markets examined by the Monopolies and Mergers Commission, he found that the average profits of market leaders (relative to the manufacturing industry average) were notably higher when the leader was 'dominant' than in a 'concentrated oligopoly'.

---

[17] The overall relationship between industry margins and the Herfindahl index for these industries was implied to be positive but with declining slope.

[18] Recent studies have typically used one of two rich and relatively new data sets: the Strategic Planning Institute's PIMS data or the Federal Trade Commission's Line of Business data. They include Gale and Branch (1982), Martin (1983), Ravenscraft (1983), and Kwoka and Ravenscraft (1986). Schmalensee (1985) attempts to distinguish the relative importance of industry and firm effects on profitability.

(Dominance is defined as a leading firm having a market share of about 50 per cent and its nearest rival having less than half the leader's share; a concentrated oligopoly is where the two leading firms have a combined market share of 50 per cent.) Leading firms' profits in concentrated oligopolies were in turn higher than those in the remaining industries. Using a sub-sample of 42 firms for the period 1972–4, Utton then regressed relative profitability on market share, and most of his specifications produced significant and positive correlations between the two. Although the Commission sample is definitely not random and the analysis here confined to partial correlations (excluding the influence of barriers to entry, growth, etc.), there seems to be no reason to think that further experiments in the UK will not produce the type of results commonly found in the USA.

The natural extension of this line of approach is to examine why the gains from market power are uneven, and this has led to the analysis of strategic groups and mobility barriers (Caves and Porter (1977)). Whereas entry barriers describe obstacles to movement *into and between* industries, mobility barriers comprise similar obstacles *within* the industry. Mobility barriers are thought to emerge from the selection of competitive strategies by firms within the industry (to produce highly differentiated products, to integrate into distribution, etc.). Those which select the same strategies form relatively homogeneous strategic groups, which are then protected from challenges from outside and are thought able to develop within-group patterns of collusion. The evident empirical problem with this analysis is quite how to identify strategic groups. No work of this type has yet been attempted for Britain.[19]

To conclude, the British evidence does give some support for a positive profits–concentration relationship. However, the relationship is weak, probably complex and non-linear, and is often estimated imprecisely. Moreover, even thus qualified, a positive relationship has not been observed in the 1970s with British Census of Production data. Attempts to distinguish the effects of collusion from the effects of efficiency have had some success, but have indicated that a simple model of such effects may not be rich enough to explain the data. We have indicated one further avenue which has been pursued with new data sets in the USA, and the limited attempts thus far to follow this line in Britain. In the following section we shall describe two rather different paths which have been followed in recent empirical work in industrial economics.

---

[19] Empirical work for the USA includes Newman (1978), Porter (1979), Caves and Pugel (1980), and Oster (1982).

3. NEW DEVELOPMENTS IN THE ANALYSIS OF MARKET PERFORMANCE

The analysis of market performance has evolved considerably since Bain's early study. The previous section indicated some advances achieved within the framework laid out by Bain: the use of other independent variables such as barriers to entry, the estimation of systems of equations, the examination of the shape of the profits–concentration link, and efforts to probe the market power or efficiency debate. In this section, two rather different approaches will be outlined: the examination of the pattern of competition within individual industries, and the examination of the persistence of market power.

The first of the new approaches we consider could be regarded as having emerged from concern with the dependent variable typically used in the structuralist studies. As we have seen, a correlation between market structure and average profits (the rate of return on capital or the price–cost margin) may be interpreted as reflecting either collusion or the superior efficiency of market leaders. The problem arises because one is using rates of return to make inferences about pricing behaviour. Theory suggests that prices will be raised relative to costs, but since it is difficult to observe prices and costs, various profits measures are used as proxies. (There is continuing controversy over which of the available profit measures, if any, best fits the purpose.)[20] Ideally one would wish to examine the effect of market structure on prices, holding marginal costs constant. Profits are not really the appropriate variable to use in examining this type of conditional prediction, since they do not satisfactorily hold constant the various influences that market structure might have on costs. Bias is bound to result if variations in marginal costs across industries are correlated with the market structure variables of interest.

One response to this problem is to consider the effects of market structure on prices. Here, one needs to consider single industries with differing structural characteristics, as with a series of regionally distinct markets for a particular product. Studies of this type on the USA (for example, Geithman, Marvel, and Weiss (1981)) have often found stronger relationships than those studies focusing on measures of profits.

However, one can push further with this type of data and try to infer from prices, costs, and market structure the conduct which underlies any observed discrepancy between prices and marginal costs. The starting-point for an exercise of this kind is the observation that a profit-

---

[20] Weiss (1974) and Scherer (1980, ch. 9) cover the issue. Controversy has been regenerated by Fisher and McGowan's (1983) strong claims about the inadequacy of using accounting data to describe economic returns; see Kay and Mayer (1986) for a response. A comparatively recent attempt q to overcome the difficulties is to use Tobin's q, e.g. Salinger (1984).

maximizing firm chooses output to equalize marginal revenue and marginal cost. At any level of output, marginal revenue depends upon the demand curve facing the firm and on the pricing behaviour of its rivals. In exactly the same way that one uses information on outputs and inputs to make inferences about the parameters of a production function, or data on prices and quantities to test restrictions on the parameters of consumer demand functions, one can use basic data on prices, outputs, costs, and demand, together with the marginal cost equals marginal revenue condition, to infer what the conduct of industry members must have been in order to have generated the observed data. Since different types of behaviour (for example, dominant firm pricing, Cournot behaviour, competitive price taking) generate observably different price–output configurations in equilibrium, one can infer which of these conduct types appears to have occurred.[21] Notice in addition that one is able to 'correct' for correlations between market structure and costs in such an exercise: the 'collusion or efficiency' ambiguity does not cloud interpretation of the results.

To date, the only example of this type of work on UK data is the recent paper by Borooah and van der Ploeg (1986). In contrast with the American literature which focuses on specific industries, Borooah and van der Ploeg examine a series of broad industries (food, mechanical engineering, textiles, etc.) over the period 1954–79. For each industry, they estimate input demand and output demand functions, and from the resultant estimates of price elasticity and conjectural elasticity they derive a measure of monopoly power. The ranking of these measures across their ten industry groups was unrelated to the ranking of aggregate concentration across industries, suggesting quite different areas of policy concern. Although an interesting exercise, we imagine that a wide variety of industry cost and demand conditions are suppressed within the group aggregates. To investigate individual industries requires extensive gathering of data. In principle, such empirical work could form part of merger and monopoly investigations, although we acknowledge that such an approach bears little resemblance to current policy.

The final new approach we shall mention concerns the dynamic performance of industries. Attention is here shifted from the consequences of market power at any one point in time to the question of whether high prices and profits persist over time. Clearly, relatively transitory positions of market power are unlikely to arouse much concern. Therefore, what

---

[21] For recent examples, see Gollop and Roberts (1979), Appelbaum (1982), and Roberts (1984). Geroski, Phlips, and Ulph (1985) survey the literature. An extension of the approach is to model how conduct changes over time (e.g. Porter (1983), Geroski, Ulph, and Ulph (1987)) or to predict the conduct consequences of a merger (Baker and Bresnahan (1985)).

matters is how rapidly monopoly positions and their associated returns are eroded by the threat or fact of new entry.

Recent work in this area has aimed to develop time series descriptions of the profitability of firms, either in isolation or grouped together to capture common industry effects. One can then determine how rapidly above-average rates of profit converge toward long-run levels, and attempt to explain this intertemporal performance. It emerges from recent studies that although profits in British industries are not, on average, particularly high by American or European standards, positions of above-average profitability tend to persist for relatively longer than elsewhere.[22] It also seems to be the case that there is a notable variation in performance within industries, and therefore industry characteristics can explain only part of the observed patterns (Cubbin and Geroski (1987)).

The picture of a sluggish competitive process, which the persistence of profits suggests, is mirrored by studies of the stability of leading firms' market shares (Shaw and Simpson (1986), Utton (1986), Geroski (1987)). Whilst it is not obvious that market shares ought necessarily to decline— if leaders are more efficient or have continued access to some specialist resource, for example—the very slow pace of observed decline suggests that even when leading firms lose their edge, their replacement by relatively more efficient rivals can take an extremely long time.

4. CONCLUSIONS

We observed at the outset that one reason for interest in the type of work surveyed in this chapter is that it might provide clear guidance for policy. If concentrated industry structures are found to be directly related to high profits, an important policy objective should be to reduce levels of concentration or at least to prevent their increase. The work surveyed in Section 2 provides limited support for such a policy: the concentration–profits relationship in the UK is weak, non-linear, and dependent on other factors; it seems to have disappeared in the 1970s.

Nevertheless the subsequent work surveyed in this chapter suggests that it would be unwise to conclude on this point. The material covered in Section 3 suggests two important further issues. First, the growing awareness of limitations with previous approaches and of the need for sound theoretical underpinnings in empirical work has led to a move from cross-sectional work to close studies of particular industries. Such studies certainly validate concern that the impact of market power is more complex than is allowed for in simple concentration indices, but in many

[22] Geroski and Jacquemin (1986) compare the UK with France and West Germany; for the United States, see Mueller (1986).

cases market power most certainly does exist. Second, there has been a broadening of perspectives from examination of the current level of market power to investigation of its duration. On this score, empirical work has indeed found that whatever the current dimensions and determinants of profits, a speedy competitive process should not be relied upon.

This type of work does, however, forsake the direct lessons about industry structures which were suggested by the original cross-sectional studies. Can anything be retained from the original approach, or modifications of it? We would suggest that the chief lessons to be learned here are from those studies which emphasize the impact of *market share* on profits—a lesson the duration of profits studies took on board from the outset. Thus, although concentration does not appear to have a clear impact on profits, more recent studies from the USA suggest that market share does. Factors which augment large market shares and remove the dampening effect on profits of large *rivals'* market share—i.e. factors such as mergers—may well have substantial impact on profits. A merger policy based on this premiss may therefore seem most justified than one relying on the concentration doctrine, even though there has been only limited confirmation of such results for Britain.[23] Since horizontal merger policy in Britain has never been based on opposition to all increases in concentration, a weakening of policy could not therefore be justified by reference to empirical work in industrial economics.

REFERENCES

Appelbaum, E. (1982), 'The estimation of the degree of oligopoly power', *Journal of Econometrics*, **9**, 283–94.

Bain, J. S. (1951), 'Relation of profit rate to industry concentration: American manufacturing, 1936–1940', *Quarterly Journal of Economics*, **65**, 293–324.

—— (1956), *Barriers to New Competition: Their Character and Consequences in Manufacturing Industries*, Cambridge, Mass.: Harvard University Press.

—— (1959), *Industrial Organisation*, New York: John Wiley.

Baker, J. B., and Bresnahan, T. F. (1985), 'The gains from merger or collusion in product-differentiated industries', *Journal of Industrial Economics*, **33**, 427–44.

Borooah, V. K., and van der Ploeg, F. (1986), 'Oligopoly power in British industry', *Applied Economics*, **18**, 583–98.

Bradburd, R. M., and Over, A. M. (1982), 'Organizational costs, "sticky" equilibria and critical levels of concentration', *Review of Economics and Statistics*, **64**, 50–8.

Caves, R. E., Khalilzadeh-Shirazi, J., and Porter, M. E. (1975), 'Scale economies in statistical analyses of market power', *Review of Economics and Statistics*, **57**, 133–40.

---

[23] The extent to which the market share arguments can be tested is severely limited by the nature of data currently available.

—— and Porter, M. E. (1977), 'From entry barriers to mobility barriers: conjectural decisions and contrived deterrence to new competition', *Quarterly Journal of Economics*, **91**, 421–34.

—— —— Spence, A. M., and Scott, J. T. (1980), *Competition in the Open Economy: A Model Applied to Canada*, Cambridge, Mass.: Harvard University Press.

—— and Pugel, T. (1980), *Intra-industry Differences in Conduct and Performance: Viable Strategies in U.S. Manufacturing Industries*, Monograph Series in Finance and Economics, New York University Graduate School of Business Administration.

Clarke, R. (1984), 'Profit margins and market concentration in UK manufacturing industry: 1970–76', *Applied Economics*, **16**, 57–72.

—— and Davies, S. W. (1982) 'Market structure and price–cost margins', *Economica*, **49**, 277–87.

—— —— and Waterson, M. (1984), 'The profitability-concentration relation: market power or efficiency?', *Journal of Industrial Economics*, **32**, 435–50.

Comanor, W. S., and Wilson, T. A. (1967), 'Advertising, market structure and performance, *Review of Economics and Statistics*, **49**, 423–40.

—— —— (1979), 'The effect of advertising on competition: a survey', *Journal of Economic Literature*, **17**, 453–76.

Cowling, K., and Waterson, M. (1976), 'Price–cost margins and market structure', *Economica*, **43**, 267–74.

Cubbin, J. S., and Geroski, P. (1987), 'The convergence of profits in the long run: inter firm and inter industry comparisons', *Journal of Industrial Economics*, **35**, 427–42.

Davies, S. (1979) 'Choosing between concentration indices: the iso-concentration curve', *Economica*, **46**, 67–75.

Demsetz, H. (1973), 'Industry structure, market rivalry, and public policy', *Journal of Law and Economics*, **16**, 1–9.

—— (1974), 'Two systems of belief about monopoly', in H. J. Goldschmid, H. M. Mann, and J. F. Weston (eds.), *Industrial Concentration: The New Learning*, Boston: Little, Brown & Co.

Dickson, V. A. (1982), 'Collusion and price–cost margins', *Economica*, **49**, 39–42.

Donsimoni, M. P., Geroski, P. A., and Jacquemin, A. P. (1985), 'Concentration indices and market power: two views', *Journal of Industrial Economics*, **32**, 421–34.

Fisher, F. M., and McGowan, J. J. (1983), 'On the misuse of accounting rates of return to infer monopoly profits', *American Economic Review*, **73**, 82–97.

Gale, B. T., and Branch, B. S. (1982), 'Concentration versus market share: which determines performance and why does it matter?', *Antitrust Bulletin*, **27**, 83–105.

Geithman, F., Marvel, H., and Weiss, L. (1981), 'Concentration, price and critical concentration ratios', *Review of Economics and Statistics*, **63**, 346–53.

Geroski, P. A. (1981), 'Specification and testing the profits–concentration, price and critical concentration ratios', *Economica*, **48**, 279–88.

—— (1982a), 'Interpreting a correlation between profits and concentration', *Journal of Industrial Economics*, **30**, 305–18.

Geroski, P. A. (1982b), 'Simultaneous equations models of the structure-performance paradigm', *European Economic Review*, **19**, 145–58.

—— (1983), 'Some reflections on the theory and application of concentration indices', *International Journal of Industrial Organization*, **1**, 79–84.

—— (1987), 'Do dominant firms decline?', in D. A. Hay and J. S. Vickers (eds.), *The Economics of Market Dominance*, Oxford: Basil Blackwell.

—— and Jacquemin, A. P. (1986), 'The persistence of profits: a European comparison', mimeo, Louvain la Neuve.

—— and Masson, R. T. (1987), 'Dynamic market models in industrial organization', *International Journal of Industrial Organization*, **5**, 1–13.

—— Phlips, L., and Ulph, A. (1985), 'Oligopoly, welfare and competition: some recent developments', *Journal of Industrial Economics*, **33**, 369–86.

—— Ulph, A. M., and Ulph, D. T. (1987), 'A model of the crude oil market in which conduct varies over time', *Economic Journal,* Supplement, **97**, 77–86.

Gollop, F., and Roberts, M. (1979), 'Firm interdependence in oligopolistic markets', *Journal of Econometrics*, **10**, 313–31.

Hannah, L., and Kay, J. A. (1977), *Concentration in Modern Industry*, London: Macmillan.

Hart, P. E. (1975), 'Moment distributions in economics', *Journal of the Royal Statistical Society, Series B*, **138**, 423–34.

—— and Morgan, E. (1977), 'Market structure and economic performance', *Review of Economics and Statistics*, **25**, 177–93.

Hitiris, T. (1978), 'Effective protection and economic performance in UK manufacturing industry', *Economic Journal*, **88**, 107–20.

Holtermann, S. E. (1973), 'Market structure and economic performance in UK manufacturing industry', *Journal of Industrial Economics*, **22**, 119–40.

Hughes, A. (1989), 'The impact of merger: a survey of the empirical evidence for the UK', in J. A. Fairburn and J. A. Kay (eds.), *Mergers and Merger Policy*, Oxford: Oxford University Press.

Kay, J. A., and Mayer, C. P. (1986), 'On the application of accounting rates of return, *Economic Journal*, **96**, 199–207.

Khalilzadeh-Shirazi, J. (1974), 'Market structure and price–cost margins in United Kingdom manufacturing industries', *Review of Economics and Statistics*, **56**, 67–76.

Kwoka, J. E. (1979), 'The effect of market share distribution on industry performance', *Review of Economics and Statistics*, **61**, 445–53.

—— (1981), 'Does the choice of concentration measure really matter?', *Journal of Industrial Economics*, **20**, 445–53.

—— and Ravenscraft, D. J. (1986), 'Co-operation v. rivalry: price–cost margins by line of business', *Economica*, **53**, 351–63.

Lyons, B. R. (1981), 'Price–cost margins, market structure and international trade', in D. Currie, D. Peel, and W. Peters (eds.), *Microeconomic Analysis*, London: Croom Helm.

—— Kitchen, P. D., and Hitiris, T. (1979), 'Effective protection and economic performance in UK manufacturing industry: comments and reply', *Economic Journal*, **89**, 926–41.

Martin, S. (1979), 'Advertising, concentration and profitability: the simultaneity problems', *Bell Journal of Economics*, **10**, 639–47.

—— (1980), 'Entry barriers, concentration and profits', *Southern Economic Journal*, **46**, 471–88.

—— (1983), *Market, Firms and Economic Performance*, New York: New York University Graduate School of Business Administration.

Mueller, D. C. (1986), *Profits in the Long Run*, Cambridge: Cambridge University Press.

Newman, M. (1978), 'Strategic groups and the structure–performance relationship', *Review of Economics and Statistics*, **60**, 417–27.

Nickell, S., and Metcalf, D. (1978), 'Monopolistic industries and monopoly profits or, are Kellogg's cornflakes overpriced?', *Economic Journal*, **88**, 254–68.

Oster, S. (1982), 'Intra-industry structure and the ease of strategic change', *Review of Economics and Statistics*, **64**, 376–83.

Phillips, A. (1972), 'An econometric study of price-fixing, market structure and performance in British industry in the early 1950s', in K. Cowling (ed.), *Market Structure and Corporate Behaviour*, London: Gray-Mills.

Porter, M. (1979), 'The structure within industries and companies' performance', *Review of Economics and Statistics*, **61**, 214–28.

Porter, R. (1983), 'A study of cartel stability: the Joint Executive Committee, 1880–1886', *Bell Journal of Economics*, **14**, 301–14.

Ravenscraft, D. J. (1983), 'Structure–profit relationships at the line of business and industry level', *Review of Economics and Statistics*, **65**, 22–31.

Roberts, M. (1984), 'Testing oligopolistic behaviour: an application of the variable profit function', *International Journal of Industrial Organization*, **2**, 367–83.

Salinger, M. (1984), 'Tobin's q, unionization and the concentration–profit relationship', *Rand Journal of Economics*, **15**, 159–70.

Scherer, F. M. (1980), *Industrial Market Structure and Economic Performance*, 2nd edn., Chicago: Rand McNally.

Schmalensee, R. (1977), 'Using the H-index of concentration with published data', *Review of Economics and Statistics*, **59**, 186–93.

—— (1985), 'Do markets differ much?', *American Economic Review*, **75**, 341–51.

—— (1989), 'Interindustry studies of structure and performance', in R. Schmalensee and R. D. Willig (eds.), *Handbook of Industrial Organization*, Amsterdam: North-Holland.

Shaw, R., and Simpson, P. (1986), 'The persistence of monopoly: an investigation of the effectiveness of the UK Monopolies Commission', *Journal of Industrial Economics*, **34**, 355–72.

Shepherd, W. G. (1972), 'Structure and behaviour in British industries with US comparisons', *Journal of Industrial Economics*, **21**, 35–54.

Strickland, A., and Weiss, L. (1976), 'Advertising, concentration and price–cost margins', *Journal of Political Economy*, **84**, 1109–21.

Utton, M. A. (1986), *Profits and the Stability of Monopoly*, Cambridge: Cambridge University Press.

Waterson, M. (1980), 'Price cost margins and successive market power', *Quarterly Journal of Economics*, **94**, 135–50.

Waterson, M. (1984), *Economic Theory of the Industry*, Cambridge: Cambridge University Press.

Weiss, L. W. (1974), 'The concentration–profits relation and antitrust', in H. J. Goldschmid, H. M. Mann., and J. F. Weston (eds.), *Industrial Concentration: The New Learning*, Boston: Little, Brown & Co.

White, L. (1976), 'Searching for the critical concentration ratio: an application of the switching regimes technique', in S. Goldfield and R. Quandt (eds.), *Studies in Non-linear Estimation*, Boston: Ballinger.

7

The Evolution of Merger Policy in Britain

JAMES FAIRBURN*

1. INTRODUCTION

The aim of this chapter is to provide an overview of the operation of merger policy in Britain from the introduction of controls on mergers in 1965 to the end of 1986. The structure of the paper broadly reflects the two-stage procedure characteristic of British policy, whereby a limited number of the many merger proposals falling within the scope of the legislation are first selected by the authorities for further consideration, and these few are then examined by the Monopolies and Mergers Commission against a broad public interest standard. Thus, following a brief description of the legislation, Section 2 will examine the initial selection decision: which types of mergers have been referred to the Commission, and how the types and number of references have changed over time. The section is concerned with establishing the broad pattern of policy. Section 3 then focuses on the operation of the Commission: how it has dealt with the various issues it has been required to consider, for example, how it establishes the effect of a particular merger on competition. Section 4 contains some concluding comments on the overall operation of this two-stage policy, and offers some tentative policy recommendations.

2. MERGER POLICY

Inherited Institutions

The first modern competition legislation preceded the institution of controls over mergers by some seventeen years. The 1948 Monopolies and Restrictive Practices Act set up a Commission (composed of prominent lawyers, economists, businessmen, and trade unionists) to inquire into the effects of restrictive agreements and monopoly firms in the manufacturing

* Lecturer in Economics at the University of Sussex.

sector. The Commission had to establish whether such practices and situations operated against the public interest, a loosely defined criterion incorporating business efficiency and competition among other considerations. The Commission investigated in depth individual industries referred to it by the Board of Trade. Its reports showed a general hostility to the effects of agreements between firms to restrict prices, share markets, and deal only with agreed customers. However, little direct government action resulted and the number of industries considered was tiny in comparison with the estimated pervasiveness of such restrictions. As a consequence, new legislation was introduced in 1956. The Restrictive Practices Court was established to consider restrictive agreements of certain types. The presumption was that such agreements were harmful and would be outlawed unless they could be shown to be justified according to certain specified criteria, the so-called 'gateways'. In practice the new Court interpreted the generous gateways tightly, and as a consequence many agreements were abandoned and overt cartelization of manufacturing industry rapidly diminished in the early 1960s.

During the years in which the new legislation was becoming effective, the Monopolies Commission continued to operate, albeit on a diminished scale, examining industries where there were single monopolists or groups of jointly dominant firms. Certain of its reports showed that one important way of establishing or strengthening a monopoly position was by means of merger with competing firms, for example Wall Paper Manufacturers had repeatedly countered its diminishing market share by multiple mergers with rivals, and in the tobacco industry the leading firm Imperial Tobacco was found to have a substantial interest in its rival Gallaghers. At the same time the pace of merger activity was quickening and in some cases clearly replacing recently condemned agreements with tighter links. Other contemporary events highlighted the importance of merger, the most notable example being ICI's hostile, and ultimately unsuccessful, bid for Courtaulds, the other principal domestic manufacturer of man-made fibres, in 1961–2.

The antipathy to large-scale take-over battles, and the growing realization that the monopolies legislation provided only a belated and ineffective response to mergers, led to agreement on the need for further legislation. The Conservative government's 1964 White Paper included proposals for the control of mergers, and these measures were largely adopted in the incoming Labour government's 1965 Monopolies and Mergers Act. The Act adopted the administrative means of control familiar from the monopoly legislation. Mergers, like monopolies, were to be referred to the Commission by the relevant government department, at that time the Board of Trade. The Commission would then have six months, or exceptionally up to nine months, to ascertain whether the merger proposal would be expected to operate against the public interest, the vague standard set out in 1948. The Act provided the government with the means to halt a merger proposal while the investigation was under way (a provision absent in the preceding White Paper).

The adoption of the public interest investigation by the Commission rather than a more specific prohibition enforceable in the Court—as with the restrictive practices legislation— indicated the lack of a clear stance on horizontal mergers. Furthermore, the legislation was to apply to mergers creating or strengthening a one-third share of supplies, or where the book value of assets acquired exceeded £5 million. Thus vertical and conglomerate mergers, as well as mergers between competing firms, could be referred.[1] The general and flexible nature of the provisions was indicated in the government's introduction of the legislation:

Mergers involving large firms are not, of course, necessarily harmful to the public interest—I should like to make the point—but the power of a giant, especially of two giants united, might be such as to stifle competition, or the empire created might be too large for the most efficient use of resources. In judging all these cases, however, I would propose always to remember what mergers can in certain cases do to achieve greater strength for our economy at home and abroad.[2]

This latter feeling, that mergers were often a powerful means of restructuring British industry, was further emphasized in contemporary policy developments. In particular, in 1966 the Industrial Reorganization Corporation (IRC) was established to promote rationalization, a manifestation of the feeling that British firms were frequently too small to compete effectively on world markets. The IRC was staffed largely by businessmen and little constrained by formal procedures. Its principal role proved to be the encouragement of mergers in industries it determined to be too fragmented. It typically proceeded by determining in its opinion the most efficient firm in an industry, and promoting mergers around that base. This prompted Caves's (1968, p. 321) caricature of British industrial policy: 'In order to achieve industrial efficiency, find the most efficient firm in Britain and merge the rest of them into it.' Clearly the ethos behind the establishment of the IRC, and the direct actions of that body, would have an important influence over the early phases of merger policy.

---

[1] In speaking on the second reading of the bill, Douglas Jay, then President of the Board of Trade, commented on likely candidates for referral: 'One obvious case, I think, is where competition in a vital industry might be markedly reduced. That is why we have provided, as an alternative to the criterion of monopoly, the size of assets test, so that what are called vertical or diversifying mergers could be investigated if the public interest required' (reprinted in the 1978 Green Paper, *A Review of Monopolies and Mergers Policy* (Department of Prices and Consumer Protection (1978)).) The specific concerns with non-horizontal mergers are not evident from this statement.

[2] Douglas Jay, reprinted in the 1978 Green Paper.

The First Phase of Policy, 1965–1973

In this and following parts of this section, the operation of merger policy will be sketched out principally using information on the references made to the Commission. Table 7.1 gives the details up to 1973, thus taking us through the intensive merger activity of the late 1960s and early 1970s, and stopping before the first full year of operation of the Office of Fair Trading (see below).

The most notable feature of Table 7.1 is the paucity of references, and the reference question merits further attention. In 1969 a Board of Trade pamphlet noted that between July 1965 and April 1969 only 10 of the 350 mergers falling within the scope of the legislation had in fact been referred. The same pamphlet also gave details of the referral process, revealing the existence of the Mergers Panel. The Panel was a non-statutory body comprising representatives of the Board of Trade and other government departments which had an interest in the particular proposal at issue. Its task was to assess the information gathered by the Board of Trade about the merger proposal and decide whether to recommend a referral to the Commission.[3] Although the Minister was not bound by the Panel's recommendation, this was evidently the forum in which most of the contentious issues would be discussed. The pamphlet listed many criteria relevant to the reference decision, including questions of efficiency as well as competition, but gave no indication of how the various factors were weighed against each other. The Panel's procedure was evidently no simple screening process, but rather in contentious cases might amount to the *de facto* public interest inquiry when no reference was ultimately made. However, the Panel's investigations were completed in much shorter intervals: it typically took no more than a few weeks to come to a decision, compared with the Commission's standard six-month inquiries.

The clearest evidence of conflicting objectives arose through the parallel operation of the Commission and the IRC. Mergers between competing firms were likely to be a central concern of the Commission and the majority of early references did indeed involve horizontal mergers. (The Commission's analysis is considered below.) In the same period, the IRC sponsored approximately 50 mergers (Hindley and Richardson (1983), Hague and Wilkinson (1983)). These included the formation of British Leyland, and the merger of GEC with first AEI and then English Electric. In addition there were a whole string of mergers, many of which

---

[3] Knowing of the existence of a merger proposal did not prove a major difficulty. Although there was no formal notification procedure, the time limit within which a reference must be made began when the proposal became public knowledge. In practice, voluntary notification became common to expedite the referral decision.

Table 7.1. Merger references to the Commission, 1965–1973

Year	Reference	Public interest finding
1965	BMC/Pressed Steel	Not against
1966	Ross Group/Associated Fisheries	Against
	Dental Manufacturing/Amalgamated Dental	Not against
	Dentists' Supply Co/Amalgamated Dental	Not against
	GKN/Birfield	Not against
	BICC/Pyrotenax	Not against
1967	UDS/Burton	Against
1968	Barclays/Lloyds/Martin[a]	Against
	Thorn/Radio Rentals	Not against
1969	Unilever/Allied Breweries	Not against
	Rank/de la Rue	Against
	Marley/Redland	Abandoned
1970	Burmah Oil/Laporte Industries	Abandoned
	British Sidac/Transparent Paper	Against
1971	(Pulp paper and board-making activities in UK of)	
	Reed International/Bowater Paper	Abandoned
1972	Beecham/Glaxo	Against
	Boots/Glaxo	Against
	Sears Holdings/William Timpson	Abandoned
1973	Tarmac/Wolseley-Hughes	Abandoned
	Glynwed/Armitage Shanks	Abandoned
	Whessoe/Capper-Neill	Abandoned
	British Match/Wilkinson Sword	Not against
	Bowater/Hanson Trust	Abandoned
	Davy/British Rollmakers	Against
	Boots/House of Fraser	Against
	London & County Securities/Inveresk	Abandoned

Note: A listing of completed reports is contained in Appendix A at the end of this book.

[a] The Commission objected to the proposed mergers between Barclays and Lloyds and between Barclays, Lloyds, and Martins. It stated that it would not object to either large bank merging with Martins. The findings were not by the requisite two-thirds majority but were none the less complied with.

Source: Annual Reports on the Monopolies and Mergers Commission, various years, HMSO, London.

showed similar characteristics to those which were referred. Indeed in one case, the IRC sponsored a merger of the trawling interests of the Ross Group and Associated Fisheries, a full merger of the two companies having previously been found against the public interest by the Commission. More generally, it has been suggested that the prime role of the IRC, certainly in those cases where it did not directly provide finance, was to establish that a merger proposal would not be referred to the Commission.[4]

This first phase of policy therefore confirmed the impression established on enactment of the merger legislation, that relatively few mergers were thought to give rise to public interest concerns, and saw the parallel operation of a policy clearly antagonistic to merger control. What of the mergers actually referred to the Commission?

The earliest references involved mergers with an impact on competition. The majority were horizontal, i.e. concerning competing suppliers of a product, although the first reference (*BMC/Pressed Steel*) and certain subsequent ones (*Dentists' Supply Co/Amalgamated Dental, Thorn/Radio Rentals*) involved vertical issues through the merging of firms at successive stages of the production process. Certain of the initial references were also characterized by the fact that the Board of Trade had not used its power to halt the merger, and thus the Commission was confronted with a completed transaction. Although this did not seem to affect the finding in *GKN/Birfield*, in *BMC/Pressed Steel* considerable emphasis was placed on assurances given by the company not to discriminate in supplies, and in *BICC/Pyrotenax* the Commission seemed clearly hostile to the merger but reluctant to carry this through to the breakup of an established concern.

The reports failed to show much evidence of a consistent approach by the Commission. Of the early horizontal mergers, the Commission objected to *Ross/Associated Fisheries* and *UDS/Burton*, and as noted was clearly hostile to *BICC/Pyrotenax*. In each case it emphasized the impact of the merger on parts of the fish, menswear, and cable markets. In other cases where the impact on market share was just as substantial (*GKN/Birfield, Dental Manufacturing/Amalgamated Dental,* and *Thorn/Radio Rentals*) it cleared mergers, having placed emphasis on such factors as the buying power of customers—the motor manufacturers and Ministry of Health—and imminent technical and demand changes in the television industry. The lack of predictability clearly weakened the contrast between merger policy and other policy initiatives: one could not say with certainty that the IRC had encouraged mergers to which the Commission would have taken exception. The point remains, however, that the characteristics of the two sets of mergers were similar, and consistency would require that they at least be referred.

In the early 1970s, as shown in Table 7.1, the Commission's stance on this type of merger strengthened considerably, with adverse findings in

---

[4] Young and Lowe (1974) refer to the close working relationship between the IRC and the Mergers Panel, and Hindley and Richardson (1983) cite the example of GEC/AEI where a merger had previously been contemplated but where IRC sponsorship ensured that no reference to the Commission would be forthcoming.

each of *British Sidac/Transparent Paper*, *Davy/British Rollmakers*, *Boots/House of Fraser*, and the Glaxo mergers. In the latter two cases, this was despite fairly low shares of industry output, and the *Beecham/Glaxo* case in particular showed the Commission resisting an argument that an increase in scale was required for the domestic drug companies to compete effectively in what was an international market. Instead, the Commission stressed the importance of there continuing to be a number of decision-making centres in the allocation of research expenditures. Yet at the same time as the toughening of policy was shown by this case, the potential for anomalies in the referral process was also displayed. The original bid for Glaxo by Beecham had initially been cleared: only when the rival bid by Boots emerged was it decided to make the reference to the Commission.

The last feature of the early phase of policy to which attention will be drawn is the commencement of referrals of conglomerate mergers. Given the concern expressed at the scale and nature of earlier bids, such as ICI/Courtaulds, it was not surprising that the merger procedures would be applied to this type of proposal. Equally the Commission had already been drawn to comment on conglomerate issues in previous references, for example its discussion of the likely impact of the *UDS/Burton* merger on management capabilities. In outright conglomerate mergers, such issues would form the heart of the Commission's inquiries. The first such references were *Unilever/Allied Breweries and Rank/de la Rue*, referred and reported on in parallel in 1969. Although the Commission did not see any exceptional merits in the huge, agreed Unilever/Allied Breweries proposal, it opposed only the contested Rank/de la Rue bid. A take-over was thought likely to have an adverse effect on the management of de la Rue, with the probable loss of personally established technical exchange agreements, and this was the central reason for the Commission's opposition. This report was important in that it drew the Commission firmly into an involvement with the mechanics of take-over bids and a potential role as arbitrator in disputes between the companies involved. The lack of any other clear stance on conglomerate mergers was evident in *General Observations on Mergers*, published as an annexe to these two reports. Here the Commission noted the increased size of recent proposals, and expressed concern at the buildup of giant firms through equity-financed acquisitions and at the financial instability and managerial weaknesses which might result. Its only specific recommendations, however, concerned post-merger disclosure of accounting information, and these were not followed up. Thus the early referrals marked the beginning of a policy of conglomerate references, in which the object of the inquiries was by no means clear at the outset. Although there were few other conglomerate references in the period covered in Table 7.1—only *British*

Match/Wilkinson Sword of those resulting in reports—this was to be an important facet of merger policy subsequently.

The Middle Years, 1974–1983

The initial phase of policy had then established the ground rules on which subsequent policy would operate. The net of merger policy was cast widely, bringing many mergers of diverse types within the scope of control, but it was evident from the outset that relatively few cases would be drawn in. It was clear that the selection of references was as important a part of policy as subsequent consideration of particular mergers by the Commission. Within this framework, the 1960s and early 1970s had indeed seen the referral of diverse types of merger—horizontal, vertical, conglomerate—and a broad range of issues considered by the Commission, from a merger's likely effect on prices to its impact on the morale of incumbent management.

The atmosphere in which policy was to operate was to be different in several respects from 1974 onwards. Overt official encouragement of large-scale mergers had ceased with the disbandment of the IRC in 1971, and the high level of merger activity of the late 1960s and early 1970s had given way to the gentler pace of activity which characterized the next ten years. This had limited impact on the workings of policy, since there continued to be a fairly constant stream of proposals falling within the scope of the legislation each year.[5] Yet although the amount of work faced by the Panel and the Commission did not decline, the background against which they worked would be less frenetic and it remained to be seen whether policy standards would be clarified as a result.

The early 1970s had also seen an important change in the institutional setting of policy. The 1973 Fair Trading Act, in addition to modifying the market share and public interest criteria of the competition legislation,[6] established the Office of Fair Trading (OFT) to oversee competition and consumer protection legislation. In the competition sphere, the head of the OFT, the Director-General of Fair Trading ('the Director-General'), took over the duties of the Registrar of Restrictive Practices, and became responsible for referring monopolies to the Commission and overseeing any subsequent actions that were called for. In the area of mergers, there were fewer changes. The Director-General was not given

[5] More detail on numbers of qualifying references and mergers is given in the final part of this section.

[6] The market share criterion was reduced from a one-third to a one-quarter share of supplies. The new public interest criteria placed somewhat more emphasis on competition than previously—the exact wording is given in the appendix to Borrie (1989) and further discussed by Swift (1989)—but the specified criteria remained only factors 'among other things' which the Commission had to consider.

primary responsibility for making references, as with monopolies, but was simply charged with keeping informed of current merger proposals. He took over as the head of the Mergers Panel, but recommendations made were still not binding on the Secretary of State. Although the operation of policy became somewhat better documented, it was not then essentially altered by the 1973 Act.

Table 7.2 gives details of references in the period. The table first shows a general increase in the rate of referral in the early 1980s compared with the mid- and late 1970s, 1977 apart. One consequence of this was that in the early 1980s there was a sufficient number of reports on horizontal mergers that one could begin to ascertain the Commission's criteria of judgement in a way that is less true of the intermittent reports of the first half of the period. This question will be taken up in Section 3.

Yet in this period, in particular, the competitive ramifications of mergers were only part of the story. There was also a series of referrals of conglomerate mergers. The hostile bid of Amalgamated Industrials for Herbert Morris was referred, and when that was prevented, the resultant bid by Babcock and Wilcox was also directed to the Commission. Lonrho's efforts to control House of Fraser were the subject of three separate references from 1978 to 1984, and take-overs of Anderson Strathclyde, Illingworth Morris, and Sothebys were each the subject of notable references. The last example was the foremost case of a reference being courted by an incumbent management and proving the crucial element in its defence against an unattractive bid which did not, however, raise any competition issues. Sothebys was faced by a bid from an American company. Following a substantial lobbying effort, the reference was made, against the advice of the Director-General. The consequent pause gave Sothebys a chance to find a 'white knight', A. Alfred Taubman. Although that bid was also referred, the first bid was soon abandoned, and following a token clearance of the Taubman bid by the Commission, the way was thus cleared to proceed.

The elements present in these examples were also evident in other references where some competition issue might also be involved. A majority of references involved contested take-overs, with the parties involved taking full opportunity to set out what they considered to be public interest issues. Other elements which repeatedly featured were foreign take-overs, as with the bids by Eurocanadian Shipholdings, Hongkong and Shanghai Banking Corporation, and the Enserch Corporation amongst others, and the regional question, where a series of bids for companies based in Scotland—Alginate Industries, House of Fraser, Highland Distillers, the Royal Bank of Scotland, Anderson Strathclyde—were referred between 1978 and 1982. The following section will examine how the Commission responded to this diverse set of concerns.

Table 7.2. Merger references to the Commission, 1974–1983

Year	Reference	Public interest finding
1974	Eagle Star/Sunley/Grovewood	Not against
	Charter Consolidated/Sadia	Not against
	Sears Holdings/The Nottingham Manufacturing Company	Abandoned
	NFU Development Trust/FMC	Not against
	Dentsply International/AD International	Not against
1975	Weidmann/Whitely	Not against
	Norvic Securities/W Canning	Abandoned
	Eurocanadian Shipholdings/Furness Withy/Manchester Liners	Against
	Amalgamated Industrials/Herbert Morris	Against
1976	Pilkington/UKO	Against
	Babcock & Wilcox/Herbert Morris	Against
	Fruehauf/Crane Fruehauf	Not against
	BP/Century Oil	Against
1977	Provident Financial Group/Cattle's (Holdings)	Abandoned
	Associated Engineering/Serck	Abandoned
	Sketchley/Johnson Group Cleaners	Abandoned
	Smith Bros/Bisgood Bishop	Not against
	Rheem International/Redfearn National Glass	Abandoned
	Rockware Glass/Redfearn National Glass	Against
	United Glass/Redfearn National Glass	Against
	Derritron/British Electronic Controls	Abandoned
1978	Lonrho/Scottish & Universal Investments/House of Fraser	Not against
	Hepworth Ceramic Holdings/H & R Johnson-Richards Tiles	Abandoned
1979	GEDC/Averys	Not against
	FMC Corporation/Alginate Industries	Not against
	Merck/Alginate Industries	Not against
1980	Hiram Walker-Gooderham/Highland Disillers	Against
	Blue Circle/Armitage Shanks	Not against
	S & W Berisford/British Sugar Corporation	Not against
	Compagnie Internationale Europcar/Godfrey Davis	Not against
	Grand Metropolitan/Coral Leisure Group	Abandoned
1981	Enserch Corporation/Davy Corporation	Against
	Lonrho/House of Fraser	Against
	European Ferries/Sealink	Against
	British Rail Hovercraft/Hoverlloyd	Not against
	Hongkong & Shanghai Banking Corporation/Royal Bank of Scotland	Against

Year	Reference	Public interest finding
	BTR/Serck	Not against
	Argyll Foods/Linfood Holdings	Abandoned
1982	Rowntree Mackintosh/Huntley & Palmer	Abandoned
	Nabisco Brands/Huntley & Palmer	Not against
	ICI/Arthur Holden	Not against
	Great Universal Stores/Empire Stores	Against
	Charter Consolidated/Anderson Strathclyde	Against
	Sunlight Service Group/Johnson Group Cleaners	Against
	Initial/Johnson Group Cleaners	Against
	Prosper de Mulder/Midland Cattle Products	Abandoned
	Linfood Holdings/Fitch Lovell	Not against
	The Enterprises of Alan J. Lewis/Illingworth Morris	Not against
1983	London Brick/Ibstock Johnsen	Not against
	Redland/Ibstock Johnsen	Abandoned
	Hepworth Ceramic Holdings/Steetley	Against
	GFI/Knoll International Holdings/Sotheby Parke Bernet	Abandoned
	A. Alfred Taubman/Sotheby Parke Bernet	Not against
	Pleasurama/Trident Television	Against
	Grand Metropolitan/Trident Television	Against
	Trafalgar House/ P & O	Not against
	GKN/AE	Against

Source: Annual Reports of the Director-General of Fair Trading, various years, HMSO, London.

The Recent Past, 1984–1986

Table 7.3 outlines references made between 1984 and 1986. The first entry in the table, Lonrho/House of Fraser, was the last of a kind. This was the third time the bid had been referred. In the first case, in 1978, the two companies had been linked by Lonrho increasing its share in House of Fraser through a bid for Scottish and Universal Investments. The Commission had cleared this stake, but explicitly noted that a greater level of control might give rise to public interest issues. When Lonrho did increase its shareholding, in 1981, a further reference had been made and the Commission in turn had found increased control likely to operate against the public interest. The third reference arose as the bitter board-room disputes between Lonrho and House of Fraser continued and Lonrho attempted to increase its representation on the House of Fraser board.

Table 7.3. Merger references to the Commission, 1984–1986

Year	Reference	Public interest finding
1984	Lonrho/House of Fraser	Not against
	Scottish & Newcastle/J. W. Cameron	Abandoned
	Dee/Booker McConnell	Not against
	BET/Initial	Not against
1985	Imperial Group/Pernaflex	Abandoned
	Scottish & Newcastle/Matthew Brown	Not against
	British Telecom/Mitel	Not against
	McCorquodale/Richard Clay	Abandoned
	Elders IXL/Allied Lyons	Not against
	BET/SGB	Not against
1986	GEC/Plessey	Against
	Imperial Group/United Biscuits	Abandoned
	Guinness/Distillers	Abandoned
	Cope Allman/Cleveland Strip	Abandoned
	Norton Opax/McCorquodale	Not against
	Hillsdown Holdings/S & W Berisford	Abandoned
	Tate & Lyle/S & W Berisford	Against
	London International/Wedgwood	Abandoned
	P & O/European Ferries	Not against
	Feruzzi/S & W Berisford	Against
	Strong and Fisher (Holdings)/Garnar Booth	Abandoned
	Trusthouse Forte/assets of Hanson Trust	Not against
	Gulf Resources and Chemicals Corporation/Imperial Continental Gas	Abandoned

Source: As Table 7.2.

Soon after the reference, an internal Department of Trade and Industry review of the operation of mergers policy concluded with what has become known as the Tebbit Guide-lines: 'my policy has been and will continue to be to make references primarily on competition grounds'.[7] Henceforth, it seemed clear that hostile conglomerate bids of the Lonrho/House of Fraser type would no longer be referred. Indeed, the House of Fraser saga was to provide confirmation of this change. When the Commission's investigation was extended for a further three months, the Lonrho stake was sold off to the Alfayed Investment Trust. Despite the heat engendered by the previous contest, and despite the fact that very little was known of the new owners of this prestigious British company, no reference of the new merger situation was made, despite considerable political clamour for this to be done.

[7] For further discussion, see Borrie (1989) and Swift (1989).

The Tebbit Guide-lines then marked a change of emphasis in reference policy, although the elements of that change—consistent referrals of horizontal mergers and an awareness of the difficulties of providing an opportunity to refer contested bids—had been apparent some time before then. Subsequently the majority of references have indeed focused on competition issues. For the most part, these have involved horizontal mergers, often in fairly small or regional markets, although much larger mergers (for example, *GEC/Plessey*) and vertical mergers (for example, *British Telecom/Mitel*) have also been referred.

The Tebbit Guide-lines retained the option that some mergers not involving competition issues might be referred to the Commission, and inevitably subsequent attention has focused on what the scope of this exception might be. The first evidence was produced by the 1985 reference of the Australian company Elders IXL's bid for the huge food and drink manufacturer Allied Lyons. This was notable for the relative size of the two companies, and the consequent facts that the bid was highly leveraged—Elders would have to borrow heavily to finance the acquisition—and then to pay off this debt, Elders planned to sell off certain parts of the Allied Lyons group. These were evidently thought to be issues involving the public interest, and although the Commission cleared the bid in autumn 1986, another highly leveraged bid (Gulf Resources/Imperial Continental Gas) was also referred later that year.

This pattern of references and these exceptions, however, meant that merger policy had limited impact on the merger boom of 1985 onwards. No matter how large or bitterly contested a bid was, if no competition issues were involved a reference was unlikely. A final feature further limited the overlap between merger policy and the merger boom. The Imperial Group/United Biscuits and Guinness/Distillers bids were initially perceived to arouse competition concerns in the snack food and whisky markets respectively, and both were referred to the Commission. These references clearly reduced the bids' chances of success, since Hanson Trust and the Argyll Group had rival bids for the Imperial Group and Distillers respectively. However, in both cases the initial bids were then abandoned, and arrangements made to sell off certain interests in the markets of concern, should the revised bid succeed. These arrangements were cleared by the competition authorities, and the contests allowed to continue. Although United Biscuits subsequently lost out to Hanson Trust, Guinness won control of Distillers and duly sold off the specified whisky interests.[8]

---

[8] Similar proposals were adopted in Dixon's and Mills and Allen International's bids for Woolworth and London and Continental Advertising Holdings; see 1986 Annual Report of the Director-General of Fair Trading, p. 28. For further discussion, again see Borrie (1989) and Swift (1989).

These arrangements were clearly consistent with the newly declared goals of policy. If the authorities were concerned with the impact of a merger on competition, and if that part of a bid which gave rise to such a concern could be removed to the satisfaction of the authorities, the objectives of all parties would be achieved. Such arrangements did, however, reinforce the recent changes in policy. Two or three years previously, a contested bid could have been referred to the Commission and the arguments of the competing parties analysed in detail. Now, bitterly contested bids involving large public companies were not only not examined, but furthermore the policy concerns were dealt with in an abrupt manner to ensure that the bids could proceed with minimal interruption.

Most of the large bids of 1985 and 1986 were not then subject to scrutiny by the Commission. The resistance to this new stance was apparent at the close of the period, in the latest of the £1 billion plus bids. This involved BTR, one of the most notable of the new conglomerates, and Pilkington, a family-controlled glass manufacturer located in the north of England and noted for a record of intensive research and innovation and of good labour relations. The bid arose as the controversies surrounding Guinness's take-over of Distillers threw new doubts on the ethics and merits of take-over, and in an atmosphere in which the short-term focus of the City—typified by its favourites, BTR—was widely and adversely contrasted with the long-term needs of industry, as represented by Pilkington. Despite considerable pressure for a reference from the company, its work-force, and MPs of all parties, the proposal was not referred to the Commission, and considerable relief was apparent when BTR subsequently retired from the contest as Pilkington's value was revised upward by the market.

Referral Policy: Conclusions

The preceding discussion has described how referral policy has progressed through a number of phases to the current one of primary concern with competition issues. It remains to gather together here some overall figures and general discussion.

Tables 7.4 and 7.5 illustrate a central facet of referral policy, namely that it has always selected from the large number of proposals satisfying the qualifying criteria only a very few for further consideration by the Commission. Table 7.4 gives the annual figures, and shows how the total varied with the overall level of merger activity in the first ten years covered, but has subsequently kept at a fairly continual 160 to 260 proposals per year (to this extent justifying a comment made in the text above), until 1986. This has been accomplished by twice raising the qualifying assets criterion, from £5 million to £15 million in April 1980 and

Table 7.4. Merger proposals qualifying for consideration by Mergers Panel, 1965–1986[a]

Year	£5m. criterion	£15m. criterion	£30m. criterion	Actually considered	References made[b]
1965 (part)	48			48	1
1966	63			63	5
1967	96			96	1
1968	133			133	2
1969	126			126	3
1970	80			80	2
1971	110			110	1
1972	114			114	3
1973	134			134	8
1974	141			141	5
1975	160			160	4
1976	163			163	4
1977	194			194	8
1978	229	103		229	2
1979	257	131		257	3
1980	182	140	115	182	5
1981		164	105	164	8
1982		190	122	190	10
1983		192	129	192	9
1984			223	223	4
1985			192	192	6
1986			313	313	13

[a] The assets criterion was raised from £5m. to £15m. on 10 April 1980, and to £30m. in July 1984. The back projections show how many mergers would have qualified had the higher criteria prevailed in preceding years.

[b] Including more than one bid each for: Amalgamated Dental, Glaxo, Redfearn National Glass, Alginate Industries, Royal Bank of Scotland, Johnson Group Cleaners, and Trident TV.

Source: As Table 7.2.

then to £30 million in July 1984, as shown in the table.[9] The absolute number of references made, and the proportion of qualifying mergers referred, has varied substantially from year to year. However, Table 7.5 makes it clear that the proportion remains low, and fairly consistent over longer periods at around 3 per cent.

[9] Although with an assets criterion in place, this procedure is clearly justified in principle by the inflation of asset values, in practice it has been applied erratically (reducing qualifying proposals by over a half—on the basis of the 1978–9 overlap—for the increase to £15 million, and by about a third—using 1981–3 figures—for that to £30 million). Moreover, the

Table 7.5. Merger references and abandonments, 1965–1986

Period	Total qualifying mergers (1)	Referred to Commission (2)	(2) as percentage of (1) (3)	Referred mergers abandoned (4)	(4) as percentage of (2) (5)
1965 (part)–70	546	14	2.6	2	14
1971–5	659	21	3.2	9	43
1976–80	1,025	22	2.1	7	32
1981–5	997	37	3.7	8	22
1986	313	13	4.2	7	54
TOTAL	3,540	107	3.0	33	31

Source: As Table 7.2.

Two related factors are relevant here. First, the approach initially taken by policy-makers, and continued to date, was to assume only 'special' cases merited examination, rather than, say, referring large classes of horizontal merger. Second, the Commission's capacity is somewhat fixed, and the referral authorities must be conscious of this fact. Although the Commission has been able to cope with the sort of numbers experienced to date—in addition to examining monopolies and anti-competitive practices and conducting efficiency audits of nationalized industries—any substantial change in referral policy would entail adding to its capacity.[10] Thus there are considerable forces placing bounds on current referral policy.

Table 7.5 also illustrates that a substantial proportion of referred mergers are subsequently abandoned by their participants (a factor obviously easing demands on the Commission's time). To discuss the reasons for this requires further consideration of the Commission's approach, its predictability, and cost in terms of time taken and resources expended. Are

presence of the criterion is ultimately questionable. It clearly brings proposals with no competitive ramifications within the scope of the legislation, and as Hughes's discussion (1989) of the OFT evidence illustrates, these have constituted an increasing proportion of the total. With the shift in attention to competition, this could clearly be revised, although large mergers will continue to be the subject of what non-competition concern remains. For competition mergers, an assets criterion—certainly one which focuses on the large firm as opposed to, say, combined size—is a less obvious requirement. However, as a practical matter it would continue to be easier to make references on the basis of assets, as has been the case in the past, rather than to use more contentious market share figures. Clearly the decision on such matters depends on the type of regime in place—as discussed in the remainder of the text—and the capacity allocated to the enforcement agencies.

[10] As discussed in subsequent sections, reforms of merger policy need not necessarily take this route, but might choose instead to simplify the analysis of mergers and thus reduce or even generally eliminate the role of the Commission.

proposals abandoned because participants recognize they will be opposed by the Commission? I shall return to this question (with no clear answer) subsequently: suffice at this stage to note that, to the extent that this is true, it suggests that merging firms consider they still have a chance of averting reference altogether, or else would have dropped the proposal at birth.

Given the wide scope of the qualifying criteria, it may not be surprising or interesting that so low a proportion are referred. Of more concern is the treatment of particular classes of merger, specifically substantial horizontal mergers. At the outset it must be admitted that accurately characterizing mergers not reported on by the Commission is difficult, because the report itself tends to throw much light on the exact nature of the firms and the markets in which they operate, information which is not generally available elsewhere. Nevertheless there are three sets of evidence which suggest that there have been important ambiguities in the referral process.

First, there is the existence of the IRC in the early years of merger policy. As noted above, there is little doubt that IRC-sponsored mergers were often similar to those considered and sometimes prevented by the Commission in the 1960s. The sources cited earlier give further details.[11]

Second, there are some data available giving the market share breakdown of merger proposals satisfying the qualifying criteria. Gribbin (1974) provided this for the period 1965 to mid-1973, and the 1978 Green Paper (Department of Prices and Consumer Protection (1978)) extended it through to the end of 1977. Table 7.6 displays the two sets of figures, and extracts data for a period in the mid-1970s. Unfortunately, no subsequent data are available.

Table 7.6 can first be used to modify the impression given by the overall breakdown of merger proposals into horizontal, vertical, and conglomerate categories given annually by the OFT and reported by Hughes (1989). Horizontal mergers have accounted for the majority of the total (albeit a declining majority in recent years), or typically over 100 such mergers per annum. Table 7.6 shows (column 2) that if a minimum market share is introduced into the calculations, this proportion declines to around a third for the 1960s and early 1970s, and further to only 12 per cent in the mid-1970s. (This decline is obviously of some intrinsic interest, given the indication that the policy stance altered and the Commission's attitude appears to have hardened around this period.) Moreover, these figures also modify a common presumption that to resort to a guide-lines approach, whereby any merger satisfying a minimum market share might be referred, would put unbearable strain on the system of control. Thus,

---

[11] Ellis (1971, pp. 286–95) discusses referral policy in the early years.

Table 7.6. Qualifying mergers which qualified on the basis of market share

Period	Total	Total as percentage of all qualifying mergers	Total for which specific figure available	Market share created			
				25–50[a]	50–80	80–100	50–100
1965–mid-1973	281	281/798 = 35%	239	118	74	47	121
Mid-1973–1977	92	92/764 = 12%	87	46	34	7	41
TOTAL	373	373/1 562 = 24%	326	164	108	54	162

[a] Market share criterion was changed from 33% to 25% in November 1973.

Sources: Row 1: Gribbin (1974), table 6; row 3: Green Paper (Department of Prices and Consumer Protection (1978)), appendix table 6, p. 111.

on the mid-1970s basis, adopting a 25 per cent market share guide-line would increase references to about 20 per year, a substantial but hardly earth-shattering increase.[12]

The figures in Table 7.6 can next be compared with the actual operation of policy. In the period to 1977, only 25 horizontal mergers were in fact referred (using the Green Paper definitions to ensure comparability: p. 111, appendix table 7). This is evidently still only a small proportion of the total given in the table (326) and, more worryingly, only a fraction of those mergers creating or strengthening a market share of 50 per cent or more (162). Clearly not even all mergers creating market shares of 80 per cent or more (54) were referred, possibly not even those 7 in the mid-1970s, as policy strengthened.

These figures suggest that in a substantial number of cases, mergers creating a strong presumption of danger of monopoly abuse were not even put before the Commission. It is apparent from Gribbin's (1974, p. 72) analysis that one reason for this is that many of the mergers were very small. Thus of the 281 proposals in the top row of the table, 70 per cent (193) did not separately satisfy the assets criterion, and as a class had average target firm assets of £1.9 million. More precise figures would be needed to increase our understanding of referral decisions, and would also be valuable on a continuing basis.[13]

[12] Of course, all this conjecture depends on how mergers are subsequently treated. If the Commission were to make no move toward such presumptions, a great many wasteful reports would be produced: I return to this in Section 4. Alternatively, if the guide-lines became the centre of policy, i.e. no merger was allowed which infringed them, the figure would fall from 20 to zero as proponents of merger declined to waste their time planning mergers which would certainly be outlawed. See Hay's (1989) discussion of the 1968 US guide-lines.
[13] It should again be noted (see footnote 9) that it is not obviously that because a merger is small it deserves no policy attention. There is obviously not much sense in applying an

The third set of evidence relating to anomalies in the referral process concerns the Director-General's advice to the Secretary of State. The Director-General is charged by law with keeping the state of competition in the economy under review: of those contributing to the referral process (the parties to the bid, other government departments represented on the Mergers Panel, the Secretary of State), he is the one most likely to advocate the cause of competition, an issue which is a principal concern of the legislation. Therefore the referral process can be criticized when his advice is rejected, particularly when that advice is to refer a merger.[14] There have been ten such instances to date.[15] To cite the explanation of the most recent:

The Secretary of State accepted that some detriment to competition could result from the acquisition, but took the view that in the particular circumstances of the case this was not serious enough to outweigh the employment and efficiency benefits to be gained from the probable strengthening of the United Kingdom fibreglass industry. (Annual Report of Director-General of Fair Trading for 1986, pp. 26–7)

As is clear from the legislation, it is this type of trade-off which the Commission is there to perform, and which it is given six months to do. If the fairly common pre-emption of such an inquiry before reference suggests that the Commission's procedures are too slow, then an obvious direction of policy reform is indicated. If it suggests that the Commission would not have come to the same conclusion, an obvious question as to the Secretary of State's particular expertise in these matters is raised. The doubts surrounding these issues are perhaps sufficient to consider giving the Director-General sole charge of making competition references. As

expensive policy procedure to a market which would not possibly justify it in terms of monopoly profits or welfare loss averted. To the extent that small markets are liable to be swamped by the effect of a large new entrant, or a rush of foreign competition, this conclusion is reinforced. However, policy based on guide-lines, for example, need not be costly in this sense.

[14] There are two known instances—A. J. Lewis/Illingworth Morris, GFI/Knoll/Sothebys (and by implication a third, consequent on the latter, A. Alfred Taubman/Sotheby's)—when a reference was made contrary to the Director-General's advice. Given that these did not involve competition, and that a case *can* be made for public scrutiny of *specific* non-competition issues, the criticism of these is less.

[15] Since 1978 details have been given in the Annual Report of the Director-General of Fair Trading. The 1978 report (p. 10) cited Imperial Group/broker chicken business of J. B. Eastwood Ltd as the third, and other sources (e.g. Whish (1985, p. 519)) suggest Tate and Lyle/Mandre Garton and Woolworth/Dodge City were the previous two. The subsequent cases, including referrals against advice, are (with year of annual report and page reference): Thorn Electrical Industries/EMI and Calor Gas/Clogas (1979, p. 41); A. J. Lewis/Illingworth Morris (1982, p. 29); GFI/Knoll/Sothebys, Blue Circle Industries/Aberthaw and Bristol Channel Portland Cement, Dalgety/agricultural division of Rank Hovis McDougall (1983, p. 29); Nestlé SA/UK subsidiary of Carnation Company (1984, p. 30); Cannon Group/Screen Entertainment, and Owens-Corning Fibreglass Corporation/two fibreglass plants of Pilkington Brothers (1986), p. 26).

noted above, this is essentially the procedure with monopoly inquiries. Complementary changes in the remainder of policy and extensions on this general theme will be pursued in Section 4.

The evidence above leaves some doubt as to the extent of anomalies in the referral process. Do the Director-General and Secretary of State simply sometimes differ, but essentially pursue the 'correct' policy, or do they and the system conspire to neglect dozens of mergers which are harmful to competition? It does not seem sensible to address this question without first considering the other half of policy: what the Commission does with the references it receives. This is the purpose of Section 3.[16]

3. MERGERS AND THE COMMISSION

The previous section has established that British merger policy has gone through several phases. The policy began in an atmosphere clearly supportive of mergers and industrial restructuring, with the consequence that few mergers were referred to the Commission and attention in large part lay elsewhere. As support for merger subsided in the 1970s, policy was left unfocused, a characteristic emphasized by the fact that policy had been extended to cover mergers involving no competition issues. This lack of clarity as to why mergers were referred in turn allowed an increasing politicization of policy in the late 1970s and early 1980s, as supporters and opponents of particular mergers saw the chance to use this state of affairs to their own advantage, seeking to win or avoid a reference to the Commission. This in turn brought its own reaction when in 1984 the Tebbit Guide-lines pulled policy sharply back to a concern with the impact of mergers on competition.

These changes have meant that the Commission has been presented with a broad array of issues to consider, against a changing background of public and political attitudes toward merger. This section considers how the Commission has responded. What gives importance to these questions, and ultimately what has allowed such changes in priorities to

[16] To pre-empt the following discussion somewhat, the Commission has rarely shown concern at mergers creating market shares below about 30 per cent. On this basis, research at the Institute for Fiscal Studies by Andrew Bird could not find many instances of substantial horizontal mergers which had not been referred in the early 1980s. Using market research and trade journal sources, a picture of many merging industries was built up. These drew attention to the cement merger noted above (footnote 15), but no other merger appeared to create as much as a 20 per cent market share, and many were in these terms trivial. The deficiencies of such research are the accuracy of the sources used—reaffirming the desirability of the authorities themselves revealing more data on non-referred cases—and the coverage. Thus the study could not mimic the referral process by confirming information on all cases which were referred. The impact of sales of subsidiaries, less well covered in the financial press, is partly to blame.

occur, is that the Commission's deliberations are little constrained by the legislation. The Commission is required to establish whether a merger is expected to operate against the public interest, and the ways in which this is so, but in so doing must take into account 'all matters which appear to [it] in the particular circumstances to be relevant'. Thus it is fully able to pick up the particular issues in any given proposal, and base its findings upon them.

A broad distinction can be made between those mergers that involve questions of competition and those that do not. There are several obvious types of competition issue, such as when actual or potential competitors merge or when a supplier of a product or input merges with one of its customers. I shall begin with issues not involving competition.

Non-competition Issues

In a number of reports, non-competition issues have been to the fore. Often the question evidently at issue here is one of management efficiency: whether the incumbent management or the acquiring management will run the company better. Other distinct issues suggested by various references are whether the merger will have an adverse impact on the regions, whether a foreign take-over would be desirable, and whether the financing of a merger might give cause for concern.[17] Attention has primarily been given to those cases where the Commission has indeed considered that a merger should be prevented on such grounds, and we examine these presently.

A more general point to make first is that even if the Commission does not ultimately reject a merger on the basis of these issues, its analysis will still be conditioned by such matters. This is best illustrated by the growth of references of contested bids. Very few of the earlier references concerned contested bids, but a much higher proportion of references in the 1970s and early 1980s were opposed by the target firm's management. Indeed, as indicated in Section 2, obtaining a reference to the Commission came to provide an important potential defence against an unwanted bid. This had the consequence that much of the Commission's time was spent accepting, qualifying, or rebutting the various contentions of the parties involved. However the arguments are ultimately treated, this process tends to give shape to the Commission's inquiries and reports. The point is that the impact of non-competition considerations should not be measured solely by the number of mergers prevented on

---

[17] The balance of payments and employment are two other considerations which have been mentioned. However, conclusions on these matters have not generally been independent of those on efficiency.

such grounds: the availability of such defences has meant they have been a principal preoccupation of the Commission.

This leads to the first of the non-competition issues, the question of management efficiency. Given both the prominence of evidence submitted by the parties involved and the broad scope of the public interest criteria, it is not surprising that the Commission has been drawn into this question. If two companies are vigorously disputing which of them is best suited to managing a group of assets, it is tempting for the Commission to express its view.

On several occasions the Commission has objected to mergers which were thought likely to have adverse effects on management efficiency and morale. The argument was first used in *Rank/de la Rue*, and has subsequently been used to protect the management of Glaxo against Beecham, Herbert Morris against both Amalgamated Industrials and Babcock & Wilcox, and House of Fraser against Lonrho.

The regional question has surfaced on a number of occasions, with one particular 'region', Scotland, being a central concern in a series of reports in the period 1979–82. The Commission showed itself to be concerned with employment and career prospects in Scotland and the need to prevent Scotland becoming a branch economy, and this led to the prevention of Standard Chartered's bid for the Royal Bank of Scotland, and a majority finding against the Charter Consolidated/Anderson Strathclyde proposal. The latter became notable because it was not accepted by the Minister of State.

In three further reports the Commission has perceived foreign ownership to be undesirable, at least in part because of the nature of the industries involved. Thus the Commission accepted that it was 'advantageous' to have a British owned and controlled transatlantic shipping company (*Eurocanadian Shipholdings/Furness Withy/Manchester Liners*). (The benefits consisted of having a close knowledge of, and paying particular regard to, the interests of British traders.) It was thought necessary for a contract engineering company to be perceived to be British controlled because of the importance of national identity in securing overseas contracts (*Enserch/Davy*). Finally, the foreign take-over of a British clearing bank was thought likely to impair the Bank of England's control of monetary policy (the Hongkong and Shanghai Banking Corporation/Royal Bank of Scotland proposal).

The most topical of the non-competition issues to be considered is the impact of the financing of a merger. Whereas referral policy and the stance of the Commission currently suggest that the issues outlined above have been down-graded, this particular issue has been the subject of recent concern. It was the reason behind the referral of the first conglomerate merger proposal since the Tebbit Guide-lines, *Elders IXL/Allied Lyons*.

In its report, the Commission accepted that the financing of a bid might be a public interest issue. If a bid for a major public company were likely to lead to severe financial weakness in the new group, it was not sufficient simply to rely on the market to patch things up after the group had contracted or even collapsed. The particular issue at hand was where a bid was largely financed by debt, so that the group would have a high level of gearing and be exposed to a risk of further borrowing and financial constriction if profits did not subsequently live up to expectations.

The Commission examined the levels of gearing and interest cover of Elders's bid on two different projections, and concluded that in this case there was little risk of financial problems. The company had plans to reduce the gearing ratio, in part by selling off Allied Lyons's food division. The Commission also seemed reassured by Elders's recent connections with Broken Hill Proprietary Company and by the reputation of the consortium of banks financing the bid, which had put limits on how far Elders could borrow. The proposal was therefore cleared, but the Commission conceded that less desirable bids of this type might emerge, and invited the Bank of England and the Stock Exchange to consider what might be an appropriate response. One alternative is clearly that further bids might be referred to the Commission for a similar type of analysis, and this therefore remains an active issue.

One final issue should be mentioned, even though it has not been the central concern of any inquiry in the way that those outlined above have. This is the loss of information which results when one company's accounts are submerged within another's, with the consequent danger that poor post-merger performance can be concealed from investors. The disclosure issue was first mentioned in *General Observations on Mergers*, the annexe to the first two conglomerate merger reports. On some subsequent occasions, the Commission has required assurances that separate disclosure of the results of specified activities be given after a merger (*British Match/Wilkinson Sword, Berisford/British Sugar*), although in *Blue Circle/Armitage Shanks* it thought this would be an unfair obligation to place on the company. Nevertheless, the latter report did include recommendations for changes in company law to reduce management discretion in making disclosure decisions.

Competition Issues

The impact of a merger on competition seems the clearest subject of public policy concern. Within this area there are, however, a number of diverse issues ranging from minor overlaps between two companies' fields of operations to the outright merger of two (or more) substantial and direct competitors. This section will commence with the less direct cases.

A general worry with a merger might be that it enables the new group to subsidize certain of its activities from the profits made elsewhere. This has not been a common concern, with the Commission usually accepting firms' arguments that they run activities as separate profit centres and that it would be irrational to cross-subsidize. One exception was *Blue Circle/Armitage Shanks*, the merger of powerful producers of cement and ceramic sanitary-ware. Before allowing the merger to proceed, the Commission required assurances that the group would not grant special discounts to builders' merchants on certain products if they took other products from the group, and that it would not generally use cement profits to reduce the prices on other lines. It was clearly suspected that the group might engage in predatory activity designed to harm Armitage Shanks's competitors. A clear alternative here—and perhaps a necessary alternative, given the unclear force of the assurances—would be to examine any instance of such conduct under the anti-competitive practice provisions of the 1980 Competition Act.

A more common, but related, issue arises from vertical mergers which join together suppliers and customers. For example, firm A might be a producer of a product which is used by firm B. If they merge, firm B might be required to use firm A's product rather than take its supplies from firm A's competitors, although it would otherwise have chosen not to do so. Implicit in such a change is that firm A's product is being subsidized within the new firm, perhaps to the detriment of A's competitors.

Such interlinkages are common in modern diversified firms. In certain cases they may seem almost incidental and the merger would not generally be called vertical. In *Lonrho/House of Fraser* (1981), Lonrho was seen to produce textiles of the type sold in Fraser department stores. One of the Commission's objections to the merger was the danger that Lonrho's textiles would be promoted unfairly in this way, and assurances that this would not be done were not accepted.

In other cases the vertical links between firms have been a more central concern.[18] However, vertical mergers remain comparatively rare, and the Commission's attitude to them has not been clear. One prerequisite for any objection to such a merger is the presence of market power in the activities concerned. In the Boots/Glaxo proposal, for example, the question arose of whether Boots could use the control of a drugs wholesaler

---

[18] Competition law's hostility to vertical mergers and vertical restraints more generally, particularly the foreclosure and leverage arguments (the idea that a monopolist can extend or leverage its market power into other markets), has been one of the central concerns of critics of antitrust in the USA, for example Bork (1978). Krattenmaker and Salop (1986) suggest there may sometimes be a basis for concern in such practices. See also Williamson (1983) for the argument that vertical mergers involving concentrated industries may enhance entry barriers by requiring simultaneous entry into the two activities; Williamson also describes the US Department of Justice guide-lines' approach to the issue.

to its advantage by discriminating in supplies away from other retail chemists. Since drug wholesaling was fairly competitive, this was not thought to be a danger. By contrast in *Pilkington/UKO*, UKO was the only domestic producer of mass-produced lenses, and one of the Commission's objections to the merger was that UKO would be required to take more of its supplies of lens blanks from Pilkington than it would otherwise choose to do. However, market power does not constitute sufficient grounds for an objection: *BMC/Pressed Steel* involved the take-over of a substantial producer of vehicle bodies by one of its customers. Here the Commission was content to rely on assurances that pressed Steel would continue to supply the other vehicle producers.

The most recent such case, *British Telecom/Mitel*, was also the largest to come before the Commission for some time. This concerned BT's backward integration into the manufacture of telecommunications equipment through merger with Mitel, a Canadian-based manufacturer of private automatic branch exchanges (PABXs). There was no doubt of BT's dominant position as telecommunications network operator, and the Commission thought it very likely that BT would be able to divert business to such a subsidiary, given its influence over technological specifications for links with the network and the favourable position of its staff as routine contacts with customers and sole source of advice on equipment. The case was also complicated by the fact that BT's main business was regulated, and thus the distortions in favour of a manufacturing subsidiary might have provided a means of exercising BT's market power which it would not otherwise have. The Commission recommended that the merger should be prevented unless severe restrictions were placed on BT's ability to favour Mitel. In the event, only much weaker restrictions were sought by the Secretary of State (Gist and Meadowcroft (1986)).

The final category to be considered involves the merger of competing firms. This is the largest category, and to keep the analysis tractable and topical, the chapter will concentrate on the Commission's reports produced from 1980 onward.[19] As indicated in Section 2, there were few clear guide-lines from the earlier period. In the 1960s the Commission had objected to some mergers involving large combined market shares but let others pass. The Commission's stance seemed to toughen in the early 1970s with its objections to the merger of both Boots and Beecham with Glaxo, but the signals from later in the decade were less clear. Charter Consolidated was allowed to merge with Sadia and Weidmann with Whitely despite high market shares, whilst the Boots/House of

---

[19] For further discussion of earlier periods, see Rowley (1968), Sutherland (1969), Ellis (1971), Pickering (1974, 1980), Pass and Sparkes (1980), Colenutt and O'Donnell (1978), and Utton (1975).

Fraser merger was prevented despite low ones. More generally there was only an intermittent flow of reports and an increasing propensity to consider issues other than competition. Both of these complications have been mitigated in the 1980s.

The first step in such inquiries is to determine an appropriate market definition. This entails a certain amount of simple gathering of facts, establishing what the firms' interests are and how they overlap, but where firms are diversified or products complex there may be many such overlaps and this stage of the inquiry consequently prolonged.

Beyond this basic stage, market definition will have both a product and a geographic dimension. Thus the Commission will have to consider which products are close substitutes for the output of the merging firms, and over what area competition extends.

Product market definition involves looking for a gap in the chain of substitutes between products. However, such a gap may not be obvious. In *Nabisco/Huntley and Palmer*, for example, the Commission considered markets for biscuits and savoury snack foods (crisps, nuts, and snacks). These two products were seen to be distinguished from each other and from confectionery by such factors as price, taste, place of sale, child or adult appeal, size, and nature of wrapping. But the Commission also had to consider whether the biscuit market should be subdivided into markets for savoury, plain, or chocolate biscuits (it decided not), and precisely where the boundary between biscuits and confectionery lay. To cite some well-known brands: is a Penguin or a Club a biscuit? What about a Kit-Kat?

Another example is provided by *British Rail Hovercraft/Hoverlloyd* and *European Ferries/Sealink*. These reports placed hovercraft in the same market as cross-Channel ferries. They also distinguished several types of demand for such ferry services: accompanied vehicle traffic, through passengers to continental destinations, and excursionists. Survey analysis suggested that the various routes were often regarded as close substitutes by travellers with vehicles, and in particular that the Anglo-French crossings should not be considered separately from Anglo-Belgian crossings. For through passengers, a further dimension came into play, and here the Commission outlined market shares for travel to Paris and Brussels, with air transport showing the largest share.

Product market definition therefore presents a number of conceptual problems and requires a considerable amount of time and attention. Where there are difficulties in distinguishing a product, the Commission may stress supply characteristics, i.e. factors specific to the industry rather than the market. For example, *GUS/Empire Stores* concerned firms conducting catalogue mail-order selling. Clearly the products here will face close substitutes in corresponding products—clothes, shoes, household goods, etc.—sold in the shops. Nevertheless the Commission stressed factors to some extent specific to the mail-order industry—the use of agents and catalogues, the provision of credit, the right to return goods—and focused subsequent analysis on firms operating here.

Geographic market definition involves considering how competition is localized by transport costs or the immobility of the goods or services produced. The two situations which command particular attention are when markets are highly localized and when products are traded on world markets, although in principle there is a complete spectrum between the two extremes. Examples of the first were found in *Dee/Booker McConnell*, which considered local competition between cash and carry wholesaling depots, and *Scottish and Newcastle/Matthew Brown*, which involved competition between pubs in Cumbria. Rather than precisely analyse each local market, of which there may be dozens or hundreds, the Commission's approach here has been to examine the typical distance a customer will travel, and on this basis measure how many local monopolies currently exist and how many more would be created by the merger. A less satisfactory approach, evident in the retailing side of *Linfood/Fitch Lovell* and *Dee/Booker McConnell*, is simply to measure regional as well as national levels of concentration, rather than pressing further to consider the state of local competition of particular shops.

At the other end of the spectrum, although the impact of imports will be acknowledged, international markets have been considered less often than might be imagined. Where markets are not to some extent insulated by transport costs, other factors may impinge. Thus in *GEC/Plessey*, the Commission was willing to concede that there was an international market in public switches (telephone exchanges), but in other sections of telecommunications equipment and more particularly in defence electronics, the purchasing policies of the Post Office (less so under British Telecom) and the Ministry of Defence had meant that effective competition extended only among domestic producers. Thus for truly international markets one had to look to such cases as passenger cruises (where the competition was potential rather than actual, see below) in *Trafalgar House/P & O*, and the scotch whisky market, characterized of course by the fact that all production was within the UK, although 85 per cent of output was exported.

Table 7.7 presents a summary of the market definitions used in the Commission's reports since 1980. This emphasizes the fact that in many cases, most obviously *GEC/Plessey*, a range of different markets were involved. Clearly it is not possible to discuss each in detail here. Indeed the Commission may not be able to conduct as full an inquiry as one might wish. Examples include the localized markets noted above, and

Table 7.7. Market definitions

Reference	Market definition
Hiram Walker/Highland Distillers	Malt whisky distilling
Godfrey Davis/Europcar	Car rental
British Rail Hovercraft/Hoverlloyd	Cross-Channel ferry services; ferry services to Northern Ireland
Nabisco/Huntley and Palmer	Biscuits; savoury snack foods
GUS/Empire Stores	General catalogue mail-order selling
Sunlight/Initial/Johnson	Textile maintenance: laundry dry-cleaning linen rental cabinet towel rental
Linfood/Fitch Lovell	Cash and carry wholesaling; grocery retailing
Pleasurama/Grand Metropolitan/Trident Television	London casinos
Hepworth/Steetley	Refractories: high alumina bricks basic bricks dolomite bricks sliding gate systems
Trafalgar House/P & O	Deep-sea passenger shipping; cargo shipping (Europe–Australasia)
GKN/AE	Engine components: pistons piston rings cylinder liners plain bearings
Dee/Booker McConnell	Cash and carry wholesaling; grocery retailing; grocery purchasing
BET/Initial	Textile maintenance: workwear rental cabinet towel rental dust mat rental
Scottish & Newcastle/Matthew Brown	Beer retailing in Cumbria
GEC/Plessey	Telecommunications equipment: public switches transmission systems PABXs various other products;

Reference	Market definition

GEC/Plessey (*cont.*)	defence electronics:
	   radar
	   avionics systems
	   underwater defence systems
	   communication systems

BET/SGB	Access industry:
	   offshore scaffolding
	   industrial and petrochemical
	     scaffolding
	   other major projects
	   hire and sale of equipment

Norton Opax/McCorquodale	Personalized cheques; lotteries and promotional games
P & O/European Ferries	Anglo-Continental freight transport; Northern Ireland freight transport

Godfrey Davis/Europcar, where distinctive local, national, and international markets were discussed but data presented only for the aggregated total market.

Having defined the market, the Commission will then begin to assess competition within it by computing the market shares of the merging firms and their competitors. Two questions then arise. Do market shares adequately describe the state of competition and the merger's effect upon it? If they do, then what levels of market share are liable to lead to the prevention of a merger? It will be convenient to address these issues in reverse order.

Table 7.8 presents the Commission's estimates of combined market share of merging firms, in particular markets considered relevant. The table should be interpreted with considerable caution, since it illustrates only particular markets from those analysed by the Commission. Thus the overall refractory, engine components, and access industry shares are presented for *Hepworth/Steetley*, *GKN/AE*, and *BET/SGB* respectively, whereas for *Sunlight/Johnson*, *Initial/Johnson*, and *GEC/Plessey* certain specific markets are given. Some other reports are omitted due to the approach to the local markets outlined above. Finally in certain cases the market definitions seem somewhat arbitrary, although these definitions figured in the Commission's conclusions; for example, *Hiram Walker/Highland Distillers* shows the share of quality malt whisky distilleries excluding those owned by Distillers (since Distillers was considered to be self-sufficient in malts, and unlike other whisky suppliers did not operate in the market for whisky fillings). The table would give a somewhat different impression if the whisky share were adjusted downward, or

Table 7.8. Combined market shares of merging firms

Merger	Combined market share (%)	Against public interest	Market definition
Linfood/Fitch Lovell	7.3		Grocery retailing in south
Europcar/Godfrey Davis	8.5		Cars available for rental
British Rail Hovercraft/ Hoverlloyd	19.5		Accompanied vehicle traffic
BET/SGB	22.5		Access industry
Hiram Walker/Highland Distillers	28.0	Yes	Quality malt whisky distilleries
Hepworth/Steetley	39.0	Yes	Refractories
BET/Initial	41.0	a	Combined workwear, cabinet towel, and dust mat rental
McCorquodale/Norton Opax	43.0		Personalized cheques
Nabisco/Huntley and Palmer	43.0		Savoury snack foods
Initial/Johnson	45.0	Yes	Cabinet towel rental
GUS/Empire Stores	47.0	Yes	General catalogue mail-order
P & O/European Ferries	52.0		Continental freight ferry services
GEC/Plessey	59.0	Yes	PABXs
Sunlight/Johnson	60.0	Yes	Linen rental in London
Trafalgar House/P & O	66.0		Passenger cruises from UK
Pleasurama/Grand Metropolitan/Trident Television	67.0	Yes	London casino takings
GKN/AE	71.0	Yes	Various engine components
Sealink/European Ferries	71.0	Yes	Accompanied vehicle ferry traffic to Continent

[a] The Commission clearly regarded the merger as having adverse effects on the public interest, speaking of 'a *prima facie* detriment to competition' (para. 8.40) and of this outweighing any benefits from the merger (8.40). However, due to BET's existing shareholding, these consequences were seen to be 'inherent in the existing situation' and 'not properly attributable' to a full merger (8.41), and the merger was therefore not prevented.

if different sectors of the textile maintenance or access industries were considered.

Keeping these caveats in mind, can any general statements be made about the Commission's treatment of market share in these reports? Beyond the fact that mergers involving low market share—say under 30 per cent—are likely to be allowed, and those involving very high combined market share—over 60 per cent—will probably be prevented, it would seem not. Clearly such statements are imprecise and leave a broad range of market share where the Commission's finding is unpredictable. This contrasts somewhat with the position found in an earlier paper (Fairburn (1985)), where although there was an uncertain intermediate range, this was narrower (20 to 40 per cent) and the Commission would typically prevent mergers creating or strengthening the largest market share in any reasonably concentrated market. Thus mergers involving a combined market share of over 40 per cent would normally be blocked. Such an impression is reinforced by the Commission's statements in reports of the time, for example in *GUS/Empire Stores* (para. 8.23):

It seems to us that where a company in an already highly concentrated market or market sector further strengthens its position by acquiring a competitor, this may be expected *prima facie* to be inconsistent with the objective of maintaining and promoting effective competition in that market.

Subsequent findings such as those in *Trafalgar House/P & O*, *BET/SGB*, *McCorquodale/Norton Opax*, and *P & O/European Ferries* clearly do not take such a strong position against increases in concentration, and this leads to the other of our questions. When do market shares fail to give an adequate representation of the state of competition within a market?

Market shares may give a fairly good representation of the state of competition when they truly reflect firms' underlying capacities to pro-duce for that market, and where those capacities are largely fixed through time. They are liable to be less informative when these conditions do not apply, where output can be readily expanded, and where other firms can transfer capacity from elsewhere or establish new capacity in the market. Thus an obvious extension to the analysis of concentration would be to consider the process of new entry and possible barriers to new entry. (For further discussion of the Commission's analysis of barriers to entry, see Littlechild (1989).)

In each of the cases where the Commission has cleared mergers which would produce a combined market share of over 40 per cent, new entry has been considered to provide an important discipline on any attempts by the group to restrict output and raise prices. In *Trafalgar House/P & O*, the merged firm accounted for 70 per cent of cruises from UK ports and 45 per cent of fly-cruises from the UK (where passengers are flown to foreign ports from which cruises begin), about which the Commission remarked, 'These are large market shares, which in most cases would give us serious concern about a proposed merger' (para. 7.12). However, it continued: 'An even more important feature of this market is the ease of entry into it. Ships, which are the principal capital assets used by cruise operators, are by their nature very mobile and readily redeployed in response to market demands' (para. 7.13).

Likewise, the costs of marketing such cruises—the only cost in the case of fly-cruises—were seen to be low, and some recent new entry had in fact been detected. Similarly, in the personalized cheque printing market the Commission found that the requisite technology was readily available and entry by other security printers was feasible, and in the freight ferry markets examined in *P & O/European Ferries* new entry was again considered practicable and some evidence of recent entry presented in support of this. (In each case the Commission also considered whether the new firm could successfully engage in predatory pricing, i.e. cutting prices to deter entrants or eliminate existing competitors, and concluded that it could not.)

In the personalized cheque printing and freight ferry markets, a further factor thought likely to limit any danger of increased prices was the buying power of the banks and haulers' associations. Buying power has often featured in the Commission's reports, although precisely what is at issue is unclear. (In these reports the Commission indicated the ability to bargain with suppliers for better prices: hence the presence of alternative suppliers rather than existing market shares was thought relevant.) A similar argument was used in the majority finding in *Nabisco/Huntley and Palmer*, which allowed the merger despite the high share of savoury snack foods. The buying power of the British Steel Corporation and the car producers was not, however, deemed important enough to mitigate the effects of the *Hepworth/Steetley* and *GKN/AE* mergers on the refractory and car components industries respectively.

Finally, *Dee/Booker McConnell* was in part concerned with the other side of the coin, a merger possibly increasing buying power. The merged firm would be the largest purchaser of groceries if its retailing and wholesaling interests were combined (there was some question as to whether this would be done). Despite the concern expressed elsewhere about the buying power of multiple retailers, this was not considered a major issue and the merger was allowed to proceed.

One further area in which market shares have been considered deficient indicators of the state of competition is where there are indivisibilities on the demand side. This has been illustrated in two recent reports. In *BET/SGB* a combined market share of 46 per cent of the offshore scaffolding sector (which 'would normally imply a considerable degree of market power') was seen to reflect the firms' current holding of a few large contracts. In fact there were a number of firms—around a dozen—actively competing for such contracts, and hence the market share was measure of success rather than strength. (Buying power was again seen to be an element in this market.) In *GEC/Plessey* similar arguments were used to opposite effect. Thus in different defence electronics markets—various radar and communications systems, torpedoes, and sonar—one of the firms held current contracts and thus had large market shares whilst the other had none. What the Commission emphasized was that the firms had in the past competed for contracts and were among few domestic firms that could do so in future. On the basis of this loss of potential competition, the Commission objected to the merger. (The Commission also objected to various actual reductions in competition in telecommunication products, and to the reduction in competition in research and development.)

Therefore potential competition has been considered important on a number of occasions, most often where it is seen to diminish any adverse impact of a merger on competition. *GEC/Plessey* represented an exception in that here, potential competition itself was harmed. Although a reduction in potential competition was also used as an argument against the mergers in *Sunlight/Initial/Johnson*—where the firms owned laundry facilities which might in the absence of merger be used as the basis of expansion into a number of the product markets—it has not been used elsewhere. Of course, any conglomerate merger represents a diminution of potential competition, since the acquiring firm could enter the market directly rather than by take-over. However, it would seem most relevant in mergers which just miss the horizontal classification, i.e. where the firms supply similar but not identical products or where they supply the same product in different geographic markets (often called product-extension or market-extension mergers). Nevertheless in reports such as *London Brick/Ibstock Johnsen*, where the firms produced different types of bricks, and *Standard Chartered/Hongkong and Shanghai Banking Corporation/Royal Bank of Scotland*, where the bidders were banks outside the clearing bank system, potential competition was not stressed. Given the large market shares required for prevention of horizontal mergers, more frequent objections on the more uncertain basis of reduced potential competition would seem unlikely.

One issue which has not been mentioned so far is the possibility of increases in market power being offset by any cost savings attained through merger.[20] Although the Commission has on a number of occasions looked quite closely at potential cost savings, for example in *Nabisco/Huntley and Palmer*, it has not generally considered this type of trade-off. This may seem surprising in view of the wide scope of the legislation and the prevalence of arguments about rationalization when it was enacted. The principal reason seems to be the lack of quantification of

---

[20] The trade-off was first analysed by Williamson (1968) and is further considered in the 'Introduction' in Fairburn and Kay (1989).

the degree of market power following a merger.[21] The Commission appears to ask whether or not a merger would have an effect on competition, and its answer is never sufficiently precise to then enter into a subtle calculation of the net effect of market power increase and cost reduction combined.

The Commission and Mergers

Three brief points can be made in conclusion to this section before proceeding to some overall analysis of British merger policy. First, the diverse merger reports show the Commission attempting to establish a broad range of 'public interest' standards on issues which have been presented to it. Questions such as the suitability of foreign ownership in particular areas, the general impact of a merger on a regional economy, or the implications of a radical new means of financing a merger can be considered difficult ones to judge in an objective and consistent manner in a public forum.[22] This difficulty is reflected in apparent inconsistencies from report to report and in dissenting opinions within the Commission.

Second, the procedures which enable the Commission to consider thoroughly and afresh the repercussions of a highly leveraged bid, for example, hamper it in other ways. The structure of the inquiries draws out the particular rather than general facts of the case in question, allows participants to dictate the agenda of the investigation, and down-grades cross-referencing between reports.

Third, these matters are seen to be problems particularly in the Commission's handling of competition. Here the Commission repeatedly has to confront questions such as how we can judge the state of competition in a market and what is an unacceptable restriction of competition. Yet although the same issues come up repeatedly—market definition, effects of potential competition—it is hard to trace the Commission's reasoning from report to report, or even to perceive that it regards such continuity as an important matter.

---

[21] There are also, of course, problems on the cost side: how precise are the plans of the parties involved? Would they be achieved anyway if merger were prevented?

[22] To these could be added the general concern with disclosure and the more recent problem of merger financing. An earlier specific example was *Eagle Star/Sunley/Grovewood*, which examined the effects of a building society taking over property companies at the time of the secondary banking crisis.

I would not classify all the disputes about managerial efficiency in the same way. However, in several of these there was evidently doubt about the suitability of the individuals involved to take charge of their targets, for example *Alan J. Lewis/Illingworth Morris* and the Lonrho/House of Fraser cases. This would seem a broad public interest objective, paralleled in company law.

4. CONCLUSIONS

Rather than repeat the conclusions of Sections 2 and 3, this section will concentrate on three themes—scope, predictability, and, to a lesser extent, timing—pertaining to the overall operation of merger policy. The *scope* of British policy is clearly perceived as an important issue, as is reflected in the 1984 Tebbit Guide-lines. The legislation clearly entitles the Commission to consider issues not involving competition: the question is which, if any, of these matters can be dealt with effectively in this way? Is it a requisite part of a regional policy to have controls on mergers, or can regional policy objectives be secured in a more direct way? Over what set of industries is review of foreign investment appropriate? There has been doubt about the effectiveness of merger policy in these areas, and they do not seem to form part of current objectives. However, new 'public interest' issues do arise on occasion—witness the highly leveraged bid for Allied Lyons—and it may well be appropriate to retain the current flexible procedure against similar contingencies in future. For this reason, it looks unlikely that the predictability of policy in this area could be greatly increased.

There remains the question of whether policy should extend to consideration of the merger process more generally. There is considerable evidence that the market for corporate control does not function smoothly. Is it then appropriate for the Commission to try to separate valuable take-overs from those based on speculative motives and poorly thought-out plans? Indeed should many more mergers be subject to this test, and the test made easier for the Commission by reversing the burden of proof?[23] Although such a case can be made, the problem is that it entails the Commission becoming involved in what are very public and often very bitter disputes between companies, with no guarantee that its expertise in such matters will go unchallenged. Indeed in the more recent cases such as *Taubman/Sothebys* and *Lonrho/House of Fraser* (1985), the Commission itself seems to have been aware of this fact, and to have stepped back from acknowledging that there are public interest issues with which it should be involved. There is also a possible alternative to merger policy in this area, which is to displace the merger process by improving internal monitoring of companies' performance, an issue discussed in the 'Introduction' in Fairburn and Kay (1989) and by King (1989).

There is little doubt that merger policy should extend to the effects of mergers on competition, and it is here that the matter of *predictability*

---

[23] Reversal of the burden of proof has been considered by Meeks (1977) and O'Brien (1978). See also George (1989).

holds more force. The question is essentially whether standards can be set out in advance, or whether the details and refinements of each issue have to be considered for each case. I have suggested above that the Commission's procedures, more suited to broad public interest investigations, overemphasize the specific at the expense of what is general. This could be changed by directly requiring the Commission to refer to its previous decisions, perhaps by making a general reference on horizontal mergers to allow the Commission to clarify its own rules. For further reasons given below, I suggest instead that the OFT be brought more directly into proceedings, taking on a role before the Commission.[24] There would then be a clear advocate of competition and less reliance on the arguments of the parties involved. The OFT would have a strong incentive to draw out the common themes and to force the Commission to confront the key issues directly. At present the Commission returns to matters it has acknowledged in previous reports, but attempts little quantification and thus leaves it unclear why the balance between them may have shifted since a previous similar case.

In the conclusions to Section 2, I made further suggestions on the referral stage of policy which complement the recommendations above. It seems anomalous that the Secretary of State should be able to prejudge events by not referring a merger which has been shown to give rise to concern on competitive grounds. I suggested that the referral decision be taken out of his hands, although it may be appropriate for him to retain responsibility for public interest references of the type described above. The OFT would be in charge of taking on cases involving competition, and as part of this would have to clarify its decisions at the current reference stage.

Turning now to the question of *timing*, it is clear that a reference may be a handicap to a bidding company in that it gives at least six months for share prices to alter adversely and new bidders to arrive on the scene. I think that the answer to this lies more in the arguments on predictability than in any direct attempts to compress the Commission's investigation into a period shorter than six months. The Commission has a lot of issues to cover, and has to prepare its findings for public scrutiny. In any particular case, the recommendations above suggest closer scrutiny of the relevant issues rather than the reverse. However, the point is that the pro-

---

[24] The role of the OFT, or to be precise the Director-General, in merger policy is less developed than in other areas of competition policy. In the field of restrictive practices he is charged with taking cases to the Restrictive Practices Court, and has some discretion to allow non-significant agreements. With monopolies, he makes the references to the Commission in almost all cases, and negotiates and monitors undertakings which result. Under the 1980 Competition Act, he is charged with the preliminary investigation of anti-competitive practices: although this may only be the prelude to reference to the Commission, in many cases the investigation ends here.

posals aim to develop clear standards, and that once these exist, the number of cases will diminish. With a standard in place, any inquiry then becomes essentially a matter of establishing how the facts of the case correspond to the standards. In most instances, it will be possible for the parties to the merger to resolve such questions. Realizing that a merger proposal would infringe the standards would result in the proposal not being made. Only difficult or novel cases would then require consideration before the Commission. Of course, it may be possible in advance of any reference to reorganize some proposals so that they do not infringe the standards. In this sense the recommendations here merely continue a recent development in existing policy.

On the question of what the standards might be, I shall be less committal. However, for horizontal mergers it seems there are two positions one can take. First, one could essentially identify competition with market concentration, and set thresholds in terms of market shares (or of some more complete index of concentration). This would give a very predictable policy. There has, however, been growing doubt in the economics literature that this is an appropriate stance.[25] Second, one can inquire more directly into the effects of a particular merger on the state of competition within that industry. Rather than simply measuring the outcome of the current state of competition—the firms' market shares—this involves inquiring somewhat more closely into why those market shares arise and what this entails. Do we see only a few firms each with large market share because there are extensive scale economies in production, meaning that to produce efficiently for the industry one has to be large in relation to it? Are current firms' reputations in the eyes of consumers a valuable asset which cannot readily be duplicated? If such factors are present, mergers between such competitors should not be allowed, since they have the likely effect of raising price with the consequent loss to society. That market processes might in time rectify matters through new firms entering the industry is not a suitable defence. Such adjustments take time and use up resources, and the incumbent firms will have been placed in a stronger position to defend themselves. Finally, trade-offs with decreased costs should not generally be attempted.

Vertical mergers have typically proved more difficult to evaluate. It seems clear that the only effective inquiry to pursue here is into the underlying economic effects.

These are admittedly somewhat vague criteria, and at a disadvantage to market share standards in terms of predictability. However, market shares are one step away from the problem, and in detailed examination of an industry this will become apparent. The proposed criteria also allow

---

[25] See the references in Fairburn and Geroski (this volume).

one to get to grips with situations in which market shares are clearly misleading. Furthermore, they are the type of factors which the Commission currently employs, as was shown in Section 3, although less emphasis is placed here on outright market dynamics.

Finally I should note that the emphasis in this section is on the proposals as a means of dealing with perceived problems with current policy—anomalies in referral decisions, uncertainty as to policy standards, etc.—rather than on the particular details of the proposals. Although they seem a feasible means of developing policy from existing arrangements, considerably more attention must yet be given to changes to the law and the institutions of policy before they could be implemented.

REFERENCES

Bork, R. H. (1978), *The Antitrust Paradox: A Policy at War With Itself*, New York: Basic Books.

Borrie, Sir Gordon (1989), 'Merger policy: current policy concerns', in J. A. Fairburn and J. A. Kay (eds.), *Mergers and Merger Policy*, Oxford: Oxford University Press.

Caves, R. E. (1968), 'Market organisation, performance, and public policy', in R. E. Caves (ed.), *Britain's Economic Prospects*, London: Allen and Unwin.

Colenutt, D. W., and O'Donnell, P. P. (1978), 'The consistency of Monopolies and Mergers Commission merger reports', *Antitrust Bulletin*, **20**, 51–82.

Department of Prices and Consumer Protection (1978), *A Review of Monopolies and Mergers Policy: A Consultative Document*, Cmnd. 7198, London: HMSO.

Ellis, T. S. (1971), 'A survey of the government control of mergers in the United Kingdom', *Northern Ireland Legal Quarterly*, **22**, 251–300 and 459–97.

Fairburn, J. A. (1985), 'British merger policy', *Fiscal Studies*, **6**, 1, 70–81.

—— and Kay, J. A. (eds.) (1989), *Mergers and Merger Policy*, Oxford: Oxford University Press.

George, K. (1989), 'Do we need a merger policy', in J. A. Fairburn and J. A. Kay (eds.), *Mergers and Merger Policy*, Oxford: Oxford University Press.

Gist, P., and Meadowcroft, S. A. (1986), 'Regulating for competition: the newly liberalised market for private branch exchanges', *Fiscal Studies*, **7**, 3, 41–66.

Gribbin, J. D. (1974), 'The operation of the Mergers Panel since 1965', *Trade and Industry*, 17 January.

Hague, D., and Wilkinson, G. (1983), *The IRC: An Experiment in Industrial Intervention*, Hemel Hempstead: George Allen and Unwin.

Hay, G. (1989), 'Merger policy in the US', in J. A. Fairburn and J. A. Kay (eds.), *Mergers and Merger Policy*, Oxford: Oxford University Press.

Hindley, B., and Richardson, R. (1983), 'United Kingdom: an experiment in picking winners—the Industrial Reorganisation Corporation', in B. Hindley (ed.), *State Investment Companies in Western Europe: Picking Winners or Backing Losers?*, London: Macmillan.

Hughes, A. (1989), 'The impact of merger: a survey of empirical evidence for the UK', in J. A. Fairburn and J. A. Kay (eds.), *Mergers and Merger Policy*, Oxford: Oxford University Press.

King, M. (1989), 'Take-over activity in the United Kingdom', in J. A. Fairburn and J. A. Kay (eds.), *Mergers and Merger Policy*, Oxford: Oxford University Press.

Krattenmaker, T. G., and Salop, S. C. (1986), 'Anticompetitive exclusion: raising rivals' costs to achieve power over price', *Yale Law Journal*, **96**, 209–93.

Littlechild, S. (1989), 'Myths and merger policy', in J. A. Fairburn and J. A. Kay (eds.), *Mergers and Merger Policy*, Oxford: Oxford University Press.

Meeks, G. (1977), *Disappointing Marriage: A Study of the Gains from Merger*, Cambridge: Cambridge University Press.

O'Brien, D. P. (1978), 'Mergers—time to turn the tide', *Lloyds Bank Review*, October, 32–44.

Pass, C. L., and Sparkes, J. R. (1980), 'Control of horizontal mergers in Britain', *Journal of World Trade Law*, 135–59.

Pickering, J. F. (1974), *Industrial Structure and Market Conduct*, London: Martin Robertson.

—— (1980), 'The implementation of British competition policy on mergers', *European Competition Law Review*, 177–98.

Rowley, C. K. (1968), 'Mergers and public policy in Great Britain', *The Journal of Law and Economics*, **11**, 75–132.

Sutherland, A. (1969), *The Monopolies Commission in Action*, Cambridge: Cambridge University Press.

Swift, J. (1989), 'Merger policy: certainty or lottery?', in J. A. Fairburn and J. A. Kay (eds.), *Mergers and Merger Policy*, Oxford: Oxford University Press.

Utton, M. A. (1975), 'British merger policy', in K. D. George and C. Joll (eds.), *Competition Policy in the UK and EEC*, Cambridge: Cambridge University Press.

Whish, R. (1985), *Competition Law*, London: Butterworth.

Williamson, O. E. (1968), 'Economies as an anti-trust defense: the welfare trade-offs', *American Economic Review*, **58**, 18–36. Reprinted with corrections in C. K. Rowley (ed.) (1972), *Readings in Industrial Economics*, London: Macmillan.

—— (1983), 'Vertical merger guidelines: interpreting the 1982 reforms', *California Law Review*, **71**, 604–17.

Young, S., and Lowe, A. V. (1974), *Intervention in the Mixed Economy*, London: Croom Helm.

8

Free Trade in Companies: Does Nationality Matter?

LESLIE HANNAH*

It is government policy to welcome . . . investment and in normal cases the nationality of the new owners (foreign or British) is immaterial. However there could be exceptional cases where foreign ownership might affect the public interest—for example in relation to a sector of strategic importance or in cases where the nationality of the owner might affect export prospects.

> Office of Fair Trading, *Mergers: A Guide to Procedures under the Fair Trading Act 1973.*

Only this much is certain, all . . . nations have a character, and that character, when once taken, is, I do not say unchangeable . . . but the least changeable thing in this ever varying and changeful world.

> Walter Bagehot, *Literary Studies*, ch 3.

. . . managers should not be protected from, nor shareholders deprived of the benefits of, the ordinary forces of competition in a capitalist economy.   *J*

> R. G. Smethurst, note of dissent to Monopolies and Mergers Commission, *Report on Proposed Merger of Royal Bank of Scotland*, 1982.

1. COSMOPOLITANISM AND FOREIGN OWNERSHIP

Economists contemplating the last forty years of international investment and the growth of the foot-loose multinational often welcome the free-trading, cosmopolitan approach to foreign ownership which has been encouraged by (and has itself strengthened) these trends. Certainly it is difficult for Europeans to take a hard line against foreign investment on the basis of their collective, past experience, whether as investors or as hosts. European capital was heavily involved in the USA in the early twentieth century and European multinationals have remained strong and recently expanded there. The leading economy in Europe—West

* Professor at the London School of Economics and Political Science.

Germany—has a higher degree of foreign (mainly US) multinational penetration of its home economy than any of its major competitors. It is not obviously impoverished by that direct investment. There have been concerns expressed in Germany and elsewhere in Europe about the loss of national sovereignty through foreign investment, but most European states have distinguished themselves at least as much by wooing foreign investors with competitive incentives to establish new factories as by trying to inhibit the process.

When it comes to the take-over by foreign interests of already existing domestic assets, the atmosphere has been only marginally less cosmopolitan. Indeed, many of the major US subsidiaries in Britain or Germany have their origin in such take-overs. The case for allowing a take-over of a domestic firm by a foreign one is (in an ideal liberal world) not fundamentally different from the case of a purely domestic take-over bid. For the cosmopolitan liberal, there is a general prescription in favour of permitting the market in corporate control to act as a discipline on corporate management. There is no need to prevent either domestic or foreign take-overs unless significantly enhanced monopoly power results.

This relaxed view of foreign take-over bids is by no means universal, and it would be foolish to ignore the special concerns which foreign take-over generates. The last time the world developed such optimism about the movement of trade, people and institutions in a free international environment—the mid-nineteenth century—was only a brief interlude. It was followed by imperialist wars in which foreign ownership was a major issue of contention, not to speak of world wars and revolutions in which all the five largest exporters and importers of capital—the USA, Germany, Russia, France, and the UK—expropriated the interests of many of the foreign corporations previously established on their territories. It may well be that we have now developed more sophisticated international co-operation in matters of economics and politics and will be able to avoid a similar fate. Yet, the neuroses about foreign control which are emphasized in wars and revolutions, do exist at other times. They touch concerns which are human, deep, and not necessarily in areas where economists can pretend to understanding or knowledge. Nationality matters to a lot of people and certainly to a lot of governments. On the other hand, the cosmopolitanism that decorates much international political debate is paper thin.

Within the liberal post-war consensus, there have been vigorous warning voices of dissent. General de Gaulle—backed by the French intellectuals' distaste for the American challenge to their culture and economy—discouraged and hamstrung US multinationals in France. Even where there was a generally welcoming stance, as in Britain and Germany, concerns were expressed, and sometimes discriminatory public purchasing policies were used against foreign firms. More recently, European and Japanese take-overs in the USA have caused a flurry of American criticism of foreign ownership: a rich irony in view of the continuing dominance of America's own multinationals abroad.

Foreign take-overs, moreover, are not only criticized in the 'victim' countries. There are also headquarters country concerns: for example, that firms going abroad will take investment or jobs with them that could have stayed at home. (The special case of South Africa, too, creates anxieties about participation in an apartheid economy which affects victim and acquirer alike.)

The argument is increasingly heard, even in the more liberal countries, that reciprocity should be a condition of liberal treatment. There is now growing concern that Japanese companies, in particular, despite their recent attempts to brush up their internationalist images, enjoy protected home markets and freedom from take-overs which US and UK companies lack.

Similar issues are of increasing concern within Europe, where restrictions on take-over are more widespread and diverse than in Britain. The pressures of the single European market will intensify both intra-European merger activity and overseas interest in gaining a foothold inside 'Fortress Europe' or whatever liberal regime emerges. The spread of merchant banking and merger broking in Europe, the greater freedom of international capital movement where exchange controls previously inhibited outward investment, and the pressure from wider markets and increased competition to increase the scale of European business will propel issues of foreign ownership to the fore. European governments—and the European Commission—will face a range of nationalistic arguments against foreign ownership.

This chapter considers the major economic arguments raised in the debates so far. In Section 2 the *laissez-faire* argument is outlined. Sections 3 and 4 examine the economic case for stopping foreign take-overs. Section 5 considers the present proposals for European Community (EC) initiatives on take-overs and the implications of calls for corporate control.

2. THE *LAISSEZ-FAIRE* ARGUMENT

The case for free trade in the control and ownership of companies has some parallels with the case for free trade in goods and services, in both its strengths and its weaknesses. Some countries may be good at growing fruit, some at making motor cars, some at offering bank accounts. By the same token, some may be good at managing orchards, others at managing car factories, others at managing banks. Given such differentials, countries can profitably specialize in the activities in which they have a comparative advantage. This will often result in trade of goods and services, notably where the factors of production are not very mobile across borders. But there is no reason why it should not instead result in transfers of ownership and management, if the comparative advantage lies essentially in the supply of capital, enterprise, or management organization but not in other factors. In an analogous way to the operation of comparative advantage under a regime of free trade, a regime of free ownership could lead to mutual economic gains. While British owners, managers, and workers in large sectors of the car industry may find that they cannot compete in the global car market, Japanese owners and managers may be able to employ British managers and workers in a British car factory and create a viable subsidiary here because of their superior skills.

As in the case of the car industry, the complexity of production processes, diversity of markets, and varying mix of skills (of both firms and countries) will often in modern industrial conditions result in some combination of international trade and multinational ownership. It is increasingly the case that trade between advanced industrial nations takes place not just at arm's length between companies, but as part of the planned transfer of goods and services *within* multinational firms themselves.

There may be a wide and complex range of objectives which lead a foreign firm to attempt an agreed merger with (or to bid for control of) a national one. These will normally no more be the concern of public policy than other everyday management decisions. Indeed there should arguably be some policy preference for widening the international arena in which such decisions are made. Import competition keeps domestic producers—who may be too few to permit effective competition—on their toes. Why should not competition in take-over bids from outsiders also enliven the market for corporate control? This market depends crucially on a pool of potential bidders being available to pose a credible threat to incumbent managers of quoted companies. This is arguably the most effective way that shareholders can ensure that managers act in the owners' interest, and use the corporate assets most effectively. Recent developments in British capital markets have made it easier to mount bids against even the largest British companies, and Hanson Trust, BTR, and their like do an excellent job of posing a general take-over threat. Yet they can tackle only a small proportion of the possible areas of managerial inefficiency in the corporate sector, and every take-over itself reduces the number of potential bidders. A paucity of potential bidders limits the effectiveness of the take-over threat, and, if Hanson's profits are a guide, it may lead to high profits being made by the few bidders who are available.

Such problems will presumably be limited if the universe of potential bidders is expanded to include overseas companies. Increasing competition in the bidding process to levels faced by firms concentrating on normal business activities would drive bidders' profits down to levels earned in such activities, and this is to be welcomed. The benefits of internationally open bidding processes would not stop there, however. Foreign owners and managers are not just more of the same kind of bidders we already see in Britain, but bring a welcome diversity of skills. Japanese, American, Dutch, and Greek companies clearly in some respects have different skills from each other and from British ones. Yet they may be reluctant to venture overseas. The more generally welcoming the domestic climate is to such bids, the more likely foreign companies are to be willing to incur the extra risks of an overseas bid, deriving from exchange-rate fluctuation or unfamiliarity with the foreign environment.

There are, of course, arguments which cast substantial doubt on the merits of the take-over mechanism as a whole. It may lead to an increasingly short-term perspective by company managers, who forget the need for a long-term strategy, under the paradoxical pressure to achieve short-term profit in order to resist a bid and prolong their own incumbency. The costs of the expensive procedures involved in successful and unsuccessful contested take-over bids may substantially offset efficiency gains from the overall process, and alternative means of improving managerial efficiency could prove superior. (Kay (1988) has estimated that £500 million was spent on contested bids in 1986 on accounting, public relations, merchant banking, and other fees: rather more than is spent on management education.) Moreover, where bidders do enhance shareholder values, they may do so only at the cost of breaking implicit contracts with other stakeholders (for example, suppliers or employees). This in the long run destroys the capacity of the economy to sustain relationships and investments built on trust, and may again outweigh the efficiency benefits of the take-over threat. These are real issues which explain some of the reluctance of countries like Japan and Germany to follow domestically the relatively liberal approach to contested take-over bids adopted in the USA and Britain. They apply, however, with equal force to both domestic and foreign take-overs.

There are, by contrast, some arguments against take-overs which apply exclusively or with special force to foreign take-overs of domestic firms. They may be summarized as:

1. the strategic industries argument
2. the headquarters versus branch plant economy argument
3. the reciprocity argument.

Most of the *economic* arguments which have been used against foreign take-overs in recent years can be resolved into one of these three basic approaches.

3. THE 'STRATEGIC INDUSTRIES' DEFENCE

The strategic argument is distinctively applied in defence manufacturing industries. Within the EC, despite extensive discussions on co-operation in defence production on a bilateral basis and within NATO, only a small fraction of national defence budgets is spent on foreign equipment; Thomson-CSF in France, or Daimler-MBB in Germany, or GEC and British Aerospace in Britain are clearly seen by their governments as national champions in a highly secret business. When competition in war was fundamentally a question of mass production of hardware, countries often wanted their own defence factories on their territory, but foreign ownership as such was not a crucial concern: it could be (and was) expro-priated in the event of war. In the post-war age of nuclear deterrence, with increased technical sophistication of little-used equipment, it is secrecy and national control of access to information that are paramount.

This need not bar foreign take-over of defence production completely, especially if the acquiring company is a friendly power. Thus the German electrical giant Siemens was recently allowed to take over part of the Plessey defence electronics business. There were, however, still perceived limits: the British government felt obliged to transfer coding activities to the British-owned GEC. The Ministry of Defence also placed restrictions on the level of information which the British directors can give to their German superiors: an unusual amalgam of trust and distrust which does credit to Whitehall's capacity for creative fudging (though the sceptic might justifiably wonder at its implications for the functioning of the resulting business organization).

There are very few cases of this kind even in the defence industries. That has not prevented creative arguments absurdly extending the label 'strategic': indeed everything from Coca-Cola to dyestuffs has at different times been defined as 'strategic' by different governments. Recently one of the most fashionable candidates has been banking. The Bank of England, in the early 1980s, made it clear that it would use its formal and informal powers to block the take-over by foreigners of any of the major London clearing and merchant banks. In its evidence to the Monopolies and Mergers Commission (MMC), it opposed the take-over of the Royal Bank of Scotland by the Hongkong and Shanghai Banking Corporation. The Bank pointed to the difficulty of maintaining the stability of the banking system in times of crisis if foreign owners were not as sensitive as

British ones to its informal network of control, particularly if they were under countervailing pressure from their own shareholders or regulators. The Commission were rightly sceptical of the Bank's arguments (though they recommended against the merger on other grounds).

Since then the Bank of England has itself moved more towards formalizing its methods of regulation and thus weakened any force its original argument may have had. The Bank retains its powers to prevent foreign take-over, but it is clear that it will now use those more selectively than it did earlier in the decade. In 1989, Deutsche Bank was permitted to make an agreed bid for Morgan Grenfell, a leading City merchant bank, following an attempt by the French Banque IndoSuez to position itself for a take-over.[1] The Hongkong and Shanghai Bank was permitted to buy a minority stake in the Midland Bank, and then to move towards a fuller merger. The Midland was also permitted to strengthen its own capital base (weakened by an ill-considered take-over of its own in California) by selling its Clydesdale Bank subsidiary to an Australian Bank which is using this Scottish base to extend southwards. The new powers of building societies to demutualize have also opened up alternative routes for foreign banks to acquire a substantial position in the British retail banking market. If British banking is still a 'strategically' protected industry, the protective walls are now much lower.

Arguments on the strategic nature of a particular sector have been made in other countries and industries but the recent tendency has been for such views to be eroded. The holding company Société Générale occupied such a central role in the Belgian economy that many considered it inconceivable that the Belgian government would permit a foreign take-over. Mr de Benedetti's successful bid did, however, show that another EC predator was acceptable. Many governments protect their supposedly 'strategic' industries from foreign investment by nationalizing them, but the privatization process in the 1980s has eroded this protection too. The British government has in some cases attempted to extend the protection abandoned with public ownership by a variety of devices. The simplest and most effective has been deliberately to discriminate against overseas buyers: Austin Rover was sold to British Aerospace at a very low price despite the probable willingness of Ford, Volkswagen, or Honda to pay a substantially higher price reflecting the company's true value. More commonly, shares in privatized companies have been sold to the general public and financial institutions. In some such cases the government has retained a 'golden share', giving a temporary or permanent veto power over changes in control. This has been of limited effectiveness: for example, both General Motors and Ford precipitated the govern-

---

[1] *Financial Times*, 28 Nov. 1989, 1.

ment's withdrawal of their veto by making competitive approaches to the privatized Jaguar in 1989, a year before it was due to expire, and Ford successfully gained control. Where the government *has* taken actions against foreign predators—as in the case of BP or the privatized water companies—it has, significantly, done so on competition policy grounds, compelling the Kuwaitis to reduce their large holding in BP and referring the stake-building in privatized water companies by French water interests to the MMC.

There are still many inhibitions on take-over of allegedly strategic industries, but Britain clearly stands at the more liberal end of a wide spectrum of government behaviour. The recent tendency in most countries in the EC is to move further that way. The somewhat cavalier use of the term 'strategic' and the difficulty of defending the label in all save a small minority of cases are partly responsible for the policy retreat.

This is not to say that the national pursuit of an 'industrial strategy' is dead. Indeed, in both the EC and the USA the idea of supporting national champions in strategically important industries has gained an increasing number of advocates in recent years. Many of them base their case on the alleged success of such policies as practised by Japan's Ministry of International Trade and Industry in the great post-war boom. This effectively broadens the definition of a strategic industry to include anything that the supporter of the industry considers will be capable of achieving significant competitive advantages in the long run, even if it does not seem to exhibit them now. Comparative advantages in modern manufacturing rarely derive from natural advantages of the country in question. They are more commonly based on a capability developed over time, and subject to economies of scale and learning effects which make them difficult for others to copy successfully unless they are given temporary 'infant industry' protection.

Such ideas are alive and well in Brussels and among many member governments, including (if one may ignore some of its rhetoric and judge from its support of, for example, the Airbus) the British government. 'Eurochampions' in other areas like electronics may emerge from the subsidies which have already been given. Strategic criteria in this broader sense will remain acceptable arguments in the Commission's consideration of Euromergers. Such sentiments will not be uncontentious, but they are likely to sweeten rather than delay mergers between putative EC partners. The Commission may, it is true, tend to inhibit bids by Japanese or American companies, but fears in those countries of 'Fortress Europe' are certainly exaggerated on its performance so far. Japanese companies have anyhow shown a very marked preference for European investment on greenfield sites rather than take-overs of existing firms. By contrast, American companies have been engaged in intensive merger activity in

Europe, but without any serious restraint by national governments or Brussels (see Geroski and Vlassopoulos, this volume).

4. THE 'HEADQUARTERS EFFECT' DEFENCE

We have so far spoken of ownership as if that was all that mattered in foreign companies, but in fact the ownership of shares in modern companies is fluid and international. National investors have generally favoured domestic companies familiar to them, but this is changing rapidly; the dominant institutional investors in particular are more frequently spreading their investments internationally. Best guesses are that Britain, at the end of the 1980s, held some US $180 billion of foreign equities, Switzerland $120 billion, the USA $60 billion, and Japan $40 billion.[2] There are many British shareholders in the Hongkong and Shanghai Bank, and many foreign ones in the Midland or the Royal Bank of Scotland; there were many British shareholders in Ford and American shareholders in Jaguar when the take-over occurred. Control by shareholders is, moreover, often diffuse and ineffective and foreign shareholders are hardly likely to change this. Why then should we be particularly concerned with the foreign *registration* of a company, if the option of acquiring a share in it is likely to be freely available to British investors, while 'British' firms might be owned by foreigners? What appears to cause concern is not just the ownership, but the blow to national pride and the desire for local control implied in take-over by a company *headquartered abroad*. At the extreme, there is a fear that the taken-over company will decline, to become part of a 'branch plant' or even a 'screwdriver plant' economy, in which multinational subsidiaries merely assemble products that are conceived, managed, and marketed elsewhere.

This view is partly fuelled by a concern for the quality of jobs. The suspicion is that the place where a company is headquartered will be where the most important and interesting jobs are done: where, for example, R & D jobs and product development activities are based, and, above all, where *all* important employment decisions are taken. While, in principle, companies might be expected to locate their various activities where costs are minimized and their gains maximized, in practice they may show a tendency to favour the centre. Multinational companies will, of course, have a variety of management styles, varying degrees of centralization of different activities, and varying degrees of delegation of authority to national and local units.

None the less, we only have to think of the gradual drift of corporate

2 *The Economist*, 16 Dec. 1989, 95.

head offices from the provinces to London in the twentieth century to appreciate how the 'headquarters effect' can impoverish provincial centres. The MMC, for example, has reported that in life insurance offices still headquartered in Edinburgh the proportion of professionally qualified to total staff was similar to that in 1965, but where a take-over by a southern company had occurred the qualified staff had declined by 34 per cent (though there was virtually no change in the total number of staff) (MMC (1982, p. 73)). The quality jobs, it was implied, had moved to London, permanently impoverishing the Scottish skills base in this industry.

The difficulty in assessing such evidence is weighing it against the unknown: what would have happened in the absence of merger. The surviving Edinburgh companies—implicitly the control group in the MMC's study—may not have been the same as the ones taken over. Indeed to the extent that the discipline of the market for corporate control is the dominating factor in take-overs, it seems more likely that the ones taken over were those with weak Scottish management. The alternative to take-over might not have been continuing strong and independent Scottish companies, but declining or bankrupt ones in which the quality and quantity of jobs lost might well have been greater.

None the less fears of this kind were influential in blocking foreign take-overs in Britain in the early 1980s: the majority of the MMC inquiry into the Hongkong and Shanghai Bank's bid for Royal Bank of Scotland, for example, stated 'the degree of control and management exercised by Scots from Edinburgh, the scale of the company and the importance of it and its industry for Scotland lead us to conclude that removal of management and control of the group from Scotland would be a serious detriment' (MMC (1982, p. 86)). There were other, similar cases, but after 1984 the government (partly because of concern that the 'headquarters effect' defence would become a popular barrier to take-over bids) made it clear that such defences would not be generally entertained, and that competition considerations could be paramount in future references to the MMC.

In the case of R & D jobs, there is precious little evidence that Britain has suffered from its vulnerability to multinational take-over. Indeed while there is a *general* tendency for multinationals to locate R & D jobs in the home country, American multinationals in particular seem to choose Britain as a favoured location for R & D facilities. The proportion of all R & D financed from abroad has increased rapidly in recent years: from 4 per cent of all British R & D in 1968 to 12 per cent today.[3]

---

[3] Organization for Economic Co-operation and Development statistics on R & D quoted by Paul Stoneman, unpublished paper to British Association for the Advancement of Science (1989 meeting).

The reasons for this are clear. The British have an excellent university system producing a relatively cheap and plentiful supply of high-quality research and development personnel. Yet managers of British firms are not fully capable of employing them profitably to exploit their national competitive advantage. (The poorly educated and trained mass of the British workforce also provides a poor base for exploiting any product innovations they generate at the manufacturing stage.) American multinationals have therefore moved into Britain to make up for its native deficiencies, putting scientists and engineers to profitable work who would otherwise have emigrated or been wastefully used elsewhere. US companies have preferred this to employing Americans because of the relative costs of the two locations, and have not been inhibited by any pro-American prejudice from shifting part of their R & D budget away from their headquarters, when it proved profitable to do so.

This has been a success story both for the British workforce and the American owners partly because their common language, culture, and institutions have created a special business relationship between Britain and the USA which has overcome some of the problems for the host country of foreign investment and control. Any artificial attempt to create wider equal treatment under 'most favoured nation' type rules, so that everyone behaves like American multinationals in Britain, is arguably doomed to produce disappointment. 'Foreign plot' theorists will inevitably prosper while the multinational falls short of complete cosmopolitanism: as is evident, for example, in the writings of Robert Reich and others in the USA on Japanese penetration of the US economy (e.g. Reich and Mankin (1986)). Not until Japanese subsidiaries in Europe and the USA prove themselves both genuinely willing to participate in European or American life and mutually acceptable as corporate citizens (like US corporations in Britain) can they expect to receive truly equal treatment, nor, for that matter, to mete it out on rational economic grounds to their host country subsidiaries. The evidence is, though, that they are, in their own interest, trying hard. Certainly in the US, Japanese firms are ensuring a large flow of quality jobs (with high value added per worker and a high R & D concentration) to confound their critics.[4] In Britain, too, Japanese firms like Sharp are reviving British competence in consumer electronics and investing heavily in R & D as well as in the pure assembly functions.

In most large industrial economies the 'headquarters effect' is *not* a serious problem. Typical levels of foreign penetration are only in the 10–20 per cent range. The current levels of take-over bid activity noted in

---

[4] See a study by Edward Graham and Paul Krugman, for the Institute for International Economics, as reported in *The Economist*, 16 Dec. 1989, 79–82.

Geroski and Vlassopoulos, this volume, will not profoundly alter this situation.

The threat to national job quality, for peripheral European countries like Britain, comes not from foreign take-over, but from the dangers of an overcentralized federal Europe, which might generate powerful centrifugal forces compelling firms to locate near the locus of European government, a process akin to London's baneful impact on the provinces in the twentieth century. Edinburgh's business autonomy has survived (whereas firms in the English provinces have succumbed to increasing centralization of political and financial forces in London) partly because Edinburgh retained separate legal, governmental, and financial institutions. By the same token, the Europe of the 1990s will present a greater or lesser threat to the companies headquartered in its peripheral constituent parts in proportion to the extent to which it is a highly centralized or a federal Europe. The less power is centralized to give an artificial advantage to companies located at the centre, the more benignly can peripheral regions look upon take-overs from other countries, for such take-overs may confer management advantage and competitive strength on the regional economies, rather than taking them away. By contrast, the more uneven the playing-field, the more real and justified will be the pressure for protection of the vested interest of peripherally located firms.

Until the political dice give more serious weight to this kind of effect (and in the Scottish case the serious industrial effects of overconcentrated government did not emerge for more than 200 years after the Union), it is safe to conclude that our resources would be better devoted to overcoming the real management and other weaknesses which lead to foreign take-over: to attacking the root causes of British economic weakness, rather than inhibiting foreign take-overs which are often merely part symptom and part cure of the disease.

5. THE 'RECIPROCITY' DEFENCE

In principle, the benefits of free trade are available to any country which unilaterally lowers its tariffs; it is not necessary for others to reciprocate. In practice, governments have always been inclined to use their own tariffs as a bargaining counter to get others down.

In the case of free trade in companies the principle is the same. Unilateral adoption of the principle need not be damaging: indeed if the take-over mechanism is benign, it is in any country's interests to maximize its favourable effects by opening the process to foreign bidders, irrespective of what they themselves permit foreigners to do. In practice, in the market for corporate control, that is what usually happens, and on the rare occasion when it does not the concept of reciprocity is a difficult one to pin down.

None the less reciprocity arguments were increasingly heard in the 1980s both from governments and from victims of take-over bids. The principles can get rather confused. Mrs Thatcher, for example, tried to get James Capel (the British stockbroking subsidiary of the 'foreign' Hongkong and Shanghai Bank which she successfully stopped buying the Royal Bank of Scotland) a seat on the Tokyo Stock Exchange by threatening to block the progress of Japanese financial institutions in London if they did not get equal treatment in Tokyo. However, British firms are not uniformly in favour of getting British-style treatment abroad: victims of take-over bids, for example, are not averse to exploiting international regulatory confusion to thwart their predators. The UK's BAT Industries, for example, defended itself from the mixed-nationality Hoylake take-over bid by lining up US state insurance regulators to oppose a bid with basically British implications. Businessmen can be pardoned if they are not always sure which take-over jurisdiction they are operating in, much less whether they can respect national standards in complex situations.

Strict reciprocity requires that foreigners should not be allowed to bid unless they in turn allow foreign bids on roughly the same terms. Thus the British chocolate manufacturers, Rowntree PLC (unsuccessfully) opposed a take-over bid from Nestlé, the Swiss chocolate manufacturer, on the grounds that Swiss restrictions on foreign share ownership would prevent a similar bid for Nestlé. Similarly, US telecommunications regulators argue against foreign ownership of US telecommunications companies unless the bidding company's country also enforces free markets in telecommunications.

Yet reciprocity can undermine the principle on which national regulation is based, and in some cases, such as banking regulations, this is too great a problem for even the more liberal regimes such as the USA or Britain to accept. In these cases a more realistic target for government negotiations is 'national treatment', i.e. that the same treatment should be available under law to foreign companies as applies to domestic companies. The European Commission has in general abandoned the idea of harmonizing national rules directly in many fields and the 1992 initiative essentially represents a commitment to the 'national treatment' approach within Europe: EC firms will generally have to be treated as national ones are, and the hope is that competition will ultimately reduce the diversity of national approaches. It is clear, however, that there is likely to remain a good deal of leeway on reciprocity in bilateral bargaining, particularly in the heavily regulated industries.

The key case to generate calls for reciprocity in the UK was the hostile take-over of Rowntree by Nestlé. The British government at the time adopted a robustly *laissez-faire* attitude, and Rowntree fell to the Swiss. This strengthened concerns about the inequity of British management being subject to take-over bids from foreigners who were not themselves vulnerable. Swiss companies have to some extent tried to defuse such overseas criticism by liberalizing their shareholding structures. More importantly, the British government has vigorously pursued the issue of reciprocity in take-overs with the European Commission, with the aim of levelling the playing-field in the twelve member countries (though in line with its general approach it has argued *against* the EC demanding reciprocity from *non-EC* states like Switzerland in its merger laws).

There is some prospect of the EC countries moving to liberalize take-overs, under pressure from Brussels and elsewhere. The European Commission has submitted an action plan for reducing or eliminating the barriers to take-over. In some member countries, for example, the Netherlands, the national authorities and stock exchanges had already moved to liberalize their merger and take-over rules in anticipation of EC requirements. European regulation may well have its biggest effect in countries like the Netherlands and Germany, though changes are likely to be slow. There, measures such as proxy voting, companies buying their own shares to frustrate a hostile bid, cross-shareholdings, and restraints on dismissing directors make hostile take-over bids for publicly quoted companies virtually impossible.

The case for forcing such countries to reduce such barriers is, however, far from clear on efficiency grounds. This may seem surprising in view of what has been said above. In Britain, where take-over bids are permitted and even encouraged, I have suggested that there are only very limited cases where intervention to prevent foreign bidders is justified. That is *not* the same as establishing the case that the Anglo-Saxon style of corporate control (with the competitive take-over bid mechanism as a central element) is efficient. On the contrary there is a good deal of circumstantial evidence for the view that countries which choose alternative methods of disciplining and changing corporate management perform better (see Franks and Mayer, in this volume). In particular, firms which overcome pressures for short-termism, establish implicit contracts of trust with their employees, or have active bankers or investors able to intervene to change management directly when it is required, may have a strong competitive advantage. There is no logical reason for their governments to destroy those advantages merely to satisfy Anglo-Saxon tastes for take-over freedom. We may, then, expect considerable resistance to the European Commission's take-over proposals if they threaten such relationships.

Whatever the Commission decides, the main inhibitions on take-over in most countries are not easily subject to regulation.[5] Even in Britain about a third of the largest enterprises are not (practically speaking) likely to fall to a hostile bid. Some are subject to protection by golden shares or the Banking Act, others are still government-owned, and many which are publicly quoted are owned by families or trusts whose slice of the equity is large enough to constitute a blocking vote. Such situations are substantially more common in the other EC countries, where equities play a markedly smaller role in industrial financing (the UK accounts for only about an eighth of the EC's gross national product but nearly half of its equity market capitalization). It is hard to see that changing as a result of legislation.

The most likely scenario for the next decade is for the market in corporate control to remain much as it is now in the UK, while there are slight extensions and liberalizations of it in the continental EC countries. Will that lead to the unfair exposure of British firms to EC predators, severe limits on British take-over activity in Europe, and an increasing take-over gap, as is sometimes alleged? (for example, Blackhurst and Lorenz (1984)). On the performance so far, there is little evidence for this (see Geroski and Vlassopoulos, this volume).

Most mergers (the overwhelming majority, even in Britain) are agreed mergers, not contested take-over bids. These are possible (though no doubt conducted in different ways when the ultimate threat of a hostile bid is barred)[6] in all European countries, and Britain has been no laggard in taking advantage of them. British mergers and acquisitions specialists, like Kleinwort Benson, Schroders, and Warburgs, dominate the European field of merger and acquisition advice,[7] and British companies in the later 1980s were the dominant acquirers in EC countries (see Geroski and Vlassopoulos, this volume). While many large British companies—Eagle Star, Peachey Properties, Morgan Grenfell, Metalbox Packaging, and RTZ Chemicals—have fallen to EC acquirers, the agreed bid has been the norm, not the hostile take-over. American, Swiss, Japanese, and Australian acquirers together have, moreover, been at least as important as EC ones. Of those countries, America is already almost as open as the UK to bidders, while the policies of the Swiss and Japanese are more likely to be influenced by investor pressure or US diplomacy than by British initiatives.

It is quite conceivable that in the next decade the internationally comparative evidence for or against take-over bids as an efficient discipline on

[5] For a survey, see Coopers & Lybrand (1989) for the DTI.

[6] It would be interesting to measure whether a country sells its assets more cheaply or dearly allowing contested bidding rather than allowing inhibitions on them. A priori arguments can go both ways.

[7] 'Bidding business', *The Economist*, 20 Jan. 1990, 114.

management will be more decisive. Certainly the increases in bidding activity at a variety of paces within the different EC countries will provide additional evidence on which a case for or against take-over bidding may be built. Until that time, it seems sensible to permit a variety of national approaches to the market in corporate control, to celebrate the spirit of 'vive la différence' rather than to impose central Brussels standards in areas where we are far from understanding the merits of otherwise of such standards.

6. CONCLUSION

There is every reason, in countries which make take-over bids a principal method of discipline on corporate management, for increasing the efficiency of the process by welcoming foreign bidders on an equal footing. But there is no clear evidence yet that the active (some would say hyperactive) market for corporate control which exists in the USA and the UK is a blessing others would do well to emulate. They may sensibly decide that would be prejudicial to their own alternative institutional incentives to economic efficiency, which have proved so formidable in the international market of the post-war decades, though they may well allow some increased pressure for efficiency in careful controlled liberalization of their take-over process. It would not, however, be surprising if such liberalization were paralleled by increased regulation of the take-over process to control its excesses in the most liberal economies like the UK and USA, in the event of another take-over boom in the 1990s.

REFERENCES

Blackhurst, C., and Lorenz, A. (1984), 'Britain up for grabs', *Sunday Times*, 3 December, p. 11.

Coopers & Lybrand (1989), *Barriers to Takeover in the European Community*, Department of Trade and Industry, London: HMSO.

Kay, J. A. (1988), 'The economic role of mergers', *London Business School Journal*, Summer.

MMC (Monopolies and Mergers Commission) (1982), *Report on Proposed Merger of the Royal Bank of Scotland*, Cmnd. 8472, HMSO.

Reich, R., and Mankin, E. D. (1986), 'Joint ventures with Japan give away our future', *Harvard Business Review*, March–April.

9

European or National? The Community's New Merger Regulation

MATTHEW BISHOP*

1. INTRODUCTION

Since September 1990, mergers taking place in the European Community (EC) have been regulated under a new merger regulation. After sixteen years of unsuccessful negotiations, undertaken with varying degrees of enthusiasm and occasional hostility, the EC member states agreed, in December 1989, to this new system of community-wide merger regulation, based around the Competition Directorate of the European Commission. The negotiation of this regulation raised questions reaching to the heart of current debates about the future economic and political development of the Community, and particularly issues of national sovereignty. These questions will continue to be debated. A central plank of the new merger regulation is to be reassessed in the years to 1994.

The new merger regulation has, however, been broadly welcomed, and its practice mostly uncontroversial. UK Trade Minister, John Redwood, called the regulation 'very important . . . providing more certainty for companies about who exactly is determining the fate of their mergers'. Leon Brittan, the European Commissioner responsible for competition policy, emphasized the link between merger control and the single market programme, and that the European Community has 'for the first time a single framework in which take-overs and mergers with a Community dimension can be dealt with, recognizing the importance of maintaining fair competition throughout the single market'. Less optimistically, however, there are fears that, in the words of one City lawyer, 'the regulation will remove many of the uncertainties which have bedevilled merger control in the Community . . . only to replace them with a new set of uncertainties'. The political controversy surrounding the first merger to be vetoed by the European Commission, in October 1991, reinforces these concerns.

* Matthew Bishop is a journalist with *The Economist*.

Helpful comments on an earlier draft by Stephen Kon of S. J. Berwin & Co., Evan Davis, Paul Geroski, John Kay, and David Thompson are gratefully acknowledged. The usual disclaimer applies.

This chapter describes the previous system of merger control (Section 2), examines and compares the new merger regulation (Section 3), and discusses the implications of these changes, both for businesses and for national merger authorities (Section 4). The conclusions are set out in Section 5.

In particular, the regulation sought to introduce a 'one stop shop'. This aimed to end 'double jeopardy'—the considerable uncertainty facing businesses about whether a potential merger would be investigated by national or European merger regulators—or both. The new regulation tackles this problem by referring only the very largest cross-border mergers to the European Commission, whilst relying on the various merger control authorities within the member states to regulate the remainder.

I focus on three key issues. First, and as there is a broad consensus on this point, briefly, on what criteria should mergers be approved or prohibited? Second, how should responsibility for regulating mergers be allocated between the Commission and member states? Third, how can merger regulation in the Community be undertaken most efficiently?

Discussion of the first of these issues is built on an important assumption about the economic rationale for merger control: that it should concentrate on establishing and preserving competitive market structures. The reasons for this assumption are summarized briefly below (for a more detailed discussion see, for example, Fairburn and Geroski, this volume).

Advocates of a merger will generally cite one of three major benefits. Merger can reduce costs by enabling companies to exploit economies of scale and scope. Efficiency can be increased by replacing poor management through a competitive market for corporate control. Merger can enable two companies that are performing poorly against foreign rivals to form a 'national champion', able to compete internationally. Each of these arguments has some validity. However, economists recognize that mergers can have both beneficial and detrimental effects on companies and society. In particular, merger can have a large anti-competitive effect. Merging companies can gain market power, thus both reducing the pressure on them to be efficient, and allowing them to raise prices. It is not appropriate, therefore, to adopt a generalized stance either pro or anti mergers *per se*. Any merger will have both the possibility of benefits and of anti-competitive costs. Merger authorities inevitably face a pragmatic assessment of the relative size of these costs and benefits.

This raises a number of problems. First, the anticipated gains from merger are likely to be overstated by the merging companies (or the acquirer, in the event of hostile take-over). This is the natural consequence of normal managerial and political motivation. Management may claim that a merger will bring forth economies of scale and scope, the replacement of inefficient management with superior skills, or the advantages of being an effective international competitor. However, they will be equally attracted by the market power and protection from competition that might accompany such benefits. Similarly, politicians may value the increased political influence deriving from 'national champion' arguments. Second, regulators have to choose between spotting potential anti-competitive behaviour in advance—with the risk that a merger might be wrongly opposed, and the benefits unnecessarily forgone—or allowing a merger to proceed, but reversing it if the merged firm behaves anti-competitively in practice. Experience has shown that regulating market structure (i.e. stopping mergers that might lead to anti-competitive behaviour) is often more effective than conduct regulation (penalizing actual anti-competitive behaviour). This is discussed in detail in Kay and Vickers (1988).

In view of the problems described above, I argue, and assume throughout this discussion, that proposed mergers promising scale economies in return for reduced competition should be treated with considerable scepticism. Although the possibility of such mergers should not be ruled out entirely, the claims of competition should be presumed superior until clearly proven otherwise.

The second area of concern—whether regulation should be undertaken at the national or European level—goes to the heart of debates about sovereignty and the future development of the European Community. I build my argument on the principle of subsidiarity—that activities should be carried out at the 'lowest' efficient level (on a hierarchy rising from the individual citizen, through local and national governments, to transnational authorities), a principle fundamental to the Community. I conclude that subsidiarity provides a powerful rationale for regulation of cross-border mergers by the European Commission in preference to member states. However, I question whether the new regulation will properly allocate mergers between state and European level. The size of the companies merging may not be a good indicator of the consequences for the Community of their merger.

The third issue—efficiency of regulation—centres on the new regulation's introduction of clearer procedures and explicit timetables. At the heart of these changes is the allocation of each merger to one, and no more than one, competition authority—the 'one-stop shop'. I suggest, however, that the 'one-stop shop' may be seriously flawed. Although the previous system of multiple regulation was undoubtedly unpopular, I suggest that it was uncertainty about merger procedure that posed the most serious problems facing companies considering merger, rather than the existence of several regulators. The proposed increase in the jurisdiction of the Commission raises legitimate fears of over centralization and regulatory capture. There is considerable doubt about the ability of the Commission's Competition Directorate to meet the timetables it has been set, purely because of the volume of work likely to be required, and the low staffing levels in that particular section of the Commission. Yet, at the same time, the new regulation relies on the extremely varied national merger regulations for controlling all but the largest mergers. As many of these smaller mergers will have some impact on the competitiveness of Community markets, I conclude that the new regulation is itself in need of further modification, though not in the manner presently favoured by many in the Community.

In the discussion throughout the chapter I refer to mergers in a broad sense, embracing the wide variety of legal arrangements within and throughout the European Community that are covered by merger control legislation. These legal arrangements control the general process by which broadly independent companies come under some, or an increasing, degree of common control. The most common examples are friendly merger, friendly acquisition of one company by another, and hostile/contested take-over. However, when I describe a particular set of merger regulations in detail, I provide a more precise definition of the mergers covered by those regulations.

I also note in passing that the absence of a consistent Community legal framework means that friendly merger across national borders presents extreme practical difficulties. Thus, most cross-border arrangements will involve one company acquiring a majority shareholding in another, with both companies remaining legally independent. This would change were the Community directives on company law harmonization within the European Community to be implemented.

2. ARTICLES 85 AND 86

When the European Community's founding document, the Treaty of Rome, was drafted, no mention was made of mergers—largely because the mergers taking place at, and prior to, that time had little economic impact. There was, therefore, no explicit provision for merger regulation in the Community. This did not prevent the European Commission exerting some control over mergers, however, and, from 1972, when it opposed the merger of Continental Can and Thomassen Drijver,[1] the Commission's influence steadily grew. By the late 1980s, a framework for the control of mergers and acquisitions had emerged, developed

---

[1] For details and discussion of the cases cited in this chapter see e.g. Euromoney (1989), Kluwer (1988), the annual reports of the Organization for Economic Co-operation and Development Committee on Competition and Law, or Reynolds (1989).

incrementally from changing legal interpretations of Articles 85 and 86 of
the Treaty of Rome.

Much of this legal debate took place informally, outside the courts—as
throughout the 1970s and 1980s, the Commission only ever took one
formal decision to prohibit a merger, and that decision was subsequently
overturned. Instead, the Commission, when approached, would indicate
to the companies which were proposing to merge the decision it would
most likely take, were a formal decision to be necessary. On the occasions
when the Commission has suggested informally that it would oppose a
merger, the companies concerned have generally regarded this as a sufficient deterrent, declining to subject the Commission's informal 'decision'
to judicial examination. It is not surprising, therefore, that the procedures
emerging from this informal, 'quasi-judicial' process have been complex,
somewhat unpredictable, and driven largely by legal rather than economic
requirements.

After 1972, the Commission mostly relied on Article 86 in regulating
mergers; Article 85 was only considered relevant to mergers after 1987,
and there remained considerable controversy as to its precise meaning
and application to mergers. I therefore begin my analysis of the previous
merger control regime by examining the scope and implications of Article
86.

Article 86

Article 86 states that 'any abuse by one or more undertakings of a dominant position within the common market or in a substantial part of it
shall be prohibited as incompatible with the common market in so far as
it may affect trade between member states'.

Article 86 was first interpreted as applying to mergers in 1972, when
Continental Can sought to merge with a subsidiary of a Dutch can producer, Thomassen Drijver. From then on, the Commission focused on
three key areas in deciding whether or not Article 86 applied to a particular merger—market definition, existence of dominance, and abuse of
dominance. Each area is examined in turn.

In defining the relevant market, the European Commission took
account of all closely substitutable products—both from the perspective
of the consumer and the producer. In assessing substitutes, the
Commission considered both actual and potential competition. For
instance, a proposed merger between Pont-a-Mousson and Stanton &
Staveley (1974), which would have given the combined company more
than a 50 per cent share in the Community market for ductile iron pipes,
was allowed to proceed because there was significant competition from,
among other alternatives, concrete, steel, and plastic piping. Equally, on

some occasions, a manufacturer may have a large market share—and appear dominant—because other companies choose not to enter the market. Such companies might, however, enter that market should the incumbent company seek to abuse its position by raising prices. The Commission also stressed the importance of accurately defining the relevant geographical market.

2 The meaning of 'dominant position' was best defined, in the 1978 judgement on the United Brands refusal to supply Olesen, as 'a position of economic strength enjoyed by an undertaking which enables it to prevent effective competition being maintained in the relevant market by giving to it the power to behave to an appreciable extent independently of its competitors, customers and ultimately of its consumers'. In assessing this, the Commission emphasized the importance of market share. A market share of 40 per cent or more justified an initial presumption of dominance, and a market share of more than 80 per cent was taken as sufficient proof of a dominant position. The Commission also took account of the existence of potential entrants, barriers to entry, technological superiority, pricing behaviour, and ownership of important vertical assets.

3 Demonstrating actual abuse of dominant position proved a substantial and difficult task—particularly as the Commission initially employed a very tight definition of abuse. Abuse, it was held, occurred when the only companies remaining in the market were those whose behaviour depended on the dominant company. Subsequently, the investigation of Hoffmann–La Roche's customer loyalty rebate scheme resulted in the adoption of a modified definition. This focused on action which has 'the effect of hindering the maintenance of the degree of competition still existing in the market or the growth of that competition', and suggests that any merger with a significant impact on the structure of competition in any Community market could technically be an abuse, if either company involved already has a dominant position in any Community market.

Article 86 provided good criteria with which the Commission could regulate mergers. However, the procedures associated with Article 86 were inadequate in terms of the process by which the Commission became aware of mergers, the extended timetable within which the Commission operated, and the resulting uncertainty regarding their intentions. Most strikingly, although the European Commission had enormous powers to frustrate and prohibit mergers, Article 86 did not require companies involved in mergers to notify the Commission before a merger was completed. Instead, the Commission had to rely for its information on newspaper reports, complaints from customers or rival companies, or voluntary self-notification by the companies involved in merger.

Article 86 also failed to provide any effective formal mechanism for assessing proposed mergers in advance. There was some provision for 'interim measures' to delay merger pending investigation—but this required the Commission to demonstrate that a merger was 'likely to cause serious and irreparable damage to the party seeking its adoption, or which is intolerable for the public interest'. This requirement was strictly applied, and the use of interim measures rarely even threatened, not least because the Commission was reluctant for investigations to become a regular part of the defensive armoury of any firm faced with hostile acquisition.

The absence of prior control reflected the powers available to the Commission, and the need to demonstrate actual rather than potential abuse of a dominant position. In cases where a completed merger was found to violate Article 86, the Commission could order the sale of any shares and assets, such that competition was completely restored. (Thus, it is argued, powers to control a merger in advance were unnecessary, as the Commission could remedy the situation afterwards.) There was also no procedure for declaring a merger null. Article 86 could technically be applied only to completed mergers. Because the costs of merger are substantial, there is great advantage to knowing in advance whether a merger will be allowed to continue. Thus, in the mid-1980s the Commission began to show greater interest in the use of prior controls. However, this interest failed to produce any significant changes.

There was no time limit within which the Commission had to either begin or complete an investigation. Thus, some mergers were not investigated until some years after they were completed—for instance, the Commission's investigation of the proposed merger between Berisford and British Sugar (1982) was not called for until sixteen months after the merger had been cleared by the UK's Monopolies and Mergers Commission (MMC). The lack of a comprehensive notification procedure also resulted, inevitably, in some inconsistency in the treatment of mergers that are basically similar.

Companies became more and more dissatisfied with this pervasive uncertainty about how the Commission would treat any proposed merger; and in such an environment companies considering merger were often discouraged from doing so. To combat this negative bias, an informal procedure for advance vetting of mergers grew up. Many companies proposing to merge sought clarification in advance, consulting the Commission informally prior to proceeding with a merger, and obtaining a non-binding (but usually accurate) opinion on whether the Commission would be likely to investigate the merger if it were completed. Thus, although the Commission could not prevent an undesirable merger in advance, companies were, in practice, unlikely to proceed with a merger if they were aware that it was likely to be ruled out by the Commission.

Likewise, an informal system of sanctions against undesirable mergers evolved. The Commission's formal powers, although far-reaching, were difficult to enforce and suffered from various bureaucratic disadvantages. These included, for example, numerous lengthy internal procedures such as translating all documents into nine languages. The informal options available to the Commission include writing letters of warning, setting out changes in the composition of the merger that the merging companies would need to make if they were to avoid formal proceedings, and press releases stating the Commission's detailed objections to a particular merger. However, the reliance on informal procedures had the notable disadvantage that mergers could be called off on a preliminary view, rather than on a thorough investigation of the facts. Obviously, if a company disagreed with an informal decision, it could proceed with merger and put the decision to test in the courts. However, the costs, both financial and in time, made such an action impractical.

Article 85

Article 85 focuses specifically on anti-competitive agreements rather than market positions. It treats as being 'inconsistent with the common market', 'all agreements between undertakings, decisions by associates of undertakings and concerted practices which may have as their objective or effect the prevention or distortion of competition within the common market'.

For an agreement to fall under Article 85 it must both involve competitors and have an impact on the commercial conduct of *either* party. Such agreements include the acquisition of legal or *de facto* control over a competitor; provision for commercial co-operation; creation of a specific structure likely to be used for such co-operation; the possibility of the investing company increasing its influence over its competitor and perhaps to take control later; relationships between parties outside the community (global co-operation); rights of representation on the board of the company; special voting rights; and pre-emption and option rights.

Until relatively recently, Article 85 was not thought to apply to mergers, as it was assumed to refer only to companies that remained fully independent after an agreement was reached. However, this view changed in 1987 following the European Commission's investigation into the acquisition of a minority shareholding in Rothmans by Philip Morris. Although this was not itself a merger, and both companies remained independent, the Commission's summing up of the investigation implied a much broader role for Article 85 than was either necessary to deal with the issues raised by the Rothmans/Philip Morris case or had been previously assumed.

Article 85 was not applied to mergers before 1987 for two main reasons. It was assumed that, first, Article 85 could not apply to permanent changes in the structure of undertakings, and, second, it could not apply to simple changes in the ownership of property. The Rothmans/Philip Morris decision indicated that, whilst taking an equity stake in a competitor does not automatically constitute conduct restricting competition, it may have some influence on the 'commercial conduct of the companies in question so as to restrict or distort competition'. Thus, some mergers will, of themselves, fall within the scope of Article 85.

The precise circumstances in which Article 85 applied to mergers was never satisfactorily resolved. Article 85 certainly covered mergers to which the owners of both companies agreed; and to voluntary transfers of shares that could lead to restrictions on competition. Whether a takeover was agreed or hostile was not thought to be important in this context; more complex were the tricky legal questions about whether individuals selling shares should be treated in the same way as companies and institutions selling shares (see Reynolds (1989)) for a discussion).

These difficulties indicate why Article 85 was never applied, and was only crucial to the outcome of one case, the proposed acquisition, in 1988, of the Irish Distillers Group by a consortium involving Grand Metropolitan and Allied Lyons (although it was also used informally to persuade GEC/Siemens to modify the conditions of their acquisition of Plessey). In this case, the Commission threatened to take interim measures under Article 85—and this threat was sufficient to deter the bidders from their original plans. However, there is little doubt that if the new merger regulations had not been agreed, Article 85 would have come to play a far more prominent role in Community merger control.

Article 85, unlike Article 86, had a formal procedure for notifying agreements. Agreements covered by Article 85 had to be notified to the Commission if the parties involved wished to obtain official exemption from the oversight of the Article or avoid certain fines. However, this requirement applied to a variety of potential infringements of the Article, including some but not all mergers. It was not, therefore, a comprehensive system of merger notification—although the increasing application of Article 85 to share transfers provided companies considering merger with a strong incentive to notify the Commission voluntarily. Notification under Article 85 could take place after the implementation of an agreement, thus the Commission could not always exercise prior control. As with Article 86, competitors of merging companies could also notify the Commission of potential infringements of Article 85.

Article 85, unlike Article 86, did give the Commission powers, exercised through the relevant national courts, to nullify an agreement. This presented few problems when a merger was being assessed in advance. However, nullifying a merger agreement after a merger has taken place poses difficult practical questions. Nullification implies the restoration of the situation that existed prior to the agreement. Yet, restoring share ownership to thousands or millions of former shareholders would have been an immense task, complicated by technical uncertainties about whether Article 85 actually applied to individual shareholders (see Reynolds (1989)). The Commission might instead have considered limiting the voting rights attached to shares as a more practical alternative to restoring ownership, had the new regulations not been agreed.

At its discretion, the Commission was able to exempt agreements from further investigation under Article 85. However, such an exemption had to be for a fixed time period—and this obviously presented problems in situations of permanent structural change such as mergers. Companies may be deterred from merger if they are uncertain about how long it would be allowed to continue. One solution here might have been to offer extremely long exemptions, similar to leaseholdings in the UK property market.

Problems with Articles 86 and 85

The absence of merger control from the Treaty of Rome clearly did not prevent the evolution of a workable Community system of merger control. However, despite achieving a number of notable results, particularly in the latter years of the 1980s, the system that emerged contained a number of serious flaws.

First, the inability to vet mergers before they took place increased the costs that would have been incurred by companies had the European Commission finally ruled against a merger. Once completed, the costs of unravelling a merger far exceed the costs of not implementing the merger in the first place.

Second, although once referred to the Commission, a merger would be evaluated on broad economic criteria, the process by which mergers were referred was founded on a somewhat unsatisfactory series of legal precedents. The most critical divergence between the legal and economic approaches lay in the treatment of dominant position. Article 86 focused on the abuse of dominant position—regulating the conduct of companies—whilst economists are increasingly concerned to regulate market structure (see Kay and Vickers (1988)). This is because the kinds of market structure in which a dominant position can exist are relatively familiar, whilst actual instances of abuse of any dominant position are notoriously difficult to prove (the Commission's 'dawn raids' on companies, in the hope of finding incriminating documentation, illustrate these problems well). Article 86 failed, however, to prohibit the creation of dominant position, only its abuse. Article 85, which did regulate structure, was too limited in scope to overcome the inadequacies, in this respect, of Article 86.

Third, the Commission had no power to positively approve a merger under Article 86 (although some approval by using exemptions was allowed under Article 85), casting doubt on a merger's long-term viability. In particular, in cases in which the Commission had no objection to a merger, it would simply take no further action. Thus, it would remain open to a national authority to prohibit the merger—the normal hierarchy of authority between the Community and member states would in practice (though not in theory) fail to apply. This contrasts sharply with cases in which the Commission decided to prohibit a merger. On these occasions, national authorities did not, however, have the power to approve a merger that the Commission had disallowed (although it should be emphasized here that this is only accepted practice: such hierarchies of power have never been tested fully in the courts). Uncertainty also arose from the lack of any time limit within which the Commission had to decide whether to investigate a merger, and by the failure to create any clear procedure for deciding whether a merger should be investigated by national or Community authorities. This 'double jeopardy'—the risk that a merger would be investigated by two or more regulatory bodies, national or European—provided one of the strongest motivations for the new merger regulation.

Fourthly, the informal system of regulation that developed may have generated a degree of inequality in the treatment of relatively similar mergers. For instance, proposed mergers involving BA, British Sugar, and Pilkington, among others, were attacked by the Commission, whilst others of similar magnitude, such as Electrolux/Zanussi, Alfa Romeo/Fiat, and Philips/Grundig were not. As Reynolds (1989) succinctly observes, 'there seems no logical reason for this'—although more cynical observers might detect a markedly higher success rate for merging companies with aspirations to become 'European Champions'. Also, it led to decisions being taken on the basis of less than rigorous analysis. An informal decision would be provided relatively quickly following a fairly superficial treatment of the issues. The large number of informal decisions also limited the extent to which the Commission's decisions were subject to rigorous scrutiny in the courts.

Finally, as Articles 86 and 85 grew in importance, the number of referrals (particularly under Article 85) increased rapidly. Without the new merger regulation, the growing role of the Commission in merger regulation would probably have exacerbated this effect, with its accompanying administrative difficulties. An increasing number of companies would have sought informal approval from the Commission, despite having no legal obligation to do so, simply because of the uncertainties surrounding the Commission's powers and intentions in the field of merger regulation. Together, these defects present a powerful argument for improved Community merger regulation. It is to the new regulation that I now turn.

3. THE NEW EUROPEAN MERGER REGULATION

As I have seen, prior to 1990 the European Community had no formal system of merger regulation. The Community's founding document, the Treaty of Rome, makes no mention of mergers and, despite the proposal of a merger regulation in 1973, little progress was made in formalizing merger control until 1987, when the original 1973 Directive was revived by then Competition Commissioner, Peter Sutherland. After substantial amendment, the new regulation was approved in December 1989, to come into force in the autumn of 1990. The key elements of the new regulation are outlined below.

The new merger regulation makes a clear division of responsibility for merger control between the European Commission and national governmental bodies. All mergers of companies with a combined world-wide turnover of more than 5 billion Ecus (£3.5 billiion) will be scrutinized solely by the European Commission, subject only to two qualifications. First, each company (or at least two companies, if more are involved) must have a turnover within the Community of more than 250 million Ecus. Second, a merger is exempt from Community control if either company generates two-thirds or more of turnover within one member state. Council of Ministers minutes also indicate that mergers with combined turnover of between 2 billion and 5 billion Ecus may be investigated by the Commission, but only at the request of a relevant member state. However, this right is not part of the body of the regulation. Mergers meeting these criteria must be notified to the Commission no later than one week after the conclusion of the merger agreement.

The member states have agreed to reassess the 5 billion Ecus turnover threshold within four years, with a view to reducing the threshold to 2 billion Ecus. This lower threshold was discussed extensively during the negotiations of the new regulations. However, it was opposed by, among others, the UK, and because of the need for a unanimous vote, a higher threshold satisfying the UK had to be agreed. When the threshold is reassessed, only a qualified majority will be necessary to bring about a change; thus, a lower threshold stands a greater chance of being adopted.

The definition of mergers covered by these notification criteria includes all concentrations resulting from the merger of two or more previously independent undertakings and the acquisition of direct or indirect control of a previously independent undertaking by another undertaking, or by one or more persons already controlling at least one undertaking. The creation of a joint venture performing on a lasting basis all the functions of an autonomous economic entity (and which does not involve the co-ordination of the competitive behaviour between the parties to the joint venture or between either party and the joint venture) also falls within the definition. (Distinguishing between these different types of joint venture is clearly a complex task—and is directly addressed by the Commission in a Commission Notice setting out examples of various types of joint ventures.) Joint ventures not falling within the regulation's definition of concentration may, none the less, be subject to scrutiny under Articles 85 and 86.

Once notified of a merger, the Commission has six weeks in which to decide whether to initiate proceedings. If it decides not to proceed, letters stating that the merger is compatible with the common market are issued to the undertakings concerned, and the relevant authorities in the member states. If the Commission decides that there is a prima-facie case for further investigation, it has a maximum further four months in which to investigate the merger, at the end of which it must declare whether or not the merger is compatible with the common market.

Investigation may include the examination of books and other business records, making copies of all or part of such records; and entering premises, land, or means of transport of the undertakings concerned. However, the purpose of the investigation must be specified in advance in writing, and the relevant national merger authority informed. The Commission is also required to consult with the undertakings involved throughout the investigation process, since it can only object to a merger if the investigated companies have first been able to comment on the detail of the objections cited. Throughout an investigation, the Commission works with the relevant national authorities, communicating with them and, where appropriate, employing their skills. The national authorities are kept informed throughout the investigation; some investigations are carried out by member authorities working with Commission officials, and the opinions of these authorities must be sought throughout. Before any final decision is taken to prohibit a merger, the Commission must also consult an advisory committee on concentrations comprised of one or two representatives of each member state. The Commission is required to take 'the utmost account' of the advisory committee's opinion of its decision; indeed, the advisory committee may require the publication of its opinion along with the Commission's final decision.

Member states are not able to overrule decisions reached by the European Commission, unless given specific permission to do so by the Commission. However, member states may intervene where a concentration threatens public security, the plurality of the media, or the security of financial services. Also, the European Commission has agreed to waive any right to investigate mergers falling beneath the notification threshold that may have followed in the past from the application of Articles 85 and 86. Such decisions are now entirely under the jurisdiction of the relevant member states.

In exceptional cases, a member state may argue that a particular merger under investigation by the Commission, whilst having no undesirable impact within the European Community as a whole, restricts competition in a distinct market *within* that state's borders. If the Commission so wishes, it may allow the relevant national authorities three weeks in which to judge whether the merger does have such an effect.

The new regulation makes no presumption either for or against mergers. Rather, the Commission will find a merger to be incompatible with the common market only if it has both a 'community dimension and creates or strengthens a dominant position in the common market, or a substantial part of it'. When deciding whether a dominant position exists, the Commission must take account of various factors, including:

1. market position and economic and financial power of the firms concerned;
2. the possibilities of choice of suppliers and consumers;
3. access to supplies or markets;
4. the structure of the markets affected, having regard to actual and potential, domestic, European, and international competition;
5. barriers to entry (legal or *de facto*);
6. the trend of supply and demand for the goods or services concerned.

The definition of a market will in no way be assumed to correspond to either national or Community geographical borders, unless this is indicated by the analysis above.

Mergers which, because of the market share of the firms concerned, are unlikely to impede effective competition are presumed to be compatible with the common market; this presumption exists in particular where the merging firms do not have a market share of over 25 per cent in the common market as a whole or in any substantial part of it.

There are a number of sanctions and powers available to the Commission if it finds a merger to be incompatible with the common market. If the merger is still at the proposal stage, the Commission may decide to prohibit it, or, in the event of a completed merger, require the breaking up of the undertakings such that competition is adequately restored. Lesser measures, such as requiring modifications to a merger arrangement, are also available. In addition, the Commission may fine undertakings up to 10 per cent of annual turnover for failure to abide by the Commission's ruling on merger, or to implement agreed modifications. The Commission may also impose lesser fines of up to 50,000 Ecus for incorrect notification or non-notification of a merger; for the supply of incorrect or misleading information in notification or during investigation; for the failure to supply requested information; or for the refusal to submit to investigation. Delays in meeting Commission requests may also be penalized by fines of up to 100,000 Ecus a day.

The new regulation clearly represents a significant change from the previous regime. I now consider the differences in depth, and assess the likely effectiveness of the new controls. Before turning to the fine details of the new regulations, however, I first examine the context in which they will operate, and which will more than anything determine their success or failure—the evolution of strong European institutions and their relationship with sovereign states.

4. SUBSIDIARITY, CENTRALIZATION, AND THE NEW MERGER REGULATION

Conclusion

How should the task of regulating European mergers be divided between the European Commission and the member states? Deciding which mergers should be assessed by the Commission and which by national merger authorities provoked fierce debate. Some member states, including the UK and West Germany, preferred the Commission to vet only the very few largest cross-border mergers (if it had to have any role whatsoever), with national regulators assessing the remainder. Other member states want the Commission to have far greater authority. This conflict reflects both differences between the existing merger regulations operated by the member states; the political debate between centralists and federalists in the European Community; and genuine differences of economic interest.

It would clearly be possible, if administratively and financially costly, for the European Community's merger regulation to be entirely centralized in Brussels—or entirely decentralized to the member states. However, the Community's fundamental commitment to the principle of subsidiarity suggests I look for a decentralized solution where possible.

Subsidiarity is the principle that decisions should be taken at the 'lowest' possible level—by all those (or their representatives) affected by the decision, and by no one who will be unaffected by the decision. The most clear statement of this principle in the context of the Community to date came in a report by the European Parliament (1990):

The principle of subsidiarity implies that the (Community) will be required to perform those tasks which can be carried out more effectively by the institutions of the (Community) than by the Member States acting independently, because of their importance or effects or for reasons of more effective implementation. The Community therefore intervenes only in a subsidiary capacity and in accordance with a principle . . . whereby each level is granted powers only because these cannot, given their nature and scope, be exercised efficiently and effectively at any other level.

This definition is vague about precisely which tasks should be undertaken by the Community—grounds of 'importance' could easily become a catch-all justification for centralization, for example—and the definition will no doubt be improved over time. However, I am able to make the presumption that merger regulation should be carried out by national regulatory authorities, unless it can be shown that they will not perform this task adequately. I can also demonstrate that using the most decentralized definition of subsidiarity suggested by the European Parliament there is strong justification for Community regulation of certain large mergers. This decentralized approach, 'assigns to the Community level only those tasks the dimension or effects of which extend beyond national frontiers'.[2]

In applying the principle of subsidiarity to merger control in the European Community, the lowest practical level at which merger regulation can be exercised is by regulators appointed by member governments—such as the MMC, or the West German Federal Cartel Office—and the highest level is the European Commission. Clearly, using my decentralized definition, there should be no objection to a national merger authority regulating a merger involving two domestic firms with no international trade effects. There is no way in which the decision reached by the regulator in those circumstances can give the country concerned an unfair advantage over another member state—although the regulator's decision may clearly be to the disadvantage of its own national population. Although the Commission might be able to regulate such mergers more efficiently, I argue that the inadequacy of domestic institutions, when this has no clear cross-border repercussions, is a matter for the domestic electorate at the ballot box; the Commission should play no part in such decisions, regardless of how poor it considers those decisions to have been.

Where mergers concern companies involved in cross-border trade, there is potential for opportunism by the regulator on behalf of its narrow national interest. For example, a domestic company may have an

[2] This contrasts with a more centralized alternative 'based on the idea that the states will transfer to a higher level only those tasks which are essential and which will be better accomplished at Community level than by the states acting individually'.

opportunity to strengthen its international competitiveness by reducing domestic competition through merger. If the domestic regulator is able to allow such a merger, it may benefit its own citizens—workers, shareholders, taxpayers—at the expense of those in the other nations in which the newly merged firm will operate.[3] In other words, there are costs to the merger that arise outside the jurisdiction of the regulator—they are 'externalized'. The solution to this problem is to 'internalize' these costs by ensuring that the regulator's jurisdiction extends to the entire market in which the merging companies operate, so that the regulator is indifferent between the residents of different countries. This notion of 'equal treatment' is the vital difference between national and European level regulation, as many national regulators already base their decisions on technical criteria similar to those of the Commission, yet can reach very different conclusions.

There are, in theory at least, three ways in which such 'equal treatment' regulation of cross-border mergers could be achieved, and these vary greatly in efficiency. First, each country affected by a merger could be given the right to veto the merger and would be able to carry out its own independent investigation and decision procedures. This has obvious potential inefficiencies because of duplication.

Second, the various states concerned could negotiate bilateral or multilateral agreements to delegate the regulatory task to one member authority. Obviously, this carries the risk that a particular merger would be regulated in the interests of the regulating nation. However, this risk could be minimized by regularly rotating the regulatory responsibility. The greater the number of national markets affected, however, the more complex the process of negotiating workable bilateral arrangements becomes.

A third, and more practical, option is for all the nations affected to delegate regulation to a single authority (preferably one that is already operational) with jurisdiction over the market(s) concerned—in this case, the obvious institution is the European Commission. This avoids the unnecessary duplication of resources, and removes much of the considerable uncertainty within the business community regarding regulatory intentions and procedures that often arises in merger.

Thus, I conclude that *there is a strong justification for Community regulation of all mergers significantly affecting more than one member state.* However, national authorities should be free to regulate in whatever way they wish all mergers with solely domestic impact.

Recognizing that there is a strong case for Community-level merger regulation of cross-border mergers should not, however, be confused with

---

[3] Assuming, of course, that this benefit exceeds the cost resulting from reduced domestic competition—something that is assumed more often than it is achieved.

support for wholesale centralization of merger control in Brussels. I have already seen that one of the most often used arguments for the new regulation was that it would allow a 'one-stop-shop'. That a 'one-stop-shop' is desirable seems to have been widely accepted, almost without question. It is somewhat ironic that legislation designed to promote competition should fail to be alert to the dangers of monopoly for a regulator as much as any other organization. Indeed, the history of regulation, both at the national and Community level, suggests that there are significant benefits to be gained from 'competition' amongst regulators, much as in the rest of the economy. The lack of such a competitive element in the new regulation may prove to be a serious weakness.

Conclusion

One of the few strengths of the Community's previous merger control regime was the element of 'competition' that existed between the national authorities. Under that regime, a number of mergers—such as those between British Airways and British Caledonian, GEC/Siemens and Plessey—were better regulated because of the 'conflict' between national authorities and the Commission, although the costs arising from this 'double jeopardy' should not be underestimated.

An initial investigation of the British Airways/British Caledonian case by the MMC resulted in the terms of the merger being modified, with British Airways forfeiting rights to fly on certain routes. However, the European Commission was not satisfied with this outcome, and investigated the merger for itself. Its findings led it to require further changes to the merger arrangements, including the forfeit of additional routes. (Less satisfactory, however, was the unnecessary duplication of resources during the simultaneous MMC and European Commission investigations of the Minorco/Consolidated Goldfields merger; the MMC concluded that the merger should be prohibited, and the European Commission reached the same conclusion a fortnight later.)

Furthermore, a degree of 'competition' between regulators can be an important safeguard against regulatory capture—regulators acting on behalf of the companies they are supposed to be regulating (see Kay and Vickers (1988)). It can also minimize the extent to which competitive advantage is conferred arbitrarily on a merged company through differences between national and European regulations.

It is clear that competition between regulators is, by definition, virtually incompatible with the 'one-stop-shop'. This need not mean, however, that all of the benefits of 'competition' between regulators must be lost in the new system. The value of European-level regulation is that decisions should not be biased in favour of one country against another; however, the European Commission has no advantages over national authorities in terms of access to information, informal cultural access to management, or staffing. In all of these areas, national authorities are better placed than the Commission. Thus, a division of roles might offer a better way forward—national regulators collecting information, with the Commission setting the terms of the investigation and being responsible for taking the final decision.

The separation of roles might be even more effective were the Commission to delegate initial decisions to a national authority (selecting one of the authorities of the countries concerned), and concern itself primarily with monitoring national decisions, overturning them only when necessary. Also, the emphasis on subsidiarity would be further strengthened by allowing countries affected by a merger to veto any Commission involvement by unanimous agreement amongst themselves as to the appropriate decision. (It would be surprising if such a right were exercised in other than exceptional circumstances.)

Fears about the 'one-stop-shop', and suggestions that the roles of Commission and member states be distinct yet in tension are no mere theoretical niceties. It is vital that a wholesale centralization of the merger regulation process to Brussels is avoided. In addition to substantial administrative inefficiencies, it would forfeit the limited but important benefits of the remaining potential for competition between regulators, so increasing the risk that companies will concentrate their considerable lobbying resources on, and succeed in, 'capturing' the Commission. Add to this the inevitable subjectivity involved in merger regulation (how to define a market, how to measure the degree of competition, and so on), and it becomes clear that a 'captured' regulator could be a considerable asset to a company contemplating, or, indeed, seeking to avoid, merger.

Having outlined the principles on which merger regulation should be based, and the issues relevant in determining whether merger regulation should occur at the national or European level, I now consider the implications of the new merger regulation in detail.

Implications for the New Regulation

It is immediately apparent that in all three areas of concern—the criteria by which mergers are regulated, the allocation of regulatory responsibility between member states and the European Commission, and efficiency— the new regulation has considerable advantages over the previous *ad hoc* system. First, much of the procedural uncertainty has been removed. There is now a formal notification system, an explicit and binding timetable, and the ability to approve acceptable mergers. Second, the need for European-level regulation of mergers with a significant impact on Community markets has been explicitly recognized.

Third, the criteria on which merger regulation will be based, though still inevitably subject to some discretion, now firmly emphasizes getting market structures right, rather than relying on controlling the conduct of the companies operating within these markets. Superficially attractive, but, as the discussion above indicated, ultimately spurious, arguments about economies of scale and the creation of 'European Champions' have been firmly rejected. (However, there is a disturbing vagueness in allowing the Commission to take account of likely 'technical and economic progress' in reaching its decision; already industrialists in areas of high technology change can be heard justifying mergers between the large European companies in order to ensure European success in the 'global markets of the future'. The UK experience of the 1960s' mergers provides a salutary warning.) Significantly, the creation of a dominant position is now sufficient grounds for prohibition of a merger, whereas previously a dominant position had to be 'abused'.

In terms of efficiency, a more serious criticism has been made (see earlier discussion) of the limited opportunity for 'competition between regulators' that has followed from the commitment to a 'one-stop-shop'. The Commission is obliged to consult national authorities during investigations, and to give substantial weight to the advisory committee comprising representatives of the states whose companies are involved. This is welcome, as far as it goes—and might arguably be strengthened by the oversight of the member states. However, if the interests of different states in a particular merger vary, this scrutiny is unlikely to be effective, thus allowing the Commission a relatively free hand. It is, therefore, likely that the Commission will itself undertake the bulk of the practical work involved in an investigation—much of which could comfortably be delegated to the national authorities (so according more closely with the spirit of subsidiarity).

This will impose severe limitations on the Commission's relatively small competition staff. Indeed, there are legitimate fears that the practical demands of regulating the forty to fifty proposed mergers per year that the Commission expects may be such as to cause considerable delays. If these fears are only partially realized, one of the major advantages of the new system—its speed and predictability—may be undermined.

Fears of regulatory capture are not without basis. In October 1991, the Commission blocked a French/Italian acquisition of de Havilland, a Canadian aircraft manufacturer. Although the decision made sense on competition grounds, it provoked a fierce political row within the Commission, and might well have been voted down on the casting vote of the (French) president of the Commission, Mr Delors, who in the end abstained. One way to reduce the potential for political fudging and the promotion of 'European Champions' by stealth would be to delegate the regulatory function to an independent European Merger Office, along similar lines to the German Federal Cartel Office. With a clear mandate to promote competition, such an independent body would not prevent political interference but, by requiring the Commission to publicly over-turn an unpalatable decision, it would make such interference more obvi-ous and thus a more painful option for the Commissioners. Equally worrying problems arise with regard to the allocation of responsibility for regulating particular mergers. The Commission has voluntarily aban-doned its rights to investigate certain cross-border mergers falling beneath the referral turnover threshold—many of which it would previously have been able to investigate under Articles 86 and 85. The Community has already acknowledged this potential weakness by committing itself to reassessing the threshold, with the probability of lowering the threshold to 2 billion Ecus. However, this problem highlights more fundamental problems with the turnover referral threshold.

In the discussion above, I observed that the basis for prohibiting merger should be the presence of an anti-competitive effect. Yet, mergers are to be referred to the Commission primarily on the basis of absolute size, rather than market structure. It is quite conceivable that there will be many mergers which have a significant anti-competitive impact, affect-ing more than one country, that will not be investigated by the Commission because the combined turnover is too small. Such mergers will thus be subject only to regulation by national merger authorities. To the extent that national regulations differ, and whilst acknowledging that some countries may choose to delegate an investigation to the Commission, many essentially similar mergers may receive arbitrarily dif-ferent treatment. This may undermine some aspects of the single market.

The likely size of this problem is presently unclear, though it may be considerable. Previously the Commission would have been able to inter-vene in cases where inadequate national regulation allowed a merger to proceed to the detriment of the Community as a whole. Now it is unable to do so. One possible solution is to reduce the referral threshold to a level at which it embraces all conceivable mergers that might create a 25 per cent share in the common market or any substantial part thereof. This is the direction in which the Community appears to be moving. However, with the proposed reduction in the referral threshold, this would vastly increase the number of referrals to the Commission, present-ing significant administrative difficulties, and strengthening fears of over-centralization.

Similar criticisms can be made of the exemption from Community merger regulation of mergers involving a company that generates two-thirds of its turnover in one member state. This exemption might allow, for example, a country to prevent foreign entry into its domestic markets by approving mergers giving domestic companies substantial market power. Although the exemption appears to accord with the principle of subsidiarity, involving, for example, only domestic producers with no international trade, it would in fact impose an external cost on the foreign companies unable to enter the national market. Thus, it should in principle be regulated by the Commission.

Another challenge for the Commission will be dealing with the competition implications of deals that remove potential competitors rather than actual competitors from the market. It is quite likely that cross-border mergers will connect firms in similar industries, serving different geographical markets. It may be that in such a merger, the number of actual competitors in either market is unchanged. Each market was dominated by one firm, and each market will still be dominated by one firm, even though it will now be the same firm whereas before it would not have been. This is an issue that has already been raised in the UK with respect to mergers between water companies, and also in the defence sector. The belief is that firms in different geographical markets but within the same industry hold a pro-competitive presence because they represent credible potential entrants to the market.

The degree to which potential competition should be considered a factor in preventing mergers is complicated, and involves weighing up the effectiveness of the potential competition in the absence of a merger. Many firms would maintain the only way that they can be effective is to merge, and this was an argument voiced in the case of Nestlé's take-over of Rowntree. The new regulation does require the Commission to look at potential competition. It will find that, to the extent that the single market/'1992' programme removes barriers to cross-border entry, potential competition will increase. It may well be that many mergers that would previously have been considered 'anti-competitive' will in future be deemed acceptable because of the greater number of potential competitors. The new merger regulation may thus have considerably less impact than is currently envisaged. The Commission should also make clear its attitudes to mergers between companies that meet the reference criteria in terms of turnover within the Community, but which are both registered outside the Community.

Finally, by allowing solely national jurisdiction over mergers in sectors where a concentration is considered threatening to public security, the plurality of the media, or the security of financial services, the regulation prevents the Commission from overseeing the restructuring of some of the most important areas of current and potential merger activity. In both cases, ending the exemptions from Community regulation would greatly increase the number of mergers referred to the Commission, and thus the administrative burden.

There are, then, a number of potential weaknesses in an otherwise attractive system. The extent to which these weaknesses will undermine the regulation will only become apparent when it is operational. However, the weaknesses do not lie in the fundamental principles underlying the regulation, and there is every probability that they will not present insuperable difficulties.

conclusion

5. CONCLUSIONS

The new European Community merger regulation represents considerable progress from the *ad hoc* regime which preceded it. Mergers will now be regulated on clear economic criteria, designed to ensure a competitive single market. Many of the uncertainties associated with the earlier regimes will be removed.

Some criticism of the new regime is based on doubts about whether the 'one-stop-shop' principle of merger control will actually be achieved. By the end of 1991, it appeared to be working fairly smoothly; however, the early 1990s have been a relatively quiet period of merger activity. Even so, this is not quite the essence of the matter as the threshold level of 5 billion Ecus does not capture all mergers which might have anti-competitive effects on Community markets with borders extending beyond a particular state. Indeed, the exemptions based on domestic turnover, and for certain industrial sectors, may mean that the European Commission regulates only a very few mergers. Yet the solution favoured by many in the Community—simply lowering the threshold—is a recipe for bureaucratic overload and inefficiency, presenting substantial difficulties as well as risking failure to meet the Community's commitment to subsidiarity.

The need is not for a clear demarcation between Community and national merger policies but for greater integration between them—which would, incidentally, require the development of merger policies in the many Community states which currently have weak provision. There is in reality no distinction between mergers with a Community dimension and those without—indeed the notion that there is itself contradicts the single market concept. There are mergers where local issues are most important, others where national and international issues are critical, and some which raise issues at all levels. There are some cases—as the regulation acknowledges—where local and Community arguments point in different directions, and others—as the regulation does not acknowledge—where competition between different regulatory authorities ensures more effective scrutiny.

I would like to see an outcome in which the Commission (or an independent delegate body) worked closely with national competition agencies and subcontracted much of its work to them. The issue has not developed in this way because the regulation is the product of a battle for authority between Brussels and—particularly—London and Bonn, and a battle for content between—particularly—Bonn and London on one axis and Paris and Rome on another. As the Community matures, I hope that the regulation will evolve in ways which reflect the needs of economics more than those of diplomacy.

REFERENCES

Euromoney (1989), 'The regulations governing mergers and acquisitions across the European Community', *International Financial Law Review*.

European Parliament (1990), 'Report by Giscard d'Estaing on the principle of subsidiarity'.

Fairburn, J. A., and Kay, J. A (1989), *Mergers and Merger Policy*, Oxford: Oxford University Press.

Kay, J. A , and Vickers, J. S. (1988), 'Regulatory reform in Britain', *Economic Policy*, No.7.

Kluwer (1988), 'Merger Control in the EC'

OECD (annual), 'Competition policy in OECD countries', annual report of the OECD Committee on Competition Law and Policy.

Reynolds, M. J. (1989), 'Application of Articles 85 and 86 to mergers', paper given to 8th Annual Conference, International Anti-Trust Law.

10

Recent Patterns of European Merger Activity

PAUL GEROSKI* and ANASTASSIOS VLASSOPOULOS†

1. INTRODUCTION

There is widespread agreement with the view that the full potential of the internal European market has yet to be realized. Many politicians and business people think that industrial restructuring through merger may be an important part of the process of change brought about by completing the internal market in and after 1992. European enterprises are thought to have been held back from fully exploiting scale economies by the limited size of their own national markets and, as a consequence, are too small to be competitive in world markets. The solution, it is thought, is the development of competitive advantage achieved through the enhanced cost efficiency that rationalization may bring, and merger is one way to realize these scale-related benefits.

Our goal in this chapter is to describe merger activity both within Europe and between Europe and the USA, tracing patterns of activity from the early 1980s when the promise of a single European market began to be taken seriously. The data suggest that cross-border merger activity is a very modest proportion of total merger activity and that most cross-border mergers take place across the Atlantic. On the whole, it is difficult to see such a pattern of merger activity as being consistent with a rational response to the opportunities opened up by 1992.

* Professor of Economics at the London Business School.

† At the time of writing this chapter Anastassios Vlassopoulos was a Research Officer at the Centre for Business Strategy at the London Business School, and now works in private industry.

This article first appeared in Business Strategy Review, 1, No. 2, 1990, published by the Centre for Business Strategy, London Business School.

The authors are grateful to John Cubbin, Paul Simpson, and David Thompson for comments on an earlier draft. The usual disclaimer applies.

2. MERGER ACTIVITY IN THE EC, 1983–1987

The most striking feature of European merger activity is the enormous differences in the number of mergers that occur in different countries. Table 10.1 shows that the UK accounted for most European mergers, and, as a consequence, most of the value involved in such transactions. The combined turnover of all firms involved in mergers in the UK amounted to nearly 8 per cent of UK gross domestic product (GDP) and 41 per cent of UK Gross Fixed Capital Formation. France, West Germany, Italy, and the Netherlands also recorded mergers adding up to more than £1000 million in total, although in none of these four countries did the total value of mergers exceed 1 per cent of GDP by much. At the other extreme, Luxemburg and Portugal experienced only 3 mergers between them. By any historical standard, the merger rate in Europe over the period 1983–7 was enormous. The number of mergers per year increased approximately threefold over the period, and in almost every year, the annual percentage increase in the number of mergers exceeded 33 per cent. The majority of these mergers were strictly national (that is, between two firms with the same nationality).

Table 10.2 shows the breakdown of national, community, and international mergers by sector over the period. The majority of mergers occured in chemicals, electrical and mechanical engineering, food, and paper. Chemicals alone accounted for just over 40 per cent of the total

Table 10.1. Acquisitions by country, 1988

Country	Value		Combined value as a percentage of GDP	Combined value as a percentage of gross fixed capital information
	No. (m.)	(%)		
Belgium	160.5	0.3	7.8	41.3
Denmark	260.5	0.6	0.2	1.1
Eire	379.3	0.8	0.5	2.6
France	5,079.9	10.5	4.1	22.4
Italy	2,337.1	4.8	0.3	1.5
Luxemburg	6.6	—	0.5	2.6
Netherlands	1,522.4	3.1	0.2	1.0
Portugal	6.3	—	1.2	5.8
Spain	1,355.3	2.8	0.1	0.1
UK	35,378.8	73.0	0.6	2.8
West Germany	1,987.9	4.1	1.0	4.9
TOTAL	48,474.6	100.0		

Source: Coopers & Lybrand (1989).

Table 10.2. European mergers by sector and type, 1983–1987

Sector	National	Total
Food	92	122
Chemicals	117	252
Electrical engineering	70	104
Mechanical engineering	92	133
Computers	5	6
Metal goods	58	72
Transportation	36	54
Paper	63	92
Extraction	30	43
Textiles	27	36
Construction	58	75
Other manufacturing	14	21
TOTAL	662	1,010

Source: The European Commission's *17th Report on Competition Policy*. The data were constructed from an examination of the merger activities of the largest 1,000 firms in Europe. As such, they are likely to capture most of the larger mergers initiated in Europe, and since large firms are rather more likely to initiate cross-border mergers than smaller ones, the data will almost certainly understate the degree to which merger activity is contained within national borders.

number of mergers recorded by these four sectors, and for about 25 per cent of all mergers. Furthermore, the number of mergers in each of these sectors increased year by year throughout the period, most dramatically in food, where it rose from three in 1983 to fifty-two in 1987. Of the four, chemicals is the most community merger-intensive sector. Less than 50 per cent of all mergers in chemicals were national, while two-thirds or more of all mergers in food, and the two engineering sectors and paper were national. The least merger-intensive sectors appear to be construction, computers, extraction, and other manufacturing. Between them, these four accounted for a mere 14 per cent of total mergers during the period, less than in the chemical industry alone. Between two-thirds and three-quarters of the mergers in these four sectors were national.

The merger picture outside manufacturing is less well documented, and we have only been able to track down figures for the period 1985–7. Two hundred and forty-nine mergers occurred over these three years (compared with 738 in manufacturing). Nearly 70 per cent of the mergers in the service sectors were national (which is similar to manufacturing). Breaking non-manufacturing down into three broad sectors—distribution, banking, and insurance—reveals distribution to be the most merger-intensive, accounting for just over 50 per cent of the total.

Table 10.3. European mergers by combined turnover of firms involved, 1983–1987

Sector	Less than 500m. Ecus	Between 500m. and 1,000m. Ecus	More than 1,000m. Ecus
Food	29	13	78
Chemicals	49	31	155
Electrical	38	10	51
Mechanical	25	24	75
Computers	2	0	4
Metal goods	24	6	36
Transportation	18	9	23
Paper	40	11	27
Extraction	9	1	31
Textiles	16	5	11
Construction	14	13	43
Other manufacturing	7	3	10
TOTAL	271	126	544

Source: The European Commission's *17th Report on Competition Policy*. The data were constructed from an examination of the merger activities of the largest 1,000 firms in Europe. As such, they are likely to capture most of the larger mergers initiated in Europe, and since large firms are rather more likely to initiate cross-border mergers than smaller ones, the data will almost certainly understate the degree to which merger activity is contained within national borders.

Table 10.3 shows a breakdown of total European merger activity by size of merger for those mergers in Table 10.1 for which reliable data were available. Clearly, most of the mergers recorded in the data are large, but the averages in Table 10.3 conceal an important shift away from the very large mergers. The percentage of mergers in which the two partners had a combined turnover of 1,000 million Ecus fell from 75.2 per cent of the total in 1983 to 56.4 per cent in 1987. Mergers in which the combined turnover of the two parties was less than 500 million Ecus, on the other hand, rose from 13.6 per cent to 33.3 per cent of the total in 1987. Large mergers seem to be particularly common in food, chemicals, computers, and extraction. By contrast, small mergers were more common in paper and textiles.

Most of the size thresholds proposed as markers of the different jurisdictions of national and European Community (EC) merger regulations have fluctuated in the 2,000 million to 5,000 million Ecus range. Over the period 1983–7, slightly more than 50 per cent of all mergers exceeded 1,000 million Ecus, suggesting that between perhaps at least 25 per cent and 35 per cent of all mergers are likely to come under the purview of EC authorities if a threshold of 2,000 million Ecus is chosen. If past trends continue, chemicals and the two engineering industries will be the industries most affected by EC policy. However, there is very little reason to think that size thresholds are a very good way of isolating those mergers that national authorities may have trouble in regulating. Problems of national regulation arise whenever the activities of economic agents exceed the domain of national political jurisdiction, circumstances where it makes sense to invoke a supra-national regulatory authority. Clearly, the types of mergers that are likely to give national merger authorities some cause for concern and open up scope for effective regulatory action at the EC level are community mergers. These amounted to 238 over the period 1983–7, a mere 24 per cent of the total. Thus, whether size thresholds or some more sensible targeting of community mergers are used to delineate the respective domains of national and EC merger policy, the bottom line seems to be that between a quarter and a third of mergers are likely to be affected by any rule that is not too extreme, and that many of these are likely to be in the chemical industry, if past trends continue.

The first column of Table 10.4 shows the percentage of acquisitions within the EC made by national firms in nine of the twelve EC members in 1988. Belgian and Luxemburg firms, for example, only acquired other firms resident in the EC when they initiated a merger outside Belgium

Table 10.4. Cross-border mergers in 1988 (total acquisitions by national firms in selected countries)

Country	Percentage of acquisitions in the EC	Acquisitions of national firms by country
Belgium + Luxemburg	100	94
Denmark	47	41
France	69	61
Italy	74	57
Netherlands	60	70
Portugal		55
Spain	93	97
UK	32	53
West Germany	41	43

Source: *M & A International*. They collect information from the press on all the acquisitions and mergers that take place in Europe, cross classifying them by the national of the acquiring and acquired company. This data source records rather more mergers than the one used in Tables 10.1 and 10.3 and it seems possible that it is more accurate in recording cross-border mergers than national ones.

and Luxemburg, while only 32 per cent of the non-national acquisitions of UK national firms took place in the EC.'It is evident that UK firms show a lack of interest in acquiring EC partners; German and Danish firms are also relatively non-EC oriented. National firms in the remaining six countries chose EC partners two out of every three times they selected a non-national partner.'The second column of Table 10.4 shows the same story from the point of view of who acquired the national firms that disappeared through merger in each of the nine countries. For example, 94 per cent of those Belgian firms that were taken over by non-Belgian firms were acquired by firms located in other EC countries. By contrast, 41 per cent of Danish, 43 per cent of German, and 52 per cent of the UK firms that disappeared through cross-border mergers were swallowed up by other national firms located in the EC. As before, the UK, Germany, and Denmark stand out as having markets for corporate control that are relatively non-EC oriented. In most of the rest of the EC, national firms that lose their national identity through cross-border mergers usually do so through merger with another EC firm.

The story told in Table 10.4 reflects not only the willingness of national firms in the different EC countries to seek out merger partners in other countries, but also the extent to which they are forced to do so by the particular way that the market for corporate control operates in their home country. By all accounts, the UK capital market is the most open in Europe, and, while it is not surprising to find foreign firms acquiring UK firms on a regular basis, what is surprising is to find that a similar story applies to West German and Dutch firms. The explanation for this may lie in the details of how capital markets operate in the different European countries. West German and Dutch firms are reputed to enjoy the protection of large shareholdings controlled by banks or family concerns, and a variety of institutional devices (such as limitations on voting rights, two-tier boards, etc.). Perhaps more fundamentally, there are also cultural differences in attitude towards the relative rights (and responsibilities) of management and shareholders in the different countries in Europe, and these undoubtedly colour the cross-border merger patterns that we observe.

Table 10.4 needs to be read in conjunction with Table 10.1. The simple fact is that the UK stands out as being the most merger-active country, recording more than twice as many community or international mergers as France, the second most active country in Europe. Further, both the UK and the French share of merger activity rose steadily throughout the period. West Germany is the third most merger-active country, with a merger rate running at about 60 per cent of that of France. Merger-active countries are, by and large, those most involved in cross-border merger activity.

3. TRANSATLANTIC MERGER ACTIVITY

A particularly interesting feature of cross-border merger activity is the extent to which it is transatlantic rather than purely trans-European. US and Canadian firms are fairly active acquirers of European firms, but, more interestingly, European firms (led by those in the UK) are very active acquirers of North American firms. Nearly 30 per cent of the cross-border acquisitions that were examined in the last section involved the acquisition of US or Canadian firms by European firms, 11 per cent involved the acquisition of European firms by US or Canadian firms, and 40 per cent of all the cross-border mergers recorded involved the acquisition or sale of a European firm by or to a North American firm.

Table 10.5 shows national mergers in the USA, acquisitions of US firms by non-US firms, and acquisitions of non-US firms by US firms. US merger activity has been high and generally increasing throughout the 1980s, but it seems to have peaked in 1986 and has fallen off slightly since then. In the peak year of 1986, nearly 9 per cent of US mergers involved the acquisition of US firms by foreign ones, while just over 4 per cent of US acquisitions involved a domestic firm buying out a non-US firm. Acquisitions by foreign firms rose as a percentage of US merger activity after 1986, reaching nearly 16 per cent in 1988. Acquisitions of foreign firms also rose slightly post-1986, reaching a level of 5.5 per cent in 1988.

Table 10.5. US merger activity (number of transactions)

Year	US buys US	Non-US buys US	US buys non-US
1980	1,300	170	113
1981	1,964	266	83
1982	1,960	222	139
1983	2,075	111	148 .
1984	2,729	182	149
1985	3,001	206	184
1986	3,799	329	166
1987	3,367	326	190
1988	2,882	447	158

Source: *Mergers and Acquisitions*. To be included in this data base, a transaction must involve a US firm and be valued at more than $1m. In principle, this data source is less inclusive than that used in the previous section. In practice, it lists nearly 300 fewer acquisitions of US firms by Europeans than the previous one (which added US and Canadian firms together), and about 26 fewer purchases of European firms by US firms.

As in Europe, most US mergers are national affairs, but the domestic orientation of US merger activity is far more marked than that of European firms. What, from a European perspective, looks like a relatively large number of acquisitions of European firms by US firms and of US firms by European firms is, by US standards, pretty small. Mergers are far more common in the US than in Europe, and it is that and not a marked interest in Europe by US firms which accounts for most of the transatlantic merger activity that we observe.

Table 10.6 shows the countries that have provided most of the non-US firms acquired by US firms. As with European cross-border mergers, US firms display a strong tendency to acquire Canadian firms. Slightly—but perhaps only slightly—less attractive as a source of merger partners is the UK, which provides a third of the acquirees of US firms. Taken together, three-quarters of the rather meagre total of US mergers that are not national involve seeking out Canadian or UK partners. The remaining foreign acquisitions of US firms were concentrated in Europe, involving France, West Germany, and Italy.

Table 10.6 also shows the national identity of the major buyers of US

Table 10.6. Cross-border merger activity by US firms, 1988

Country	Transactions	
	Countries attracting US buyers	Countries most active in the USA (acquisitions)
UK	36	188
Canada	49	46
West Germany	10	27
France		
Italy	7	
Australia	7	
Netherlands		
Switzerland		
New Zealand		
Hong Kong		
TOTAL	109	

Source: *Mergers and Acquisitions*. To be included in this data base, a transaction must involve a US firm and be valued at more than $1m. In principle, this data source is less inclusive than that used in the previous section. In practice, it lists nearly 300 fewer acquisitions of US firms by Europeans than the previous one (which added US and Canadian firms together), and about 26 fewer purchases of European firms by US firms.

firms. It is clear at a glance that the most important acquirers of US firms are UK firms, which alone accounted for just over 50 per cent of all acquisitions of US firms over the period 1985–8. At quite some distance away in terms of their quantitative importance as predators are Canadian firms who account for nearly 20 per cent of total acquisitions. Perhaps more interesting, the importance of the UK as a buyer of US firms noticeably increased throughout the period. Of the foreign-based acquisitions of US firms in 1985, 42.3 per cent were accounted for by UK firms, and their share of total acquisitions rose steadily throughout the period, reaching 56.6 per cent in 1988. Canadian firms declined in importance, accounting for 25.5 per cent of acquisitions in 1985 and only 13.9 per cent in 1988. Neglecting the UK, European firms accounted for a mere 9 per cent of the total foreign acquisition of US firms, less than the total number of take-overs initiated by Japanese firms.

4. CONCLUSIONS

Putting together the data on European and American cross-border mergers, three overall conclusions emerge. First, cross-border mergers are a small percentage of total merger activity. They constitute a quite small percentage of US mergers, and no more than a modest share of European mergers. Second, the most important flow of cross-border mergers takes place across the Atlantic, and most of that occurs between the US and the UK. This is almost certainly the result of the extremely open nature of the capital markets in both countries, as well, perhaps, as a similarity in business cultures. Aside from the UK, the only other European countries that engage in any substantive cross-border merger activity are France and West Germany, and in both countries a fairly high percentage of cross-border mergers involve US partners. Third, a striking feature of cross-border merger activity is that it goes hand in hand with increases in total merger activity. Although it is only speculative, the impression that one gets from the data is that increases in cross-border merger activity occur when increases in total merger activity deplete the stock of attractive domestic partners enough to make it worth while for merger active firms to begin to seek out partners abroad. There is, it appears, a hierarchy of choice for most acquiring firms, and that hierarchy ranks domestic partners above foreign partners, and, for European firms, US partners no lower than other European partners.

Looked at as a European response to completing the internal market in 1992, the pattern of merger activity that we have observed is hardly impressive. Most firms seem to be domestically oriented in their choice of partners, and their choices of foreign partners often lead them out of

Europe. From a North American point of view, 1992 and the single European market does not seem to be a particularly strong magnet, and those US firms who feel the need to establish a European position appear to regard the UK as the natural country in which to extend their observations.

REFERENCE

Coopers & Lybrand (1989), *Barriers to Takeover in the European Community*, Department of Trade and Industry, London: HMSO.

11

Continental Mergers are Different

EVAN DAVIS*, GRAHAM SHORE†,
and DAVID THOMPSON‡

1. ABSTRACT

In recent years, business has been heavily preoccupied with two themes: merger and acquisition activity, and the development of the European Single Market. The topic of this chapter combines the two: continental mergers. The authors argue that the costs and benefits of continental mergers are different from those of their domestic counterparts, and they need to be handled in different ways. This has implications both for the form of integration and for the way in which it is implemented. Most important, it is relevant to the selection of the right partner.

2. INTRODUCTION

With the developing single market, there has been an enormous increase in merger activity in the European Community (EC). Whilst much of this activity reflects more general trends in acquisition activity—and is confined in scope within national borders—there has nevertheless been an underlying increase in cross-border activity and, in particular, a shift in UK acquisitions from the USA to Europe (see Geroski and Vlassopoulos (1990)).

Does this hold out the promise of industrial restructuring in Europe in response to the challenges of the single market, or will this turn out to be

* Economics Correspondent at the BBC. Evan Davis was a Research Fellow at the Centre for Business Strategy at the London Business School when this chapter was written.

† Managing Director of Shore Capital & Corporate, a corporate finance house specializing in advice on mergers and acquisitions and deal structuring.

‡ David Thompson was previously a Senior Research Fellow at the Centre for Business Strategy, London Business School.

The material for this paper has been drawn from chapters 3, 4, and 5 of *Continental Mergers are Different: Strategy and Policy for 1992*, a report of the Centre for Business Strategy published in 1990.

The authors acknowledge modelling help from Stefan Szymanski, research assistance from Ann Whitfield, and helpful comments on an earlier draft from John Cubbin and Paul Geroski. The usual disclaimer applies.

as disappointing as previous waves of UK merger activity? In this chapter
we argue that continental mergers will be different. The *benefits* of integration will be different because the motivation is more likely to be the
prospect of entry into new markets rather than financial factors or the
exploitation of scale economies. The *costs* of integration will be different
because the pattern of ownership and control of companies are different
as also is the acquirer's access to information on prospective target companies.

These observations have several important implications for strategy:
firstly the best *form* of integration will often be different—partial integration (through joint venture or minority share stakes) may be preferable to
full merger. Second, *choosing a partner*—will be different. The objective is
both to identify partners who will be capable of facilitating entry into
new geographic markets but who will also have adequate incentive to do
so.

3. THE BENEFITS OF INTEGRATION ARE DIFFERENT

Why have firms been tempted to engage in European mergers? The general justification of merger is that it can combine under-used resources in
one company with complementary under-used resources in another. Two
firms operating under capacity, for example, can share fixed costs and
benefit from economies of scale. A firm with good management can combine with another firm with bad management to become a larger firm
with good management. A firm with good ideas but no money can combine with a firm with lots of cash but few ideas.

Of course, value is not created by the mere existence of complementary
resources. There must also be some reason why the firms that have complementary resources cannot get those which they want directly: why the
cash starved firm cannot get cash; or the badly managed firm good managers. If this cannot be achieved via market transactions, however, then
merger may be the cheapest way to use all resources fully. Analysts
would describe the complementary resources as providing a synergy that
creates value to the merged entity, meeting the so-called '2 + 2 = 5'
criteria, describing the types of synergy discussed in the corporate strategy text-books (for example, Ansoff (1965)).

In some form or other, this is the argument most commonly used to
justify previous rounds of merger activity. The resources involved are
usually loosely specified, covering any corporate assets or forms of competitive advantage which can contribute to the productive process. And
these resources often tend to be intangible. For example, an argument
frequently maintained along these lines would take the form that one

company has certain strengths that the other lacks, and that the merger allows those strengths to be more fully exploited. These strengths are an asset of one company that can be more fully exploited by merger with another.

Whatever the motivation for integration, however, the goal should be to create value from a combined entity that would not exist in the two components separately. This criterion justifies a merger when the combination will be capable of achieving things that the two on their own could not achieve. In particular, it does not hold if the merged entity only looks more attractive than the acquirer on its own because the target company is itself so much better than the acquirer that it raises the average of the two taken together.

If the recent round of continental merger activity was motivated by the same factors as the various waves of domestic merger, the arguments used to justify them would derive from the desire to achieve greater market share and economies of scale, the most common argument for merger in the 1950s and 1960s (exemplified in Cook and Cohen (1958)). Economies of scale almost universally derive from the fact that certain inputs—if inputs are taken to include all the intangible things that go into the production chain—do not need to be increased pro-rata as the amount produced is increased. Once the costs of buying them have been incurred, they should be spread as widely as possible. An example would be the operation of a branch banking network. It may be important to have a branch in every high street and the minimum efficient scale of a branch can mean that there is spare capacity for most banks within each branch. For Spanish banks, this spare capacity has been considerable and they have found that it is easier for banks that have merged to rationalize their branch network, than to have each bank offering a service in half the high streets. A similar example is the claim that the two parties to a merger can shed duplicated capacity by merging. This implies that there is unused capacity in both firms. Neither firm can shed it, but if both firms were together, they would be able to do so.

More recently, attention has switched to merger as a means by which good managers expand their domain at the expense of bad managers, and this also conforms to the framework outlined here. The good management is under-used in that it can take on a larger empire without damaging its effectiveness, and the badly run firm needs good management; and when significant costs have been sunk in establishing the badly run firm it will be better to salvage it than destroy it. The view of synergies as matching complementary resources with spare capacity can be seen as a general description of most of the good—and indeed many of the bad—arguments given for mergers.

The evidence is, however, that different arguments are being used to justify cross-border deals. They are based less on factors such as exploitation of economies of scale, or merely increasing market share, and more on providing a means of entry into new markets. This proposition is supported by analysis of the reasons offered for mergers reported in the *Financial Times*. Table 11.1 provides a breakdown of reasons based on all the articles in the paper from two months—July 1985 and July 1990—that have been classified under 'merger', 'acquisition' or 'take-over bid' by Reuter's Textline service. Of course, the categorizations are subjective, numerous reports fall into grey areas, and the results are based on a small sample and are of little statistical significance. But the main feature to emerge, not altogether surprisingly, is that accounts of cross-border mergers are heavily couched in terms of geographical extension of

Table 11.1. Motivations for integration stated in *Financial Times* reports

	July 1985			July 1990		
	Domestic	Cross-border	Total	Domestic[b]	Cross-border	Total
No. of mergers with no reason stated	63	11	74	66	44	110
No. of mergers with some reason stated	64	27	91	24	37	61
Total no. of deals[a] reported			165			171
No. of reasons mentioned[c]	64	31		30	57	
Of which (percentages)						
Expansion	50	26		20	25	
Geographical expansion/ entry to new markets	8	45		10	35	
Vertical expansion	3	6		7	5	
Efficiency/Economies of scale	11	6		20	10	
Diversification of product range	14	6		13	10	
Target in distress or a good buy	9	10		20	10	
Other	5	0		10	4	

[a] Not all the deals were successfully completed.
[b] Includes several mergers across the border of East and West Germany.
[c] More than one reason is offered for some deals.
Source: Centre for Business Strategy analysis of Reuter's Textline database of *Financial Times* articles cagetorized under 'merger', 'acquisition', or 'take-over bid'.

activities. In contrast, the most important stated factor for domestic mergers is general 'expansion'.

In the time that has elapsed between the two periods covered, there has been no very marked change in the motivations cited for cross-border integration. But the number of cross-border mergers increased substantially over that period, in line with evidence from other sources. Expansion has fallen in importance for domestic mergers, and distress or the purchase of a 'good buy' has increased; and general expansion has increased somewhat at the expense of geographical expansion in the cross-border cases. Nevertheless, the overall findings are consistent with the view that the factors motivating cross-border deals are distinct from those motivating domestic mergers.

The conclusion this suggests is that the motives for continental merger relate to geographical expansion, and that the synergies that correspond to this motive are correspondingly different as well. If the geographical extension of markets is the objective, then the aim of the merger may, for example, be to acquire a distribution network in one country for a product that would be hard to sell there otherwise, or the complementary resources to be matched together could, for example, be the good product design from a firm in one market with the local intelligence held by a firm in the other market.

Combining with foreign firms can be a means of expanding trade and thus exploiting technology that is currently used only in the home market. By linking up good producers in one country with companies that can distribute their products abroad, or even assemble the final item, consumers will be offered effective choices that they would not otherwise have had. In foreign markets, information can play a more important role in determining successful or unsuccessful performance than in domestic mergers. There is a substantial amount of evidence that consumers require some assurance when they buy a product that they will not get something very different from what they are expecting. This manifests itself in high profits accruing to reputable brands in industries where consumers are unable to quickly judge for themselves the quality of what it is they are going to buy. Familiar brand names are one means by which consumers can receive reassurance, because familiar names carry a stock of goodwill which the owners will be reluctant to damage. Local names are both more familiar to consumers and often provide a better assurance of redress in the event of an adverse outcome. So for quite good reasons, nationalistic buying is something which exporters will face, and which they can overcome by setting up deals with local firms. Citibank's poor record in entry to the UK retail banking industry in 1984 to 1986 provided a striking example of how little credence can be given to a large international brand name in a new and uninformed market.

Matching the information needs of firms in different markets does appear to provide a potential synergy. Information has sunk cost characteristics, and is one input into the industrial process which is inexhaustible—one which does not get used up as production increases. It does not necessarily become capacity constrained when the firm expands. The sorts of information that might generate synergies are technical and market know-how.

Contrast this with the motives and corresponding synergies of domestic mergers. Expansion *per se* is not a good reason for merger, for while it presents a motivation for combining firms—the merged entity will certainly be bigger then either of the separate parts—it does nothing to suggest that actual performance will be improved. Expansion is a good justification only if we believe that it builds competitive advantage through, say, economies of scale or efficiencies through rationalization. Its record at doing so is not encouraging, as countless studies of previous rounds of merger activity have shown (see, for example, Meeks (1977)).

So while market entry is not, *by itself*, a source of competitive advantage, it can unlock the value of the competitive advantages that either of the firms may have by enabling the advantages to be extended to new markets. In this respect, mergers motivated by the desire to enter new markets appear to be directed more toward the exploitation of potential synergies than their domestic counterparts, and it is at least not surprising that multinational diversity has a stronger link to profitability than product diversity (Grant, Jammine, and Thomas (1988)).

Examples of cross-border integration based on information synergies abound, some of which are mergers, others of which are share swaps and some of which are limited technology transfer deals or distribution licensing deals.

1. The car industry: this is one where there has been a strong belief in the existence of economies of scale. It is equally characterized by extreme nationalistic buying (domestic producers do well in the home market) and high rewards to good engineering. The Honda (UK)–Rover share swap is the outcome of several years of collaborative work: Honda has passed much needed engineering expertise to Rover; Rover has provided sales and a label to put on to Japanese-designed cars in a market in which nationalistic purchasing is endemic. Fiat's collaboration in Eastern Europe is of the same type—local production remains important to the East Europeans, but the local automotive design base is years behind the West.

2. The food industry: again, a great deal of merger activity has occurred. Some is justified in terms of economies of scale, but in other areas, there is a high degree of branding and proprietary products flourish. In the confectionery sector, the Nestlé–Rowntree take-over was

justified on the grounds that Rowntree had an insufficient infrastructure in Europe, and that Nestlé had a distribution network with spare capacity. Also, the Rowntree distribution network provided access to confectioners, while Nestlé was stronger with food sellers. Both might benefit from better access to the other. Another interpretation of the merger was that Rowntree had a skill in developing countline products, and that Nestlé wanted the skill: it took over Rowntree to buy the 'architecture' which had proved so successful to Rowntree. Similar arguments have been made in the case of BSN acquisitions—such as HP and Worcester Sauce—and the Bulmers–Perrier distribution deal.

3. The electronics industry: again, this is an industry in which a large portion of the value added can be attributed to the design and engineering process, which has the characteristics of being inexhaustible. The link between AT and T and Olivetti was designed to give the Italian firm access to AT and T technology, while giving the Americans access to the very protected Italian market. Similar arguments have been advanced by Philips in its various joint ventures.

4. The pharmaceutical industry: this is a sector in which the bulk of costs are research and development; and marketing and distribution to doctors. The latter is handled on a more personal and local basis than, say, most consumer product advertising. The success of Glaxo's link with Hoffmann–La Roche in the distribution of Zantac to the USA exemplifies the typical exploitation of a synergy (see dell'Osso (1990)). More recently, the link of SmithKline and Beecham was said to provide geographical synergies (Beecham in Europe, SmithKline in the USA and Japan) and skill complementarities (Beecham at research and SmithKline at development and promotion).

5. The accountancy profession: in the accountancy industry, the emergence of large international practices has been the result of benefits from the cross-border spread of reputation. Multinational firms and their stakeholders want accountants they can trust in new markets, and they go to 'Big Six' firms with this in mind. Thus, if a 'Big Six' name can be attached to a local unbranded accountancy practice, it generates value for both firms. There is, however, no such synergy to justify the trend for merger between the very large companies; these mergers are very likely to be based on a misperception that increasing market share provides a form of competitive advantage, or that there are further economies of scale in accounting which even large firms have not realized.

4. THE COSTS OF INTEGRATION ARE DIFFERENT

Implementing a continental merger poses different practical problems and consequently different costs, to those normally experienced in domestic or transatlantic deals. Choosing a partner is a different process, effecting the transaction involves different considerations, and both structuring the deal and making it work are different.

Differences when Selecting Targets

Large acquirers find that, on average, their targets on the Continent have to be smaller than they would prefer because aggregate concentration is lower there, and the few large companies that there are tend to be bid proof (see Shore (1990)). At the same time, contested take-overs are rare because of technical and ownership barriers (see Coopers & Lybrand (1989)). The result of these two characteristics is that merger is typically by agreement and involves 'merger' in the literal sense rather than take-over by an acquirer. Banking shareholders with a close strategic management role are often more important than the more passive, but less loyal, Anglo-Saxon institutional shareholder. And continental partners are accustomed to, and comfortable with, cross-shareholding between partners. These differences mean that continental merger strategy is in practice about seeking smaller companies as large partners, not large victims to capture and swallow.

Differences in Transacting

When effecting the transaction, three differences between continental and domestic practice are critical. The first problem is in determining a reference price to set a fair value on a continental target. Second, problems arise from variations in accounting conventions between countries and the consequential problems in interpreting reported earnings and asset values. Third, there are particular tax implications of cross-border deals.

The Reference Price Setting a reference price for an Anglo-Saxon deal is made much easier by the well-developed status of the equity markets and their role in the market for corporate control. A comparable yardstick is not available for many potential continental merger targets.

Anglo-Saxon deals often begin from established values of quoted companies. Suitably adjusted, these can guide even private 'trade' deals. Discounted cashflow techniques can then serve as a cross-check. However, using stock market rules of thumb is much less likely to be reliable in the case of a continental merger target. Continental stock markets are not typically markets in corporate control. Usually only a small proportion of a company's shares are held by shareholders uncommitted to the Board of the company. Thin markets in shares are rarely sound guides to the purchase value of the companies being traded. Whilst the lack of an open market in corporate control hinders both purchaser and vendor, this loss of transparency increases uncertainty and hence transaction costs.

Accounting Information Inevitably in a merger negotiation, the valuation discussions will depend on an assessment of current and prospective financial performance. Great weight will therefore rest upon the financial accounts of the parties. Whilst it is generally recognized in business circles that preparing financial accounts is a judgemental activity, not an exact science, and that accounts must be interpreted in the light of the objectives of those preparing them, using accounting information is still more problematic in cross-border mergers.

The problems arise because there are a number of important differences of principle between continental accounting and the principles and policies used in Anglo-Saxon jurisdictions. Many of these arise from the varying roles of financial accounts in tax computations. On the Continent, the treatment of property as an asset is usually more conservative, with restrictions on revaluing the asset to reflect changing market values (the Netherlands and to some extent Belgium are the exceptions to this), and on the whole permitted asset lives are shorter. Unlike in the UK (although similarly to the USA) continental accounts usually treat goodwill on acquisition as a charge against profit and loss rather than against reserves. (This generally reflects practice rather than principle.) The treatment of finance lease obligations varies. On the Continent, profits on long-term contracts tend to be taken at completion (primarily for tax reasons). There are also differences in the treatment of currency gains and extraordinary items. Finally, other than in the Netherlands, provisions for deferred tax tend to be lower than those made in the UK.

The impact of these differences varies depending upon the business and circumstances of the company to which they are applied. A study by Touche Ross (1989) provides a more detailed analysis. In so far as it is possible to generalize, it can be said that applying continental principles will typically show lower earnings and a lower return on capital than applying British principles. However, the only certain and universal conclusion is that the results will be different. The EC is attempting to harmonize company accounting conventions across the Community as part of the 1992 programme. However, this is unlikely to have any bearing on European mergers for some considerable time. As Touche Ross conclude, 'As far as we are concerned, we will be satisfied if the main accounting differences . . . are settled before January 1st, 2000!' In the interim, deal-makers face the extra transactions costs of accounting re-presentation to ensure that they are using a consistent method of measurement.

Taxation The field of cross-border taxation can be even more compli-cated than that of accounting. Although the EC's harmonization pro-gramme embraces taxation, the differences between countries in corporation tax rates and treatments remains large. Particular, otherwise commercially attractive, deal structures may have adverse tax conse-quences. Tax planning will inevitably be a significant element of the direct costs of the transaction.

Differences in Deal Structuring

Merger on the Continent is likely to be with a family-run business and is quite likely to involve the purchase of less than 100 per cent interest. Even if it is a 100 per cent acquisition, the acquirer will probably need to have the family management involved after completing the deal. Whilst periods of management transition are not unusual for domestic purchases of family-run firms, the fact that the merger is with a company in a different country makes it especially important for the acquirer to be assured of management continuity. The transition, if there is to be one at all, will need to be over a long period.

As a result, many continental mergers are structured more like venture capital deals than acquisitions. This is because the principle of venture capital is that an outside shareholder, often holding a minority stake, provides finance advice and assistance to a growing business which is entrepreneurially owned and managed. Whilst continental mergers are intended to be marriages, not mere capital injections, many of the same deal-structuring provisions apply.

For example, a typical venture capital contract includes explicit protec-tion for minority shareholders. These might include rules on dividend policy and restrictions on changes in business direction without the con-sent of the minority; provisions for seats on the Board; regulations on the flow of management information; procedures for determining senior managerial salaries and incentives; and agreements on the disposal of shares.

Merger partners, where there is a minority interest, usually seek to cement the merger more closely over time. As well as arrangements for the disposal of shares, option agreements for converting shares held post-merger in the smaller of the companies into shares of the larger party are often appropriate.

It is important that merger terms retain financial incentives for the management, and limit the demotivating effect on the recipient of receiving a large cash sum. Preferably, this is done by insisting that where cash is paid most of the cash is used to develop the business further or is dependent on future performance (i.e. a modified 'earn-out'). Option arrangements may also play a large part in encouraging the managers of the merger partner to want the merger to succeed.

Thus acquirers have to adopt different and more calculated deal structures if the parties are to achieve a fair deal and to create the right incentives. These structures need to be tailored to each deal and the careful planning they involve is another element in the cost of the transaction.

Achieving Integration

Clearly, there is little point in merging businesses to secure the benefits of integration only to leave each business as a completely separate managerial unit without more than occasional contact with other units. However, the dependence of managers in one country on their new partners in the other country for knowledge of local market and business conditions is at a maximum just after a merger, when the partners are still new to each other. Local knowledge must be used, but integration must begin before all momentum is lost; so how should intergration proceed?

Time and trouble are needed to achieve successful merger. A long premerger courtship can help, as can careful planning of new structures and responsibilities before consummating the deal. But any cross-border merger plan must recognize the importance of differences in business culture. It is striking that even mergers between British and North American companies founder because of cultural problems. Commonality of language and superficial similarities in methods hide more fundamental differences. A comprehensive study of the human factors in acquisitions examined, amongst other things, the cultural impact on US companies of being bought by a British company (Hunt, Lees, Grumbar, and Vivian (1987)). They found that:

British companies seriously underestimate the degree of ignorance about the British business environment amongst North American managers. For them, selling to a British company is much more of an uncertain process than selling to another American company. Consequently, there is a greater need for social reassurance regarding acquisition motives, the buyer's management style, and the long-term intentions for the acquired business. This is particularly important for private companies which are being sold for reasons of expansion or succession.

How much greater force such an observation has for continental mergers! This study stressed that carefully regulated interfaces between the merging companies played a central part in achieving successful merger. When key individuals were nominated on each side to act as a buffer, this

helped to minimize frictions. Establishing agreed mechanisms for transfer-
ring methods, know-how and market intelligence can also help. All these
measures require frequent personal contact and may need to include
international management training sessions; frequent social as well as
business meetings; exchange of internal communications material; second-
ments; and the posting of foreign managers to head office.

Building a cross-border collegiate spirit in a company is time consum-
ing and expensive. But without doubt, it provides scope to gain
significant international competitive advantage if an industry is seeing its
national boundaries erode.

5. THE FORM OF INTEGRATION IS DIFFERENT

We have argued that the nature of both the benefits, and also the costs,
of continental integration will typically be different from those of domestic integration.

The implication is that the cost-benefit trade-off, which determines
whether integration is the preferred strategy, will also be different. The
particular nature of continental mergers means that types of integration
which fall short of full merger—for example minority share swaps or
joint ventures—are likely to have particular advantages. This is especially
likely to be the case if the benefits and costs of integration increase at a
different rate with the size of the acquirer's stake in the target. In these
circumstances, a minority share stake—or joint venture—might enable
firms to obtain a disproportionate slice of the benefits of integration without incurring a similar proportion of the costs.

In practice there are a number of ways in which various types of partial integration might be used to achieve the benefits of full merger.
Williamson (1983) identifies the use of 'hostages'—for example, through
the extension of credit—to sustain trading relationships which might
otherwise be eroded by opportunistic action. The establishment of partial
integration between the partners—for example, through a joint venture—
is a particularly pronounced form of hostage exchange. Where imperfections in contractual arrangements arise from asymmetric information
between the parties, then partial integration provides a means of reducing
this—particularly where it involves cross-board representation between
the two companies concerned. More generally, partial integration provides both a signal of commitment to the trading relationship—actions
which damage one party now damage both—and also signals the possibilities for retaliatory action should the other partner seek to 'cheat' on the
agreement.

A case will serve to illustrate some of these principles. The manufacture of machines for making cigarettes provides a classic example of a buyer–seller relationship in which both parties have significant sunk costs. A cigarette-making machine is a very specific product and, because the tobacco industry has few participants, a supplier has a very limited range of alternative customers. The danger that suppliers will not be able to recover the costs already sunk in the development of their product is thus real. However, buyers face a similar problem. The market for cigarette-making machines is also highly concentrated. Furthermore, these machines are long-lived assets which are progressively refurbished over their economic lives. A tobacco company with an installed machine base would thus face significant switching costs in moving to another supplier. The possibility of expropriation by the seller from the buyer thus also arises.

These stylized facts are reflected in the development of cigarette-making machines in the UK. In 1927, the two principal tobacco companies each took a 24 per cent share stake in the major manufacturer—Molin's—in order to secure developments in technology whose implementation was being delayed by financial constraints faced by Molin's. Associated with this were various supply agreements which, in particular, provided guarantees on the availability and prices of spare parts for installed machines. BAT's stake—raised to just under 30 per cent when Imperial pulled out—has continued into the 1980s. Whilst the advantages to both parties of integration are clear, BAT considered that full integration would not be desirable because the management skills required to run a machine manufacturing business were different to those associated with the company's main products—which required more market-oriented skills.

This case is not an isolated example. In practice, partial integration is a highly significant characteristic of industrial organization. A study by Meadowcroft and Thompson (1987) showed that just under 30 per cent of quoted industrial and commercial companies in the UK have a minority share stake (greater than 5 per cent) held by another industrial or commercial company. Whilst some of these stakes appear to be held as a first step in preparation for a take-over bid, the majority—estimated at 80 per cent—reflect longer-term partial integration between the two companies concerned.

We expect partial integration to be equally important in the case of continental mergers. Whilst there are examples of continental mergers which aim to exploit scale or scope economies, we have argued that this will not be the most important consequence of the developing European Single Market. More relevant will be the lowering of administrative barriers to permit market entry by firms from one member state into the geographic—'home turf'—markets of another. A range of new opportunities will thus emerge for firms with comparative advantage in products or production processes to export their expertise.

Entry into new markets will, as we have argued, usually require trading arrangements with companies in the target country; in some cases to carry out distribution or marketing, in others to carry out production, in others to implement combined R & D. We have already noted that in the domestic UK context, integration which is motivated by a desire to improve the efficiency of trading relationships is frequently implemented through a minority shareholding, in preference to full merger. We expect this to be especially true in the case of continental mergers. Furthermore, we have argued that cross-border mergers show specific costs of integration additional to those found in the domestic context. The result is that the 'cost' side of the cost-benefit balance is likely to be greater than in the case of domestic mergers. In consequence, partial integration will more frequently be the appropriate solution in the case of continental mergers.

The expansion policy followed by Heineken during the 1980s provides a good example of this type of strategy. The preferred route of expanding into a new geographic market is through partial integration with a domestic producer in order to secure access to local brand advantage and distribution networks. In 1984–5 alone, Heineken acquired stakes in companies in France, Spain, the Cameroon, and in South America. But not only Heineken can do this.

6. CHOOSING A PARTNER IS DIFFERENT

If, as we have argued, continental mergers are primarily about market entry, what criteria can be used to judge whether matches are suitable?

Because the achievable synergies relate to information flows, of one kind or another, the primary goal is to find complementarities in the resource base of the companies. A good way of deciding whether two parties are suitably matched is to look at the customers at whom they aim their products and then to compare this with those to whom they actually sell their products. The best combinations are those where:

1. the two companies both want to sell to the same customers;
2. they have different strengths in accessing those customers—i.e. one is stronger in marketing and distribution than the other, or has a better or more familiar name;
3. they have different skills in supplying the customers—i.e. they produce different products, or the one with the worst access to the customers has clearly the better product.

A bad match is very likely if both companies have the same access to the customers, and the same skills at supplying those customers. Just as, under the theory of comparative advantage, countries with the same relative strengths have fewer grounds for trade than those with very different strengths, firms with exactly the same performance have fewer grounds for integration than those with very different performance, and indeed, integration is unlikely to be favoured at all. In that case, there would be few net gains from the merger and the gains of one party will only accrue at the expense of the other, unless the combination results in other advantages—such as economies of scale in production or increased market power—to the firms concerned.

It is equally important that the two firms are aiming at the same target: if one aims its sales at long-distance lorry drivers and the other is producing hand cream for housewives, the match is unlikely to be a good one. If, in contrast one is concerned to sell a hand cream in French chemists and the other makes shampoo for the French market, the match would be likely to generate benefits. The Honda/Rover match is perfect, because the buyers of Rover in the UK were identical to the target buyers of Honda, while Rover had better access to them, and Honda could furnish them with better engineered cars.

A specific way of measuring the suitability of two parties in these terms would be to look at the proportion of one firm's primary target customers who are already served by the other and vice versa. The higher this proportion, the greater the knowledge that the second will have of suitable distribution channels, and the more likely it is to have a reputation that will be of value in selling the first's product. In establishing the exact suitability of a partner, a firm should be concerned with two types of mismatch: lack of cover, which would arise where a high proportion of its target customers are not accessible through its potential partner, and unnecessary dilution, where a high proportion of its potential partner's customers are not part of its target customer base.

To make it worth buying a firm, that firm should reach an appreciable proportion of the target customer base; to make it cost effective, it must probably not reach too many others. It would be expensive to buy British Telecom merely to access potential buyers of peanuts. Coverage is the important variable, and is worth paying for. Dilution is rarely too severe a problem, but does extend all the problems of integration without generating any important benefits. It will severely detract from a possible partner if the dilution makes the deal expensive. It will also be worse than useless in the case where one product needs to be marketed in a focused way and sold on image.

Of course, coverage will be near 100 per cent, and dilution near to zero, when the two companies involved are strong potential—but not actual—competitors. This observation suggests an immediate paradox. Whilst co-operation reduces the costs of entry—by sharing marketing and distribution costs, for example, or by saving transport costs through overseas production—it also means that the rewards from successful entry have to be shared. In circumstances where the preferred partner is a potential competitor who is already well established in the domestic market, then co-operation forgoes the opportunity of eroding his market share (but insures against him aggressively resisting entry).

These interactions can be investigated using a model developed by Szymanski in which two firms are deciding whether to set up a joint venture. (See Szymanski and Thompson (1990) for more details.) If successful, the joint venture will enable both parties to reduce their costs of production. But where the prospective partner is also a potential competitor—that is, already incumbent in the market which is to be entered—then co-operation in development expenditures will shape the competitive advantage of the two companies once entry has taken place. Three possible scenarios can be stylized if the entrant decides to go it alone rather than co-operate in development expenditure:

1. in the first, both companies successfully reduce costs: in these circumstances it would have been better to co-operate and economize on development expenditure;
2. in the second, both companies' development expenditures end in failure; again co-operation in development would have reduced each company's share of the project;
3. in the third, one company undertakes a successful development whilst the other company's project ends in failure. In this case the successful company usually benefits from going it alone; the higher development costs which are incurred by going it alone are more than offset by the competitive advantage which results from successful development

From this stylized outline of outcomes it is intuitively clear that the decision on whether to go for integration or whether to go it alone will be determined by three main factors. The first is the size of the reduction in development expenditures which can be achieved by going for integration compared to going it alone. This will be determined by the complementary resources which can be matched; the skills, products, and processes available to the two companies. The second is the likelihood that events will follow each of the three scenarios outlined above, and the third is the size of the pay-off that might be achieved by being the successful company in scenario three. Importantly the size of this pay-off will be determined by whether the erstwhile partner is also a strong potential competitor.

If we look at Figure 11.1, we can see that in circumstances where the potential partners produce non-competing (or only weakly competitive) products, we are in a situation where co-operation in development has no direct bearing upon the two companies' relative competitive advantage. Integration will be the preferred entry strategy, providing the synergy

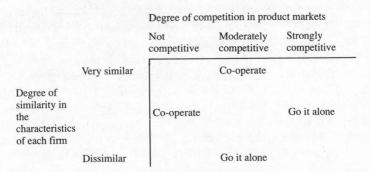

Fig. 11.1 When is it worthwhile to co-operate in development?

benefits are not outweighed by the increased costs of organizational control.

However, when we look at potential partners who are also strong product market competitors, then a different set of conclusions emerges. In this scenario it is usually more profitable—under a wide range of demand and cost conditions—for the larger firm to go it alone. In effect, the possibility of securing a significant competitive advantage by undertaking development expenditures alone outweighs the risk that the competitor is able to match the development—leaving their relative competitive position unchanged—whilst the benefits of sharing the development expenditures are forgone. In some circumstances the smaller firm is also better-off going it alone. More significantly, even where the smaller firm would prefer to co-operate, its advantage in doing so is typically smaller than the profits which would be forgone by the larger firm in substituting co-operation for going it alone. The implication of this is that in many circumstances, strong competitors will not find it mutually worthwhile to co-operate in development expenditures. Agreement is only likely to be achieved on terms which act to the disadvantage of one or other of the parties. In other words, this type of agreement shows severe danger of a 'winner's curse'—success in reaching agreement is achieved only in circumstances which lead to reduced profitability.

The most important exception to this conclusion arises in circumstances where co-operation in development provides the basis for collusion in the final product market. Where this possibility arises then co-operation will usually be the most profitable strategy. The public policy implications of this are clear; co-operation in development between strong competitors will often (although not always) only be worthwhile where this is expected to lead on to product market collusion.

A good partner is thus one which already serves the customers which

the entrant is seeking to serve, and additional customers. The ideal partner—on this criterion—will be a company selling an identical product to
the entrant; but for these incumbents, co-operation is unlikely to be
worthwhile. How is this dilemma to be resolved? The solution is to identify a partner which offers the required synergies—in distribution, marketing, production, R & D, or whatever—but which is not a strong potential
competitor in the product market.

A good example is provided by Perrier's expansion into the emerging
UK market in mineral water. Perrier is distributed in the UK by Bulmers,
which clearly has well-established expertise in the distribution of bottled
drinks. The two companies' products—mineral water and cider—are,
however, only weak competitors. More generally, where the domestic
market has several different participants then a fruitful partner may be
the one with which the entrant is likely to be in least direct competition,
as Honda were with Rover, for example.

7. STRATEGIES FOR EXPANSION IN EUROPE

In this chapter we have discussed two respects in which 'continental
mergers are different'. First, we believe that the nature of the benefits will
be different. It seems likely that the main source of advantage from integration will be to facilitate entry into new geographic markets after 1992.
The opportunities for further significant exploitation of scale or scope
economies in Europe do not, with the exception of one or two sectors,
appear great. The most important consequence of the single market will
be to increase the opportunities for cross-border market entry, but integration will often be a favourable strategy for achieving this expansion
because of the difficulties which arise in trading relationships based on
contracts or spot-market deals.

Second, however, we consider that the costs of integration will be
different. Differences in the pattern of ownership and control, in business
culture, in accounting conventions and, most basically, in language all
mean that the costs of continental merger will be both different in
nature—and higher—than in the domestic context.

What do these observations mean for strategy? One result is that full
integration will often not be necessary to achieve the requirements for
market access; furthermore full integration will often not be cost-effective
because of the many specific features which raise the costs of continental
mergers. The conclusion which this suggests is that partial integration—
minority shareholdings, or joint venture—will often be the best strategy.

A second conclusion is that choosing a partner will require firms to exercise different skills and criteria: it involves identifying a company with which the required synergies can be exploited to establish market access. Unfortunately, the most promising candidates in some respects—companies selling to the same target market—are often likely to be least promising in other respects—they are direct potential competitors, who will not want to do a deal except on terms which are disproportionately favourable to them. The solution is to search out a company with the skills and expertise to offer the required synergies but whose business is not directly in competition. And once a potential partner has been identified, a whole range of questions needs to be resolved to get the right deal—questions relating to the valuation of the target, to the structure of the deal, to the achievement of the potential benefits of integration. The development of the single market has signalled an upsurge in continental mergers which echoes the waves of merger activity in the UK in the 1960s and 1980s.

In the past, however, domestic merger activity has not provided much of a stimulus to successful domestic performance. It would be easy to argue that continental mergers are going to have an equally disappointing impact on European economic performance. And indeed there is evidence that some continental mergers have not been either well conceived or well executed.

Nevertheless, we remain more optimistic than analysis of the domestic experience alone would suggest. Domestic mergers were primarily about creating economies of scale—which as it transpired were illusory—within single markets. Many continental mergers are about using new opportunities offered by 1992 to actually create single markets by enhancing the penetration of successful products into previously closed domains. In some of these cases at least, the outcome should be that 'European Champions' are created by more effective competition within Europe, not by the mere awarding of medals.

REFERENCES

Ansoff, I. (1965), *Corporate Strategy*, New York: McGraw Hill.

Cook, P. L., and Cohen, R. (1958), *Effects of Mergers*, Cambridge Studies in Industry, London: Allen and Unwin.

Coopers & Lybrand (1989), *Barriers to Takeover in the European Community*, Department for Trade and Industry, London: HMSO.

dell'Osso, F. (1990), 'Defending a dominant position in a technology led environment', *Business Strategy Review*, **1**, No. 2, 77–86.

Geroski, P., and Vlassopoulos, A. (1990), 'European merger activity: a response to 1992?', in *Continental Mergers are Different: Strategy and Policy for 1992*, Centre for Business Strategy Report, London Business School, 22–46.

Grant, R. M., Jammine, Azar P., and Thomas, Howard (1988), 'Diversity, diversification, and profitability among British manufacturing companies, 1972–84', *Academy of Management Journal*, **31**, No. 4, 771–801.

Hunt, J. W., *et al.* (1987), *Acquisitions—The Human Factor*, London Business School, London: Egon Zehnder International.

Meadowcroft, S. M., and Thompson, D. J. (1987), 'Partial integration: a loophole in Competition Law?', *Fiscal Studies*, **8**, No. 1, 48–82.

Meeks, G. (1977), *Disappointing Marriage: A Study of the Gains from Merger*, Cambridge: Cambridge University Press.

Shore, Graham (1990), 'Continental mergers: differences and deal making', in *Continental Mergers are Different: Strategy and Policy for 1992*, Centre for Business Strategy Report, London Business School, 85–104.

Szymanski, S., and Thompson, D. J. (1990), 'Expansion in Europe: what is the best form of integration?', in *Continental Mergers are Different: Strategy and Policy for 1992*, Centre for Business Strategy Report, London Business School, 64–84.

Touche Ross (1989), *Accounting for Europe—Success by 2000 AD*, London: Touche Ross.

Williamson, O. E. (1983), 'Credible commitments: using hostages to support exchange', *American Economic Review*, September.

Appendix A
The Commission's Merger Reports

1966

Jan.   The British Motor Corporation Ltd and the Pressed Steel Company Ltd. HC 46 (1965–6)

May   Ross Group Ltd and Associated Fisheries Ltd. HC 42 (1966)

Aug.   The Dental Manufacturing Co Ltd or the Dentists' Supply Co of New York and the Amalgamated Dental Co Ltd. HC 147 (1966)

1967

Jan.   Guest, Keen, and Nettlefolds Ltd and Birfield Ltd. Cmnd. 3186

May   British Insulated Callender's Cables Ltd and Pyrotenax Ltd. HC 490 (1966–7)

Sept.   United Drapery Stores Ltd and Montague Burton Ltd. Cmnd. 3397

1968

July   Barclays Bank Ltd, Lloyds Bank Ltd, and Martins Bank Ltd. HC 319 (1967–8)

July   Thorn Electrical Industries and Radio Rentals Ltd. HC 318 (1967–8)

1969

June   Unilever Ltd and Allied Breweries Ltd. HC 297 (1968–9)

June   The Rank Organisation Ltd and The De La Rue Company Ltd. HC 298 (1967–8)

1970

Nov.   British Sidac Ltd and Transparent Paper Ltd. HC 154 (1970)

1972

July   Beecham Group Ltd and Glaxo Group Ltd, The Boots Company Ltd and Glaxo Group Ltd. HC 341 (1971–2)

1973

Oct.   British Match Corporation Ltd and Wilkinson Sword Ltd. Cmnd. 5442

1974

Apr.   Davy International Ltd and The British Rollmakers' Corporation Ltd. HC 67 (1974)
June   Eagle Star Insurance Company Ltd and Bernard Sunley Investment Trust Ltd and Grovewood Securities Ltd. Cmnd. 5641
July   Chartered Consolidated Investments Ltd and Sadia Ltd. HC 345 (1974)
July   The Boots Company Ltd and House of Fraser Ltd. HC 174 (1974)

1975

June   Dentsply International Incorporated and AD International Ltd. HC 394 (1974–5)
July   The NFU Development Trust Ltd and FMC Ltd. HC 441 (1974–5)
Aug.   H. Wiedmann AG and BS & W Whitely Ltd. Cmnd. 6208

1976

May   Amalgamated Industrials Ltd and Herbert Morris Ltd. HC 434 (1975–6)
Oct.   Eurocanadian Shipholdings Ltd and Furness Withy and Company Ltd and Manchester Liners Ltd. HC 639 (1975–6)

1977

Feb.   Babcock and Wilcox Ltd and Herbert Morris Ltd. HC 175 (1976–7)
Mar.   Pilkington Brothers Ltd and UKO International Ltd. HC 267 (1976–7)
May   BP/Century Oil. Cmnd. 6827
Aug.   The Fruehauf Corporation and Crane Fruehauf Corporation Ltd. Cmnd. 6906

1978

Feb.   Smith Bros Ltd and Bisgood, Bishop & Co Ltd. HC 242 (1977–8)
May   Rockware Group Ltd, United Glass Ltd, Redfearn National Glass Ltd. HC 431 (1977–8)

1979

Mar.   Lonrho Ltd and Scottish and Universal Investments Ltd and House of Fraser Ltd. HC 262 (1978–9)

July FMC Corporation, Merck & Co, Inc, Alginate Industries Ltd. HC 175 (1979–80)

Sept. The General Electric Company Ltd and Averys Ltd. Cmnd. 7653

1980

Aug. Hiram Walker-Gooderham & Worts Ltd and the Highland Distillers Company Ltd. HC 743 (1979–80)

Oct. Blue Circle Industries Ltd and Armitage Shanks Group Ltd. Cmnd. 8039

1981

Jan. Compagnie Internationale Europcar and Godfrey Davis Ltd. HC 94 (1980–1)

Mar. S & W Berisford Ltd and British Sugar Corporation Ltd. HC 241 (1980–1)

June British Rail Hovercraft Ltd and Hoverlloyd Ltd. HC 374 (1980–1)

Sept. Enserch Corporation and Davy Corporation Ltd. Cmnd. 8360

Dec. European Ferries Ltd, Sealink Ltd. HC 65 (1981–2)

Dec. Lonrho Ltd and House of Fraser Ltd. HC 73 (1981–2)

1982

Jan. The Hongkong and Shanghai Banking Corporation, Standard Chartered Bank Ltd, The Royal Bank of Scotland Group Ltd. Cmnd. 8472

June BTR Ltd and Serck Ltd. HC 392 (1981–2)

Sept. Imperial Chemical Industries PLC and Arthur Holden & Sons PLC. Cmnd. 8660

Oct. Nabisco Brands Inc and Huntley & Palmer Foods PLC. Cmnd. 8680

Dec. Charter Consolidated PLC and Anderson Strathclyde PLC. Cmnd. 8771

1983

Jan. The Great Universal Stores PLC and Empire Stores (Bradford) PLC. Cmnd. 8777

May The Sunlight Service Group PLC and Johnson Group Cleaners PLC and Initial PLC and Johnson Group Cleaners PLC. Cmnd. 8868

May Linfood Holdings PLC and Fitch Lovell PLC. Cmnd. 8874

Aug. The Enterprises of Alan J. Lewis and Illingworth Morris PLC. Cmnd. 9012

Aug. London Brick PLC and Ibstock Johnsen PLC. Cmnd. 9015

Sept. A. Alfred Taubman and Sotheby Parke Bernet Group PLC. Cmnd. 9046

Dec. Pleasurama PLC and Trident Television PLC and Grand Metropolitan PLC. Cmnd. 9108

1984

Feb. Hepworth Ceramic Holdings PLC and Steetley PLC. Cmnd. 9164
Mar. Trafalgar House PLC and the Peninsular and Oriental Steam Navigation Company. Cmnd. 9190
Mar. Guest, Keen, and Nettlefolds PLC and AE PLC. Cmnd. 9199

1985

Jan. The Dee Corporation PLC and Booker McConnell PLC. Cmnd. 9429
Feb. The British Electric Traction Company PLC and Initial PLC. Cmnd. 9444
Mar. Lonrho PLC and House of Fraser PLC. Cmnd. 9548
Nov. Scottish & Newcastle Breweries PLC and Matthew Brown PLC. Cmnd. 9645

1986

Jan. British Telecommunications PLC and Mitel Corporation. Cmnd. 9715
May BET Public Limited Company and SGB Group PLC. Cmnd. 9795
Aug. The General Electric Company PLC and The Plessey Company PLC. Cmnd. 9867
Sept. Elders IXL Ltd and Allied Lyons PLC. Cmnd. 9892
Sept. Norton Opax PLC and McCorquodale PLC. Cmnd. 9904
Dec. The Peninsular and Oriental Steam Navigation Company and European Ferries Group PLC. Cm. 31.

INDEX